PAUL THE FIRST OF RUSSIA

Paul I
Emperor of Russia.
from a drawing attributed to the Empress
Marie Feodorovna his wife

in the collection of H.I.H. the Grand Duke
Nicolas Mikhaïlovitch.

PAUL THE FIRST OF RUSSIA, THE SON OF CATHERINE THE GREAT

BY K. WALISZEWSKI

ARCHON BOOKS
1969

First published 1913
Reprinted 1969 by permission of William Heineman Ltd.
in an unaltered and unabridged edition

SBN: 208 00743 1
Library of Congress Catalog Card Number: 69-19221
Printed in the United States of America

CONTENTS

v

INTRODUCTION

THE tragic figure of the son of Catherine the Great is one of the most enigmatic in history, and also one of the most discussed. Mad monarchs have been common enough, and in the second half of the eighteenth century such an affliction hardly called for remark. George III in England and Christian VII in Denmark were the contemporaries of the Czar Paul, whose case however presents some special features.

In the first place was Catherine's son really mad? Till lately it seemed to be admitted that he was so, at any rate in the last years of his life. The events of his reign of nearly four years were unanimously regarded as the grotesque and disastrous result of the uncontrolled caprice of a demented tyrant. All this is now contested, and in the last few years there has been a complete reversal of the received opinions both of Paul's character and intellect and of the value of his work.

The progress of science, both medical and historical, has made it necessary to revise to some extent views formerly accepted, but the reaction has been carried to extremes. In the eyes of his most recent Russian biographers Paul is not merely not a lunatic; he has become almost a great man. They are not content to celebrate his great qualities and his brilliant talents; they incline to think that he had genius. His reign, far from having been a series of cruel misfortunes for his subjects, as used to be supposed, was in the opinion of these historians a period of beneficent activity and development which, had it not been cut short by the death

1

of the sovereign, might have been the beginning of un-exampled prosperity and greatness.

How is it that we have deceived ourselves so long and so grossly ? How was it that Paul's own mother shared the common delusion to such an extent that she did all she could to exclude him from the throne ? Moreover, if he is really worthy of the place in the Pantheon of great sovereigns which is assigned to him by his new apologists, how do they reconcile this historic eminence with the eccentricities of his mind and character which they do not deny, and with the calamities which they admit were the consequences of his government.

All this gives a new aspect to the problem and the following pages may help to indicate a solution.

Minute as the investigations of Paul's intellectual and temperamental evolution have been, all the factors have not been taken into account. Influences of even greater moment than heredity, education and environment have escaped the notice of the inquiries. It is a plausible supposition, but not an ascertained fact, that his reputed father Peter III was really the author of his existence. Thus the theory of congenital mental instability is no sound basis for argument. He was opposed to the ideas of his mother and for twenty years he spent his time in violently attacking a policy and a government which with all its faults gave Russia a power and a prestige which she has not since recovered. Paul meditated, plotted and prepared the overthrow of this system, and when he came to the throne he endeavoured at least to carry out his design. Entangled for a moment in the anti-revolutionary league he left that alliance in order to join hands with the hero of the 18th Brumaire and to take a share with him in the destruction of the old order of things in Europe and in the partition of the world. To what does all this point if not to a close and clear relationship with the mob of unbalanced contemporaries who suffered as he did from the political and moral hysteria of the time. He may have been neither a Holsteiner nor a Romanof ; he was certainly the true child of the Revolution which he affected to detest and to combat. He was neither insane, in the pathological sense, nor even weak-minded. But he was capable of the most astounding madness and folly because, being himself a mediocrity, he was touched by a kind of collective frenzy which turned stronger heads than his. In spite of this he was admired in his own time and has been extolled since, because most people readily mistake violence and recklessness for the vigorous inspirations of genius.

The author hopes that if his readers will follow him in examining the facts set out in the following study they will be at least so far persuaded of the truth of his conviction as to absolve him from any suspicion of paradox or a taste for arbitrary conjecture. It is more-over to be remarked that the new school of thought which favours Paul's rehabilitation in Russia has there somewhat violently encountered the same political and social currents which shook Europe a hundred years ago.

The object of this book, and its chief interest, is to examine how far these currents penetrated and influenced the Russia of that time; how in the person of Paul I and in the character of his government they were combined with elements of stability or disorder, of conservatism or revolution. The complicated psychology of the Czar and the dramatic incidents of his career which led up to the final tragedy no doubt make him a figure of great interest. But the trials suffered during his reign by the vast country which he held in his hands and sought to mould as he thought fit are more interesting still.

For the preparation of the volume the literature of the subject has provided abundant resources which, however, were often difficult to utilise. Apart indeed from a few fragmentary and incomplete studies and the

INTRODUCTION

ordinary histories of the period the monographs, memoirs and even the printed documents of which it consists are scattered through innumerable periodical publications. I believe I have neglected nothing which is at all instructive.

I cannot claim to have similarly exhausted the other sources of information. Their multiplicity, no less than their dispersion, defies any individual effort. Some are inaccessible even in public depositories owing to the absence of the indispensable catalogue or classification. But no revelations can be expected which are likely to modify our ideas about Paul himself on the events of his time. The work of investigation has been carried very far, even in Russia, and Catherine's son with his passion for publicity lived too much in broad daylight to conceal anything essential even about his most intimate concerns. The principal documents for the history of his reign are to be found in the Collection of Laws and the publications of the official *Gazette* in which his follies and his fits of passion are writ large.

Valuable help from many quarters has compensated for the gift of ubiquity which I do not possess. Of this one example must suffice. At the Record Office in London the courtesy of the eminent head of that incomparable establishment and the assistance of his intelligent staff, enabled me to accomplish much in the space of a few days. At the very same time the helpful kindness of M. de Roudanovsky, the learned Russian Consul at Valetta, spared me the necessity of a personal visit to the archives of the island. To these gentlemen and to others whose help I have been fortunate enough to obtain I wish here to express my grateful thanks.

His Excellency M. Iswolsky, the Russian Ambassador at Paris, has also been one of my benefactors, for he placed at my disposal a large number of notes and documents collected by the brilliant diplomatist in the course of a

INTRODUCTION

doubly laborious career in which the calm study of the past has often vied with a busy participation in the great affairs of the present. I beg him to accept the expression of my sincere gratitude.

Finally, I owe a special tribute to H.I.H. the Grand Duke Nicolas Mikhaïlovitch, who has again generously favoured me, not only by opening to me his own splendid collections at St. Petersburg and Borjom, but in procuring me access to others in which I have found much that was most valuable. I hope that this book may thereby be made more worthy of the interest with which he has honoured it.

PART I

CHAPTER I

WAITING

I

PAUL was born on September 20, 1754 (old style), and was eight years of age at his father's death. His mother having usurped the supreme power he had to wait till 1796 before he came to the throne. He was convinced that Catherine's usurpation was an encroachment on his own rights, and this was the crux of the quarrel which more or less violently divided mother and son for so many years.

I have elsewhere * described this period during which their lives overlapped, but it must be briefly recapitulated here, for the Emperor Paul of 1796–1801 can only be understood by reference to the Paul of 1762–1796—the heir apparent, but also the pretender and the rebel. This aspect of the character of this unfortunate Prince has been too much neglected, but it is essential in the history of his life during the greater part of which it was a leading feature, and in many ways dominated and controlled the short but dramatic development of his fortunes.

There is still a controversy about the justice of his claims, but the question is in reality extremely simple and is complicated only by Paul's having improperly imported into it an element of " legality " which is quite

* See *The Story of a Throne*, also *The Romance of an Empress*, Book IV, Chapter II.

6

out of place. There is absolutely no justification for this. The crown which Catherine's son claimed as his by inheritance, was not hereditary at this time. It was, according to the celebrated formula of Caracciolo " elective or occupative."

From the chaos of contradictory principles which had existed since the extinction of the dynasty of Rurik at the end of the sixteenth century, Peter the Great had professed to disengage a decisive principle—" the truth of the sovereign's will "—that is to say the discretionary power of the reigning monarch to choose his successor. But though he adopted this expedient he neglected to use it, and after his death there began with his widow a disorderly series of male and female " occupiers" who were swept on to the throne by a succession of *coups d'état*.

The aunt of Peter III, having gained the throne in this way, thought fit to appeal to the law laid down by the great Czar and appointed her nephew, Paul's father, to reign after her. He, however, did not think of using the same privilege in favour of his son. Thus at his death Paul was legally nothing, and between him and Catherine the only conflict possible was one, not of rights but of ambitions. This conflict began before Catherine came to the throne and even before her husband had met his tragic end.

Already in 1760 Nikita Ivanovitch Panine, appointed Paul's tutor by Elizabeth, was plotting to dethrone Peter as Catherine afterwards succeeded in doing, but to substitute for him not his wife but his son. With such a pupil Panine hoped more easily to realise his ideal of constitutional monarchy on the Swedish model in which the sovereign power is exercised ostensibly by the sovereign but really by the minister. He failed. Catherine, better served by her audacity, her good fortune and her friendship with the Guard, succeeded.

Paul did not fail to hear of the plans previously made on his behalf and his anger was increased, not only against the winner of the game in which the stake was a crown, but also against those who had helped her to win it.

And yet, apart even from filial sentiment, his rancour was the less justified because he gained much more than he lost by what happened. He lost a highly doubtful chance. Nothing could be less certain than that his father would appoint him his successor. Peter had talked of repudiating Catherine and of marrying Mlle. Vorontsof. The second wife might have had more children and might have persuaded the Czar to give the preference to one of them. Some even thought him capable of preferring the victim of one of the earlier *coups d'état*, the Emperor Ivan Antonovitch dethroned by Elizabeth. On the other hand one of Catherine's first cares on coming to the throne was to make her son her heir at the same time as she proclaimed herself an autocrat. The only title he ever had to the empire proceeded from this act. He owed his rights to his mother and was in a double sense her creature.

Ambition and reason, however, are strangers, and between mother and son there was still the shade of the victim of Ropcha. Had Peter III lived it is probable enough that Paul would not have succeeded him. Paul was quite right not to let this consideration influence him. He was wrong to confound his legitimate resentment with claims which were not legitimate, and to confront his mother to whose throne he was heir not merely as an avenger but as a rival. This double part he played for thirty-four years and it dominated his destiny.

Catherine had probably no means of averting this calamity. What could she have done ? She could not punish the assassins of her husband, for to them she owed both her throne and the means of preserving it. She could not appease her son by her maternal kindness, for he was torn from her arms the day after she gave him birth. He was to her practically a stranger and nothing in him either attracted her affection or flattered her pride. Moreover he was a rival, and she had to reckon with the susceptibilities and the suspicions of those who were her own partisans.

Their jealousy certainly did not go the length of preventing Catherine from discharging her duties as a mother. Did she deliberately neglect these duties as has been asserted ? This charge also must be retried.

II

Paul's education has been severely criticised and certainly it cannot be regarded as ideal. It would, however, be hard to find at this period and in analogous circumstances any other which could be so described. Neither the heir of Louis XV nor the heir of Frederick the Great was in this respect better off than Panine's pupil ; and Catherine herself had not the leisure to superintend the moral and physical development of her son even after she had taken the government of Russia into her own hands.

She had nothing to do with the choice of Bekhtéief, Panine's predecessor. He was a mediocre diplomat but an honest man. He developed Paul's inborn taste for drill by inventing for him an alphabet in which the letters were lead soldiers, and his conceit by writing and printing a gazette in which everything the young Prince said or did was inserted. Catherine had then no voice in the matter.

When she had the power to intervene she wished to continue her son's education under the auspices of the most distinguished intellects of contemporary Europe. But, having read the manifesto which attributed the death of Peter III to an attack of hæmorrhoids, d'Alembert declined the honour, observing that he was himself too much liable to that affection. Diderot, Marmontel, even Saurin, followed suit. She could not dispense with Panine, who was also not her choice, without rousing the powerful party of which he was the head, and in order to supplement his instructions she was reduced to employing various obscure persons.

Panine himself, however, does not deserve all the severity and disdain with which he is treated by most of Paul's biographers. He was a sybarite, an intriguer and a debauchee, and spent the interval of these pursuits, as the French chargé d'affaires at St. Petersburg said in 1774, in embroiling the son with the mother and the mother with the son. But he was not without merit even as a teacher; in 1760 he wrote a memoir which proves this. In this he discusses the care of the physical no less than the moral health of his pupil, shows how even his play may be used to teach him goodness, and sets forth a scheme of studies which are gradually to include everything likely to be useful to a future monarch. The debauchee was also a thinker. He was in touch, somewhat distantly it is true, with all that was best in the intellectual life of his time. In spite of his half German, half French education he remained a Russian, firmly rooted in his native soil and attached to its traditions, its manners and its prejudices, but he felt on his brow the gusts which were coming from the west and his eyes were open to the new light which was dawning there.

The young Grand Duke's other masters were not contemptible. The Frenchman Nicolay had previously been a distinguished professor of mathematics in the University of Strassburg; his compatriot Lafermière was an amiable man of letters while the Russian Plechtchéief was an eminent geographer and had been trained as a sailor in England.

Panine had passed his childhood in the Baltic provinces

and was consequently a Germanophile, but he was not denationalised and prided himself on his eclecticism. True the Prussian alliance was the first article of his political creed; Frederick II was his prophet and Berlin his Mecca. But it was the Berlin of the second half of the eighteenth century in which, as every one knows, the French genius counted for much. Moreover, in the scheme of education Panine did not fail to give a due prominence to Russia.

Whether the scheme was carried out is another question. Panine had no doubt read *Émile*, the first edition of which appeared in 1762, but it was not open to him to settle in the wilderness with his pupil ; he had to contend with the pomps and pleasures of a court—and such a court ! Thus no regularity in the hours of study was possible. Paul learned his lessons as he could, between a state dinner, a play, and a masquerade; he was taken early to the theatre and probably got little food from the *Faune jaloux* or the *Folies amoureuses*, though he learned to canvass the respective merits of the ballet girls in vogue, and to express opinions such as that a prematurely faded actress " had been too much handled."

The Semiramis of the North was delighted to introduce her son to her Court and went so far as to encourage certain precocious affairs with the least innocent of her ladies-in-waiting. She did wrong; but, as it happened, neither Paul's childhood nor his adolescence suffered from these corrupting influences. Whether by natural in-clination, a natural reaction against impulses received in this way, or an aversion from everything which came from his mother, the young prince seems to have been much more ready to yield to the more austere teaching of his tutors. His religious instructor, the Archimandrite Plato, afterwards Metropolitan of Moscow, made a strong and, as it proved, a lasting impression on his boyish mind.

This restored the balance, but a more serious reproach

lies at the door of Paul's educators. The intellectual and moral nourishment with which they supplied him was always too substantial for his powers of absorption and assimilation. It was always his fate to put into his head more than it could contain. While still a child sentiments and ambitions were instilled into him which were beyond the capacity of a mind in which the emotions always had the upper hand. He was treated now much as if he were a man, and he was never allowed to forget that he was a unique man at that—the future Czar! The result was that at ten years of age he had begun to express peremptory opinions about everything and to criticise severely the established government of his country, impatient already to replace it by his own. Two currents of inspiration were confused in him. On the one hand he caressed the autocratic tradition which in his later years became a sort of delirium. On the other he yielded himself to the fascination of the chivalrous romance of Malta on which he afterwards squandered the fortune of his empire. One day he treats his chamberlains as his slaves, another he dresses them as Crusaders and makes them engage in mimic tournaments.

Yet, however contradictory were these dreams, there were even more discordant elements in the surroundings of his waking life. Panine was a constitutionalist, Plechtchéief a mystically minded freemason, Catherine herself an assiduous reader of Montesquieu and Beccaria. From them into Paul's awakening intelligence filtered liberal tendencies, humanitarian ideas, utopian schemes of reform—all the philosophy of the age. Here was a new quest and one which pleased him. But for the pretender and the rebel this dream, too, must take on the form appropriate to the double rôle. He would be a reformer like Struensée, Turgot and Joseph II. But like the revolutionaries at the other end of Europe he was aiming at the conquest of supreme power, and, more blindly even than they, he attributed to what he like them was pursuing a magic virtue which would enable him to change, if not the face of the world, at least that of the country over which he was to rule.

Panine following Rousseau had gone so far as to forbid his pupil to engage in military exercises. Catherine, under the guidance of the Orlofs, was attempting to free her army from the tradition of Prussian militarism already stamped on her son's mind. But among Paul's entourage there were partisans of the methods thus repudiated. Every day the boy heard the praises of the glory of Peter the Great, soldier, sailor and sculptor, in whose hands his people were as wax; or of the genius of Frederick, the sublime drill-sergeant who governed his subjects like a regiment; or again of the heroism of Miltiades, the rough warrior, without whom Greece, for all her philosophers, would have succumbed at Marathon. Paul's dream was to be Frederick, Peter the Great and Miltiades all at once, to eclipse Catherine without giving up philosophy, to regenerate the empire yet retain absolute power.

Paul was by nature gay, playful and full of generous impulses, but he learned very early how his father met his end, and this prompted disquietude, suspicion and hatred, as well as a feeling of humiliating degradation. With this train of thought was intertwined another, contradictory, sinister, even revolting. The thought of Peter III was constantly present within him; no less constantly was he haunted by doubts as to whether he really was his son. Catherine's conduct certainly made it uncertain, but in the eighteenth century the case was common, and yet few mothers had to face the inquisitorial curiosity of their children.

Paul was uncompromising, and in the mystery of his birth he found a new occasion for self-torment, another occasion of scandal, an additional motive for his pose of sullen mistrust. By nature expansive, he learned to hide his thoughts and control his expressions. With all his joys bitterness was mixed and he reacted against the injustice of which he believed himself to be the victim by developing an unmeasured pride and an exaggerated susceptibility.

Catherine, Nikita Panine, and their assistants were certainly far from being masters in an art of which the principles are even now not fully understood. But when he left their care Paul was assuredly neither a fool nor a rake. He surprised all who met him by the extent of his learning and charmed them by his graceful wit. He was destined to be for many years a model husband; and to the end of his days he was a passionate worshipper of Goodness, Beauty and Truth. In spite of all this he was to dig with his own hands the abyss in which were engulfed, one after the other, his happiness, his fortune and his life.

III

Catherine was planning her son's marriage before he was fifteen, and the choice she made four years later, after anxiously considering all the innumerable German princesses of marriageable age, no doubt seemed to her the most advantageous for her son. It certainly was not the one which best suited her own convenience. The mother of the selected lady was the Landgravine of Hesse who used to receive Wieland, Goethe and Herder at Darmstadt. She was an excellent woman and her daughter was reputed above the average; but it was said of her by the Prince of Waldeck, when he heard she was going to Russia: "If that woman does not cause a revolution no one will." The Empress herself seems to have been warned by her matrimonial agent the Baron von Assebourg of the ambitious character of her prospective daughter-in-law, yet she did not hesitate to accept her.

Catherine, however, was always too ready to measure

other women's characters by her own, and in this instance she was mistaken. Wilhelmina of Hesse-Darmstadt when she became a Grand Duchess under the name of Nathalie Aléxiéievna had no other ambition than to amuse herself royally. It is said that she had begun the romance which she was to carry on at St. Petersburg before she left Darmstadt and that Catherine knew of it. But it was on the ship that brought her to Russia that Nathalie for the first time met her hero the handsome André Razoumovski.

Catherine was at pains to warn her son, and did all she could to break off the *liaison* by which he was being dishonoured. Was this, as has been said, because Nathalie and her lover were intriguing with the Franco-Prussian league? Frederick II had used the "junior court" a great deal for his own purposes in the days of Elizabeth, and no doubt he would have been very glad to play the same game again; but Nathalie was not Catherine. "My wife has just sung Pergolesi's *Stabat mater* to console her for the death of Olida," wrote Paul ingenuously to Razoumovski announcing the death of a favourite dog.

Paul was predestined to tragedy and even his first experience of married life ended sadly. This time his mother was not to blame. Von Assebourg had been more or less misled himself and had entirely misled the Empress. It appeared that the Grand Duchess had had an accident which rendered her incapable of bearing children, and in April 1776, after less than three years of married life, she died in childbirth. Catherine may have searched her papers after she was dead, but if so it was probably not with the expectation of discovering a conspiracy. There is no trace of such an intrigue in the correspondence either of the Austrian Ambassador, Prince Lobkowitz, or of his French colleague and opponent the Marquis de Juigné. If Razoumovski did conspire with his mistress he escaped very easily with a temporary banishment to Revel followed in a few months by a diplomatic appointment in Italy. In the Russia of those days this was the customary punishment for compromising a Grand Duchess—not for conspiracy.

Less than three months after the catastrophe Catherine was treating with her son about a second marriage and Paul was asking eagerly, " Is she fair or dark, tall or short ? " The Empress had returned to her first idea, which, comparatively speaking, was excellent. In 1768 she had thought of Sophia Dorothea of Wurtemberg. Sophia had been her own name before she came to Russia, and the young Sophia had been born like herself at Stettin where her father, Prince Frederick Eugene of Wurtemberg like Catherine's was in command of the troops. Sophia Dorothea was the niece of Frederick the Great ; Catherine had been his protégée. But in 1768 the Princess was only nine, and since then, having given up hope of becoming a Grand Duchess, she had become engaged to Prince Louis, a brother of the deceased Nathalie.

This mattered little. The young man was rather a scamp, but he knew how to behave. He was over head and ears in debt, and, having been offered a pension of 10,000 roubles, he discovered that " he was in honour bound " to waive his claims. So in August 1776 Sophia Dorothea was already on the way to Berlin to meet her new fiancé.

She was the very model of a German princess who, like other German princesses, had been brought up to fulfil the destiny of matrimonially recruiting the Courts of Europe. A very few weeks after the affair was settled Sophia Dorothea was able to write a letter *in Russian* to her future husband, and, having learned that his tastes were serious, she talked geometry to him at their first interview. Next day she wrote a glowing letter about

16

the Prince to a friend in which she declared that she was
" madly in love " !

Physically she was well fitted to be the mother of a
large family. Her numerous portraits do not make it
certain that she was beautiful, but perhaps that is the
fault of the painters. She was certainly tall, fair and
fresh, extremely shortsighted and inclined to be stout.
At Montbéliard, the seat of the junior branch of the
House of Wurtemberg to which she belonged, and still
more at Étupes, a neighbouring semi-rustic residence in
the taste of Rousseau, the little Court was frequented by
Joseph II, Prince Henry of Prussia, Lady Craven, afterwards Margravine of Anspach, La Harpe, Raynal, Florian,
Saint-Martin, Lavater and Droz. Thus she was a mixture
cunningly blended of patriarchal simplicity and worldly
wisdom, of intellectual and artistic culture, and bourgeois
simplicity, and of German *Gemüthlichkeit* and French
refinement.

She had in her in fact the makings of an excellent wife
and an accomplished princess. Her education was solid ;
she had pleasing talents, robust virtues and a few faults,
some of which she brought with her from Étupes while
others were developed in her new surroundings. Her
parsimony was such that, if we may believe Corberon,
the new Grand Duchess did not hesitate to take over the
clothes of her predecessor and to dispute with the lady's
maids the very slippers of the defunct Nathalie. But
she also had a taste for splendour, a love of pomp
and ceremony, and a passionate interest in small Court
intrigues. She was extremely tenacious of her rank, and,
as she was herself prepared to spend the whole day from
morning till night in full dress without respite or fatigue,
she implacably imposed the same burden on all her
entourage, and was ruled by etiquette in the most intimate
details of her domestic life.

She cultivated the arts—all of them !—without much

success but with great enthusiasm and in a rather pleasing fashion—not disdaining even needlework, which the first Sophie had hated. She kept a journal, wrote volumes of letters ; both were unfortunately destroyed by the Czar Nicolas, but a few surviving fragments show how prolix they were. At Pavlovsk she collected a literary circle in imitation of that at Étupes, and she built and planted and organised theatricals for her husband, who delighted in that amusement. In addition to all this she found time to devote her energies to the great charities and educational institutions which still bear her name.

During Catherine's lifetime she had no chance of interfering in affairs of state, from which Paul was himself excluded, but she did intervene in the quarrels between the son and the mother and, with the best intentions in the world, introduced into them a new element of bitterness. After her husband's accession she took to politics, at first timidly but afterwards more and more resolutely, till at the end of the reign for one mad moment she seemed to meditate imitating the widow of Peter III. Following her example, but at a more advanced age, she bestrode a horse like a man, a pose which in view of her corpulence was wanting in grace.

Like many less gifted women she prided herself on her subtlety. In 1781 she flattered herself that she could overreach her mother-in-law. She was longing to exhibit her greatness and her husband's in the Courts of Europe, and in order to obtain the Empress's consent she made a show of assisting her policy. The Empress was not deceived, but she was glad to get rid of the troublesome couple for a time and authorised the journey while she fixed the itinerary. In the same way, while Marie Féodorovna (as she was now called) never lost an opportunity of contrasting her own impeccable virtue with her mother-in-law's failings, she was equally watchful of every chance of attaching Potemkine or Mamonof to her interests, and she often stooped to the most shameless cajolery of the favourites, compensating herself afterwards by a double allowance of prudish horror and vituperation.

In spite of all this, and perhaps partly because of it, she and Paul were at first a most devoted couple, and Marie Féodorovna for long exercised a beneficent influence on her husband. It is possible that she abused it in order to help her friends or hurt her enemies. But in 1777 Paul, who was expecting the birth of an heir, seemed to be on the point of laying aside his old restlessness, for he said that he wished to devote himself entirely to his family duties.

If this happy development was checked the fault this time was incontestably Catherine's. She had herself been the victim of an unjustifiable abuse of power when her son was taken from her; but she now proceeded to do Paul the same wrong—and on the same pretext. She believed she could bring up Alexander better than his parents. This is the usual excuse of despots.

The result was a new cause of animosity. The parents objected to the system of Locke which the grandmother proposed to adopt for the education of their child, the future Alexander I. They were not altogether unreasonable, for one of the first effects of it was to make the boy deaf in one ear and hard of hearing in the other. Catherine wished him to be accustomed to the sound of cannon from his earliest years! The parents disliked equally the employment of the Vaudois jacobin La Harpe as the tutor of Alexander and his younger brother Constantine, and Catherine herself was destined to regret this choice, which accorded very ill with others that she had also insisted on. The governor-in-chief, Nicolas Saltykof, perhaps did not deserve the contempt which Langeron and most of his other contemporaries showered upon him. He had fought bravely under Colberg in 1761. In 1812

19

he was to raise a regiment at his own expense, and in the following year to act as a sort of regent in Alexander's absence. He was certainly a resolute partisan of the most absolute autocracy, and he obtained an influence over his pupil which often carried the day against La Harpe's and explains more than one trait in the perplexing career of the future partisan of republics who was also the organiser of the Congress of Laybach.

Catherine's idea was to arrive at some sort of balance or compromise, but in appointing Saltykof she thought she would please her son and daughter-in-law, who about this time had shown some liking for him.

The younger children were given up to their parents, and the only share taken by the Empress in the education of the girls was to call in the assistance of the excellent Charlotte de Lieven, whose nobility of heart and mind disarmed Marie Féodorovna herself. " My father," wrote the Grand Duchess Anna Pavlovna in later years, " loved to have us about him and, particularly in his last years, used to send for Nicolas, Michael and me to play in his room while his hair was being dressed—the only leisure time he had. He was so kind and gentle to us that we used to love to go. He said that he had been estranged from his elder children, who had been taken from him as soon as they were born, so he wished to have the younger ones about him so that he could get to know them."

Between Saltykof and La Harpe Alexander soon fell into an unbalanced condition, but the worst consequences of Catherine's scheme of education was that he and his next brother became as much strangers to Paul as he had been to his own mother. This became more marked as Alexander grew up. Paul, not altogether without reason, thought this son's gentleness effeminate and his reserve hypocritical. The jacobinism of La Harpe aggravated the discord, though Alexander was far in fact from

20

becoming seriously entangled in such opinions. Indeed, on this point there was little real difference between the pupil of La Harpe and the pupil of Panine and Plechtchéief. Paul himself had some marked features of jacobinism about him, and on the other hand Alexander found new joys at Gatchina. He too liked playing at soldiers between two lectures on the humanitarian philosophy, and Araktchéief, the brutal organiser of his father's military amusements, disputed him with La Harpe. Thus Paul regained half his son, but he was not a man to content himself with less than the whole, and their relations were not sensibly improved.

Meanwhile, the quarrel between Paul and Catherine became more and more bitter, and the reaction made itself felt even in the narrower home circle in which he was still free to indulge his natural tastes. Ruin and desolation entered there. The Grand Duke, more and more enraged, vented his anger on his friends and ended by destroying the little happiness which remained to him. This was but the first of a series of disasters. How far was Catherine responsible for it ?

IV

Short of effacing herself and allowing her son to reign in her stead Catherine made her son's lot very acceptable. He had magnificent apartments in the Winter Palace and at Tsarskoïe, a summer residence at Kamiénnyï-Ostrof and, later on, two others at Pavlovsk and Gatchina were placed entirely at his disposal. He had a yearly income of 175,000 roubles for himself and 75,000 for his wife over and above the maintenance of his court. Paul, therefore, was well provided for, and if he was always in agonising straits for money it was because he was robbed outrageously by his stewards and bled by Marie Féodorovna's poor relations, and because he spent preposterous sums on useless building operations, on the absurd and expensive toy army at Gatchina, and perhaps also on political propaganda in connection with his "cause."

Between his tenth and eleventh years (Sept. 20, 1764–Jan. 13, 1766, old style) Paul lived with his mother and accompanied her at all Court functions, great or small, at manœuvres and out hunting. She was present at his examinations, applauded his progress and bought for him from J. A. Korff a spendid library of 36,000 volumes, since presented to the University of Helsingfors. She announced her intention of initiating him later on into the art of government and she kept her word. In 1773, at the time of the Grand Duke's first marriage, she wrote him a letter inviting him in affectionate terms to come to her once a week to hear reports read.

This has been represented as intended by the Empress merely as a supplement to the lessons he was learning from his teachers. Paul was not twenty, and for one of this age such a supplement was not to be despised. Coming from such a teacher such lessons would have attracted older pupils. But Paul wished rather to give than to receive lessons. He was already a pretender, and was about to become a reformer.

In this very year he presented to his mother a long memorandum reflecting the ideas of the two Panines, which was neither more nor less than a violent diatribe against the existing régime—its principles, its methods, and its tendencies. The author wished to change the whole policy of the Empire, foreign and domestic ; and Bezborodko, the Empress's Secretary of State, who was destined to be Paul's Chancellor, came to the conclusion that the admission of the Prince to Her Majesty's councils had not been a success. Paul understood "nothing about anything," and made everything he was told a pretext for indiscreet criticism.

22

The experiment was therefore abandoned, but Catherine had no desire to condemn her son to idleness. She refused for the moment to make him a member of her council as he wished; but in making him High Admiral she gave him a serious occupation in life. If he neglected the great administrative duties entrusted to him and interested himself only in paltry details, it was, as became clear when he came to the throne, because his intellect and his temperament debarred him from more useful activities. Moreover, he was occupied by other cares.

He thought it due to his pretensions to the throne to prepare himself theoretically for his future duties, and he was not content to fill voluminous notebooks with extracts from the memoirs of the Cardinal de Retz or Sully. He prepared the draft of an army estimate for 1786 as if he expected to be able to put it into force. In 1778, with the assistance of Peter Panine, he prepared a scheme of military reform for immediate execution, and four years later, aided by the same collaborator, he went so far as to draw up a manifesto for his accession in which Catherine's detractors all unconsciously echoed the tone of the contemporary French pamphleteers who were struggling with the Government of Louis XVI.

In spite of all this Catherine did what she could to meet the claims of her rival. She still denied him access to the Council of the Empire, where his revolutionary ideas would have been too conspicuous. But in 1782 or even earlier she admitted him to the Privy Council, where he went on understanding " nothing about anything." Paul complained to Peter, Duke of Oldenburg, one of his brothers-in-law, that he was nothing more than " a phantom in a humiliating position." If this was so it was his own fault. It was he who chose, with ill-timed ambition, to play the part of a phantom which threatened the Government. It is true that he refused to put himself at the head of a party, but he was always agitating, criticising and proclaiming on the housetops that everything was going wrong, and whether he would or no this attracted partisans who were ready to take him at his word and join in his agitation, which was not serious enough to make Catherine anxious but quite enough to annoy her.

Already, in 1764, Count von Solms, the Prussian Envoy, spoke of a plot in favour of the Czarévitch. In 1772 there were similar rumours. The following year Pougatchof came on the scene—Paul was not concerned in this insurrection, but the pseudo-Peter III hung a portrait of the Czarévitch in the place of honour at his headquarters at Berdskaïa Sloboda and declared that he had only taken up arms to help the cause of his beloved son. Paul professed indignation, but in the same year Saldern the Holsteiner led him into a dark intrigue, the purpose of which was equally treasonable. This may perhaps have been a mere piece of folly, for Shirley, the Engl sh chargé d'affaires, wrote about this time : "I am certain that he has not enough courage or resolution to act against his mother."

By temperament Paul was essentially a man of action. This was precisely what made him so impatient. He was in a great hurry to pass from thoughts to deeds. But he never dared. Between the craving which pushed him forward and the fear which held him back the only middle course was to allow others to act. Like all pretenders he attracted about him all who were discontented with the existing Government. In 1773 Lobkowitz, the Austrian envoy, announced to his Court that Paul had become "the idol of the nation." In 1775 Catherine, who had vanquished Pougatchof and triumphed over Turkey, went to Moscow to receive the homage of her subjects. It was her son who received most of the acclamation. He was overwhelmed with ovations by a delirious mob, and his false friend Razoumovski whispered in his ear, " Ah! if you only would! "

Paul listened but did nothing. Two years later Paul found an ideal domestic happiness in his second marriage, but here again, and this time through no fault of his, the blameless pleasures of his private life placed him in perpetual and irritating contrast with his mother. At this moment Catherine was commencing with Potemkine the most sumptuous chapter of her life-long romance. Paul certainly had not seen the "Sincere Confession" addressed by the Empress to the future Prince of Tauris which has recently been attached to his memoirs, and in which with unrivalled cynicism* she discussed his predecessors! It was enough that he knew the facts, which were disgusting enough in themselves. But his rancour against the authoress of the " Confession " had little to do with this aspect of her character. Potemkine himself was hateful to the Grand Duke, not because he was his mother's lover but because he was her political collaborator.

At Vienna, in 1781, he began his great tour of Europe by declaiming against his mother's Government or the men (not always her lovers) by whom it was conducted. " As soon as he had any power he would turn them out with a whipping." At Naples the traveller attacked the legislative achievements of the Semiramis of the North. " Laws! " he cried, " in a country where the Sovereign can only keep her throne by trampling them all under-foot! " At Paris he declared that he could not so much as have a faithful dog about him without his mother having it drowned. These outbursts and many other spiteful remarks about the " one-eyed one " (Potemkine) and his mistress came to Catherine's ears ; and she became aware of a correspondence which Paul carried on during

* Potemkine had complained that he was the sixteenth; Catherine protests that before him there had been only five!

his journey under cover of P. A. Bibikof and Alexander Kourakine, two of his friends. Her reprisals, which did not go beyond an order of banishment, fell on these two intermediaries alone, and yet it was Paul who was most annoyed. He was far from understanding to whom and to what he owed the flattering attentions which he received everywhere and which were so much to his taste.

On his return to Russia he accentuated his irreconcilable opposition, which he now directed against the Empress's foreign policy. In this department Catherine had made a decisive change. She had freed herself from the bondage to Prussia, in which she had been kept for eighteen years by the genius of Frederick and the partition of Poland. The Greek plan was conceived and with it came the Austrian Alliance. Marie Féodorovna, flattered by the promise of a marriage between her sister and the Archduke Francis, the heir of Leopold II, accommodated herself to the change. Paul showed himself more Prussian than ever. He exchanged oaths of eternal friendship with Frederick's successor and maintained quasi-treasonable relations with the Court of Berlin. He even went so far as to try to corrupt Count Roumiantsof, one of Catherine's diplomatic agents in Germany. In Sweden a brother of Marie Féodorovna interfered with Catherine's plans. Made Governor of Viborg by favour he used his opportunities to enter into suspicious relations with his near neighbours. As he also ill-treated his wife, a Princess of Brunswick made famous under the name of *Zelmire* by her misfortunes, Catherine dismissed the husband and took the wife under her protection. This was another cause of quarrel, which was intensified when *Zelmire*, who had been sent to the castle of Lohde in Esthonia, fell into an obscure love-affair and perished mysteriously.

In 1787 the Austrian Alliance led to the re-opening of hostilities with Turkey. Paul as a pacifist and anti-Austrian opposed the war, but nevertheless wished to take part. His wife, though enceinte, wished to go with him! This led to further unpleasantness.

The following year Sweden intervened in the conflict, and as his wife had been delivered Catherine allowed Paul's bellicose ardour to have its way. His martial pretensions were cruelly put to shame by a fit of diarrhœa brought on by a night attack. But, what was worse, he played into the hands of the enemy he was sent to oppose by receiving compromising advances from the other side. He was recalled and became more sulky and captious than ever. He corresponded in cypher with the new King of Prussia, Frederick William II, the " lout " whom Catherine could not endure, and multiplied his conversations with Count Keller, the Prussian envoy, who received the impression that " if the Prince were compelled to defend his personal safety or if the nation called upon him with one accord he would not refuse to help them."

Thus Paul followed to the end, in thought if not in action, in the footsteps of all those who have been the authors of revolutions in Russia. But Catherine, on her side, took the steps which were indicated by her care, not for herself, but for the interests of which she was the guardian.

V

As early as 1780 she had been heard to say: "I see into what hands the Empire will fall when I am gone " . . . " I should suffer if my death, like the Empress Elizabeth's, meant a complete change of the political system of Russia." As Alexander grew up the idea took a more definite shape. The future of the Empire which she was making so great became in her eyes more and more associated with the destinies of the " budding Czar," as she called Paul's eldest son, observing that he resembled his father neither morally nor physically. When the French Revolution broke out she said: " There will arise another Tamerlane or Genghis Khan who will bring these people to their senses. But that won't be in my time, nor, I hope, in Alexander's." She did not mention Paul: he was already eliminated.

Thus there came a new phase in the duel between mother and son. Paul was certainly warned. In January 1787, in the midst of his preparations for the Turkish campaign in which he failed to distinguish himself, he drew up and gave to his wife a will in which he dealt with the possibility not only of his own death but of Catherine's during his absence. If that happened Marie Féodorovna was appointed Regent, and her first step was to be the seizure of all the Empress's papers and the proclamation that all the political dispositions made by the defunct Sovereign were null and void.

But Catherine, too, had taken precautions. She made Chrapowiçki her secretary, read to her the text of the regulations made by Peter the Great for the devolution of the Throne, indicating the successive applications which had been made of his principles since the time of Catherine I. A little later she drew up a note on the reasons which had led Peter to disinherit his only son. In another note relative to the Greek scheme she fixed the rights of succession for Alexander and Constantine as if Paul did not exist.

She now seemed to have a definite design to exclude him. Could it be justified? Paul's rights were clear, and they had the more claim to be respected by the Empress as she had herself created them. But the heir she had created was also a rival and a reformer: we have seen him in the first character; it remains to see how he sustained the second.

CHAPTER II

THE REFORMER

I

ALL Europe was at this time invaded by ideas of reform. Every one wished to try his hand at it, but in Paul's case the reformer was not so much the inventor or the partisan of this or that political formula, principle or theory, as the man himself—mind, character and temperament. His ideas no less than his inclination in this direction can only be understood with reference to the personality of which they formed part.

At the time of his first marriage, between the joyous Nathalie Aléxiéievna and the lively Razoumovski, Paul nearly cast aside his morose and prematurely melancholy humour and became a disciple of Epicurus. He " made it a principle to live on as good terms as possible with everybody," and found relaxation and amusement in his wife's company. But this did not last long. At the end of a few months he was again plunged in study and reflection, though the influence of his youthful spouse was still traceable in the fondness he showed for French literature, in which, however, he did not entirely follow the taste of the time. He had little liking for Diderot, who had just arrived in Russia, probably because Catherine was ill-advised enough to appreciate this eminent representative of western culture. Paul thought " his flattery too ponderous, his enthusiasm too profound, and his knees too supple." He found it necessary, however, after the fashion of the day, to have a literary correspondent in France, and for fifteen years, from 1774 to 1789, the other Laharpe (of the Rue Saint-Honoré) fulfilled this function.

After the fifth year Paul began to be less and less charmed with the letters from Paris. He went to Berlin for his second wife and there he found one of his idols, by whom he was held for the time in undivided allegiance. He himself cannot be said to have altogether made a conquest of Frederick the Great. " I count it among the greatest obligations under which I am to your Majesty that you have enabled me to make the acquaintance of so accomplished a Prince." This is what Catherine read in a letter addressed to her by the King after the meeting. And the following is what we find in a note, probably written the same day, which was afterwards inserted in the memoirs of the philosopher of Sans-Souci. " He (Paul) seemed to me haughty and violent, which has made those who know Russia fear that his fate may be similar to that of his unfortunate father."

But Paul's enthusiasm was sincere, and Gatchina was the consequence of the impression which he formed. Germany, or rather Prussia, disciplined, policed, drilled and governed by the stick seemed to him to be the model to imitate. He began to remember with complacency that he had little Russian blood in his veins. He was indifferent to the renunciation of his claims on Schleswig, in which his mother had acquiesced in 1767. Now the reign of Peter III himself assumed an ideal aspect in his eyes. He dreamed of resuming that Prince's work which had been interrupted by Catherine, and he was so much possessed by the idea of order, method and regulation that he drew up an " instruction " for his fiancée which treated of everything from religion and morals down to the details of her dress. In his correspondence with P. I. Panine and N-V. Repnine he remains a convinced anti-militarist, almost a pacifist, but nevertheless he sketches a complete programme of reforms to be realised when he should come to the throne, the effect of which would be to militarise his country !

In all these projects, which correspond with remarkable closeness to his ultimate realisation of them, Paul was actuated by the idea of opposing Catherine. In her foreign policy the Empress was engaged in a policy of unlimited expansion and had committed herself in every direction to war, intervention and enterprises of all sorts. Paul made up his mind that Russia should stay at home quietly and " cultivate the garden," like Candide. This was to be the watchword of his policy when he came to the throne, but by that time he had pressed his mother to put down the French Revolution with her cannon. The time soon came when he was to try to do so himself, and at the moment of his death he was in the position of defying all Europe and attempting to wrest India from England!

At home he was perturbed by the discordances of race and culture which the policy of annexation had brought into the Empire. He flattered himself that he could eliminate these and even charm away the resulting class antagonisms, and the formulæ on which he relied to accomplish this miracle were precisely those employed by the French reformers of the period and were borrowed as these had been from Montesquieu, from Rousseau— even from Marat himself. Equality before the law, ordered freedom, popular education of the masses in these principles, development of commerce and industry in the interest of the people, a responsible administration based on the power, not of a ruling class but of a Sovereign equally benevolent to all—how well one knows the catalogue !

As Catherine's rival Paul professed to hate the *encyclopédistes*, but as a reformer he borrowed both their doctrines and their vocabulary. As a philanthropist he busied himself with the condition of the peasants. He saw in them the source of nourishment for all other classes, and he determined to ameliorate their lot. He was not to abolish serfage, for Peter III had had no idea of doing so, but he would define and re-establish the law as to serfs attached to manufactories and would lighten the burdens imposed on the others. He would see to it that the land, the source of all wealth, was delivered from the excessive fiscal exploitation to which it was a prey. To succeed he had merely to balance the income and the expenditure of the Treasury by putting a stop to the latter.

About 1780 Paul had already embodied all these splendid visions in draft " fundamental laws," the outline of which has been preserved. They appear again in another " instruction " drawn up for Marie Féodorovna and intended to guide her in the event of a regency. Nothing, however, got beyond the stage of vague theory. There is nothing practical or precise.

Moreover, as he wished to embrace everything in the scope of the great work of which he dreamed, he found it very hard to know where to begin. His position as claimant gave him a hint. Clearly he must first get rid of the fundamental disorder from which all other disorders sprang and of which he, as the natural heir of Peter III, was, in his own eyes, the victim. The reign of law could not be established in a country in which the investiture of the supreme power itself escaped all legal control.

A " dynastic statute " regulating the devolution of the Crown was promptly consigned to paper. But what then ? Paul's imagination failed him. Marie Féodorovna was consulted. She was a great authority on the rights of succession and their attached prerogatives, but she knew nothing about politics, and the other collaborators of the future Sovereign were equally ignorant. Their tastes and aptitudes were fully satisfied by the manœuvring ground at Gatchina, to which Paul himself was more and more attracted. There, too, it was in the company of Peter Panine and Repnine that he found the solution of the problem. Paul allowed himself to be persuaded by his two counsellors and felt that he had solved his problem. Military reorganisation, drastically conceived and executed, should precede all other reforms and bring them in its train.

Was not a well-organised army the proper environment for the development of the spirit of discipline and the sentiment of legality? The nobility would learn these principles there and would in turn inculcate them on the masses. But Peter III had absolved the nobles from the obligation of military service and they had deserted the ranks. As things were the upper classes retained the privileges and evaded the duties for which the privileges were originally given. How was he to redress the balance and secure that duties and rewards maintained a due proportion throughout the social scale? He could not repudiate what his father had done. Again the solution of the difficulty was discovered on the parade-ground. By setting an example, by becoming the first soldier of his empire, the Sovereign who shared the toils no less than the glories of his army would rally the most refractory of his subjects about him.

But even here his mind was torn by conflicting inspirations. Montesquieu wrote and Paul copied in his note-book: "The first quality of the soldier is health and strength . . . Any officer who weakens his subordinates in any way by tormenting or beating them is responsible as a murderer before God."* "And," added Paul prophetically, "an equal retribution should overtake him."

But when Paul laid aside his Montesquieu and turned to his other instructors in the military art, the Araktchéiefs and the Steinwehrs, he found them all engaged in cuffing and

---

* This is a paraphrase. Montesquieu (*Grandeur des Romains*, Chapter II), speaking of certain cruel practices attributed to Roman generals, simply wrote: "As strength is the principal quality of the soldier, to weaken is to degrade him."

beating the recruits. This stirred his emulation: he learned to cuff himself and to order floggings; and this was a contradiction from which he never emerged.

In order to escape from it he imagined the strangest expedients, such as to use his position as a Prince of the Empire to raise levies in Germany. This would secure that only foreigners would receive the beatings and the floggings. Another day with Panine or Araktchéief he would draw up a project of military colonies which was destined to be one of the great enterprises and one of the great failures of the reign of Alexander I; or again he would attack the Guard, whose privileges and political importance offended his levelling opinions and kept alive his resentment against the existing Government.

From this chaos some sensible ideas and some benevolent intentions stand out, but these are always confused and impeded by contrary impulses, and in the long run racial instincts and historic tradition carry the day against suggestions coming from without. Paul belonged to a people for whom battles and the fighting formation had for centuries been a law of existence and progress. The curious result, therefore, of his plan to put an end to dynastic crises and in particular to government by women, was that the culmination of his reforming ambition and his liberal and humanitarian aspirations was a military reorganisation which was the fundamental characteristic of the programme of his reign and the principal cause of his ruin.

II

After his appearance at Berlin in 1776 the grand tour of 1781–1782 marks a more decided change of orientation. This time Paul, in a way, appeared to greater advantage. At Vienna his seriousness, his enlightened curiosity, his simple tastes, excited admiration. He was not very fond of dancing, preferring good music or a well-chosen play, provided he was not kept up too late. His chief interests were, however, the Army and the Navy and Commercial affairs. He was indifferent about what he ate except that he preferred simple dishes. He disliked all forms of play. He was ascetic, like Robespierre and other leaders in the saturnalia of Revolution.

At Florence the younger brother and successor of Joseph II found him very intelligent and reasonable, full of sound judgments on things and ideas, and prompt to seize all the aspects and details of a question. At Paris Louis XVI and Marie Antoinette were not less favourably impressed. " The simplicity of the Grand Duke," writes the Queen,* " pleased the King very much. He seems to be very well read. He knows the names and the works of all our authors and he speaks to them as if he knew them when they are presented."

Everywhere, however, people seem to have felt that in the traveller there were really two men—one doing all he could to play the part of an " accomplished prince " with dignity and success, the other, showing himself more convincingly at times beneath this borrowed mask, the hero of a sombre tragedy. People admired his graceful manner and repeated his *bons mots,* but his obviously studied courtesy and his official gaiety were continually contradicted by some violent outburst or some bitter speech. He told the Countess Chotek that he did not expect to live to be forty-five. At Vienna a representation in his honour of Shakespeare's masterpiece had to be counter-manded because the star of the day refused to play Hamlet. " There would be two Princes of Denmark ! " For a similar reason Laharpe's *Jeanne de Naples* was forbidden at Paris during the visit of the " Comte du Nord."

On his own side Paul's impressions were different. The honour and respect with which he was received were paid through him to the great Power he represented and

* To her brother Joseph, dated June 16, 1782. Hunolstein, *Correspondance*, p. 124.

to the great Sovereign who had raised that Power to an unexampled pitch of prosperity and splendour. Paul never for a moment appreciated this, nor did it occur to him to modify in consequence his views and sentiments on the subject of these two sources of his personal consequence. He simply became more and more possessed with extravagant ideas of his own importance. He saw Europe at his feet ; his intention was that it should remain there and he was to construct his plan of foreign policy on this basis. At the same time his contact with the old monarchies of the west awakened new ideas and new ambitions in his restless mind. Versailles and Chantilly were superimposed upon Potsdam and Sans-Souci.

When he returned to Russia Paul felt more keenly than ever the position of nonentity to which he was for the time condemned. " Here I am at thirty doing nothing ! " he wrote to a correspondent. This is a customary complaint. Thus : " Affairs in Germany are in great confusion . . . it is cruel to see all this from the top of one's tower." Or again : " You tell me that politics are getting interesting. I congratulate you. Now is the time for you to shine. As for me, my business is to understand nothing of all this." And as time goes on his lamentations grow even more bitter.

He said he was doing nothing ! But every day he rose at four o'clock and kept busy a whole tribe of secretaries, aides-de-camp and collaborators of all kinds. He had at hand a library of 36,000 volumes. He was engaged in methodical preparation for his future duties as Sovereign. He prided on keeping ready for instant execution all the vast schemes of reform which he was burning to have the power to carry out. How was it that all this was insufficient to occupy all the time at his disposal ?

Alas ! The nature of his mind made the time which he could devote to these objects very limited indeed. To reflect, to analyse or to combine was not for him. His impressions invariably translated themselves into impulses and in order to think he had to act as some have to speak. This is why books themselves soon ceased to interest him. Marie Féodorovna tried to arrange after-dinner readings but could never induce him to take part. If the books were serious they bored him, if of a lighter character they seemed unworthy of his attention. Thus he became more and more nervous and irritable, until he was free to exercise his activities in a field which he believed to be without limits and without obstacles, when he threw himself upon his work with that blind fury which is characteristic of ambitions such as his.

Meanwhile he became more and more confused among the contradictory suggestions between which his thought and his will were torn. He was now without a guide. The few men whose advice by fits and starts he had consented to follow had either quitted him or he had detached himself from them. Peter Panine died in 1789; Nikita Ivanovitch had predeceased his brother by six years. But Paul had ceased to be intimate with his old teacher. The elder Panine, faithful to the principles he had learned in Sweden, had employed his last moments in drawing up a political testament, which was circulated in manuscript and was to serve as a preface to the draft of a written Constitution prepared by the same author in 1772. This for a time had been Paul's political faith, but he was now receding farther and farther from it and he turned his back on those by whom it was still retained.

In the best part of his consciousness there still lingered some traces of his old liberal aspirations, and he kept Plechtchéief about him. The result was a moral crisis which ended in a plunge into mysticism.

Freemasonry, of which Nikita Panine, N-V. Repnine and Alexander Kourakine were adherents, had received a powerful impulse in 1777 from the Duke of Sudermania, the head of the principal chapter of the Swedish Brother-

hood who accompanied his brother, Gustavus III, to
St. Petersburg in that year. The Russian lodges were
in close touch with the Prussian organisation over which
Prince Ferdinand of Prussia, Marie Féodorovna's uncle,
presided. Under the influence of Woellner and other
Rosicrucians they underwent, like them, the influence of
the reaction in favour of religion which in Germany succeeded the triumphs of philosophical scepticism. Lavater
and Swedenborg gained a following, secret societies multiplied, and freemasonry, losing its tone and original
character of humane tolerance, went astray among
alchemists, illuminati and charlatans of all kinds.

In 1782 Novikof founded a "Society of the friends of
Science" and came under the influence of Schwartz,
a Bavarian mystic. He gave himself up to the publication
of all the philosophical pietism and mysticism which
had been produced in Europe during the previous two
centuries, and through Jacob Boehme and Philip Spener
he came to Swedenborg and to Saint-Martin, who found
a second fatherland at Moscow. There the sect called
"Martinists" was founded and made rapid progress;
they had a house of their own and organised meetings
which were soon denounced by the police as hotbeds of
revolutionary propaganda. It was said that one day the
members cast lots to decide which of their number would
undertake to assassinate the Empress.

Paul had allowed himself to be drawn into this movement in 1782 or even earlier. The Grand Master of the
chief lodge at Moscow, Prince Gabriel Galitzine, was
among his warmest partisans, and correspondence
seized by Catherine showed that he was in close relations
with Novikof and the other masons in the Second Capital
of the Empire and even in a fair way to be elected Grand
Master of the Order. Already portraits of him had been
circulated representing him wearing Masonic emblems.

As usual, the police reports exaggerated and distorted

the facts. Novikof and his friends were no regicides, but they were attached on the one hand to the libertarian movement of the day, and on the other they were entangled in certain foreign relationships which were not entirely non-political. There was reason for some anxiety on Catherine's part; for too many Prussian Princes, in correspondence with the sectaries of Schwartz and Saint-Martin in Russia, were showing a suspicious eagerness to put Paul at their head.

She cut the matter short by the prosecution which sent Novikof to the fortress of Schlüsselburg in 1792 and which does her no credit. Paul, however, was screened by some of his friends and did not hesitate to disavow the others, and he was untouched by the storm. He was left free even to continue to participate in the tendencies and the practices which had provoked the Empress's severity.

He kept about him Vassili Ivanovitch Bajénof, the celebrated Muscovite architect who had been his intermediary in dealing with the lodges. He continued to correspond with Lavater and even with Saint-Martin, who had been a *habitué* of Montbéliard, and in later days, when he had abandoned freemasonry so entirely as to insult and scoff at it, he retained its impress; there was always a tendency to exaltation in the sincerely religious sentiments which he professed.

When Paul came to the throne one of his first cares was to release Novikof, whose sect was treated with marked favour, loaded with places and seemed in a fair way to predominance until Rastoptchine, jealous of their influence, succeeded in bringing about their discredit. In the meantime, in company with Mlle. Nélidof, he abandoned himself to the flood of mysticism and all the aberrations to which it was then leading. Woellner had become director of religious affairs in Prussia and was there fighting freedom of belief with the most intolerant religious fanaticism.

Paul became equally fanatical and intolerant in his political struggle with freedom of thought in Russia. Catherine, who was much less eager to combat the free-thinkers of France than her son, crushed him with the devastating remark : " You are a savage beast if you do not understand that with cannon you can do nothing against ideas ! "

He never suspected how closely akin he was to the jacobins, whom he detested and wished to annihilate. Like them, he was an idealist in pursuit of the Absolute. Like them, too, he thirsted for despotic power. After their example, he thought he would mould and fashion the human material which was not yet at his disposal. For his ambitions for reform and his impatience to realise his plans had communicated to him the dread contagion of the restlessness which was spreading from the West of Europe, in addition to that which was congenital in him or produced by the trials of his childhood.

It was at this point in his moral and intellectual development that he was surprised by the death of Catherine, which gave him what he had wanted for so long. The appearance which he presented for so short a time on the stage of history must now be described to the reader.

III

" As for his face, he did not make it, nor as some assert, did his father ; it would therefore be unjust to reproach him for it." This pleasantry of Masson evokes the physical presence of the Prince in middle life. Paul was very ugly. His nose was flat, his mouth large and full of long teeth, the lips prominent, the lower jaw protruding. These characteristics, together with his premature baldness, combined to give his pallid countenance the appearance of a death's head. His figure was fat and round and his denuded head was planted on a short and awkward body, to which its owner vainly strove to impart an air of dignity and elegance. Tchitchagof is said to have described him as a flat-nosed Lapp with movements like an automaton.

In this unpleasing whole favourable witnesses have sought to discover some agreeable details. Madame de Lieven praises the beauty of his eyes, whose expression " was infinitely soft and pleasing." She emphasises his " good manners," " his politeness to women," which clothed his person with a real distinction and proclaimed him at once " a prince and a gentleman." Though herself very sympathetic Mme. Vigée-Lebrun seems to have been nearer the truth when she said that his physiognomy lent itself very readily to caricature.

But Paul had not always been so ill-favoured. His physical, like his mental, evolution had been gradual. He passed for a pretty child, and in the gallery of Count Alexander Stroganof his portrait and that of his son Alexander at the same age of seven years were afterwards confounded. Accidents of health no doubt contributed to the unfortunate change in his appearance. In 1762 the feeble constitution of the heir-apparent was cited as a reason by the signatories of a petition praying Catherine to contract a second marriage. The same year Paul was detained by illness on his way to Moscow for his mother's coronation and in the following October his life was in danger. There were fresh crises in 1767 and 1771 accompanied by nervous troubles, which were popularly attributed either to a congenital taint or to a seizure by which the child was said to have been attacked at the time of the deposition and death of his father. There was also some talk of epilepsy.

And yet in 1768 the surgeon Dimsdale, who had been summoned from England to inoculate the little Czarévitch for smallpox, found him well developed, robust, with no trace of congenital infirmity, and in later life Paul gave certain proof of unusual physical vigour. He was a good horseman and could remain many hours in the saddle without apparent fatigue, and he developed in his way a very remarkable power of work.

His yellow complexion, however, indicated a bilious temperament, which the doctors treated with frequent purgatives, and as his life went on not only baldness but other signs of premature decrepitude, such as wrinkles and trembling of the hands, pointed to an abnormal functioning of his vital organs. At the same time his whole deportment, his clothes, his attitudes and his gait, were pretentious and theatrical, and accentuated in him the suggestion of caricature which Mme. Vigée-Lebrun with her artist's eye could not fail to perceive.

His character is still the subject of a dispute which was begun by Kotzebue and Masson immediately after his death. This dispute is explicable by the extraordinary discordance of the traits of character brought out by the parties to the discussion, which seem to belong to two entirely different people.

"The foundations of his character," writes Mme. de Lieven, "were grand and noble. He was a generous enemy, a splendid friend. He knew how to pardon magnanimously and how to repair a wrong and an injustice with effusion." "But," she adds, "he was abrupt and extreme in his resolutions, violent and resentful, and bizarre even to extravagance."

He was essentially mobile, because extremely impressionable and, even from childhood, excessively nervous. Later in life it was observed that his humours varied with the atmospheric conditions. Every morning he was in the habit of ascertaining which way the wind blew, and those about him anxiously followed the oscillations of weathercocks. Even at ten years of age he could not sleep at night if during the day he had experienced any emotion. Already also he was always impatient : in a hurry to go

to bed, in a hurry to get up, to sit down and to rise from
table. He could not rest until he was taken to the Empress's evening reception. Once there he stamped with
his feet until he was taken away.

The explanation of this chronic state of over-excitement
has been sought in a supposed attempt to poison him in
1778, the reality of which is attested by himself. But
science knows no toxic agent which is capable of producing such effects, and before he fell under the blows of
assassins of flesh and blood Paul had for long been the
victim of his imagination, which conjured up phantom
assailants. " The stories of all the Czars who had been
dethroned or murdered were ever present to his mind and
murder was in fact an *idée fixe* with him," notes De Ségur.
At Tsarskoïé-Sélo, in 1773, he found some pieces of glass in
his favourite dish of sausages, cried out that he was being
murdered, carried the dish to the Empress and demanded
the death of the criminals. In 1781, at Florence, in the
middle of a Court banquet he discovered a suspicious
flavour in the wine served to him ; immediately he thrust
his fingers into his throat to make himself vomit. Some
months later a similar incident happened at Bruges,
where, having been incommoded by a glass of iced
beer, he accused the Prince de Ligne of attempting his
life !

Always on his guard, he saw himself threatened on every
side, surrounded by enemies conspiring his ruin, by spies
who noted his slightest movement. In time this disposition of mind acquired a character very near akin
to that of a delusion of persecution.

His most usual impression, and the one which dominated
all the rest, was that of fear. He seems to have been
born in terror. He trembled all over when his great aunt
approached his cradle, so much so indeed that Elizabeth
paid these visits which were so badly received at rarer and
rarer intervals. Cowardice was, indeed, hereditary with

him, for Peter III had been a poltroon; but the vice grew upon him. It came to be noticed that Paul, though a clever horseman, never pushed a charge to the end. He was afraid at all times of everything, and even his fits of anger could not dominate this emotion. An almost infallible means of calming the fury of this strange creature was to answer him with a violence equal to his own. Like the soldier of Skanderbeg mentioned by Montaigne, who was threatened so long as he begged for mercy and pardoned when, his prayers being of no avail, he put his hand to his sword, any man who dared to brave Paul was almost certain to cow him. But few took the risk.

Always on the alert, his distrust was strengthened by the low opinion he had of men in general and of those who composed his own household in particular. As a child he was hated by his servants, whom he falsely accused of thefts of which they were in fact quite capable. And yet, like all weak men, he felt the need of giving his confidence. Thus he gave his friendship easily and as easily took it away. He was full of sudden attachments and prompt ruptures—always the most capricious of masters and the most fickle of friends.

But his misanthropy was, from another point of view, only one form of his pride, which developed beyond measure and made him extravagantly haughty in spite of his natural affability, and preposterously imperious in spite of his natural weakness. While still a child he was offended because at the theatre the audience burst into applause before he gave the signal. It was useless to assure him that the Empress herself tolerated this breach of etiquette. During his visit to Berlin as a very young man the Court was struck by his manner of acknowledging obeisances made to him, " without making the least inclination of his head, but on the contrary throwing it back and staring at the other." When he was thirty

44

years of age he ordered his coachman to be flogged for refusing to turn his carriage into an impracticable road " Break my neck if you like, but do what I tell you ! "

He sought the illusion of force in a violence which in his words and deeds was only a consequence of an absolute want of self-control. His fits of anger, unlike those o Napoleon, were never calculated. His words and gestures escaped him without the slightest control. Often indeed they were quite at variance with his thoughts or intentions at the same moment. Like all morbid phenomena which are permitted to develop unchecked this symptom gained progressively in intensity. " His violence increased day by day," observes Simon Vorontsof, " and ended by over-throwing his mind."

These crises of passion were so acute that even Paul's external appearance seemed to change. " He grew pale ; his features became convulsed and unrecognisable ; he stiffened and gasped for breath ; he threw back his head and breathed stertorously." Other observers report that " his hair stood on end " and that " his face assumed a repellent aspect." If some intimate friend tried to restrain him he would reply, " I cannot hold myself in ! "

No doubt he sometimes repented of the evil he did in these outbursts ; sometimes he even repaired his faults. But his repentance was rare and usually incomplete. He apologised to an officer whom he had struck but he would not reverse his dismissal from the army. Another officer was shot in a duel of which the Prince's mistress was the cause. Paul congratulated the opponent of the wounded man and ordered the latter to be removed to a fortress. " But if he is moved the doctors will not answer for his life. . . ." " Do what I tell you ! " And at the imminent danger of a fatal hemorrhage the subject of this barbarous order was removed by the police. " What about his mother ? " continued Paul. " She is in despair." " She is to be made to leave the town immediately." The son of a prisoner asked as a favour to be allowed to share his father's captivity. The order was given to shut him up—but in a separate cell.

The exact truth of these anecdotes, which are excessively numerous in the memoirs of the period, cannot be invariably vouched for. There is indeed reason to suspect that they are to some extent exaggerated. Masson probably invented the story of the horse which Paul is said to have condemned to be starved to death for stumbling. But in a general sense the abundance of concordant testimony on this point is very convincing, especially as the hardness of heart which Paul knew was attributed to him by most people is remarked upon by his own daughter-in-law, the wife of Alexander I, who complained that he jested cynically about the applications for help which were brought before him.

Yet he always had his moments of kindness and he could hark back to the exquisite tenderness with which he wrote to his second wife when preparing for the Turkish campaign. " You know how much I have loved you and how deeply I am attached to you. Before God and man your nature deserves not affection only but my respect and the respect of all. You were my first consoler. You have been my best counsellor. . . ."

Very early in his career the conception which Catherine's son formed of his situation in the world led him fatally into a development of brutal egotism which, so far as was possible in one of his extreme inconsequence, ended by becoming the principal motive of all his actions. His pride still imposed on him a certain dignity of attitude and magnanimity of gesture : but the dominating sentiment of self always intervened to spoil the effect.

Paul was often excessively liberal and his largesses have been exaggerated by tradition, but they were usually nothing but parade and ostentation. He was prevented from being really generous by having inherited from his

German ancestors too much of the meanness of which his second wife could not get rid even amid the luxury of the Russian Court. According to Parochine he would count the candles in his bedroom and regulate the number from day to day. As a child he would keep for his attendant one of the biscuits served to him for breakfast, but he was careful to choose the smallest. Later on, as Karamzine says, " he punished for no fault, and recompensed for no merit, and thus deprived chastisement of all shame and favour of all charm." He left Parochine in poverty after promising him a fortune, neglected Nikita Panine on his deathbed, and ill-treated Souvorof when he returned from the campaign of Italy.

Such was the character of the man, whose intellect certainly was not made to correct the errors of his heart.

IV

His intelligence, which was lively by nature, did not lack cultivation, and he profited by the careful education which he received. His scientific, historical, geographical and mathematical acquirements were respectable if incomplete. He was almost entirely ignorant of law, a subject which was little studied in Russia at that time, and in which there was little interest. He spoke several languages : German and French were familiar to him, and besides the ordinary Russian he knew the language of the Slavonic ritual. He expressed himself in writing with fluency if not with entire correctness. Without being a prodigy he could see and remember. When he crossed the Russian frontier into Prussia for the first time he was divided between admiration and sorrow. " These Germans," he said, " are two centuries ahead of us." When he returned to Gatchina he was able to reproduce with infallible accuracy the uniforms, the equipments, the exercises, the manœuvres—every feature of the Prussian military system. Grimm says of him : " At Versailles he seemed to know the Court of France as well as his own. In the studios of our artists he revealed a knowledge which doubled the value and the honour of his approval. In our lycées and academies he showed by his approbation and his inquiries that there was no kind of talent or study to which he was indifferent."

And yet Joseph II, comparing his abilities with those of Marie Féodorovna, considered the latter to be his superior. The fact is that when looked at closely, his power of assimilation as the imitator of Frederick seems somewhat limited, and he made no attempt to increase it, as he was incapable of developing and ripening the fruit of his studies by reflection.

He was not a fool, though many of the witticisms attributed to him during his stay in France are probably apocryphal. In spite of a certain contempt, which in time turned to furious hatred, he had a real taste for French wit, even in its most perverse form. He cultivated not only the epigram but the pun, and as he preferred to use the language of Voltaire when amusing himself in this way he sometimes made mistakes. He once greeted an officer whom he had summoned in order to give him a confidential office with the remark, " *Sitôt pris sitôt pendu !* " and the recipient of his favour thought he was being sentenced to death !

It was the instinctive reaction of a mind which was condemned to a constant overstrain. As late as 1800 in the middle of his most sombre preoccupations we find Paul diverting himself by tormenting with his foot from behind a servant engaged in cleaning a stove, quite delighted by the volley of insults poured forth by the man, who did not guess with whom he had to deal.

He had no other distractions. Like most nervous people he hated all kinds of sport. He rode only in order to direct manœuvres, to make tours of inspection or to accompany his wife in a ceremonial progress. His interest in art and literature was due either to affectation or compulsion. All his efforts in this direction were for the benefit of the gallery, and because in his opinion art and letters had their definite place among the occupations of a man of his rank. Frederick the Great played the flute; his admirer thought it necessary to sing romances, although—as he was hoarse in the lower notes and shrill in the upper register—his voice was exceedingly disagreeable.

He sought society, though, as a rule, it bored him, because he was too egotistical to find anything he desired to share with others, which indeed was one of the reasons for his inconstancy in friendship.

His mind was ill made and, above all, ill suited to a position of overwhelming responsibility. As a private individual Paul would no doubt have held an honourable place in the world. As a pretender, a reformer, or later as the absolute master of a great empire, he overstrained his natural or acquired faculties and thus in time the springs were broken. In other circumstances the character of the unfortunate prince would have been merely difficult. The difficulties of an abnormal situation in the first place and then the trials of omnipotence combined to make him a monster.

His character was not wanting in nobility. He had a very high, though somewhat exaggerated, ideal of the office to which he was destined. And besides he had a very keen, though perhaps not a very just, feeling for the duties which were attached to it, and an ardent desire to discharge them satisfactorily. But as his tutor Parochine predicted, " with the best intentions in the world you will make yourself detested." Twelve years later Paul proudly took up the challenge. " I would rather do right and be hated than do wrong and be loved," he wrote to a friend. But on the question of *how* he was to do right he was destined never to be at one with anybody or even with himself.

Morally, he was a poor, ill-formed creature who, as heir to the throne, made himself intolerable not only to Catherine but to most people who had anything to do with him; and his manners, no less than his designs, foreshadowed such a monarch that every one already looked forward to his reign as to a catastrophe. He made no attempt to conceal his intention to make a revolution, and in his retirement at Gatchina or Pavlovsk he created in miniature a view of what the future was to be. There he had a little kingdom arranged according to his fancy, and at the same time a field for experimenting with his ideas, his principles, his projects of reform. It was after observing him in this domain, where we must now follow him, that Catherine decided that her project of disinheriting him was both necessary and possible.

When she struck at Novikof and his co-religionists in 1792, her intention no doubt was to deprive Paul of the assistance of partisans who, she had reason to believe, were disposed to support his cause. She had yet to reckon with the family of her heir. Four years later she had reason to believe that, in that quarter also, she would meet with no resistance.

CHAPTER III

THE HEIR

I

CATHERINE presented Paul with Pavlovsk in 1777, when Alexander was born, and he was at first delighted with the gift. It is situated two leagues from Tsarskoïé and ten from St. Petersburg, in a wild corner of the country where the roads are often impassable. Five years later, however, on the death of Gregory Orlof, he inherited a splendid palace at Gatchina which had been built for the favourite by the Italian architect Rinaldi. He at once took a fancy to this new residence and Pavlovsk was given to Marie Féodorovna, who set to work to re-create her dear Étupes between a wood and a meadow, to which she gave the German names of *Paulslust* and *Marienthal*. With this she mingled some more ambitious ideas derived from Trianon and Versailles, and soon a new palace replaced the modest *datcha* of earlier years. There were gardens with the classic chalet side by side with the inevitable " pavilion of roses," and various artistic treasures, including a Flora which Catherine " irreverently " thought was like a " roadside Madonna." The taste of the whole was mediocre, as may be seen to this day.

Meanwhile, at Gatchina, Paul was doing his best to imitate Potsdam—not the Potsdam of Sans-Souci, but that other Potsdam where Frederick, deserting Voltaire, presided every morning over the drilling of his grenadiers. Orlof's old house readily lent itself to this. It was a building more massive than graceful, and might easily

51

have been taken for a barrack. It was crowded with statues of imitation marble, hideous cast metal images from one of Demidof's factories plastered with white paint. The park may well have reminded Paul of the table covered with the lead soldiers which were the delight of his childhood. The Grand Duke's entourage was soon in perfect harmony with these surroundings.

Gatchina was not a solitude like Pavlovsk. It was a place with nearly 2000 inhabitants, situated at the intersection of the main roads from St. Petersburg to Moscow and Warsaw, and already of some importance. It was here that Paul made his *début* as an administrator, and as the task was within his powers he discharged it at first not unsuccessfully. Following his best impulses and putting in practice his best ideas, he founded schools and hospitals; side by side with the orthodox *tserkov* he built Roman Catholic and Protestant churches; he encouraged the creation and development of industry; and distributed help in money and land. Even in this limited field, however, he did not entirely escape the embarrassment which all reformers experience from the complexity of their problems, and still less from the difficulties due to the mobility and violence of his temperament and the incoherence of his purposes. Soon, moreover, he was absorbed by other cares.

He had the command of a regiment of cuirassiers at Moscow in 1775, and had even then determined to reorganise it according to the Prussian fashion. For this purpose he had recruited a Colonel Steinwehr, a German who had deserted from Frederick's army. At Gatchina he was now on the point of pursuing his experiments on a large scale with troops of all arms which, like Peter the Great's "pleasure companies" at Préobrajenskoïé, were destined to form the nucleus of the military power of Russia reorganised, or rather restored in the tradition of the previous reigns.

THE HEIR

The neighbourhood of both the Grand Duke's residences was infested with brigands. He made this a pretext for requiring and permanently keeping there a battalion of marines and a squadron of his cuirassiers, and to these elements, drawn from the regular army, he afterwards added by recruiting new formations of cavalry, infantry and artillery, which progressively increased the number of men at his disposal to nearly 2000.

He had two objects : to create a basis for his projected reconstruction of the army and to criticise the work of Catherine, the whole of which he condemned, from the uniforms which Potemkine had sought to adapt to the climate and the manners of the country to the discipline and tactics in which the Roumiantsofs and the Souvorofs, repudiating Prussian models, had tried to reconcile the special genius of their people with the universal requirements of war. Paul thought their effort was blameworthy and pernicious. His soldiers, tightly buttoned into the cast-off garments of the heroes of Rosbach, powdered, gaitered and subjected to regulations which, like their clothes, were already obsolete, were made to disguise even their Slavonic names under German pseudonyms, and to please him the Pole Lipinski called himself Lindener.*

Catherine regarded these childish pastimes with an indifferent eye. Once only, apropos of a promotion, in which she saw an impertinent encroachment on her own prerogatives, she made as if she would break the toy. But she did not persist. She had given up trying to defend Paul from his own follies, and she thought that neither she nor Russia had anything to fear from them. She was only half right.

Half a century later the restorers of the palace of Gatchina projected a commemoration of the military glories which took their rise there. Marble tablets were

* *Lipa* in Polish = *Linde* in German, which means a lime tree.

to record in letters of gold the names and the deeds of the brave men who, having passed through this school, had distinguished themselves on the field of battle. But they found no one and nothing to record. Paul, with his reputation for absurdity and brutality, had attracted to his school only "the sweepings of the army," as a contemporary historian observed, and yet unfortunately throughout his reign and those of his immediate successors it was destined to leave a profound and durable impression on the military institutions of the country.

It would be unjust to say that Gatchina did not introduce some sound ideas and some useful principles, but with "the sweepings of the army" it also brought in some of the worst aberrations.

Among the dangers against which Catherine was visibly anxious to protect the Empire it is extremely unlikely that she foresaw this one. Her intention was to safeguard the future by setting aside her heir, and for the moment Gatchina helped her design if only because it detached Paul from Pavlovsk, that is, from the one solid support which still remained to him.

II

The Comte de Ségur had the pleasantest recollections of his visit to Pavlovsk in 1785. "No private family," he wrote, "ever did the honours of their house with greater ease, grace or simplicity. Dinners, balls, theatricals, *fêtes*, everything there was stamped with the seal of the greatest dignity, good form and refinement."* After spending a few days at Gatchina eleven years later the Duchess of Saxe-Coburg, the mother-in-law of the Grand Duke Constantine, complained of the insupportable ennui from which she had suffered there. "Everything was stiff and silent in the old Prussian manner. . . . The

* *Memoires*, vol. ii. p. 219.

officers of the Grand Duke's entourage are like figures cut out of an old scrapbook."

At Gatchina Paul's dearest friend and most faithful servant was Rastoptchine, and this is what he thought of his master's establishment : " One cannot see without pity and horror the proceedings of the Head of the family. . . . He seems to do all he can to make himself hated and detested." The effect produced by his ideas and his methods did not wholly escape Paul, but to him this was only another reason for persisting more obstinately in the way he had chosen. Since the disappearance of Panine there was nothing to check his worst impulses. Saltykof sought only to disarm the just suspicions with which he was regarded by redoubling his platitudes. The two Kourakines, who had been the Grand Duke's companions in youth, had little head and no character. Marie Féodorovna's literary Court, which was composed of the remains of the staff got together by Panine for Paul's education, contained no one above the second rank. Even Plechtchéief himself could only gasp and assume an air of horror. As for Rastoptchine, he pretended that he was only there as a disgusted spectator, but in reality he was engaged in the pursuit of fishing in troubled waters.

The European public knew only the heroic Rastoptchine of 1812. The man was in reality much more complicated. Of himself he said : " Scratch the Russian and you will find the Parisian, scratch the Parisian and the Russian reappears. Scratch again and the Tartar emerges." He was capable of anything, even of braving Paul, capable of remaining faithful to his master after receiving a sentence of banishment, but capable also of the basest intrigues to retard this disgrace. His wife Catherine Petrovna Protassof, was a niece of the celebrated confidante of Catherine, who had gained high rank but little esteem by that position.

Paul had better men about him and worse. Araktchéief

was better in a sense. He was a narrow-minded, under-educated man, unfit to command an army, but he had valuable qualities. Among these was a turn for order and method, an automatic precision in carrying out the instructions he received, great energy, administrative talent of a kind and a probity which, if it was not entirely incorruptible, was at least much more scrupulous than that of most functionaries of his time.

He was the son of a poor country gentleman and had been educated at the Cadet Corps School, where he taught mathematics. But his meticulous brutality made him detested by his pupils, and the director of the establishment was glad to get rid of him by handing him over to the Grand Duke to command the artillery at Gatchina. This did not change his character. It was soon said of him that he had torn off a soldier's ear with his teeth. But he never missed a drill, and perhaps his ferocious airs were really needed to keep in order the crew of brigands, drunkards and poltroons whom he had to command. The gentle Alexander himself believed that this was so.

His colleagues in the staff at Gatchina, the Lipinskis and the Kamienskis, went beyond him in savagery, and he had at any rate the advantage over them of not being always the inhuman brute whom his subordinates learned to know in the course of their duties. Outside the ranks he became almost amiable. He was the master of a hospitable house, where he would gather his officers round a samovar of an evening and explain to them the intricacies of military theory, tolerating, even stimulating, their questions and answering with patience. He ended by developing a natural aptitude for this thankless task and became an unrivalled instructor, an artilleryman of some merit for his time, and an organiser of great ability, always hard, but unsparing of himself, and as careful with public money as with his own.

The worst feature of this staff, which was to provide the

framework of the Government which succeeded Catherine's, was Koutaïssof. He was a Turk from Koutaïs who had been captured in his infancy at the siege of Bender. In the near future he was to become Count Ivan Pavlovitch, Grand Huntsman, but for the moment he was Paul's valet and barber and also his confidante, intriguing skilfully among the feminine section of the Court, and practising with much astuteness the business of a go-between.

All this suited the designs of the Empress. Neither this rascal nor any of his kind was capable of setting himself up against her decisions. She had only to lift her finger and the "sweepings" would be swept away. But, as the head of a family on which the Empire was dynastically based, Paul had in the affection of those near and dear to him a much more solid support. The malice of his servants and his own folly went far to undermine this defence.

III

Until he was about thirty Paul's relations with the fair sex had been normal, and, if not blameless, he had certainly shown no tendency to debauchery. This is sufficient to absolve Catherine from the charges which have been brought against her on this point, and it is also enough to emphasise the comparative decency with which, in her authoritative fashion, she surrounded her own weaknesses. For her personal convenience she put them under cover of a kind of state institution. She did not make them a school of vice.

Paul's amorous history no doubt began early in his career in such surroundings, but it does not seem to have gone much beyond the more or less innocent experiences which most of us pass through at the same age. Before his marriage with Nathalie Aléxiéievna, with whom he was deeply in love, Paul had mistresses, one of whom presented him with a son. Under the name of Simon

Viélikoï he served his apprenticeship in the British Navy and died in the West Indies in 1794 on board the *Vanguard*.

This adventure was no doubt preceded and followed by others, and Marie Féodorovna was often violently, and sometimes justifiably, jealous. But after some movements of revolt she reconciled herself to her husband's infidelities and the peace of the home was not seriously disturbed. In fact, during the first ten years of their married life Paul and Marie Féodorovna realised exactly the classic ideal of domestic happiness. Having many children they were perfectly happy. At this moment the scene was changed. Paul became more and more attached to Gatchina and detached himself from Pavlovsk, and Mlle. Nélidof made her appearance.

At Gatchina the Grand Duke lived in constant excitement, manœuvring the living marionettes arranged to suit his taste by Steinwehr and Araktchéief, rehearsing the part he hoped to play upon the throne and eating his heart out because his *début* was postponed. The palace was surrounded by a continuous chain of pickets who night and day arrested and interrogated the passers-by. He himself surveyed the country from the top of a tower, and if travellers took a circuitous route in order to avoid the territory thus guarded he had them pursued and put in prison. Every night by his orders the houses of the town and the neighbouring villages were searched. In the streets it was forbidden to wear round hats and cutaway coats and any infraction of this rule was severely punished. Discovering more jacobins in his neighbourhood every day, Paul ended by declaring his whole domain permanently in a state of siege. " Every day," reports Rastoptchine, " one hears of nothing but acts of violence. The Grand Duke thinks every moment that some one is wanting in respect or has the intention of criticising his actions. He sees everywhere manifestations of the revolution." He was copying the very methods of the

Revolution while he believed that he was putting it down and more particularly in governing by state of siege.

At Pavlovsk at the same time Marie Féodorovna was placidly engaged in her various occupations, literary, artistic and domestic, disturbed only by her anxiety to secure the favours of Catherine for her numerous relations. Paul highly disapproved of the compromises with his mother into which his wife was thus led, but their disaccord was now complete in every detail of their common life. While he got up before dawn to work with Steinwehr and Araktchéief she sat up all night reading books which, according to Catherine, she often did not understand. As a matter of fact, the poetry of her own country, which was then so brilliant and so moving, was unknown to her, in spite of the presence of Klinger in her suite. She had too much prose in her composition. She shared Paul's horror of the *encyclopédistes*, but she understood neither his mysticism and freemasonry on the one hand nor his dreams of greatness, his projects of reform, and his anger and impatience on the other. It was very nice to go on living at Pavlovsk till something better came their way. Why not await like every one else, without useless disquietude, the inheritance which could not fail to come in due time ?

The attendants of the couple took part in the quarrel and embittered it. Madame Benckendorf, " dear Tilly," the friend of the Grand Duchess's youth who had followed her from Montbéliard, declared war on Mlle. Nélidof, who was so soon to be the reigning favourite. The good Lafermière, now librarian to the Grand Duchess, was at daggers drawn with Vadkovski, the factotum of the Grand Duke. All this would have mattered little had not Paul, being at variance with his legitimate consort, felt the need of some other feminine support. If he could not at once be Frederick II or Peter I he could at least, he thought, be a hero, realising an ideal of moral grandeur conceived by himself. As he could not ascend a throne he would climb the topmost summits of thought, of virtue—of love.

Towards 1790 this dream took possession of him, even to the point of hallucination. But his imagination unaided was not equal to the task of making it fit easily with the pose which he required, and he found it necessary to exteriorise his fancy and to give it a body, thereby obtaining assistance in making the giddy ascent which he proposed to himself. He had no doubt read Goethe's mysterious divagations on the "eternal woman soul" which "leads us upward and on." But he found Marie Féodorovna quite unequal to the rôle of Frau von Stein and therefore sought for some one more suitable out of doors. Helpers in this quest were not wanting. Vadkovski did his best, and also, it appears, another friend of his youth, Baron Sacken, who had just returned from an embassy to Denmark. His concern was to reconcile the interests of the present and the future, and he may well have been the agent of the Empress in this intrigue, though Mlle. Nélidof did not know it.

IV

If we may believe Mme. Rjevski, Paul could not at first endure the lady who was to be the object of so great a passion, both because of her reputed shrewishness and her undoubted ugliness. Even when he began to change his mind about her he does not appear to have yielded at first to any physical or moral attraction, but rather to some semblance of calculation which in fact was nothing but an unreasoning impulse. Vadkovski and Sacken joined in persuading him that at the Empress's Court he was believed to be ruled by his wife, and in order to prove that this was not so he forged real bonds for himself in his attempt to escape from an imaginary slavery.

The sequel did not come till later, and the beginning of the adventure did not promise anything transcendental. As early as 1786 Catherine Ivanovna was vulgarly believed to be the Grand Duke's mistress. Six years later she revolutionised the junior Court by persuading Paul to dismiss Mme. de Benckendorf. Marie Féodorovna was imprudent enough to complain to Catherine, and when Paul heard of it he forgot himself so far as to accuse his wife of preparing for him the fate of Peter III. This time the quarrel was so violent that the echoes of it reached the *Moniteur Universel* at Paris.

Mlle. Nélidof was born on December 12, 1758 (old style). She was therefore over thirty—an ugly old maid! She was educated at the *Smolnyï*, the institution for the daughters of the nobility, where Paul's mother prided herself on grafting on the little Russian savages her own particular brand of half-French half-German culture. Elegance and good manners and accomplishments were taught; the pupils were initiated into the niceties of the language of Voltaire; they were drilled in Court etiquette; and given a bias towards the cult of *Schönseligkeit*.

At fifteen Mlle. Nélidof passed for a prodigy in this highly artificial school, and her Imperial patroness had her painted by Levitski in the act of dancing a minuet. Two years later Catherine Ivanovna followed the usual career of her companions by becoming one of the maids of honour of Paul's first wife. Marie Féodorovna inherited her as she did the slippers of the deceased Grand Duchess and was far indeed from divining a possible rival in "the sallow little creature." She did not appreciate the bright clever eyes which lit up her unattractive countenance, or the grace of the slightest movement of her slender body. Paul began to like the society of the plain maid of honour. So much the better, it was thought, she would be useful when he had to be soothed or advised.

In 1788, during the unfortunate campaign of Finland,

Mlle. Nélidof, in concert with the Grand Duchess, occupied herself in lecturing the absentee. Marie Féodorovna complacently annotated the letters written by the favourite in which the latter already made it clear that she believed herself to be more intimately acquainted than any one with " dear Pavlouchka." He wrote letters to her in which he declared that his last thought would be for her if he met a soldier's death on the battlefield.

Contemporary opinion was divided on the nature of the *liaison* which followed. Most of them took the view which is most in accordance with the laws of nature and probability. Posterity has been more generous, and has inclined to adopt the platonic version which the two chief personages themselves preferred to give of it. Marie Féodorovna for a long time seemed disposed to guarantee the innocence of their relations. But she was not a prodigy of sagacity, and after similar experiences in the past her confidence did not indefinitely continue. In a letter to his mother Paul protested " before God and man " against the malignity of the public which distorted the relations of pure friendship between himself and Mlle. Nélidof, but what man has ever hesitated to lie in order to protect the woman he loved ?

There remains the testimony of the lady chiefly concerned. " Have I ever looked on you as a man ? " she wrote to Paul. " I swear that since I became attached to you I have never had such a thought. You have seemed to me a sister." These lines might seem convincing if it were certain that they were not intended for the eyes of Marie Féodorovna.

But was the writer not above all suspicion of hypocrisy ? The elevation of her character seems beyond all doubt. Her disinterestedness is proverbial. Her letters show that she constantly resisted the generosity of her protector, which she regarded as excessive and insulting. Much against her will she accepts from him one day a porcelain breakfast service but refuses the simultaneous offer of a thousand serfs.

One would fain spare the worthy bearers of a historic name the slightest pain, but history also has her rights. In a despatch of Sir Charles Whitworth, afterwards Lord Whitworth, dated February 23, 1797, mention is made of a sum of 30,000 roubles secretly paid to Mlle. Nélidof for the conclusion of a commerical treaty the advantageous character of whose terms was due in part to the good offices of the favourite. Koutaïssof, the ex-barber, received 20,000 roubles at the same time for similar services.

Whitworth was a gentleman and a *grand seigneur*, who had a great position in England. In his own country he has always had a reputation for honesty which Sir Walter Scott has acknowledged. Considerable sums of secret service money passed through his hands, and no one has ever breathed the slightest suspicion of the manner in which these were expended. During his mission at St. Petersburg Mlle. Nélidof was supplanted in Paul's good graces, but as the recipient of the Ambassador's bounty she had no successor. None of it ever reached the Princess Gagarine. This feature in Mlle. Nélidof's career seems, therefore, to be well established, and if, according to the ideas of her time, it does not seriously affect her honour it does make it hard to believe in her sincerity. It is not less certain that in other ways also she occasionally descended from the sublime altitudes in which she claimed to dwell and in which a friendly public has hitherto preserved her memory.

Both physically and mentally Catherine Ivanovna was the exact opposite of the Grand Duchess. Her air of frankness, her brusque manner, her outbursts, her fits of anger, contrasted with Marie Féodorovna's placidity, just as her generous impulses and her celestial flights were the poles apart from the pedestrian temper of the idyllic and elegiac but fundamentally prosaic châtelaine of Pavlovsk. It seems that she was at great pains to emphasise this contrast, in which it is not difficult to discover the real secret of her triumph. It is also possible that, like Paul himself, she succeeded in drowning and so transforming the material aspect of their relations in a flood of mystical reverie. The sentimental effervescence which was then proceeding from the German *Sturm und Drang*, and was being diffused over all Europe, often took the form of a spiritualisation of love, and it may have played its part in Paul's love story. But it is well known that this rapt philosophy had a coarsely sensual side.

But although she was subject to the usual lapses from sublimity, Catherine Ivanovna's was no vulgar nature. In a questionable situation she always did her best to ennoble the rôle. She sincerely believed that she had a lofty mission to fulfil, and she succeeded in at least partly justifying this claim. She gave Paul what Marie Féodorovna could not give him. She consoled and guided him; she defended him against the excesses of his sensitive temperament and the aberrations of his mind, and for the most part the influence she exercised was salutary. But it was a dishonest game and the plan of keeping the wife and the mistress in perfect harmony while it was being played could not be kept up.

After the departure of Mme. de Benckendorf the Grand Duchess, influenced by "dear Tilly's" friends, took fright. She began to grow angry and lost her child-like confidence in her husband so completely that she confided her "misfortune" to her mother-in-law. The Empress led her to a looking-glass and said, "Look at yourself, and think of the little monster's face."

She saw that the breach was hopeless and she was not sorry. Thus Marie Féodorovna demanded in vain the banishment of the favourite. Catherine Ivanovna remained at Pavlovsk, and at the beginning of 1792, when the Grand Duchess was expecting her confinement and was apprehensive of danger, she exhorted Plechtchéief not to fail in paying court to one who before long might become " a second Maintenon."

On the other hand, the watchword for the male part of Paul's entourage was, as one of them put it, " respect for the Nélidof, contempt for the Grand Duchess." And when Nikita Petrovitch Panine, a nephew of Paul's old tutor, seemed unwilling to conform, the Grand Duke observed, " The road you are taking, sir, can lead you only to the door or the window."

Paul threatened to thrash a gardener at Tsarskoïé-Sélo who had been so rash as to send fruit to the mistress of Pavlovsk ! But by this time the paroxysms of the Grand Duke's fury spared no one, not even the " divine " Catherine Ivanovna herself, though they were still accompanied by the pretence of virtue and even of holiness, and sometimes interrupted by outbursts of piety.

Mlle. Nélidof was by no means scrupulous in the means of defence which she adopted, and she made use of the support of her fellow servant in the dealings which we know she had with the British Embassy.* But she was frightened by the scandal which arose, and she made a pretence of retirement, asking the Empress's permission to go back to the *Smolnyï*, " with a heart as pure as when she left it." Paul found no trouble in persuading her to stay, but he soon made her regret that she had consented.

V

Shortly afterwards she wrote to Alexander Kourakine : " This man's heart is a labyrinth for me. I am on the point of renouncing everything." The spell was broken. More sullen, irritable and violent than ever, Paul was being swept away by the devastating torrent which was to

* See above, p. 63.

engulf all his happiness. Mlle. Nélidof's influence was much shaken, but it survived a little longer, and in 1793 Marie Féodorovna did not disdain to make use of it. The Grand Duke had refused to be present at the marriage of his eldest son, not because he objected to the union but because his relations with his mother were becoming more and more strained. The favourite intervened; he gave way, but he hated her for it, and perhaps the Grand Duchess intended that he should.

Some have seen in this incident the commencement of a new understanding whereby the two women agreed to defend the object of their common affection against himself. Such a compact was in fact concluded, but not until much later. At this time Marie Féodorovna abated nothing of her resentment. " The girl is a curse," she wrote to Plechtchéief : and their relations were such that Paul was suspected of plotting to have his wife poisoned by the instrumentality of his mistress. The Grand Duchess was, in fact, so little inclined to a treaty that Catherine Ivanovna decided to go away in good earnest. Even this decision seemed " suspicious " to the injured wife, and this time her feminine instinct was unerring.

Having decided to retire, the favourite managed things very well. She had a splendidly furnished apartment at the *Smolnyï*, " equipped with everything which taste and opulence can devise." She was pensioned and loaded with gifts both by Catherine and by Marie Féodorovna, and she played the disinterested party with more emphasis than ever, reproached Paul for " tormenting " her and " making her heart bleed " by liberalities which she did not need. She needed nothing in this haven of her choice. " Would she come back to Pavlovsk ? " " No, never ! " " For a week at least ? " " Not for a single day ! " She had said farewell for ever to Court life. And yet Rastoptchine soon observed that her absence from Court was hardly noticed, " the little witch " returned so often. And in the following spring Paul insisted, and Pavlovsk saw her again for months at a time.

It was only then that Marie Féodorovna, who despaired of getting rid of her, made up her mind to capitulate. She had not gained by Mlle. Nélidof's absence. Paul, being separated from one of the two people with whom he was accustomed to share his life, made up for it by being doubly brutal to the other. After taking away her " dear Tilly " he deprived his wife of her faithful Lafermière, who after thirty years of loyal service was exiled to the provinces, where he died in 1796. Meanwhile the heir accentuated his provocative attitude towards his mother. He now went very rarely to St. Petersburg, where he made his visits very short, using everywhere the most violent language.

Marie Féodorovna was probably unaware of the plans of disinheritance which had already been conceived and were slowly being matured by the Empress. But she knew the character of her mother-in-law well enough to understand that she could not be defied with impunity. Moreover, Paul's obstinate refusal to make any but the rarest appearances at his mother's Court practically separated the Grand Duchess from her elder sons, who, as a rule, were kept at St. Petersburg. She thought that with Mlle. Nélidof's assistance the dangers of this melancholy situation might be averted, and the triangular household was reconstituted. At first the effect seemed happy. The Grand Duchess tried to humour her husband's fancies more than she had hitherto done. She rose at four o'clock in the morning in order to accompany him to the manœuvres. He was touched by the attention, but the *rapprochement* of the two women was the only durable result of the reconciliation.

The favourite's understanding with Koutaïssof became more difficult to maintain as the difference of their temperaments and the incompatibility of their ambitions became more marked. In the course of 1795 there was some quarrel between the mistress and the valet, who set to work to give her a rival. It was not difficult. Paul allowed himself to be led with complete docility into the arms of Nathalie Féodorovna Vériguine, another maid-of-honour, undeterred by his knowledge that she was affianced to Serge Plechtchéief. Mlle. Nélidof had a right to be grieved, but she displayed an annoyance which was quite out of place in a mere friend, and in April 1796, she abruptly left Pavlovsk.

This time she kept her resolution for several months, and Marie Féodorovna, always practical and accommodating, quickly bestowed her somewhat interested kindness on the new favourite, " dear Chabrinka," as she called her, using a caressing diminutive. Mlle. Nélidof resisted Kourakine's attempts to effect a reconciliation long after Paul, who was weary of the new intrigue, had done everything to secure her forgiveness. She had her reasons for being implacable.

" No," she wrote, " nothing will ever induce me to renew a friendship so basely betrayed. . . . I care nothing for the emotions of a man capable of a series of base actions. . . . I am at present receiving endless excuses and justifications. All this only increases my disgust."

These lines were written on November 1, 1796. Some weeks later the writer addressed the following to the same person. " The more I study his heart," the heart which had so lately been the object of such violent disgust, " the more I see that we may hope that it will secure the happiness of any one fortunate enough to possess it. I wish all the world knew it ! " And very soon afterwards the recluse of the *Smolnyï* reappeared at the side of the man who but yesterday was " dishonoured for ever " but now had again become " her dear Pavlouchka." What had happened in the meantime ? On November 6/17, Paul, preparing by Catherine's deathbed to receive his heritage, had found time for a quarter of an hour's conversation with Arcade Nélidof, Catherine Ivanovna's brother, a young man of twenty-three, who the next day was promoted to be a major and an aide-de-camp. Before this the sister of this fortunate officer, like every one at St. Petersburg and even at Pavlovsk, had the strongest reasons for believing that the heir would lose his inheritance. When she decided to leave Pavlovsk the struggle between the mother and the son had reached its final phase, and among her motives for departure she named " the religious attachment which she professed for the Empress." Between the mother and the son she had chosen.

VI

It was in the summer of 1792 that the favour of Catherine Ivanovna and the consequent estrangement of Paul and his wife reached their culmination. It was also at this time that the Empress's intentions as to the succession, as confidentially expressed by her to Grimm, seemed to have taken definite shape—Alexander was shortly to marry and soon afterwards he was not only to be proclaimed heir but crowned ! The marriage of Paul's eldest son was solemnised on September 28, 1793, and a few weeks later Catherine summoned and detained for two hours César de La Harpe, who was to tell the Grand Duke and make sure of his consent to the proposed arrangement.

Alexander's nature was already so elusive and his heart so impenetrable that, skilled as she was in the management of men, the great Empress decided not herself to attempt to sound the youth or to try to gain him over. She made up her mind to use the good offices of his tutor, to whom she tried to make clear her plan without actually revealing it. If we may believe his own testimony the subtle Vaudois eluded the mission thus offered to him, and succeeded in conveying to the Empress that he did not understand its object and would be incapable of successfully discharging it. He then, according to his own account, hastened to warn Paul of the impending danger and at the same time did his best to effect an understanding between the father and the son. Catherine saw what he was doing and expelled him from Russia on the pretext of his political opinions, of which she had long known. Had she not said to him on his arrival at St. Petersburg : " Sir, you may be a jacobin, a republican, or what you please ; I think you are an honest man and that is enough for me " ?

There is probably some truth in the story, but La Harpe's expulsion did not take place until the year after the interview which is said to have led to his disgrace, by which time the growing divergence in the respective developments of the French Revolution and the policy of Russia was sufficient to account for it. It is extremely probable, however, that Catherine did not send for La Harpe merely for the sake of enjoying his conversation, and that she also tried about the same time to engage Marie Féodorovna herself in the *coup d'état* which she was meditating.

She met with unexpected opposition and abandoned the somewhat summary programme which she had confided to Grimm, though she did not give up her idea. Paul multiplied his outbursts and did his best to confirm her resolution. At Pavlovsk and Gatchina he struck terror into all about him. At St. Petersburg and Tsarskoïé-Sélo his rare appearances stupefied the Court. The pages trembled as they opened the doors before the strange visitor. The young Grand Dukes themselves shared the general impression. When he was gone the Imperial palaces resumed their usual air of festivity.

They made fun of him when he was gone ; but it was more difficult to get rid of him. In the course of 1794 the Empress went so far as to bring the matter before her council. We do not know exactly what passed. The debate was secret, but it appears that only one member raised objections, urging that the character of the Grand Duke might improve after his accession. Some say this was Count Valentine Pouchkine, some say it was Bezborodko, whose subsequent elevation under Paul's régime would thus be explained. It is improbable that Catherine would have recoiled before a single adversary, and yet it is certain that the effect of this attempt on her part was to postpone for a long time the execution of her plan. Two years later she returned to the charge, but in a manner sufficiently maladroit. She was growing old.

In June 1796, Marie Féodorovna had a third son. Though he had ceased to speak to his wife Paul had not ceased to beget children. The confinement took place as usual at Tsarskoïé-Sélo, and immediately afterwards Paul left for Gatchina. The Empress kept her daughter-in-law with her, and when she had recovered she endeavoured to persuade her to sign a note which obliged her to do her best to persuade her husband to renounce his rights in favour of his eldest son.

Catherine knew exactly what the situation was at Pavlovsk and Gatchina, where, according to Rastoptchine's later account, " The Grand Duke Alexander hates his father, the Grand Duke Constantine fears him. The daughters, *under their mother's influence*, loathe him, and they all smile and would be glad to see him ground to powder." But the Empress had reckoned without the fundamental honesty of Marie Féodorovna or without her ambition, which, though it seemed less ardent than Paul's, was none the less very strong. The Grand Duchess absolutely refused to do what she was asked, though she kept the secret of this maladroit manœuvre, which Paul never discovered until he came to go through his mother's papers. Even then he was angry with his wife for hiding the proposition from him, giving her no credit for having refused to listen to it. For, had she consented, she would of course have subscribed to her own deposition.

Catherine fumbled awkwardly. Some months later she made up her mind to treat directly with her grandson and seemed to have got her way. On September 24, 1796, at the moment when Mlle. Nélidof, as we have seen, was spurning Paul's prayers and excuses, Alexander was consenting in writing to the scheme which disinherited his father and was effusively thanking his grandmother for the preference she had shown for him. This document was found among Zoubof's papers.

Was this acquiescence merely simulated, as has been supposed ? No one, even among the most intimate friends of the future enthusiastic admirer and implacable adversary of Napoleon I, could flatter himself that he could read his thoughts. At the same moment, with the same pen, the young Grand Duke was writing to Araktchéief a letter in which by anticipation he gives his father the title of Imperial Majesty. In the correspondence which he still maintained with La Harpe he repudiated all desire for power even in the normal course of things. He hated the Court ; he shuddered at the idea of reigning. His one ambition was to escape to Switzerland and live there quietly as a private individual. On the other hand, his relations with his father at this time improved. He often escaped from St. Petersburg to join Paul at Pavlovsk or Gatchina, and he ended by acquiring some of his tastes and also some of his prejudices.

It has been conjectured that while he pretended to be doing what the Empress wanted, Alexander was concerting with his parents the means of frustrating her design. A letter to him from Marie Féodorovna, in which the phrase, " For heaven's sake keep to the plan which has been settled. Be brave and honest, my child. God never abandons innocence and virtue," occurs, has been interpreted in this sense. But we know nothing of the plan which had been decided on unless it was a project, reported by the Countess Edling to have been formed by Alexander, of evading the Empress's intentions by flying to America with his wife. Some years later, however, he assumed this crown after it had been stained with blood shed more or less with his complicity, and then too he affected disgust and talked of abandoning everything.

The problem is insoluble : all the details of this chapter of history remain shrouded in mystery. It is generally believed that Catherine at the time of her death was on the point of issuing a manifesto carrying out the sentence which she had passed upon Paul, to which it is said that she finally obtained the concurrence of the principal men in the country, such as Roumiantsof Souvorof, Zoubof, the Metropolitan Gabriel of St. Petersburg, and Bezborodko himself. But no document of this kind has come to our knowledge. There was talk also of a will which the Empress was said to have made in this sense. But Catherine knew quite well what fate awaited documents of this kind, and that politically speaking " the dead do not count."

All the evidence seems to show that she intended to settle the matter while she still lived. But she could not carry out her plan in time, and was surprised by an event with which we must all reckon and yet which so often deranges our most prudent calculations. Death decided between the mother and the son ; and in this long quarrel it was impossible to say that either side was entirely right or entirely wrong. Catherine was not without reproach ; but Maria Theresa, her great contemporary, though irreproachable, was no more successful than Catherine, though she condescended to share power with her son. In the final struggle Paul doubtless had right on his side ; but for passing over that right Catherine had an excuse of which the whole of her son's reign is a vindication.

PART II: THE REIGN

CHAPTER IV

THE ACCESSION OF PAUL I

I

On November 5/16, 1796, about three o'clock in the afternoon, Paul was taking coffee at the " Mill " at Gatchina, when a mounted man arrived at full gallop and announced the arrival of Nicolas Zoubof. The Grand Duke turned deadly pale. The brother of Catherine's favourite was a fierce giant whose intentions must be hostile. Paul had had a bad dream the previous night which still haunted him, and he had for some time had more serious reason for continual disquiet. " We are lost, my dear ! " he muttered in his wife's ear, and turning to the servant he inquired, " How many are they ? " " *They* are only one, Monseigneur," replied the man. Paul took off his hat, crossed himself devoutly, and heaved a sigh of relief.

This account, by an eye-witness, has been contradicted by Rastoptchine, who asserts that Paul was in no way alarmed, but on the contrary thought that Zoubof had brought him the good news that the negotiations for the marriage of the Grand Duchess Alexandrina with the King of Sweden had been resumed. Another account states that Zoubof was preceded by an officer who brought a note from Saltykof announcing that Catherine had had an apoplectic seizure.

It matters little ; even if Paul knew that his mother's life was in danger, Zoubof might have come to communicate her last wishes—and what might these not be ? But the giant was already on his knees before the heir apparent, and in an instant Paul must have seen that the long period of waiting was at last coming to an end.

He was overcome by an emotion which was natural, but he let it be seen that he was also much perplexed. He struck his forehead as he always did when he was much preoccupied, and demanded full details of what had happened and the probable consequences, mingling his questions with the constantly repeated exclamation " How dreadful ! " which perhaps was sincere enough. Such events produce at least a momentary thrill of disinterested affection even in the least affectionate natures. By nature Paul was far from devoid of feeling, and the news concerned his mother.

And yet anxiety seems to have been the chief cause of the agitation which he showed. He wept, ordered horses, was angry because they were not produced at once, and strode feverishly about as if he could not keep still; but when his carriage was announced he was in no hurry to get in. He grew excited and asked himself aloud, " Shall I find her alive ? " He embraced in turn his wife, Zoubof and Koutaïssof, and was visibly trying to gain time. He had his doubts still, and he was afraid.

But news kept pouring in. There was a long train of sledges on the road from St. Petersburg to Gatchina. For all his haste Rastoptchine was anticipated. Halfway to Gatchina he met Nicolas Zoubof, who was coming back in advance of the heir and was bullying the post-master at Sofia. " Give me horses, or you shall be harnessed yourself ! Horses for the Emperor ! " " What Emperor ? " Four years later, at the accession of Alexander, Marie Féodorovna was to repeat this question.

Paul did not leave until five o'clock in the afternoon, and even then made no great haste. It was eight before he reached the gates of the capital. Near the Palace of

Tchesmé he stopped his carriage, got out and conversed with Rastoptchine on the beauty of the night, which was calm, clear and comparatively warm. He looked at the moon and became sentimental after the fashion of the time, and, seeing tears in his eyes, his companion forgot the conventions of a Court and, seizing his hand, cried "Ah, sir! What a moment this must be for you!" Paul replied with a friendly pressure and said, "Wait, my dear friend, wait. I have lived through forty-two years with God's help. Perhaps he will give me strength and mind to sustain the task which He is about to lay upon me."

By this time, therefore, Paul seems to have no longer doubted that his reign was on the point of beginning. Death, however, had not yet done its work. The last reports of the doctors had been indecisive. But having seen Zoubof at his feet Paul had other reasons for reckoning with security on the event which was to follow. Already a great part of the Empress's Court was in her son's train, though the first fears of the heir had been to a certain extent justified.

II

Everything seems to show that at first there was great indecision among the important personages who were assembled about the dying Empress. The two Zoubofs, Plato and Nicolas, were there, as well as Bezborodko and Alexis Orlof. None of these men were very favourably disposed to the Grand Duke. All, moreover, were aware of what Catherine had most recently decided to do. The actual existence, indeed, of a will disinheriting Paul is vouched for only by a general popular belief at this time. Since then no one has confidently asserted that there was such a will except M. A. M. Tourguénief who, in his notes to the memoirs of Gribovski, reproaches Bezborodko with having given it up to Paul. As a poet Diérjavine

76

has written some famous lines which treat this as a fact; but as a historian he has been more reserved. But before she died Catherine might recover consciousness and speak. Alexander was already popular and might act.

According to Countess Golovine Saltykof, who was devoted to the Grand Duke, had taken care to prevent Catherine's grandson from having access to her. The precaution was useless. The young prince was restrained as much by filial respect as by the indecision of his character, and he did nothing except urge Rastoptchine to go to Gatchina, and that not until Paul was already on his way.

On his arrival Paul established himself in a cabinet next to the chamber in which his mother lay dying. The two rooms communicated, so that all who had to take orders from the son had to pass by the deathbed. " This profanation of the Majesty of the Sovereign," wrote Countess Golovine, " shocked everybody." Paul's brutal selfishness was again taking the upper hand amidst the material cares which were demanding his attention, and no doubt he was quite unconscious of this impropriety.

Catherine struggled with death until the following evening. It was not till the morning of November 6 that the doctors pronounced her condition to be hopeless. But in the country where she had so long reigned supreme the end of this great Sovereign decided nothing. The tradition is that on the day of her death Rastoptchine cajoled Bezborodko into giving the future Emperor the Empress's papers. Other accounts point to Plato Zoubof as having done this. The *Court Journal* is precise : " On the morning of November 6 the report of the physicians showed that there was no hope. The Empress's papers were sealed up by direction of the Grand Duke Alexander, Count Bezborodko and Count Samoïlof, the Procurator-General, in the presence of Prince Plato Zoubof."

It is most improbable that Paul neglected to make at

least a rough inventory before this was done, and the following story seems to indicate that he did so. Bezborodko or Zoubof is said to have directed the attention of the heir to a certain document tied up in a black riband. There was an interchange of silent interrogations. A look indicated the burning oak logs in the fire which was close at hand and the paper was reduced to ashes.

Another account has it that Paul broke the seals of two envelopes of which one contained a draft ukase sanctioning his renunciation of the throne and the other arrangements for his incarceration in the castle of Lohde. He is also said to have put in his pocket a third paper which was in fact the will which has been the subject of so many contradictory conjectures. But another version of the story is that this last document was not discovered until the papers of the Empress, which had been sealed up, were examined several days later by the Grand Duke Alexander, Prince Alexander Kourakine, and apparently also Rastoptchine. Alexander is said to have sworn his colleagues to secrecy and then to have consigned to the flames the document which made him Catherine's heir under the regency of Marie Féodorovna.

The one certain fact is that Paul was entirely reassured by the combination of circumstances which accompanied his mother's last moments, and only waited for her last breath in order to take possession of his inheritance. His first care then was to summon Araktchéief and tell him what place he intended that he should fill in his confidence and in his Government. He brought him to Alexander, and joining their hands, said, " Be united and do your best to help me ! "

The new favourite had ridden hard from Gatchina and was covered with mud. He had no change of clothes, and Alexander took him to his apartments and gave him one of his shirts. Araktchéief henceforth kept this garment as a sort of relic in a morocco case and gave directions that he should be buried in it.

The favourite of the former reign, Plato Zoubof, was now to see the ruin of his fortunes. Panting with grief and anxiety and consumed with fever he wandered up and down his mistress's apartments, finding no one who would give him so much as a glass of water! Rastoptchine claims that he was generous enough to render him this small service. Catherine still lived: it was not until a quarter to ten that Rogerson, the senior Court physician, announced that " all was over." If we may believe Tourguénief, the new Emperor immediately turned in military fashion on his heels at the door of the death chamber, put on the huge hat and took up the long cane which belonged to the uniform of Gatchina, and cried out in a hoarse voice : " I am your Emperor. Bring a priest ! "

This seems outrageous, but it is borne out by a letter from the Grand Duchess Elizabeth to her mother some months later : " Oh, I was scandalised by the little sorrow shown by the Emperor. . . . At six o'clock [on the day of Catherine's death] my husband, whom I had not seen all day came to me already in his new uniform, and the Emperor's very first thought was to arrange for the uniforms of his sons ! . . . My husband took me into the bedroom (where the Empress had just died) and told me to kneel and kiss the Emperor's hand. . . . We then went straight to church to take the oath. . . . It was horrible to see him so satisfied and so pleased."

The preparations took a long time and the ceremony of taking the oath, which was preceded by the reading of Paul's accession manifesto, did not take place before midnight. The manifesto, was drawn up by Trochtchinski, the head of Bezborodko's chancellery, and was a commonplace performance, not recalling in the least the work which Paul himself had conceived twelve years earlier in collaboration with Peter Panine.* During the ceremony the new Sovereign observed that Alexis Orlof was absent. He was no longer anxious but annoyed, and observed, " I don't wish him to forget the 28th of June ! " It was the date of the tragedy of Ropcha. Orlof was sixty years of age and the reason of his absence was simply that he had gone to bed to rest from the fatigues and emotions of the last two days. Rastoptchine was ordered to rouse him. General Arkharof, a formidable police officer, went with him. Seeing that the old man was quite exhausted they took upon themselves to be satisfied with a mere signature of the oath. But Orlof rose and placed himself before an icon with a candle in his hand instead of a taper and insisted on reading it aloud. He showed no signs of emotion.

At the same time Alexander, assisted by Araktchéief, was setting up sentry boxes with the black and white Prussian colours in the streets and placing sentinels by his father's orders.

Paul's reign had begun at last !

III

The mob loves change, and the beginning of a new reign is usually received with joy. Joy was not on this occasion the prevailing sentiment ; in some quarters quite the contrary sentiment predominated. " Words cannot describe the grief which was felt and expressed by every officer and every soldier," writes Sabloukof, an officer of the Guard ; " the whole regiment was literally in tears." Masson confirms this, though, according to him, the grief was even more general. " The principal inhabitants of the town," he writes, " were in a state of silent terror. Fear and hatred, the sentiments generally inspired by the Grand Duke, seemed to reawaken at this moment the love and regret which were due to the Empress." " It

* See above, page 23.

will be like Gatchina!" they said. Their new master was soon to justify their fears.

" Everything," says Prince Czartoryski, " costumes, faces, expressions, behaviour and occupations were changed in less than a single day." Before midday on November 7 the Court was metamorphosed. The staff from Gatchina arrived and presented a strange spectacle. " In spite of our grief for the Empress," writes Sabloukof, " we held our sides with laughter at the sight of this masquerade."

" All the brilliancy, all the majesty of the place was gone," we read in Prince Czartoryski's Memoirs. " Everywhere there were soldiers under arms. Eminent personages and high officials hung their heads among the crowd ; in their places unknown persons came and went and rushed about giving orders. . . ." " The Palace was converted into a guardhouse, everywhere you heard the heavy tramp of officers' boots and the clink of spurs."

One might be tempted to mistake this description for that of the Tuileries on the morrow of the 10th of August, 1792.

The Emperor appeared in his turn dressed as usual. He reviewed the Ismaïlovski regiment of the Guard. " During the march past we saw him rolling his eyes, blowing out his cheeks, shrugging his shoulders and stamping to show his displeasure. Then he ordered his horse Pompon and galloped off to meet the Gatchina troops which were entering St. Petersburg in state."

At the same time, according to Sabloukof, the capital assumed " the appearance of a German town of two or three centuries previously." As had been the case at Gatchina and Pavlovsk the streets were scoured by police who tore off the heads of the passers-by and destroyed all the round hats they could find, and cut the lapels of coats and cloaks. The nephew of Sir Charles Whitworth, the

British Ambassador, had himself to submit to this treatment, dandy as he was.

The descriptions given by contemporaries of the revolution which took place are, however, too highly coloured. The changes were neither so rapid nor so complete. The ukase forbidding round hats, top boots, trousers and laced shoes, and requiring the three-cornered hat, the queue and powder, buckled shoes and breeches, was not published till January 13, 1797, and Catherine herself had already proscribed " large cravats which hide the chin." The " personal liberty " which her subjects enjoyed was very strictly limited. On the other hand, Paul was at first too eager to enjoy his power to abuse it. Having satisfied his resentment in a few cases in which his personal feelings were deeply engaged, he went so far as to confirm in their offices most of the high officials and Court dignitaries whom he had so lately spoken of flogging from their places. He left old Ostermann nominally in charge of the Ministry of Foreign Affairs, which Catherine had in fact directed herself in the last days of her reign, assisted by Bezborodko, Markof and Zoubof. He even respected vested interests so far as to raise this worn-out diplomatist to the rank of Chancellor. In this department no one but Markof was dismissed, while in the Household Kalytchof, then Marshal of the Court and afterwards Ambassador at Paris, shared the disgrace of Bariatinski.

The chief reason for the few dismissals which there were was the necessity for making room for the servants and friends of the new Sovereign. Araktchéief was appointed Commandant of St. Petersburg and received the fine estate of Grouzino, which in later times he was destined to make famous. Koutaïssof was, of course, not forgotten. He was created Master of the Wardrobe and was entrusted with the control of the domestic staff of the Court.

Among the papers of the Empress Paul had found a list of promotions prepared for January 1. He did not alter them in any way. Von der Hoven, the Courlander, was appointed to the Senate. Paul hated him and never would speak to him ; nevertheless he did not prevent him from entering the Upper House.

Catherine's domestics were more hardly used. One of her two favourite footmen was imprisoned in the fortress of St. Peter and St. Paul, where he went mad. The other was exiled to Orenburg. The new monarch did not spare even her confessor, Father Savva, who was prosecuted, and, though acquitted, was dismissed and banished to the provinces, though Paul gave him a pension of 6000 roubles.

He was equally generous to others of Catherine's servants, and indeed for the time was more inclined to give than to strike. In three weeks he is said to have distributed more than £40,000, not to speak of vast allocations of land which went far beyond that sum. As to decorations, they were given to everybody—even to those who did not want them, as in the case of the Metropolitan of Moscow, his old chaplain, with whom he quarrelled on this subject.

He was evidently anxious to make others share in his happiness and to make himself beloved, and his clemency equalled his liberality. All of his subjects detained by the " secret chancellery " were set at liberty ; all functionaries accused of any but grave crimes, such as murder or theft of public money, were amnestied. Novikof and Radichtchef, the author of the famous *Journey from St. Petersburg to Moscow*, were recalled from exile ; and on November 19, 1796, the Poles who had been imprisoned at St. Petersburg since the last war of independence and those employed on the works of the port of Rogerwick were set free.

Catherine herself, according to Rogerson, had intended to release " that beast Kosciuska," as she somewhat contradictorily called him, from the prison which was so unlike the conventional dungeon of the lithographs of the day. The ex-dictator of Poland occupied apartments on the ground floor of the "Marble Palace," then one of the most beautiful houses in the capital. But Paul had made up his mind to go further. He went in person, accompanied by his son Alexander, to announce to the Polish hero the decision which had been taken in his favour, and told him that he had long deplored his unhappy fate and was glad at last to be able to alleviate his sorrows.

The interview was affecting, and according to some witnesses Paul talked with all his usual lack of restraint. " You are free, but you must promise me to keep quiet. I was always against the partition of Poland, which was as impolitic as it was unjust; but what is done cannot be undone. The consent of three Powers would be necessary for the re-establishment of your country. Is there the slightest probability that Prussia and Austria would surrender their shares ? Am I alone to lose mine and weaken myself while they are reinforced ? "

Kosciuszko seems to have behaved with wisdom and with dignity. He asked and obtained permission to go to America. He did not think it necessary to decline the attentions and the presents which were pressed upon him in the most delicate manner, and he accordingly received a travelling carriage, an outfit of plate and table linen, a fine sable pelisse and even a sum of money—60,000 roubles according to the Russian, and 12,000 only according to the Polish estimate—in exchange for an estate which had at first been placed at his disposal. Marie Féodorovna graciously added a gift of her own. During his captivity the hero had amused himself by turning in boxwood or ivory. The Empress presented him with a superb turning lathe valued at 1000 roubles, as well as a collection of cameos made by her own hands. Kosciuszko in his turn presented her Imperial Majesty with a snuffbox made by himself and they parted on the best of terms.

The sequel was less satisfactory. At Washington, in 1798, the ex-dictator learned of the triumphs of the first Polish legions under the French flag. He believed himself to be in a position to take the field again at the head of an army and to fight once more for the independence of his country. He embarked in the first vessel which set sail for Europe, and on his arrival in Paris he sent back to Paul the money he had received. This was not necessary and was not even logical, as he kept the cloak and the other gifts. He accompanied this futile proceeding with a letter which is hardly creditable to his gallant memory. It began as follows:

" SIR,—I profit by the first moments of the liberty which I enjoy under the protection of the greatest and most generous of nations, to return to you the present which your apparent goodness and the atrocious conduct of your Ministers compelled me to accept."

He did not get his command, for it was vetoed by Prussia. He did not even return the money, for by the Czar's orders it was sent to London and paid into the gallant soldier's account with Baring's. He did not draw the arrears but disposed of them by will!

The incident, alas, was only too well fitted to confirm Paul in his theories of the best method of dealing with men. His own generosity, however, had not been free from alloy. There was in it much of the unreflecting spirit of retrospective criticism. Acts of unjustified or at least excessive severity were already beginning to make their appearance among the expressions of his munificence and his magnanimity, and this became a more and more marked feature of his method of government.

IV

On January 27, 1797, Catherine's successor directed that the pages containing the manifesto issued by his mother on her accession should be removed from the register of the year 1762, together with all other official publications relating to the *coup d'état* of June. Her orders given in September 1796 for a new levy of recruits were immediately rescinded. The army which had been sent to Persia was recalled. In Livonia and Esthonia the old local institutions, suppressed by the Empress, were restored. All this showed that there were to be decisive changes in the home and foreign policy of the Empire. Paul wished, moreover, that in Persia the retreat of the expeditionary corps should be effected precipitately and *without the knowledge of the Commander-in-Chief,* who was Valerian Zoubof, another brother of the ex-favourite, and who as a result very nearly fell into the hands of the Persians. The Cossack Ataman Platof succeeded in preventing this catastrophe and was rewarded by being confined in a fortress, but in Paul's mind the dominating idea was to avenge himself for the *coup d'état,* which, as he persisted in believing, had robbed him of his rights.

Before he began to carry out his reprisals he commenced by making reparation, and recalled to St. Petesburg the officers who in 1762 had taken the Emperor's part and who were now loaded with honours and attentions. Always inconsequent, however, Paul treated Alexis Orlof, " the man of the 28th of June," whom he had for a moment seemed to threaten, with marked favour. He was soon to send him into exile, but meanwhile, in the course of November 1796, the *Court Journal* twice recorded his presence at the Imperial table, where owing to mourning guests were then infrequent.

What were Paul's real sentiments towards the father

whom he took such pains to honour and to avenge? We know that he did not even believe for certain (or said that he did not believe) that he was really his son. Several months later he pressed Poniatowski, the ex-King of Poland, to reside at St. Petersburg. He asked him to dinner, and if we may believe Poniatowski's nephew he pressed the King to confess that it was possible that *he* was his father. As to Peter III, he was " a drunkard incapable of reigning."

This story can hardly be believed, but what Paul really did think can hardly be discovered from his actions, among which was the celebrated funeral of Catherine and her husband, the gruesome details of which are too well known to require reproduction here. Rastoptchine asserts that Plechtchéief, inspired by hatred, suggested the idea to Paul, whose mystical ideas, which he derived from the same source, impelled him to realise in death a reconciliation between his parents who had been at daggers drawn while they lived. It may be observed that by Catherine's orders Peter III had hitherto lain, not in the common vault of the Russian monarchs in the fortress of St. Peter and St. Paul, but in the church of St. Alexander Nevski. By reuniting the two coffins, therefore, Paul may only have intended to put things in order. It is likely enough that he himself had no precise idea of the meaning he attached to these manifestations of sentiment.

Alexis Orlof soon received an order to travel abroad, where he lived in much splendour and placidly awaited the accession of Alexander. At Carlsbad, in 1798, he celebrated Paul's name day by a brilliant entertainment and received an affectionate letter of thanks from the Czar.

Paul's conduct to Plato Zoubof was even more strange. Until December 6, 1796, the ex-favourite was not only retained in his appointment as Grand Master of the Ordnance, for which he was quite unfit, but he was treated with the utmost kindness. Two of his secretaries, it is true, were thrown into prison, but at the very same time Paul was doing his best to provide a comfortable house for their master. Zoubof was turned out of his apartments in the Winter Palace, which were given to Araktchéief, but a house, purchased and luxuriously furnished by the Sovereign, was at once presented to the evicted tenant. Paul visited the new proprietor there in company with the Empress, and the house-warming was characterised by every sign of cordiality. Champagne was served. " He who remembers the past deserves to lose an eye ! " said the Emperor, quoting a Russian proverb, and raising his glass he added: " I wish you as many happinesses as there are drops here." Then turning to the Empress, he said, " Drink to the last drop." Then he emptied and broke his glass. When tea was served the Emperor said to Marie Féodorovna, " You pour it out : we have no hostess."

A few weeks later the object of all these friendly demonstrations was prosecuted and dismissed from his post and shortly afterwards was ordered to cross the frontier. It is difficult to believe that the reason for this sudden reaction is to be found in a certain transaction about muskets, in which the Master of the Ordnance was guilty of culpable negligence. Paul knew well enough without such a demonstration how incompetent he was. Masson suggests that " having measured his man, the Emperor made up his mind that he need not fear him." But Paul was very soon to show that he was not capable of actions distinguished by so much coherence and calculation.

At this time he came into conflict with another man, whose enmity thus incurred was to prove fatal to him. Zoubof left the country via Riga, where preparations had been made for the reception of the ex-King of Poland. The august traveller was late, and as the inhabitants did not wish to lose their trouble, the ex-favourite, who was accompanied by a royal suite, received the homage of a guard of honour posted before the *Hôtel des Têtes-Noires*, where he consumed the dinner intended for the dethroned Sovereign. When Paul heard of this he sent a letter full of invectives to Baron von der Pahlen, the Governor of the province, and deprived him of his employment. It was at this time that the first stones were laid of the Michael Palace, where the dismissed governor was to exact vengeance for the insult.

Nicolas Zoubof, on the other hand, who had been promoted since Paul's accession to the dignity of Master of the Horse and had been decorated with a blue ribbon, retained both these advantages. Perhaps the new Czar was rewarding the giant for the joy he had caused him when he delivered him from his first terrors at the Mill of Gatchina.

Generally speaking, during the month of December 1796, Paul showed a more and more marked tendency to yield to the natural impulses of his sullen and vindictive temper. On the 4th the military commandant of Moscow was directed to order Princess Dachkof to retire to her estate of Troïtskoïe, in the Government of Kalouga, " to think over her memories of 1762," and she had hardly arrived there when a new ukase ordered her off in a simple *kibitka* and in terribly cold weather to Korotova, an estate belonging to her son in the northern part of the Government of Novgorod, on which there was no house.

The poor lady had to lodge in a peasant's hut, and her only distraction was to watch the melancholy procession of other exiles on the way to Siberia. One day she recognised among them a distant relative of her own, whose appearance filled her with pity and terror. He trembled all over and spoke with difficulty : his face was convulsed with pain. " Are you ill ? " she asked. " No more so than I shall probably be all my life." The unhappy man had been an officer of the Guard : he had been accused with some of his comrades of saying things offensive to the new Emperor and had passed through the torture chamber.

The princess escaped more easily. In the following March Mlle. Nélidof and Marie Féodorovna hit upon the plan of making Nicolas, the Emperor's youngest son, present a letter to his father which persuaded him to allow Catherine's old friend to return to Troïtskoïe. But whether in his cruelty or in his mercy, it is impossible to discern any logic in Paul's conduct in cases of this kind. In that of Plato Zoubof he may on reflection have decided to strike at his mother's lover as being a representative of all that was hateful and scandalous in the favouritism of the previous reign. But almost at the very same moment he gave the title of count not only to Dimitriéf Mamonof, who gained his favour by his numerous infidelities to Catherine, but also to Zavadovski, who had done nothing to recommend himself to the Czar's good graces. In 1799, on the contrary, he exiled Korsakof for no apparent reason from Moscow to Saratof, though Countess Stroganof and others had victoriously disputed his favours with the late Empress.

There was still another living testimony to Catherine's guilty loves. In 1764 she had been at least tempted to marry Gregory Orlof and to substitute the son she had by him for the son of Peter III as the heir to the throne. This son was named Alexis Bobrinski and was a highly disreputable person. Yet one of Paul's first acts was to recall him from Livonia, where he was expiating numerous peccadilloes. He received him with open arms, asked him to dine at his table, gave him, on November 12, 1796, the title of count, a house and lands, the rank of major-general with the command of the fourth squadron of the Horse Guards and the ribbon of St. Anne. At a Court reception he treated him publicly as his brother. It is true that a month later he was forgotten, and Alexis, sobered by his recent marriage with Anne Ungern-Sternberg, daughter of the Commandant of Revel, went to live quietly in the country.

Paul's activity, however, from the first was not limited to such more or less innocent caprices.

V

It was the army which received the first-fruits of the work of reform for which Paul thought that he had more than sufficiently prepared himself. At the review of the Ismaïlovski regiment of the Guard, which took place the day after his accession, the officers were already required to appear in "Gatchina kit." They were much embarrassed. The shops were shut, and how were they to obtain the tall canes and the gloves with wide cuffs which were necessary? They had to do as best they could, and this was a mere foretaste of the *coup de théâtre* which their new Sovereign had long been meditating.

He paid little attention to the review; all the time his mind was running on the army of Gatchina, which had been summoned in a body to St. Petersburg and was to make a state entry that very day. Lieutenant Ratkof preceded his comrades and announced that they were at the gates; Paul embraced the messenger who returned with the Cross of St. Anne. The troops were assembled before the Winter Palace and Paul thanked them with much emotion for their faithful services and announced the rewards which he was about to bestow upon them. They were all, officers and soldiers alike, to become part of the Guard. The officers were to receive donations; the soldiers' term of service was to be reduced from twenty-five to fifteen years and at its expiration each was receive an allocation of land in the Government of Saratof.

Thus introduced into a privileged corps, the newcomers

were given further special and exorbitant privileges. This preference, combined with a whole system of re-organisation which affected the army root and branch, was accompanied by marks of contempt and insults levelled against all the other corps. Not long after this Araktchéief inspected the glorious regiment of Ekaterino-slav and insulted their standards, which the wars of Turkey had made illustrious, by calling them "Catherine's petticoats."

The veterans of all arms of the service were indignant ; but it was the Guard which felt most bitterly the infusion of the new and discordant elements which were forced upon them. It contained a hundred and thirty-two officers belonging to the oldest nobility in Russia. The newcomers were mostly Germans or Little Russians of base extraction. They had also to submit to a complete change of regulations. Paul intended that the work of the Guard, which had for long been merely ornamental, should again become serious. He brought them back to the ranks and compelled them to undergo the ordinary fatigues imposed upon the soldier.

He was quite right. But the reform was too radical in its conception and it was carried out too ruthlessly. Four years later it was to tie the tragic knot in which its author was strangled. Its immediate effect was to create a focus of opposition to the new régime, which was already far from being unanimously accepted. The favours and bounties of the Czar had done something to alleviate the alarm of the first day of his reign ; but men were disconcerted by his caprices and his eccentricities. Paul showed himself accessible to complaints and his prompt justice gained him the title of " the Russian Titus " ; but some were already apprehensive lest Titus might change into Nero. Simon Vorontsof, who in later years was one of Paul's severest critics, applauded from London the first acts of the reign. He declined, however, to come and admire them on the spot. " My health is no longer good enough," he wrote, " to permit me to attend military parades in frost and rain. It would kill me. . . ."

The hesitations of the popular mind are faithfully reflected in the despatches of Sir Charles Whitworth, the British envoy at St. Petersburg. On November 26 he wrote that although Paul had irritated some people against him he had the majority on his side. On December 5 the Ambassador was much less categorical. The multiplicity of ukases, he said, which succeeded one another from hour to hour confused and alarmed public opinion. It must, however, be observed that in the interval between these two reports Whitworth had received a note from Ostermann which destroyed his hopes that Paul would adhere to the plans of Anglo-Russian military co-operation which had been negotiated with Catherine.

On the other hand, Catherine was regarded with mixed feelings. On the very day of her funeral Tauentzien, the Prussian envoy, could report without being too obviously offensive that " The public are remarkably pleased and contented. The reign of the immortal Catherine, now that it is stripped of the phantom glory and greatness with which it was invested, is seen to have left behind it only an unhappy Empire and a Government which is vitiated in all its branches."

Tauentzien had every reason to dislike a Government which had restored the Russian alliance with Austria. But even impartial observers could not fail to see that behind the brilliant frontage of Catherine's administration there were many and great miseries. The finances were exhausted by constant wars, and corrupt administration made worse by the licensed depredations of the favourites. Discipline was relaxed in the army, where the Guard, which had now laid aside most of the military virtues, set the tone for the rest. Tauentzien and Paul himself took an exaggerated view of the failings of the political

edifice reared by Catherine, as was proved by the success
with which it survived even the extravagances of her
son. Nevertheless, the record of the past justified the
endeavours of the reformer and the hope of a brighter
future. The manifestations of enthusiasm which were
isolated in the capital seem to have been more marked in
the provinces. But even here the excitement of the first
moments of the reign was soon cooled by the appearance of
Imperial couriers bringing orders which were sadly inconsistent with the presumed virtues of the "Titus of Russia";
and by the time of the coronation of the new Sovereign
there was little left in any part of the Empire of the illusions
which his subjects for a moment had entertained.

VI

Paul did not fail to follow the advice of Frederick the
Great, which his father had neglected when he delayed
to assume the diadem of the Czars. As early as December 18, 1796, a manifesto was issued announcing that the
coronation would take place in the following April, and
by March 15 Paul was already at Petrovski, a palace built
by Catherine on the outskirts of Moscow. Custom required that before the ceremony the Sovereign should make
a solemn entry into the ancient capital, for which much
preparation was required. Paul spent two weeks on this,
but he was not thereby prevented from going into the town
every day under a fiction of incognito accompanied by
all his Court.

The palace which he was to occupy when he left
Petrovski was not yet ready to receive him. The old
Kremlin possessed no apartments sufficiently spacious
for him, and the Czar had chosen a house which
Bezborodko, a great lover of splendid buildings and
luxurious furnishing, had just built in one of the remoter
quarters in the midst of a large park. The park had to

be sacrificed, as Paul required most of it for the indispensable parade-ground. In one night all the old trees were felled, but Bezborodko got rid of his house which had been thus spoiled by ceding it to its new occupant, and he did not lose by the transaction.

The state entry took place on March 27 and the procession took eight hours to traverse the few versts which separated the two residences. Paul rode an old white horse given him by the Prince de Condé at Chantilly fifteen years before, and he obliged all his high functionaries and dignitaries to ride behind him. Most of them were bad horsemen or had become unfit for the saddle by reason of age, and it appears that this detracted from the majesty of the spectacle.

For the ceremony itself tradition still required a sojourn at the Kremlin, where the Grand Duchess Elizabeth "spent the day in Court dress seated on a trunk for want of anything more comfortable." Paul was crowned on April 5/16, 1797, on which day the gentlemen of the Court had to present themselves at the Palace at five and the ladies at seven in the morning! Paul, in addition to the usual purple mantle, wished to wear a dalmatic, a vestment of the Eastern Emperors which closely resembles a bishop's cope. He seems to have seriously thought of assuming episcopal functions as head of the national church. It is said that he proposed to officiate, to say Mass and receive the confessions of his family and his officials. He had caused vestments of great splendour to be prepared for him and had even practised the details of the ritual, without, however, succeeding, in spite of all his efforts, in eliminating from his delivery of the liturgy the tone of military command. It was only the resistance of the Holy Synod, who adroitly availed themselves of a canon forbidding *a priest who had married a second time* from celebrating the Holy Mysteries, which induced him to abandon the idea.

It is possible. Paul's fantastic disposition makes almost anything of the kind conceivable. But the title "Head of the Church," though it appeared in the law on the devolution of the throne published at this time, did not assume the character which ill-informed commentators have ascribed to it. It was defined both in the organic laws of Peter the Great, where it implied no right to interfere in questions of dogma, and in the new law, where the context makes it impossible to attach more than an administrative sense to the term. Paul never, in fact, attempted to extend his powers in this direction. He was even pleased to lay aside his sword on entering the church, in deference to a suggestion of the officiating clergy.

But he did not give up his dalmatic even during manœuvres and military parades, and the incongruity of this garment, attached to his uniform and worn over large boots, may be readily imagined. Paul was very fond of the sublime and had no feeling for the ridiculous.

The rite was performed by Gabriel Petrof, Metropolitan of Novgorod and St. Petersburg, who may well have been intended by the Czar, as has been supposed, for the dignity of Patriarch, which it seems to have been his purpose to restore. But the prelate was as simple and modest as he was learned, and in 1799 he fell into disgrace for refusing the Cross of Malta and an invitation to the opera! Plato, Paul's old chaplain, seemed to be the obvious person to preside over the solemnity, but he was already in disfavour. He had been ill at the time of Paul's accession and had delayed to respond to his master's call. Then he had refused to accept the Order of St. Andrew, the insignia of which he was, however, obliged to put on for the occasion when he took the second place at the ceremony.

For the first time in Russian history two persons were crowned on the same day : the Emperor and the Empress, on whose head Paul himself placed a small diadem.

After the completion of all the rites, the Czar read aloud in the church a Family Statute—the same which he had wor¹ed out nine years before in collaboration with Marie Féodorovna, and which regulated the devolution of the throne by primogeniture in the male line.   At the same time were published an *organic law* relating to the Imperial Family, a *statute* governing the institution of the Imperial orders, and a *manifesto* restricting the forced labour of peasants to three days and forbidding landlords to make them work on Sunday.   This document was generous in its intention but was badly drafted and, as we shall see, it was misconstrued in the most regrettable manner.

In the statute as to the orders those of St. George and St. Vladimir were not mentioned.   At the instance of Mlle. Nélidof a subsequent ukase referred to an " oral declaration " which the Czar was said to have made on the day of the coronation, which no one had heard but by which he was said to have decreed that as regards the Order of St. George things should remain as they were. The Order of St. Vladimir was not re-established until the reign of Alexander I.

Poniatowski, the ex-King of Poland, was ordered to assist at the Coronation in full royal robes, and when he tried to rest for a moment his gouty legs, which were fatigued by the extreme length of the service, he was ordered by the Emperor to stand up again.   Like every-one else in the Czar's entourage the dethroned monarch found that one day of pompous and exhausting ceremonial did not exhaust his troubles.   For a whole fortnight the ceremonies continued unceasingly, and when the King's nephew complained of this to one of the officials the latter replied, " *You* think there is too much of this : but the Czar can never have enough of it."

Day after day the Emperor and the Empress, surrounded by the Grand Dukes and the Grand Duchesses with their Courts, spent long hours in receiving homage and congratulations, of which in fact Paul never seemed to tire. The Master of the Ceremonies, in order to please him, made the same persons pass before him several times like a stage army. But the Empress remembered to have heard Catherine say that on a similar occasion her hand was swollen with being kissed, and Marie Féodorovna was much disappointed to find that her own hand showed no trace of swelling.

The only part of this tedious business which gave pleasure to the other participants was the reading during the gala dinner of a certain thick pamphlet, which was the object of a universal and passionate curiosity. It contained the list of the favours accorded by the Sovereign on this great occasion. Dinner was over before the reading was finished. Bezborodko received the title of Prince and Serene Highness, the Czar's portrait framed in diamonds and the Czarina's in a ring of great value. He also received a grant of several tens of thousands of serfs. Koutaïssof became Grand Master of the Wardrobe.

Marie Féodorovna was not forgotten. Paul made the Empress Director General of the educational establishments of the two capitals.

But these laborious weeks were not entirely given up to the exchange of homage and benefactions. The Czar daily visited the parade-ground and while there was always angry and displeased. The cuirassiers of Ekatiérinoslav, who had already been ill-used by Araktchéief because they had belonged to Potemkine, were at Moscow and suffered particularly from their master's malice. Tourguénief, who was one of the officers, was summoned by the Czar after a manœuvre, and Paul, without saying a word, pinched his arm, not by way of caress (as the Petit Caporal some years later used to pinch the ears of his Grenadiers), but with the manifest intention of hurting him. The torture was prolonged, and the young cornet had tears in his eyes, while the gentle Alexander, standing behind the Emperor with Araktchéief, turned pale. At last Paul spoke :

" Tell them in your regiment, from which I hope the news will be more widely spread, that I mean to get the spirit of Potemkine out of you. I will send you to a place where the crows will not find your bones ! "

In the course of the coming year Tourguénief's comrades were often to hear this threat. Satisfied for the moment with the effect he had produced, Paul let his victim go, but the cornet, turning swiftly on his heels, had the misfortune to catch the legs of his tormentor with his sabre and he gave himself up for lost. He did not blench, however, but went off at the parade step, and to his great surprise heard behind him, not a roar of fury as he expected, but a compliment : " A good officer ! A capital officer ! "

Whether this story be true or false, it is a good example of the methods and the policy which Paul was to follow in the exercise of the office which had now received the supreme consecration of the Church.

CHAPTER V

PAUL'S METHODS AND IDEAS

I

PAUL's ideas and, above all, his methods had such a decisive influence on the events of his reign that in order to understand the latter it is necessary to take a survey of the former.

We have already seen what his favourite models were. His first care was to imitate them as closely as possible. Louis XIV was his own Prime Minister. Frederick II, even more imperious and much more suspicious, dispensed altogether with collaborators of ministerial rank. For him mere clerks were sufficient, and it was in order to prepare their work that the King used to rise between three and four in the morning. It was then that his correspondence was laid before him—despatches from envoys abroad, reports from officers, plans for buildings, for draining marshes, petitions and complaints. He examined and sorted out everything, indicated his decisions always briefly, often in a mordant epigram. At eight o'clock this work was done. The principal aide-de-camp then revised his orders for the military administration of the kingdom, and the King went on parade or reviewed his guard, entering into every detail with the minuteness of a sergeant. Meanwhile four secretaries were hard at work preparing replies in accordance with the decisions which had been taken early in the morning by the King. He signed them when he came back from parade, and they were sent out the same day.

100

This was the part which Paul aspired to play when he in his turn became an autocrat. We have seen why it was that he was inclined to exaggerate the characteristics of his great exemplar to the point of caricature, and we shall see how inevitably he was destined to collapse under the crushing burden which he imposed upon himself. He preserved the habit of early rising to which he had been so long accustomed, and immediately imposed the same custom on all his staff. The offices of the chancelleries and the administrative colleges were lit up before dawn, and the senators themselves were ordered to sit at eight. Paul was quite incapable of achieving the reality of the rôle to which he aspired, and attached all the more importance to appearances.

His idea was to be constantly on the stage, and his one preoccupation was the effect he was producing on the audience. " Am I doing my part well ? " he asked Prince Nicolas Repnine during the coronation ceremonies. " Sometimes," remarks Countess Golovine, " one would have thought that he was a very vain private person who had been allowed to play at being king for a time and who was in haste to enjoy a pleasure which was soon to be taken from him." Again, according to Prince Czartoryski, " As soon as he appeared in public he walked with measured steps like a tragic actor. He did all he could to exaggerate his short stature, and you could see when he returned to his apartments how he resumed an ordinary manner and how fatigued he was by the efforts he had just been making to produce an effect of stately dignity and courtly grace."

In reality, then, though his ambition was rather to copy Frederick, it was Louis XIV that Paul seemed most often to imitate—not, be it observed, the discreet and laborious collaborator of Lionne or Colbert, but the pompous creator of the spectacle of Versailles. For Paul government was before all things a spectacle of which he was at once the stage manager and the chief actor. According to Whitworth, one-half of his time was occupied by absurd ceremonies and the other in futile evolutions dignified by the name of military reform.

II

" The Emperor speaks to no one about himself or about his affairs," wrote Rastoptchine ; " he orders and insists on being obeyed without comment." The idea he had of his functions led him to believe both that he was possessed of all the necessary capacities for fulfilling them and that he was quite infallible. " When He places a Sovereign on the throne God takes care to inspire him," he declared. He decided to attach chaplains to all the regiments, and for these posts the bishops placed before him a list of candidates whom they had chosen from among the least satisfactory of their subordinate clergy in order to get rid of them. Paul noticed one man who stood out from the others by reason of his great height. " What is your name ? " he asked. " Paul." The Czar started ; he saw in the similarity of names an indication from Heaven. The young priest, Paul Ozieretskovski, was invited to follow him into his cabinet, which he left as Chaplain-General of the forces, with the right to see the Sovereign at any hour of the day or night !

The Imperial sorcerer, like others of his kind, did not scruple on occasion to cook the oracles which he thus received from on high. The final syllable (*kij*) of the word *praporchtchikij* (cornets) was in a certain report carried over from one page to another. The Emperor took it for a proper name and, moved by a caprice, he gave orders that Ensign Kij should be promoted to the rank of lieutenant. He saw an expression of embarrassment and disapprobation on the faces of the staff who did not dare to explain his error, so the next day he promoted the lieutenant of the day before to the rank of captain, and some days later to that of colonel, demanding that the officer should be presented to him at once. There was consternation everywhere; the offices were turned upside down in search of the imaginary Kij. A subaltern of the name, or something like it, was found in one of the regiments quartered on the Don. He was sent for; but Paul grew impatient, and in the end he had to be told that Kij had been carried off suddenly by a stroke. " That is a pity," observed the Czar, " he was a good soldier ! "

He soon warmed to his work and aimed at surpassing his models. He established a box, of which he himself kept the key, outside one of the gates of the Winter Palace, in which his subjects were invited to deposit petitions and complaints. It was soon full, and Paul himself dealt with the contents. The expedient was at first useful and helped him to discover and redress certain abuses, but not only was the volume of correspondence greater than he expected, but he found among its contents many libellous pamphlets, put there no doubt with the object of disgusting the Sovereign with his invention, a result which soon followed.

The same desire to do everything himself without the interference of any one appears in the domain of foreign affairs. The Swedish Envoy Klingsporr, who came towards the end of November 1796 to resume the negotiations for the marriage of Gustavus IV with the Grand Duchess Alexandrina, found the Czar determined to treat directly with him. The College of Foreign Affairs was to have nothing to do with it. " The Emperor," observed the Vice-Chancellor Panine, " reads all the despatches, but does so with such haste that he cannot with the best intention in the world remember the points to which he should give his attention." What was worse, in default of the reflection and diligence which were indispensable in such a matter, Paul as in other departments displayed in foreign questions the most disconcerting caprices. Rastoptchine declares that he persuaded his master to withdraw a declaration of war against England on which he had decided by consenting to sing to him an air from a favourite opera !

In these and similar anecdotes, which will be found in contemporary memoirs, invention doubtless plays a large part. But that Paul did not even know where he was among the many problems which he attacked so boldly and so unskilfully is amply proved by ascertained facts. It is no less clearly proved that he was quite incapable of choosing the instruments of his dictatorial policy with any wisdom. He directed an inquiry into the production of sugar beets and entrusted it to an inspector of cavalry !

He despised mankind as much as Frederick did, but his distrust was not so systematic, for he was the slave of temporary attachments, which hurried him into the other extreme. As a rule, however, his suspicions amounted almost to insanity. On one occasion he examined in his casual way a set of accounts presented by his Treasurer, Baron Vassilief, and thought he had discovered a theft of four millions. He instantly flew into a passion and seized Obolianinof, the Procurator-General, by the throat, because he ventured to defend the suspected thief. Now, the sum which the Czar had failed to find in the incriminated report had been taken out by his own orders for a special purpose ! On the table before him was a note referring to this, but he had neglected to read it !

He dismissed Araktchéief, the only man at his Court who was sincerely devoted to him, because of a few yards of gold braid stolen by a soldier from some old carriages in store, because he suspected that behind this theft lay a plot of foreign Powers against his policy.

PAUL'S METHODS AND IDEAS

His entourage was a series of dissolving views in which the figures changed from day to day with his changing and unstable decisions. A contemporary drawing shows him holding a paper in each hand, on which and on the forehead of their bearer are inscribed the words, "Order! Counter-order! Dis-order!" This is only a caricature, but some pages of the *Legal Gazette* for the years 1797–1801 almost literally correspond to it. On August 20, 1798, his Majesty forbids *drojki* to be used in St. Petersburg; on October 20 this order is revoked by another over the same signature.

In nine cases out of ten the objects on which the sovereign will is directed are equally insignificant, and the decrees are usually even more unreasonable. Pursuing Potemkine with insatiable hatred, Paul was not content with abolishing all outward signs marking the tomb of the sumptuous Prince, or with destroying the monument which had been erected to his memory at Kherson. He changed to Tchernyi the name of the town of Grigoriopol, which reminded its inhabitants of the Christian name of its founder.

There was the same absence of common sense when Paul turned to greater matters, but the consequences were more serious. One day he decided to substitute pack-horses for draught-horses throughout the army. This cost five millions. Some months later the old system was resumed at the cost of a second five millions. Fortunately he did not often improvise on this scale. "We are occupied only with small matters," wrote Rogerson, in September 1797, "and these small matters show the most amazing versatility. . . . Anything may happen to a man." It happened to Stedingk, the Swedish envoy, for example, to be called out from a diplomatic dinner which he was giving and to be invited to leave at once with 50,000 men, provided by the Czar, to suppress a rebellion on the outskirts of Stockholm which was entirely imaginary!

PAUL THE FIRST

Paul's conduct as Emperor was the same as his conduct while he was still only the heir-apparent; but the exercise of power increased the violence of his outbursts, and its possession made the consequences more serious. On the parade-ground he wished to modify in some way the usual method of carrying out a manœuvre. He did not speak loudly enough and the order did not reach the officer. "Pull him off his horse," cried the Emperor, "and give him a hundred strokes!"

As in the days before he was autocrat he had his fits of repentance, and some days later he learned with satisfaction that this barbarous order had not been carried out. He thanked his son Constantine for having taken the responsibility of disobeying it, and promoted the officer who had been spared such a degrading chastisement. Most frequently, however, Paul saw to the carrying out of sentences thus pronounced, and sometimes he took it upon him to carry them out himself. On one occasion he pursued among the ranks with uplifted cane a lieutenant of cuirassiers, whose horse had splashed him with mud, but again rejoiced afterwards that his victim had evaded him. The next day he congratulated the officer on his escape. "In saving yourself you saved me too," he observed.

When a little later he met Paul at the game of which he was master, Talleyrand summed him up in one of his characteristic phrases. You can build nothing, he said, on the "peripatetic fancies"* of the Czar. The inconsequences and aberrations of his mind, which became more and more unhinged by the use and abuse of power, are established beyond all doubt; but they have been exaggerated by the imagination of contemporaries. Paul probably never gave the celebrated order on parade: "Files by the right to Siberia!" Sabloukof asserts that he never missed a parade and never but once saw

* *Volontés ambulatoires.*

the Emperor forget himself so far as to strike officers
with his cane. Again, in spite of the general belief in
the story, it is improbable that he caused a landed proprietor in the Government of Smolensk to be shot for
breach of a by-law. The similar story of his having
hanged a police official in the Government of Novgorod
on the complaint of some peasants belongs to the same
category. And yet the inability to control himself, to
which the Czar confessed, assuredly led to others, and
indeed many others, being victimised.

III

Even when he was calm his mind was quite unequal
to the task of controlling, as he wished to do, the whole
of the complicated machinery of government in its
smallest details. The College of the Admiralty, its chief
Admiral Kouchélof, and the corporation of St. Petersburg
merchants submitted ´three different and contradictory
suggestions on the subject of a projected regulation on
the subject of inland navigation. Without reading these,
or at least without understanding them, he wrote on each
the usual minute of approval and published them all !

In the complication of orders and counter-orders he
was soon completely lost. He took away the direction
of the artillery from Buxhoewden, whom he highly
esteemed, and gave it to Pahlen, whom he had recently
disgraced. Why ? Because of certain shooting practices
which had been ordered in pursuance of his own directions,
but which he had forgotten. He was portentously
meticulous and wasted his time and energies on the most
insignificant details. Thus in 1798 he wrote letter after
letter to Pahlen to discover why one inferior officer was
ill and why another was at St. Petersburg and not at
Moscow ; or, again, with what passports a certain picture
dealer had come from Vienna. Among these trifles both

he and his staff became bewildered. One night he took leave of his son Constantine at a ball, and a few minutes later was astonished not to see him in his cabinet, where it was his custom to receive in Constantine's presence the report of the officer of the guard. Immediately he became so much annoyed that he kept the Grand Duke under arrest for a whole week, sending back his letters of excuse unopened. The young prince was himself only too much given to detail, but like every one else he often failed to follow the complicated developments of his father's caprices.

"This is not the quarter-deck!" he said to a naval officer whom he saw in half-boots on parade; "go and put on your boots." The officer went and did as he was told, but the next moment Paul challenged him again: "You are not on horseback here; go and put on half-boots!" No one could hope to satisfy so exigent a master, for, though Paul always wanted something very much, he often did not know very well, and sometimes did not know at all, what it was that he wanted. He wanted a uniform for his soldiers which should exactly reproduce the form and colour of the Prussian uniform; but he also required the Russian clothmakers who were to make the cloth to use certain dyes which they declared could not produce the shade of dark green which was desired. The result was that Alexander Sabloukof, the Vice-President of the College of Manufactures, was dismissed, and, although seriously ill, was required to leave St. Petersburg at once. The result as far as he was concerned was an attack of paralysis.

Paul knew and remembered the epigrammatic turn which Frederick the Great gave to some of his decisions. In this, too, he sought to follow his model, but he did not keep these efforts for the seclusion of his Cabinet. He caused them to be inserted in the Official Gazette, where military orders appeared worded in the following fashion : " Lieutenant So-and-So was struck off the strength because he was reported to be dead. He requests that he may be reinstated because he is alive. Refused for this reason." Or again, " Lieutenant Chépiélof, of the Préobrajenski regiment of the Guard, is transferred to the Eletsk Fusiliers for ignorance of his duty, laziness and negligence, to which he became habituated while with Princes Potemkine and Zoubof, with whom one did not do one's duty, but loitered about the Palace and danced."

His orders and his censures were always mingled with insults, and sometimes very gross ones, and he acquired a habit of using the word *dourak* (imbecile) in season and out of season. In correspondence or by word of mouth every one, whatever his age or rank, was liable to have this word flung at him : Lieven, the Minister of War, because he forgot to be present at the reading of a report ; Panine, because he gave a passport without authorisation to the courier of the Austrian ambassador, Cobenzl ; an unknown person at a ball, " because he was gaping at him." No considerations of propriety or affection gave the Czar pause. Count Stroganof, an old man, the friend of many years, who had been honoured with exceptional intimacy and always treated with the greatest respect, was brutally dismissed from Pavlovsk and ordered to leave at a moment's notice because he had had the impertinence to predict rain one afternoon when Paul wanted to go out.

IV

Paul imagined himself still on the watch on his tower at Pavlovsk. But the vast empire over which he now wished to keep surveillance, as he had done over his own domain in the old days, defied his personal vigilance. However much he wished to be his own policeman, he was forced to recruit more and more assistants for this purpose. He ended by boasting that he had as many police as Russia had landowners ! It was indeed a service into which everybody was pressed. His officials were, of course, without exception engaged in it. In December 1799, for instance, Bekléchof, the Procurator-General, and Nicolaief, the Councillor of State, had to make a journey in order to report on the conduct of a certain Princess Dolgourouki at Moscow, or to inquire at Chklov into the mode of life of Catherine's ex-favourite Zoritch. This is the very spirit of the régime with which France was cursed from 1792 till 1794.

At St. Petersburg Arkharof, the military governor, and Scheidemann, the Commandant of the fortress, discharged the same duty with such strictness that even at private receptions and balls the presence of a police officer in uniform was required.

The *cabinet noir* was also developed as it had never been before. Everything was read there, even the letters which the Emperor's daughter-in-law, the future Empress Elizabeth Alexéievna, wrote to her mother. A post-office official advised the Princess not to use sympathetic ink, for in the *cabinet noir* " there was a remedy for every-thing.

In addition to its political investigations the ubiquitous police saw to the punctual execution of the innumerable regulations which were not all concerned with the shape of a hat or the cut of a coat. At the gates of the capital there were enormous notice-boards on which were set forth the endless rules which the inhabitants had to obey. They were in particular enjoined on no account to pro-nounce the word *kournossiyï* (snub-nosed), which might imply a disrespectful allusion to the Sovereign. Foreigners were subject to the code, but they, if disobedient, were threatened with " an unknown chastisement." Other provisions were aimed more especially at the French republicans, whom Paul was engaged in imitating : for though he repudiated their principles he made their methods his own. Such things are not uncommon in history. In April 1798 Benckendorf, the military governor of Riga, received orders to arrest at the frontier three French subjects, whose arrival had been announced, and to send them to St. Petersburg. At the same time it was laid down that none of their compatriots should be allowed to enter the country without a special authorisation from his Majesty in each case. Some days later this requirement was extended to *all foreigners*. Exception was made in favour of diplomatic agents and their couriers, and of persons of very high rank. Nevertheless, in the following July, when the Prince of Hesse-Rheinfels presented himself at the frontier with a passport signed by Count Panine, Paul had him rudely turned back " because he had not obtained the necessary authorisation."

The object of all this was to guard Russia against the contagion of revolution. But even within the bounds of his empire Paul multiplied the restrictions suggested by his prophylactic policy while he daily aggravated the despotism with which his subjects were governed. Many words besides " snub-nosed " were forbidden because for one reason or another they wounded his ears. Thus *obchtchestvo* (society), *grajdanine* (citizen), and even *otiét-chestvo*, the equivalent of the French *patrie*, were proscribed.

These absurdities were merely caprices ; but, generally speaking, Paul's despotism, his habit of interfering with the private lives of his subjects, sprang from his essentially patriarchal conception of his duties—a conception which implied the theory of the State as a kind of Providence. Here again, though he did not know it, he shared the philosophy of the jacobins, whom he held in such abomination. He regarded his relation to his subjects as that of a father who is responsible for his children ; accordingly he intervened in domestic disputes, family arrangements, and even in the details of housekeeping. He compelled

Princess Chtcherbatof to accept a reconciliation with her son by threatening to shut her up in a convent. He forbade Madame Khotountsof to make a contemplated pilgrimage to Bari in order to venerate the relics of St. Nicolas, because " the journey was too long and too dangerous for her." He forced another lady to give her daughter to a certain suitor, who turned out to be a thorough rascal, and he objected to Baroness Stroganof dining at three o'clock. He was taking the air on a balcony of the Winter Palace after his own dinner and happened to hear the bell announcing that the Baroness was about to dine. What! The insolent woman dared to have her dinner while he was digesting his! A police officer was immediately despatched to bid her henceforth sit down to table two hours sooner. It is even said that the Czar prescribed the number of dishes which should be permitted at dinner and supper for every category of his subjects. At the same time under the indulgent eye of Arkharof the police was conspiring with the tradesmen to raise artificially the price of food. Paul did not notice this, but he busied himself with the correction of a vicious horse which kicked and plunged between the shafts of a cart as it passed the Winter Palace.

He believed himself to be the depository not only of the Divine Power but of the Divine Wisdom, and in this capacity he expected to be obeyed without resistance and without delay. The docility and promptitude with which his slightest and most unreasonable whims were in fact carried out only led him into greater excesses.

One morning, on his daily ride, he happened to be with Arkharof when they passed the Italian Opera, an old and ugly wooden building. " This theatre, sir," said the Czar, " must disappear! " At five o'clock in the afternoon of the same day one of the Czar's equerries passing the same place was astounded to find that there was no trace of the edifice thus condemned ; five hundred workmen, by torchlight, were completing the levelling of the site.

Whether from excess of zeal or from malice those who carried out these orders were prone to exaggerate their effects or to distort their meaning. A page attracted the Czar's attention by some irregularity of dress. Pahlen was directed to imprison " that monkey " in the fortress. He pretended to think that this order applied to Siés-trzencewicz, the catholic Metropolitan, who happened to be in the same room. The prelate, who was, at that time, a favourite of the Sovereign, was accordingly locked up. Some hours later Paul as usual demanded a detailed report on the results of the incarceration he had ordered. " Did he cry ? Did he howl ? " The Emperor loved to play at being Ivan the Terrible, and to hear in detail and gloat over the sufferings of his victims. But this time Pahlen replied, " No, sir, the monkey quietly asked for his breviary."

" All this falls on our dear Emperor, who would never think of giving such orders," groaned Marie Féodorovna, who was distressed by daily incidents of this kind. But, allowing for exaggeration, Paul's personal share in these excesses was great enough to show that, like many other authors of ambitious programmes of reform, his theory and his practice were flagrantly out of harmony.

V

As heir he was in clandestine relations with Novikof, the accredited representative of the principle of the freedom of the Press. He openly patronised Von Wisine, another author of the same set, and obtained permission from Catherine for the production on the stage of his *Mineur*. As Emperor he began by confirming on February 16, 1797, one of Catherine's latest ukases, which ordered all printing

H

offices not authorised by Government to be closed, and by setting up bureaux of lay and ecclesiastical censorship. The same year the Metropolitan Plato was refused permission to set up a printing press in the Convent of Troïtsa.

The censorship bureaux were established at St. Petersburg, Moscow, Riga, Radziwillow, and Odessa, and acted on their own responsibility. In doubtful cases they were to appeal through the Procurator-General to the Emperor, who often aggravated the severity of their decrees. In December 1797 the Council of Censorship decided that the works of Voltaire were already so widely diffused in the country that it was useless to prohibit them. Paul ordered that no new copies should be allowed to cross the frontier. On another occasion he was not content to stop at the frontier certain consignments from foreign booksellers, but ordered the packages to be seized and destroyed. Here, however, as elsewhere, the Czar's policy was far from logical. In the list of six hundred and thirty-nine books censored between 1797 and 1799, we find *Gulliver's Travels*, the satire of which should have pleased the enemy of the *philosophes*, and at the very same time the works of Rousseau, including even the *Contrat Social*, were being sold without any restriction whatever.

Kotzebue's experiences of this policy as recounted by himself would appear improbable if we had not quite recently seen the same system at work. A character, supposed to be an inhabitant of the extreme west of Europe, was forbidden to describe Russia on the stage as a " distant " country. Another was not allowed to say that he was born at Toulouse, and as a rule the actors were not even allowed to pronounce the name of France. In one play this phrase occurred : " Consumed by the flame of love I must go to Russia ; there it will be very cold ! " It had to be replaced by : " I will go to Russia ; there everybody is kind " !

The Riga bureau distinguished itself by its zeal. A certain Seider, a pastor at Randen, in Livonia, had set up a circulating library. Some one failed to return a book and he advertised for it in the local paper. The book was a novel by the celebrated German author, Lafontaine; it was called *The Power of Love*, and was perfectly innocent. This, however, was not the view taken of it at Riga. Seider was denounced to St. Petersburg: the Czar ordered the " guilty person " to be arrested and " corporally punished." There was no inquiry, no examination, no defence. The unfortunate pastor was dragged before the court only to hear that he had been condemned to the knout and to hard labour in Siberia! This was precisely the procedure of the Revolutionary Tribunal which had so recently been in operation at Paris.

Seider was spared by the executioner, to whom he was wise enough to give his watch. He was, however, sent in chains to the mines of Nerchinsk, in Siberia, though he did not remain there long. He was sentenced in June 1800, and he returned to St. Petersburg in the following year at the accession of Alexander I. A dinner was given in his honour, and he received the proceeds of a collection which was made in his favour. Finally, a peaceful cure of souls was found for him—curiously enough at Gatchina—and he died there in 1834, at a very advanced age. But though his troubles were short they were none the less bitter and quite unmerited.

In April 1800 a ukase was issued by Paul forbidding the importation of all printed matter whatsoever: not even music was excepted! And yet at this very time he was applauding Kapnist's masterpiece *Chicane*, a satirical picture of the judiciary and the administration of Russia, the representation of which had always been forbidden by Catherine. The Czar accepted the dedication of the piece, without taking the trouble to read it,

When it was produced the majority of the audience received it with great enthusiasm, but the magistrates who had been pilloried indignantly protested. Paul was moved and began to think it desirable to see what he had approved. He ordered the play to be produced at the theatre at the Hermitage, and was present, accompanied only by his son. Contrary to all expectation, his verdict was favourable to the author. His vanity prevented him from seeing any attack on himself in the play, and his contempt for his subordinates was gratified. Kapnist was congratulated, made a Councillor of State, and received a handsome gratuity.

Theoretically, moreover, Paul was still a Liberal and a humanitarian as well in the ideas which he professed as in the reforms by means of which he was trying to apply these ideas in practice. But it was with him as it was in France, from which he was trying to separate his empire by a kind of Chinese wall. His ideal was as absolute as that which France was trying to realise, and in the attempt to put it into practice it fell to pieces in an outburst of violence and ferocity.

VI

On the parade-ground Paul imitated Frederick. He gave his orders and received the reports of the day ; the new officers were presented to him, rewards and punishments were announced. Like the King of Prussia, too, but with even more minuteness, he inspected his regiments. He examined each man's head, measured the length of the plaits, checked the quality and the thickness of the powder on their hair. He superintended the manœuvres " surrounded by his sons and his aides-de-camp, stamping to keep himself warm, his head bare and bald, his nose in the air. One hand was behind his back, like the great man, the other beat time, raising

116

and lowering his cane, one! two! one! two! It was a point of honour with him to endure fifteen or twenty degrees of frost without furs!" No pelisses were allowed even for aged and rheumatic generals. There was no pity for soldiers who were not good at lifting their legs in time or officers who were not good at managing the spontoon. Paul found fault even with the way the words of command were pronounced. There had been changes in these which were a fruitful source of misunderstanding. In vain did the Czar strain his nasal voice crying *march!* in the German manner, but really using French phraseology, for the words borrowed from the Prussian regulations were for the most part French. The men who were accustomed to the Russian *stoupaï!* did not move an inch, and there was a torrent of abuse and a storm of floggings.

But absorbing as these occupations were, Paul had many others which he carried on in the same place. The parade-ground was the place which Paul preferred above all others as an office, an audience room, a court of justice. He held councils there, he made appointments there to meet people with whom he had business, and it was there that he gave his decisions. From the general to the sub-lieutenant, all his military staff had to appear there every morning, and each man came in fear and trembling, not knowing what was in store for him. It might be sudden promotion or exile to Siberia, dismissal with ignominy from the service or advancement. The unfavourable event was much the commonest. A false step, a minute inattention, even a movement of suspicion in the tyrant's mind, was enough to ruin a man. Officers brought servants or orderlies with them who carried their bags, for there were *kibitkas* always ready to pick up on the spot those whom the Czar sentenced by a word to imprisonment, and the regulations required the uniforms to be so tight that it was impossible to carry even a small sum of money in the pockets.

PAUL THE FIRST

One after another careers full of brilliant promise were cut short in this way ; honourable families were decimated by the decrees of this terrible judge, who did not suspend his activities when he left the parade-ground. When he returned to his cabinet it was the civilian's turn, and the procedure of the tribunal was hardly to be distinguished from that of the court over which Fouquier-Tinville had presided a few years earlier on the banks of the Seine.

" The terror in which we live here," wrote Prince Kotchoubey, in 1799, " cannot be described. We tremble. . . . True or false, an accusation is always listened to. The fortresses are full of victims. Black melancholy has settled on everybody ; we do not know what it is to amuse ourselves. To weep for a relative is a crime ; to visit an unhappy friend is to become a *bête noire*. We are being tortured indescribably."

In the following October the prince was replaced by Panine at the Ministry of Foreign Affairs, and in a letter addressed several months subsequently to the same correspondent we read : " There is literally no one in Russia who is safe from vexation and injustice. Tyranny is at its height."

Madame Golovine, who wrote her *Recollections* in collaboration with the Empress Elizabeth, and who therefore observed an even stricter reticence than her fervent monarchical sentiments would have inspired, also speaks of the " tremblers " of both sexes whom she saw everywhere. She adds a trait to the picture, however, which is common to all ages and to all countries when there is a crisis of this kind : " When people were not trembling they were giving themselves up to the wildest gaiety. Never was there so much laughter—but often, too, one saw the sarcastic laugh change into the grimace of *terror*." The word italicised is to be found on every pen at this time.

PAUL'S METHODS AND IDEAS

Paul's mere appearance in the streets of his capital was the signal for a general *sauve qui peut*. A contemporary tells us how once he saw the Czar at some distance, and how by an instinctive movement he took refuge behind the palisade round the Church of St. Isaac, which was then being built. There he found a pensioner whose duty it was to guard the enclosure, and who observed: " *Here is our Pougatchof!* " This name contained a double allusion to the pseudo-Peter III and to the word *pougat*, which means to terrify.

Kotzebue, after a painful but quite short sojourn in Siberia, was loaded with favours by the Emperor, but he goes no further than to say that St. Petersburg itself was a more tolerable place of residence than the provinces. In the immediate neighbourhood of the new Pougatchof people ended by becoming accustomed to the danger. In the provinces they heard the distant rumblings of the storm and lived in perpetual alarms. The famous German author's first experience of Paul's methods contradict Mme. Vigée-Lebrun's testimony to the consideration then enjoyed in Russia by foreigners of distinction. He was arrested on his arrival at Riga, separated from his wife and children, and sent off to the neighbourhood of Tobolsk—for no other reason than that he was a foreigner and an author. A year later, it is true, he was summoned back to St. Petersburg, where he found a donation of an estate of four thousand peasants and the directorship of the Imperial Theatre of the capital awaiting him. The reason of this sudden change of fortune was that the Emperor had happened to examine his manuscripts which had been seized at Riga, and finding among them a short piece entitled *Peter III's Coachman*, had thought it very flattering to the memory of the victim of Ropcha.

Paul was an attentive if not a very intelligent observer, and was aware of the terror he aroused. With his usual

119

inconsequence he sometimes took a pleasure in producing this impression, while at other times he complained of it. " They take me for a terrible and insupportable person," he said to Stedingk in May 1800, " and yet I don't want to frighten any one." Some years before this his daughter-in-law reports an entirely contradictory remark. Writing to her mother of the Emperor's departure for Revel, she says : " It is always something to have the honour not to see him. Indeed, mamma, it revolts me even to hear the man spoken of, and his company is even more distasteful. Every one, whoever he may be, who has the misfortune to say something which displeases his Majesty may expect some insult which he must swallow. I assure you that except for some officers he is detested by everybody. . . . Just fancy, he had an officer in charge of the Imperial kitchen flogged because the meat was bad at dinner—flogged before his very eyes and insisted on their choosing a stout stick ! . . . I am a most respectful but far from affectionate daughter-in-law. After all, has he not said himself that *he doesn't mind not being loved if only he is feared*? "

Paul said, as he did, many contradictory things. He really desired to be loved as he really desired to be just, and yet in the annals of his short reign the page which describes the Grouzinof case, for which he was wholly responsible, is not surpassed in horror and infamy by anything in the history of Ivan the Terrible himself. Two officers of this name, colonels of the guard who had lately enjoyed not merely the favour but the especial confidence of their Sovereign, were delivered to the executioner on vague suspicion or on the pretence of proofs of which there is no trace in the papers dealing with the case. One of the victims was knouted after some pretence of judicial investigation ; the other, even before the inquiry into his conduct was complete, was condemned to be flogged without mercy by a sentence which was nothing but the Czar's ukase. The unhappy man had an exceptionally strong constitution and successively exhausted three executioners, succumbing only after several hours of agony. After this one of his uncles and three cossacks, who were implicated in the affair, were beheaded.

Having regard to the manners and customs of the age, the Emperor's almost daily order to " flog without mercy," was in the majority of cases equivalent to a capital sentence aggravated by torture. For many of the condemned exile to Siberia was in itself a punishment hardly less severe. Some were dragged into exile on foot, dragging chains behind them and falling down with exhaustion at every stage, only to be roused by the blows of their guards. Otherwise they made the journey in a *kibitka* hermetically closed except for two small openings, through one of which they received their food, consisting of a pound of black bread per day. The guards did not as a rule know the names of the prisoners, and were forbidden to speak to them or to answer any questions.

Paul took care that the exile should not escape a single hardship of these terrible journeys. In April 1800 two distinguished exiles, Prince Sbirski, formerly Commissary-General of the Ministry of War, and his assistant, Tourtchaninof, had the sores on their legs caused by the chafing of their chains dressed at Tver on their way to Siberia. For permitting this, Teils, the Governor of the town, was imprisoned in a fortress, and only the intervention of Obolianinof, the Procurator-General, saved him from a severer punishment.

And yet this man had begun his reign by breaking the chains of Novikof and of Kosciuszko, and between two outbursts of violence and cruelty there were not a few instances of kindness and generosity. He was more cantankerous than terrible, and fundamentally had nothing in common with Ivan IV. If his imitations of Frederick II ended in an even closer imitation of the

French *conventionnels,* his frenzy on occasion gave him a certain resemblance to Don Quixote. Here—little as he realised it—may be found the only shadow of excuse for him.

VII

The case of the Governor of Tver, who was punished for so justifiable an act of compassion, finds its opposite in that of Lieut.-Colonel Laptiof, a relative of Princess Dachkof, who, in order to escort the unfortunate lady to her place of exile, dared to outstay his leave of absence. Paul complimented him. " Here at least we have a man who does not wear petticoats ! " This officer's regiment being disbanded, Paul gave him another and shortly afterwards made him a commander of the Order of Malta.

The Princess was also visited at Korotova by other relatives and friends, who disregarded the order that she was to be kept in isolation. Even then Paul did not take offence, but was heard to say : " If any one has any friendship for this lady or owes her any gratitude now is the time to show it."

Court-martial sentences revised by the Czar were usually made heavier, but were sometimes reduced—often, it is true, with equally little reason. On one occasion a sub-lieutenant was condemned to death for having incited soldiers to desertion in the course of a campaign in Georgia and for having maltreated them while in a state of intoxication. Paul reduced his sentence to two months' imprisonment.

In religious matters the Czar continued after his accession to practise, after a fashion, a broad tolerance. But even here he showed his despotic instincts and his inquisitorial methods. Foreigners resident in Russia were free to profess the religion in which they were born ; but they were not at liberty to refrain from discharging the duties which it imposed upon them. They were enjoined by regulations published in several languages to neglect none of these duties on pain of being treated as rebels. In the Catholic churches, which during the previous reign had been deserted but which were now filled, receptacles were placed by the confession boxes, in which were to be placed the names and addresses and the professions of the penitents. Reports of these were submitted every day to the Emperor, and, as the tickets of absolution having became a sort of guarantee of respectability, a scandalous traffic in them soon developed.

At the same time Paul wished to separate entirely the domain of intellect from that of religion. Under Rastoptchine's influence he soon repudiated his former sympathies with freemasonry and Martinism. He dismissed Novikof from St. Petersburg and placed him again under police supervision. Year by year he became more uncompromising. In January 1801, Schirmer, a Prussian merchant, was arrested, kept on bread and water for a month, and finally sent back to his own country for projecting the organisation of a literary and artistic club.

On the other hand, it must be remembered that it was the son of Catherine who a century ago commenced the series of measures which, only recently and still incompletely, have assured liberty of conscience in Russia. This principle was proclaimed in a ukase of March 18, 1797, with some reserves relative to Catholic propaganda in the Polish provinces. Another ukase, dated March 12, 1798, authorised the "old believers" (*staroobriadtsy*) to build churches in all the eparchies. On October 27, 1800, with the consent of the Metropolitan of Moscow, this measure was extended to the capital of the Orthodox Faith.

Paul and Plato were aiming at some sort of union of dissenting sects among themselves, but beyond this they had another object more congenial to their natural sentiments. Their conciliatory attitude assisted a certain tendency among the dissenters to return to the orthodox fold, and the Metropolitan did his best to stimulate the movement by drawing up a plan of religious reunion, which received the approval of the Holy Synod but which in the end had little lasting effect. In this sphere Paul was as indecisive as elsewhere, and his acts show the same incoherence, the same mixture of noble inspirations and tyrannous abuse of power.

On the whole the bad predominated over the good, but his disordered activities were not wholly without salutary consequences. Prince Czartoryski, who had good opportunities of observation, points out one of these, by which the Polish provinces, so sorely oppressed since the partition, profited to some extent. The governors of this country were terrorised like the rest of the world, and, as the Prince observed, did not dare to practise abuses which attracted too much attention. This is a feature which is not uncommon in the history of despotic monarchies, and the reason is clear. Paul's Government was as evilly inspired and as wicked as that of the French jacobins, but it was far from being so deleterious. A single tyrant is never so bad as a hundred oppressors, and Paul's tyranny, formidable as it was, only affected a narrow circle, for the very reason that the limitations of the despot's mind prevented him from seeing very far, while the means at his disposal were equally restricted. Even in the immediate neighbourhood of the Sovereign, the Court and the higher ranks of society in St. Petersburg, people suffered less than has been represented. Mme. Vigée-Lebrun, who, according to her account, was terrorised herself, never felt compelled to shorten her stay in Russia, and after narrating the inconvenience and anxiety by which she no less than all other inhabitants of the capital were afflicted, she adds : " All this did not prevent the St. Petersburg of that time from being a very pleasant and profitable place to live in. The Emperor Paul was a lover and a patron of the arts. He was very fond of French literature. He attracted and retained by his generosity the actors to whom he owed the pleasure of seeing our great dramas on the stage, and the possession of any talent for music or painting was a certain title to his favour. Doyen, the historical painter, was honoured by Paul as he had been by Catherine, and the Czar commissioned him to paint one of the ceilings in the new Michael Palace. . . . As regards the pleasures of society, St. Petersburg left nothing to be desired."

The upper classes owed no privileges to Paul. His preferences were in fact all for the lower strata of society, who at any rate seem to have been far from having any quarrel with the new régime. Everything is relative, and the Russia of Catherine II had been anything but a paradise for the lower orders. If he was unwilling to abolish the institution of serfdom, Paul at least tried, in his usual spasmodic and unsystematic way, to mitigate its natural consequences. He endeavoured to introduce a moderating principle, and this gives him a real claim upon the indulgence and even upon the gratitude of posterity. But political systems, however meritorious, are usually overthrown rather because of their best than because of their worst features ; and Paul was not content to be the protector of the peasants or to pose as a Mæcenas. He had other very numerous and very high ambitions, for which the resources of his Government did not suffice. If all the Russians of this time were not so much maltreated as has been until recently asserted, they were assuredly governed, so long as Paul lived, in a manner contrary to good sense.

CHAPTER VI

THE CZAR'S ENTOURAGE

I

AMONG Paul's collaborators there was a certain Glinka. The following is the record of his service for four years. He was made an actual Councillor of State on April 5, 1797, Governor of Esthonia on May 30, Governor of Arkhangelsk on August 31 and on December 31 he was dismissed. On April 5, 1798, he was made Governor of Novgorod, and on December 22 he was transferred to St. Petersburg in the same office. Dismissed the service for negligence on March 2, 1800, he was made Privy Councillor and Senator two weeks later, and on July 14 he received a grant of 5000 diessiatines of land in the Government of Saratof.

This example shows how the staff employed by Catherine's son were affected by the mobility of his ideas, and it will be necessary to review this staff before we proceed to describe the events in which they took part. The history of Paul's reign both at home and abroad is intimately connected with the rapid mutations by which it was distinguished and the grand drama in which Paul played the leading part would not be intelligible without a preliminary glance at the minor characters. Some of these are already known to us as companions of Paul at Gatchina or as his mother's servants. The others may be briefly described.

As observed above, Paul began wisely by retaining most of the staff left to him by Catherine. Vice-Chancellor since 1775 and nominal Chief of the College of Foreign Affairs since Panine's death in 1785, the aged Ostermann was the decorative figurehead of this department. Paul respected this arrangement, but he was carried away by his love of show and could not resist making a change of form. He must have a Chancellor, and the title was therefore conferred on Ostermann, to whom it did no good. His head was turned by his new dignity and he envied Bezborodko his effective share in the conduct of affairs so much that on April 21, 1797, he was forced to yield the office to him.

Paul would have liked to promote Simon Vorontsof, who had defended his father and who had therefore been relegated to a sort of honourable exile at the London Embassy. But the exile was contented as he was. He preferred to retain and consecrate to pleasure the leisure afforded by this mission and the intervals of a heart complaint from which he suffered. Bezborodko was himself exhausted and would willingly have given way to any other competitor, but according to Rastoptchine the " place stuck to him more than he stuck to the place," for he was quite unable to account for several millions expended in the execution of the various offices which he held. On the other hand, Paul would not in all probability have tolerated indefinitely the presence in such an important post of one who, in the words of Cobenzl, " was the only man who could venture to remonstrate with him," and the death of the second Chancellor in April 1799, only anticipated his disgrace by a little.

The Sovereign received the news without regret. " In my service," he observed to a foreign diplomatist, " they are all Bezborodkos." According to Rastoptchine, the deceased Chancellor, in spite of his enormous revenues, continued until the end to plunder right and left. This was the tradition of Catherine's school, but the same man knew how to guide the foreign policy of Russia with a supple and a firm hand in the path indicated by the Empress, and how to maintain the prestige of his country. Paul understood neither how to choose new ministers nor how to make proper use of those who came to him from the previous reign. It was natural that he should employ a man like Nicolas Arkharof to forestall or put down the alleged rebellion of Alexis Orlof. Catherine herself had demanded similar services of this police officer, who was adroit enough, but whose talents seem to have been exaggerated by M. de Sartine, who was in correspondence with him. The great Empress put a juster estimate on his aptitudes and confined him strictly to subordinate functions. Paul at once made him Military Governor of the Capital—a disastrous step. The methods of the new proconsul (for this was the dignity to which Arkharof aspired) have become traditional in Russia, and consisted in exasperating the inhabitants by abuse of power, rudeness, vexatious interference and inquisitorial zeal, and in keeping the Sovereign in a state of continual alarm by denouncing the tendencies to revolt for which he was himself responsible.

This clever scoundrel is said to have ruined himself by the excess of his own cleverness. Returning from the coronation with Marie Féodorovna, it occurred to him to practise on the Empress herself the arts of the *agent provocateur* in which he excelled. He engaged her Majesty in a conversation filled with perfidious allusions to the *coup d'état* of 1762, coupled with flattering suggestions the nature of which it is easy to guess. She reported this to the Czar, and Arkharof was dismissed on June 17, 1797.

Besides these two personages Catherine left no civilian of more than mediocrity behind her. The great days were over and favouritism had made its blighting influence felt. In the military sphere the glorious Roumiantsof had for several years before her death been condemned to retirement, both because of his ruined health and because of the jealous hatred with which he had inspired Potemkine. But another great man remained, still full of vigour though not far short of seventy years of age, and after a brilliant

128

career still destined to further triumphs. Both time and Court intrigue had spared Souvorof.

The future Prince of Italy could be, when he liked, a very adroit courtier. He had shown his talent in this direction both with the Prince of Tauris and with his illustrious protectress. For various reasons he declined to try his hand on his new master. Paul at the outset of his reign paid him but scant attention and showed him frank hostility tempered only by contempt. The Czar was then a determined pacifist and did not expect to require this thunderbolt of war. Moreover, the old warrior was the incarnation of a school of war which the creator of the army of Gatchina was determined to annihilate. Souvorof was also believed to have been one of the signatories of the manifesto by which Catherine intended to disinherit her son; and finally, his personal appearance, no less than his mental peculiarities, however well calculated to make him the idol of his soldiers, was from other points of view less attractive.

In 1784, writing to Potemkine, asking for an independent command, he referred to himself in the following terms: " I have served for more than forty years and I am nearly sixty. My one desire is to finish my service in harness. I have been so long in the subordinate ranks that I have never acquired the usages of society, but my heart is pure. . . . Study has taught me virtue. I can lie like Epaminondas, I can run like Cæsar: I am as firm as Turenne and as just as Aristides. As I know nothing of adulation or flattery I do not often succeed in pleasing my superiors, but I have never broken my word to an enemy and I am fortunate because I command success."

The bizarre originality of this confession was of gradual growth. Ten years previously Souvorof's correspondence with the Prince of Tauris shows no trace of it. Souvorof was then a penetrating observer and an exact reporter of the facts of which he wished to inform his chief. But from

1788 onwards his letters, which had hitherto been extremely prolix, became distinguished by an *imperialis brevitas*, and betrayed a disorder in his faculties which might well have seemed incompatible with the exercise of functions involving serious responsibility. His letters are almost always a strange and almost unintelligible mixture of apothegms and interjections, more particularly when the writer uses the French language as he is fond of doing, but they clearly reveal the indomitable energy which still animates him, the thirst for action by which he is still devoured, his unabated confidence in his own genius, and his chagrin at not being able to use his undiminished powers to further a still unsated ambition.

There was no place for such a man in Paul's flock of docile marionettes. The eccentricities of the two men were so contradictory that any prolonged agreement between them was impossible. Souvorof disapproved of the military reforms of his Sovereign and described them in characteristic language. " Powder for the hair can't be used to load a musket ; ringlets are not Gatling guns ; hair-plaits are useless as fuse, and I am nothing of a German." As early as January 1797 he received a sharp reprimand for some trifling breach of the new regulations. It was, however, the open dislike, which he shared with Simon Vorontsof, for the joys of the parade-ground which particularly annoyed Paul. Souvorof was good for nothing but war, and the scientifically balanced but too short step in which they drilled the soldiers with whom he was accustomed to rush to victory excited his disgust. " It is an excellent way," he grumbled, "to do thirty versts instead of forty when you are marching on the enemy." Sulking, railing and scoffing, he retired to his estate of Kobryn in Volhynia and ended by asking to be allowed to resign. By order of the Emperor, Rastoptchine replied that the Marshal's desire had been anticipated, and on February 6, 1797, the following note was published after parade : " Field-

Marshal Count Souvorof, having said that in the absence of war there is nothing for him to do, is excluded from service for these words."

This involved the loss of the right to wear a uniform, and Paul saw no reason for making an exception. Being thus taken at his word, Souvorof did many foolish things. He solemnly buried his uniform and his decorations, and refused to receive a letter from the Emperor because it was addressed to Field-Marshal Count Souvorof, " who was no more." He diverted his neighbours at Kobryn by galloping about the village with all the children astride upon a stick, and in the following April he was sent to Kontchanskoïé, another estate which he owned in the Government of Novgorod and which was in fact his very modest ancestral domain. Here he lodged in a peasant's house, like Princess Dachkof, and appeared to be completely satisfied. Clad in a shirt and trousers and dispensing even with the shirt in summer, he continued to play with the young peasants, hobnobbed with their fathers, arranged marriages, read the Epistle in church on holidays, sang in the choir and took part in the bell-ringing.

In reality he was weary of his solitude and was much vexed by the supervision of the Commissary who, according to the custom of the time, was attached to him. He also complained of his poverty, and having quarrelled with his wife, Barbara Prozorovski, a niece of Roumiantsof, he refused to make her an allowance, though he still had an income of 50,000 roubles and a fine house in Moscow. In September he could stand it no longer and begged for mercy : " Great Sovereign, have pity on a poor old man ! Have pity on me if I have done wrong." Paul was inflexible and minuted the letter " no answer." But in the following year he too began to have regrets. His peaceful resolutions were disappearing and his entry into the coalition against France was becoming imminent. He sent Prince Gortchakof, the exile's nephew, to Kontchanskoïé with a gracious message inviting the illustrious soldier to St. Petersburg.

Souvorof was in no hurry to respond to the summons. He travelled with a deliberation well calculated to incense the most patient of masters, and when he arrived he made the Czar pay dear for the ennui of his exile. At parade he pretended to understand nothing of what was going on, shook his head and mutely interrogated the company in a way which hugely amused them. In vain Paul tried to conciliate him by accelerating the pace of the soldiers who were manœuvring. The Marshal suddenly declared that he was ill, asked for his carriage, and when it came stepped back several times before he got in, contriving to catch his sword (which was slung at his back in the new fashion) time after time on the door. But above all he peremptorily refused to re-enter the service or to accept one of the new Inspectorships of the Army, the holders of which were to be appointed without regard to seniority. Having been Commander-in-Chief, Souvorof said he was too old to learn the duties of any other post, and if he could not have a command of the same kind with a free hand he preferred to go back to Kontchanskoïé. In three weeks he did in fact go back, and shortly afterwards asked permission to go to the Hermitage of St. Nilus, where, he said, he wished to " spend the rest of his days in the service of God." To this petition he again received no reply.

Paul was not finished with the terrible man to whom was due the only ray of glory which was to illumine his dismal reign. But they were never destined to agree together, and doubtless the Czar would have succeeded no better with Roumiantsof himself, though he hastened to relieve that illustrious soldier of the semi-disgrace which he had suffered in the previous reign. The hero of the Turkish wars died in December 1796, and his death only anticipated a rupture which to all appearance was imminent.

As regards the navy, Paul thought his mother had left

him a more valuable servant in Count Ivan Tchernychof, who had been President of the College of Admiralty since 1769. This idea is another proof of the weakness of his judgment. Tchernychof was an amiable man of the world, without the slightest interest in or capacity for the career which he had by chance embraced, and in his department he played the same part as old Ostermann at the College of Foreign Affairs. The naval staff had been in all respects ill-equipped since the dismissal of the foreign officers to whom Catherine had owed her naval victories. In September 1796, Barré de Saint-Leu, one of the agents of the Directory who had been a long time in Russia, reported as follows: " Admiral Mordvinof is Commander-in-Chief in the Black Sea. He is *marin malgré lui.* . . . Vice-Admiral Ouchakof is an old woman, always making a fuss about nothing. Vice-Admiral Ribas is in a military sense quite incompetent and one of the most cunning intriguers alive. Rear-Admiral Poustochkine is bold only in making foolish speeches." Barré added that it would be quite possible to corrupt most of these officers, even Mordvinof himself, who was a " decent fellow."

Vassili Tchitchagof, the best of the Russian admirals who had distinguished themselves in the preceding reign, was already past service owing to age and infirmities. The son of this hero, Paul Tchitchagof, after completing his naval education in England, had become a post-captain and was reputed an officer of great merit. His father came to St. Petersburg to be treated for a disease of the eyes without asking permission, and Paul brutally dismissed him from the capital. The son on his side was angered by a slight which he thought had been put upon him and resigned his commission; it was rumoured that he wanted an appointment in the British Navy. He did in fact ask for a passport in order that he might go to England to marry a young lady in that country. It happened that at this very time the Czar, following a flattering suggestion of the British Government, was about to appoint Tchitchagof to be second in command of the auxiliary squadron which he proposed to send to the Dutch coast. Tchitchagof suspected a trap, and he also thought that he would be under the orders of a comrade whose services were inferior to his own. He therefore expressed a desire to serve in the Baltic and not on the coast of Holland. Paul saw in this nothing but an act of disobedience : a violent scene took place between them, and Tchitchagof was for a short time—from June 21 to July 1, 1799—imprisoned in a fortress. After this, however, the Czar's desire to please England overcame his other feelings, and he made amends for his former conduct by explaining that he thought that Tchitchagof had become infected with revolutionary ideas. He would, however, overlook this. " If you are a jacobin, imagine that I too wear the cap of liberty and am the chief of all the jacobins, and serve me ! " So Tchitchagof was made Commander-in-Chief of the squadron which was to co-operate with the British Fleet, and married Miss Proby. The weakness of the staff at his disposal compelled Catherine's heir to consent to more than one capitulation of this kind.

II

The two Kourakines, who enjoyed the protection of Mlle. Nélidof, seemed at first to be destined to have, under the Czar, the effective control of domestic and foreign affairs. Alexander Borissovitch the elder, who was to be the Russian Ambassador at Paris under Napoleon, was a friend of Paul's childhood and the companion of his European travels. In 1782 he had been compromised in the affair of the insulting correspondence intercepted by Catherine and this endeared him to his Imperial accomplice. He succeeded in securing the goodwill of the favourite without losing that of Marie Féodorovna ; he was loaded with honours and riches and held the post of Vice-Chancellor, the duties of which he was incapable of discharging even passably. In 1798 Mlle. Nélidof's influence was eclipsed for the second time and he talked of retiring. Paul was surprised and observed, " Why should he retire ? He is of no account even if he remains in office ! "

Alexis, the younger brother, in spite of his taste for Oriental luxury, debauchery and rapine, was a worthier figure. He was something of a statesman and had one or two ideas which have given him a place among the fore-runners of the work of reform carried out in the following century. As Minister of the Interior to Alexander I he was destined to carry out at his own cost an experiment which was a prelude to the enfranchisement of the serfs. Under Paul he probably inspired the few liberal measures of the reign which, though ill-conceived and even worse administered, were still a step in the right direction and a credit to their framers. As Procurator-General, however, as Member of the Council of the Empire, and as Minister of Domains he did nothing. Between the jealousy of Vassiliéf, the Minister of Finance, who thought his rival " took too much upon him," and the hatred of Rastopt-chine, who called him a scoundrel, " plundering and blundering everywhere and demanding the more with brazen assurance," Alexis Borissovitch made no headway, and in 1798 he shared his brother's disgrace.

In default of Vorontsof, who year by year became more obstinately disinclined for office, the elder Kourakine was replaced in 1798 by Victor Kotchoubey, another Little Russian and the nephew of the Chancellor, who was already failing and near death. During the uncle's life-time the nephew's office was a mere form, and a little later the Czar changed his mind again and fell back on Nikita Petrovitch Panine, a young man under thirty. Panine was another old friend. He was son and nephew to the two former inspirers of the " Pretender " : like his uncle, he was a Prussomaniac, but he was also an authoritarian like his father the General, a resolute partisan of the English alliance, and above all a sworn enemy of republican France. Hence his promotion was rapid. In 1795, at twenty-four, he was Governor of Grodno and commanded a brigade; three years later he left the army for diplomacy and was at once made Minister Plenipotentiary at Berlin. He had brilliant abilities and a precocious maturity of mind, together with an absolute if not invariably well-founded confidence in himself. He was one of those men of imperious temper who so often arise in Russia as a sort of counterpoise to the servility of her bureaucracy, and whose strong initiative every now and then asserts itself —often to the great benefit of their country. In Paul's reign such a temperament could find no scope for itself, and Nikita Petrovitch soon drifted first into culpable misconduct and then into a situation which forced him to become a conspirator, ruined his career and damaged his reputation.

In 1799 he was made Vice-President of the College of Foreign Affairs, but Rastoptchine was already President, and had secured a predominating position, though he did not receive the office of Chancellor which was left vacant. Rastoptchine reserved for himself the right of reporting personally to the Emperor (*doklad*), which even now is still the object of such bitter competition, and only left to his colleague the shadow of power and the more disagreeable duties of the office.

In November 1800 the " perlustration " of the despatches of the Prussian Envoy, Count Lusi, revealed to the Czar that the Vice-Chancellor disapproved of the embargo which was then imposed on British vessels in Russian ports, and Panine, who happened to be giving a great diplomatic dinner-party, had the greatest difficulty in securing the postponement of the publication of his dismissal for a few hours. He was sent to Moscow on November 15, 1800, as a mere senator, and a month later he had to exile himself

to his estates, where he was still pursued by the hatred of
Rastoptchine.

Rastoptchine began as aide-de-camp to the Emperor
for military administration. He was made a Count on
February 22, 1799, and on May 31 he received the
office of Postmaster-General, a new post which he held
in addition to the Ministry of Foreign Affairs. The old
associate of Gatchina days, who had then been so weary of
Paul, was now getting possession of all the power that Paul
could give him, but he continued to be as disgusted as
ever. " I am unpopular," he wrote to Simon Vorontsof,
" as being a man supposed to enjoy the confidence of a
master who inspires no love. I am suspected by several
ministers as being imbued with revolutionary principles
because I used to be intimate . . . with Count Koutaïssof, who is under the thumb of a Frenchwoman named
Chevalier, whose husband is supposed to be a violent
jacobin. . . . I shall be on my estates in three months."

He was nearer the truth than he supposed. He made a
great deal of use of the *cabinet noir* and he formed the plan
of intercepting a letter, attributing it to Nikita Panine and
thus completing the ruin of his hated rival. The intrigue
turned against its author : Panine's innocence was by
chance made manifest, and on February 20, 1801, a ukase
fulfilled the wish so insincerely expressed by the too wily
Tartar by dismissing him and appointing Pahlen as his
successor.

Pahlen, " the man of destiny," had been Military Governor of St. Petersburg since July 1799 ; but though he
was nearly sixty he had not yet revealed his real genius,
which was that of a born conspirator with a heart of
adamant, a brow of brass, a self-control which nothing
could shake and a matchless gift for intrigue.

His re-entry into the service had been partly due to the
general rearrangement of offices which followed the final
disgrace of Mlle. Nélidof in 1798, and it coincided with the

return to favour of Araktchéief after his first eclipse, which lasted only a few months. Paul's favourite collaborator had been dismissed in March 1798, but reappeared in August of the same year as Quartermaster-General of the Army, to which office was added, in January 1799 the command of the artillery battalions of the Guard and the post of Inspector-General of the Army. He soon, however, incurred the hostility of Pahlen, whose plans were impeded by Araktchéief's uncompromising fidelity to Paul.

In the following September occurred the theft of military braid which has already been mentioned. Araktchéief's brother was in command of the post at the place where this misdeed was discovered, and the Inspector-General, who was much devoted to his family, took upon himself to conceal this fact from the Emperor. He was denounced and at a Court ball on September 30 he was ordered, without further inquiry, to go home, and the following day he was put on the retired list. Paul had reason to repent of this later.

The office of Procurator-General obtained an unprecedented importance in Paul's reign, but more than any other it felt the effect of his changeable humour. After Alexis Kourakine, Paul first appointed, in 1798, Peter Lapoukhine, the father of Mlle. Nélidof's rival; then in July 1799 Alexander Békléchof, formerly Military Governor of Kamiéniéts-Podolski, of whom he had great hopes. Less than six months later, however, on February 1, 1800, he dismissed the collaborator of whom so much was expected. His successor was Peter Obolianinof, formerly steward at Gatchina, who, up till the catastrophe of March 11/23, 1801, which he was not clever enough to foresee, remained a sort of Grand Vizier, holding his own first against Rastoptchine and then against Pahlen, in civil and even in military matters. He was quite uneducated and almost illiterate, brutal in his humours and coarse in his manners, always using threats and big words. He was familiar with every one, and compelled the Grand Dukes themselves to appear at his morning receptions, and perhaps he was rather disagreeable than really maleficent. His probity was unshakable and a certain elevation of mind compensated for his uncouthness and his repellent ugliness. He was lazy, however, in spite of his ambition, and his chief gift was his power of choosing industrious subordinates, on whom and on his own dexterity he depended to keep his place, which he would assuredly not have succeeded in doing if the situation had been prolonged.

At the top of the hierarchy or in Paul's immediate entourage only two men, and these of very unequal value, were exempt from the vicissitudes which overtook even the most brilliant fortunes of the day. Admiral Gregory Kouchélof (1754–1832), who executed in a docile fashion Paul's naval ideas, retained to the end the confidence of the Sovereign, and his real worth deserved better employment. Inspirer of a new set of regulations for the Imperial Navy and author of a *Study of the Maritime Signals now in use*, Kouchélof had a profound knowledge of his profession, and in the history of naval construction, of marine topography and Russian naval education his record is an honourable one.

The other privileged person was, alas! Koutaïssof. Prince Czartoryski asserts that even after Paul's reign had begun he saw him doing the duties of a valet. On December 6, 1798, he was made Grand Huntsman. On February 22, 1799, he was created Baron, Count on May 5, and Grand Equerry on January 9, 1800. After Araktchéief's departure, the ex-barber occupied the apartments of Catherine's favourites at the Winter Palace. A little later he had rooms at the Michael Palace, which communicated with those of the Czar by a secret staircase. He was the recognised purveyor of his Majesty's pleasures, a duty which he sometimes shared with Alexander Narychkine, Grand Marshal of the Court. His fortunes remained afloat where so many foundered, but the Czar's caresses alternated with severe reproofs and were not unmixed with kicks and blows from the Imperial cane.

Prompt as he was to banish from his presence and from his government all those who displeased him, Paul throughout his reign was the plaything of the very men whom he so much despised and whom he found it so easy to cast off. The wavering thoughts and vacillating will of the Emperor were constantly the prey of contending Court intrigues fomented by these men, often baffled but always renewed.

In spite of appearances feminine influence did not play the predominant part in the politics of the period which some have been tempted to assign to it. The rule of favourites was not succeeded in Russia by the domination of mistresses. Mlle. Nélidof's reappearance at Court after the accession of her protector, her retirement in 1798 and the triumph of Mlle. Lapoukhine, were events which made their mark on contemporary history, but for different reasons. Paul's fair friends and mistresses did not rule him. They never had the capacity to do so if they sometimes had an inclination to try. Even after his definite quarrel with the idol of his youth, which at the same time placed him in almost open hostility with Marie Féodorovna, Paul continued for a time to pursue the same foreign policy as before the rupture—a policy to which the contribution of the two women had been only indirect. But the dismissal of Mlle. Nélidof and the ruin of the credit gained for the Empress by her reconciliation with the favourite had another decisive effect. It resulted in the disgrace of a whole clientèle who, when deprived of Mlle. Nélidof's support, had to give place to a new set of people of different passions and tendencies to whose domination Paul, a despot in name rather than in fact, at once succumbed.

III

Mlle. Nélidof, to whose mind the mere idea of a reconciliation with Paul before his accession was insupportable, had completely changed her mind. Her understanding with Marie Féodorovna was now complete and was destined to be lasting. The Empress henceforth laid aside all suspicion and no longer insisted even on being a party to the correspondence which passed between the favourite and " her dear Pavlouchka." Mlle. Nélidof's adversaries were much disturbed by this. Rastoptchine was the life and soul of this party, and in his letters to Simon Vorontsof he never ceased to denounce the manner in which the associates of the Sovereign and his mistress were " stealing the Government."

He exaggerated the danger. The two Kourakines, owing to incapacity in the one case and indolence in the other, were not in a position to exercise a predominating influence. And Marie Féodorovna and Mlle. Nélidof themselves never succeeded in establishing their ideas in this domain, though they sometimes tried. One reason for this was that they had no ideas to establish, but rather sentiments, which were always generous but sometimes imprudent. Their true task was to calm the Sovereign and to mitigate the effects of his anger. Mlle. Nélidof mingled her endearments with remonstrances which were often lively enough, and she did not shrink on occasion from scolding her protector. She stood loyally by her ally, and once when Paul lost his temper at dinner and ordered the Empress to leave the table she rose to follow her. " Stay, mademoiselle," said the Czar. " Sir, I know my duty," retorted the favourite.

To soothe and restrain the Emperor and to obtain pardons and reprieves were her chief preoccupations during this part of her career. She was not always successful, but even Koutaïssof occasionally owed it to her that his long-suffering back escaped the painful correction by which it was threatened. She had no great confidence in the return of her favour at Court and she prudently retained her rooms at the *Smolnyï* and appeared more and more rarely at the palace. In the summer of 1797 she required a great deal of persuasion before she would go to Pavlovsk. The old dissensions between her and Paul were on the point of reviving. She came however, was present at the autumn manœuvres, and, at a ball given at Pavlovsk, she once more enchanted Paul, in spite of her forty years, by dancing a minuet at his request, in which he thought her performance exquisite. " We were like two old portraits," says Sabloukof, who was her partner and wore a uniform after the fashion of Frederick the Great. But the very next day the inevitable friction recommenced, and Rastoptchine and his friends were not alone in rejoicing at its return and accentuating it as much as they could. The Grand Duchess Elizabeth wrote as follows to her mother about the " abominable passion " of her detested father-in-law :

" Mlle. Nélidof is the only person who has any influence with the Emperor and she entirely dominates him. The Empress condescends to her in the basest manner . . . and *she* is the person who should replace my mother, in whom I should have (as she wishes) a blind confidence ! Tell me, dear mamma, if you think such a thing is possible ? You must know that this winter there was a quarrel between the Emperor and the Empress, who went off after dinner in full dress—there had been a party—to the convent where Mlle. N. lives to ask her to bring about a reconciliation between her and her husband ! You should see how angry my husband is on these occasions. ' What follies mamma commits,' he often says ; ' she doesn't in the least know how to behave.' "

It should be added that, though their intentions were excellent, the ideas of Catherine Ivanovna and her august friend were not always equally well inspired. Paul would have run serious risks by reducing Bezborodko, as he said, " to the rank of an encyclopædia " and conducting his foreign policy himself with the aid of Alexander Kourakine, as the patronesses of that foolish person desired. Faithful to the programme traced by Catherine, the Chancellor was against all idea of armed intervention against the Republic in France. The Empress and Mlle. Nélidof were full of romantic ideas, and, obedient to the suggestions of the French *émigrés*, they did all they could to influence the Emperor in a contrary direction. They went so far as to favour the Catholic propaganda which was being diligently developed by the Chevalier d'Augard, the Abbé Nicolle, and other apostles of the same type. Jealousy prevented Catherine Ivanovna from assisting for the same purpose the enterprises of the celebrated Princesse de Tarente, whom, on the contrary, she caused to be exiled from the Court as soon as she arrived in Russia. On the other hand, she did everything in her power to support the Papal Nuncio Lorenzo Litta and his brother Count Giulio, the envoy of the Knights of Malta, and thus contributed to involve Paul more deeply in the mad enterprise into which the two Italians were enticing him.

Her part was, in fact, no more important than that of the fly on the coach. But the Court camarilla under her protection knew how to make the most of her influence. In order to get rid of them Bezborodko joined forces with Rastoptchine and Koutaïssof, who forgot the benefits he had received from the favourite and suggested to his associates the idea which was to lead to their triumph. Mlle. Nélidof pretended that none of her influence depended on sensual attractions. The contrary was soon to be proved to her.

An intrigue was set on foot which was to take advantage of the amorous instincts which had been reawakened in Paul by his more or less platonic passages with the graceful performer of the minuet; but at first it failed, and

Rastoptchine for a moment fell into disgrace. Paul's fondness for his wife temporarily revived and his desire to please her went so far that he had a huge wooden pavilion—now the Constantine Palace—built at Pavlovsk to accommodate the Duchess of Würtemberg, whom he invited to pay a visit to his daughter. Marie Féodorovna's ill-luck, however, would have it that at this very time news arrived of the death of her mother, to whom she was much attached and whose presence would have been so helpful to her. The result was that her health was seriously shaken and she was unable to accompany her husband on a projected journey to Moscow. Paul left her on May 5, 1798, taking with him Koutaïssof and preceded by Bezborodko, and the allies thus had an unhoped-for opportunity of planning their revenge, which in fact was not long in coming.

IV

Catherine's son, as we have seen, had always had reason to be pleased with the welcome he received in the old capital. On this occasion also he felt that he was more appreciated there than at St. Petersburg. Koutaïssof insidiously led Paul to think that he knew why this was so and at first refused to say more, but when pressed he said : " The fact is that here people see that you are what you are, good, generous, and magnanimous ; and you yourself get the credit for it. *There* they say, ' it's the Empress, or Mlle. Nélidof, or the Kourakines.' "

" Do people suppose that I allow myself to be governed ? "

" Unfortunately they do ! "

" Very well, they will see ! "

The vanity of independence was to lead Paul into the very same trap which had been set for him by Mlle. Nélidof.

During the coronation festivities he had already become

more interested than was quite proper in two young ladies named Lapoukhine, the daughters of Peter Vassiliévitch. According to Countess Golovine, Marie Féodorovna and Mlle. Nélidof had taken alarm on the occasion of this first meeting and had done their best to shorten the Czar's stay in so dangerous a neighbourhood. He now met them for the second time, when they were on the look-out for a revival of his former impression. Anne, no doubt encouraged by interested parties, flirted openly with the Emperor at a ball. Her charms were wholly physical. She had black eyes, very white teeth and an air of innocence which was not wholly affected. One of the conspirators drew Paul's attention to her manœuvres, observing, " She is madly in love with you." Paul laughed and said, " She is a baby!" The baby, however, attracted him, and Koutaïssof was only too delighted to open negotiations in which the only difficulty was the exigencies of her ambitious step-mother. Mme. Lapoukhine stipulated for considerable advantages for herself and her husband, and also insisted that she should not be separated from her lover, Fiodor Ouvarof, an officer of the garrison at Moscow. At the last moment, however, Mlle. Lapoukhine hastened matters by declaring that if they did not come to terms she would leave for St. Petersburg alone, so the bargain was settled.

Paul was so deeply absorbed in the preoccupations of this intrigue that, contrary to his usual custom, he had given only a very divided attention to the grand manœuvres which preceded his departure for Kasan. Always impatient and in a hurry he was on the point of entering his carriage without awaiting the return of Koutaïssof from a final interview with the family of Anna Petrovna. " The journey will be terrible," thought Peter Obreskof, the Emperor's secretary, who was walking feverishly up and down in front of the palace looking out for the returning negotiator. At the last moment the ex-barber arrived in his troïka at a gallop, exclaiming, " Victory ! All is settled ! "

As a result, Field-Marshal Count Ivan Saltykof, the director of the neglected manœuvres, received expressions of satisfaction which he did not expect. But the relatives of the new favourite were even more warmly complimented. If we may believe the contemporary account, all the best society of Moscow, with a very few exceptions, rushed to the aristocratic Tverskaïa Street where the Lapoukhines lived. Countless icons were carried there, and in accordance with a rite used upon high occasions were passed in procession over the body of Anna Petrovna, who lay on the ground and was plentifully sprinkled with holy water. In innumerable private chapels Mass was said for the safe journey of the family. Peter Lapoukhine was a senator in the department of Moscow. He was transferred to St. Petersburg in the same capacity until some higher destiny could be found for him. His wife took with her Ouvarof, who was promoted. Rastoptchine, who was soon to benefit by the intrigue but who was at the moment temporarily in exile, described her as " an immoral, ill-bred woman."

The consequences of what had happened did not appear until after Paul's return to Pavlovsk in June 1798. No sooner had the Czar arrived than he was in a hurry to go away again, which was a bad sign. Paul's attitude to his wife, favourable or the reverse, could always be exactly measured by the length of time that he was willing to spend at Pavlovsk. At the same time he showed violent displeasure with Alexis Kourakine. The Bank of Assistance for the Nobility, of which this protégé of Mlle. Nélidof was still manager, was turning out badly, though it was said that he himself was far from being a loser.

Marie Féodorovna tried in vain to re-conquer the affections of her husband, and in order to keep him at home she even went so far as to throw one of her women in his way.

Paul accepted this substitute for Mlle. Lapoukhine, who had not yet arrived, and indeed kept her till a much later period; and Marie Féodorovna, following the constant usage of the time, very charitably cared for the children she had by the Czar. With less prudence she took upon herself to write to the new favourite in a threatening tone, forbidding her to come to St. Petersburg. The result was that she had to beg the Emperor " to spare her, at any rate in public."

Mlle. Nélidof was no better treated. As before, she showed herself ready to retort. Paul said to her in the presence of the Empress : " If you only knew how bored I am," and she replied : " If you only knew how you are boring us ! " But this settled nothing ; " dear Pavlouchka " only grew more angry and vented his spleen on the allies of his friend. In July 1798 the Senator George Nélédinski, Buxhoewden, and Serge Plechtchéief himself were dismissed in turn. The protectors of Mlle. Lapoukhine were reaping the fruits of their stratagem. Mlle. Nélidof followed her friends into retirement and wrote to the Empress in the following year from the Castle of Lohde : " How I should bless his name if only he had not sought to injure others ! . . . It is his misfortune that he never knows how much pain he inflicts. . . ." Her part was played out, but Marie Féodorovna retained for her an affection which became all the more constant because it was withdrawn from the stormy atmosphere of Court life.

On August 1, 1798, Peter Lapoukhine dined at Court. A week later he succeeded Alexis Kourakine as Procurator-General. Shortly afterwards he was sumptuously installed in the house formerly occupied by Admiral Ribas on the Neva Quay, and his wife and younger daughter were made respectively lady-in-wating and maid-of-honour. On August 18, Mlle. Nélidof's brother was dismissed in his turn. On the 24th, Rastoptchine was reinstated in his old office.   On September 9 the Vice -Chancellor, Alexander Kourakine, was dismissed, and Koutaïssof reached the pinnacle of his fortunes by being made a count along with Pahlen, who was by no means flattered by the association.

On October 3 the new favourite appeared at a ball and for the first time was admitted to the Sovereign's table, her position at Court thus becoming in a sense semi-official. She was a kindly person and more gentle than her predecessor; but she followed in Mlle. Nélidof's footsteps, doing her best like her to appeal to the clemency or the generosity of the master, weeping or sulking when she was unsuccessful, but generally speaking falling short in the elevation of sentiment and nobility of ideas which had distinguished the preceding régime.   The same was the case with all those whom her good fortune raised to power.

Her father, the Procurator-General, was not a bad sort of man, and in his new post he showed a spirit of justice, moderation and relative disinterestedness which has been recognised by all his contemporaries.   His intelligence was, however, very limited, and his political influence was nil.   Mme. Lapoukhine's one idea was to sell as dear as she could promises of patronage which were often illusory.   She and her husband were loaded with benefactions.   Paul bought for his favourite's father from Prince Stanislas Poniatowski the fine Little Russian estate of Korsoun ; on January 19, 1799, he gave him the title of Prince, and on the 22nd of the following month he was granted that of Serene Highness.   The Czar also directed that the device *Blagodat* (divine grace), said to be a translation of the Hebrew name Anne, should be added to the family arms.   Paul was still mystically inclined, though he had dismissed Plechtchéief.   A portrait of the Sovereign surrounded with diamonds, the ribbon of St. Anne, the Grand Cross of St. John of Jerusalem and the right to use the Imperial livery were also granted to this fortunate family.

Peter Vassiliévitch prided himself on being a philosopher, and his one idea was to secure the advantages he had gained. Life at Court was not without its drawbacks for the parents of the brilliant daughter. Madame Zagriajski turned her back on the new Princess in such a manner that Paul could see her do it, and then courtesied deeply to her, saying at the same time in a very loud voice, " By order of his Majesty ! " On June 7, 1799, the new Prince resigned all his offices, leaving an honourable memory of his tenure of that of Procurator in the ukase of December 17, 1798, forbidding the corporal punishment of persons over seventy years of age. He did not reappear until the reign of Alexander I, when he was first a member of Council and then, in 1803, Minister of Justice. Finally, until his death in 1816 he held the position of President of the Council and of the Committee of Ministers.

Mlle. Lapoukhine remained at Court, spoiled, flattered and worshipped. " It is a passion of the days of chivalry ! " wrote Rastoptchine.

V

Like her father she left politics alone and was all but ignorant of their existence. In all other matters she was the ruler of the town and the Court. Paul had forbidden the waltz at Court balls as being immodest. The new favourite showed regret, and this was enough to secure the withdrawal of the prohibition. Anna Petrovna, whirling in the arms of Dimitri Vassiltchikof, was applauded by the Czar just as her predecessor had been in the chaster evolutions of the minuet. She revolutionised the fashions and even the rules of etiquette. Catherine, who was by origin a German and by education a Frenchwoman, had prescribed *Russian* costume for her ladies on gala days. Though he was an enemy of

France, Paul had reversed his mother's decision and had decreed that the Russian costume should be replaced by the *robe à la française*. One word of regret from the favourite and the Russian dress was again obligatory. Mlle. Lapoukhine's tastes were rather common, and crimson was her favourite colour. This led to another reform. The uniforms of the officers of the Guard must henceforth be of this colour as previously the Court singers had been dressed in green in honour of Mlle. Nélidof. A warship just built received the name of *Blagodat*, and the favourite presided officially at the launch as godmother !

On pretext of vindicating his entire independence with the aid of " the Divine Grace," Paul was in fact abandoning himself to a sort of amatory delirium, in which the insignificant Anna Petrovna was only the central figure. He was ferociously jealous, however. On one occasion he caught his mistress flirting with a stripling of seventeen, named Alexandre de Ribeaupierre, and he promptly sent off the young Adonis to Vienna as *attaché* to the Embassy there. And yet he wished it to be believed that his own passion was purely platonic, and easily induced Marie Féodorovna to appear convinced of this. She was used to it and did not hesitate to cajole the new rival as she had done the others. She carried this so far that Rastoptchine was indignant. Later on, in a conversation with Prince Kotchoubey, Alexander himself is said to have been more sincerely convinced of it by " positive assurances," which he said he had received from his father on the subject, " both verbally and in writing."

To convince others, and perhaps also himself, of this obvious untruth, Paul had considered how best to marry the favourite. At first he made as if to offer her Ribeaupierre, whom, however, he sent away. His next choice was Victor Kotchoubey, who excused himself on the ground that he had already made choice of a wife. Finally, with greater apparent generosity, the amorous Sovereign yielded to the preference expressed by Anna Petrovna herself for Prince Paul Gavrilovitch Gagarine, a great scamp, who, however, was recalled from Italy, where he was serving under Souvorof, and was soon in the running for the post of Vice-Chancellor!

The young people seem to have been for some time in somewhat tender relations and to have been corresponding in secret. The Prince was a poor officer, but a better poet, and Joukovski, the editor of the *European Messenger* afterwards published some of his verses. More probably, however, Mlle. Lapoukhine merely sought in this marriage, which was not a happy one, a respectable name, while her Imperial lover thought that it would offer all the advantages (which he had already experienced) of the *ménage à trois*, without any of the restrictions.

When she had become Princess Gagarine, the favourite followed all the movements of the Court, and at Pavlovsk she had a comfortable abode of her own near the Pavillon des Roses, where the Emperor could join her without being seen, though indeed he made no secret of his visits. At St. Petersburg he provided her with more luxurious quarters, which he constructed out of three houses he had purchased on the Neva Quay and had had thrown into one. In a neighbouring mansion Koutaïssof installed Mme. Chevalier. The pupils of the Cadet Corps were ordered to avert their eyes when they passed these houses. Every day the same carriage conveyed the master and the valet to the scene of their respective pleasures, and soon the rumour spread that the actress, having chosen a crimson robe for the part of Phèdre, was competing with the Princess, whom she was thus flattering, for the affections of the Sovereign.

VI

Round this double intrigue revolved a whole society of a very questionable sort. There was Mme. Gerber, governess and afterwards companion to the favourite, who was still young and rather pretty. She used to figure discreetly in the daily interviews between the Sovereign and the object of his affections, and perhaps found means of advancing her own interests. There was M. Chevalier, the husband of the actress, formerly a dancer and an intimate of Collot-d'Herbois, whom he had assisted at the massacres of Lyons. He was now wholly occupied in making money out of his wife's success. Mme. Chevalier's identity cannot be certainly established, as several actresses of the same name are known to have existed at this time. One of these, a *pensionnaire* of the Théâtre Louvois in 1792, had figured in the republican fêtes as the Goddess of Reason, and it was probably the same lady that honoured the Théâtre français and the pleasure resorts of St. Petersburg with her presence. She was a friend of Barras, and when she formed the purpose of displaying her talents in Russia she offered him her services. It is more certainly established that she was in the pay of the First Consul's police at St. Petersburg. Born at Lyons about 1774, her charms were by this time a little faded, but they were reinforced by a good deal of grace and even more assurance. When she rode abroad she was followed by two grooms like the Emperor himself, and she eclipsed by her luxury even more than by her talent Mlle. Valleville, her rival at the Théâtre français. Her friendship with the Czar's favourite enabled her to make enormous sums by benefit performances. On the lists, which were known to be submitted to Koutaïssof and even to the Emperor himself, boxes at 1000 roubles and more were quite common. Her husband, whose insolence surpassed that of the most audacious of his class, received the subscriptions with the air of a pasha. Besides being manager of the theatre he held the rank of a major of infantry and wore the uniform of the Order of Malta !

In the same set there was also a young woman named Mrs. Gascoyne, the daughter of an English doctor named Guthrie, and wife of a Scotchman who managed the mines of Oloniets, and mistress of the new Prince Lapoukhine. Mr. Guthrie's post was in the public offices, where he was well looked after. If some business was about to be concluded he was allowed to delay the final formalities and to make money by offering to complete the transaction within twenty-four hours—for a consideration.

Paul, who was something of an actor himself, rather liked theatrical society. Frogères, a member of the French company, had the *entrée* of the Imperial cabinet, and the actor and the monarch were often seen walking arm in arm. They talked of French literature and sometimes of more frivolous matters. Perhaps, anticipating Napoleon, Paul sought in this companion another Talma. But Frogères was better at buffoonery than at the art of deportment and noble attitudes. He was admitted to the private parties at Court and there exercised his talents, sometimes at the expense of the Grand Dukes themselves.

About the beginning of 1800 the ex-favourite, who very soon wearied of Lohde, begged permission to return to St. Petersburg. Paul granted her request in courteous and even kindly terms, but he did not give up his new acquaintances or his new pleasures. It was in vain that Marie Féodorovna tried to return to the old habits: Koutaïssof and Princess Gagarine, Pahlen and Panine took good care that it should not be so. After having promised to attend a reception at the Empress's, where he knew that he was to meet his former idol, he sent word at the last moment that he would not come.

The correspondence between the Empress and her friend at this time makes it quite clear that they were both incapable of even understanding the skilful but cunningly masked manœuvres of their common enemies. They praised to the skies Pahlen and Panine, the very men who were already conspiring to kill the object of their affections ! From this moment Mlle. Nélidof became prematurely aged : her face was full of wrinkles ; her complexion the colour of lead. Yet she was to survive Marie Féodorovna by eleven years, though she never quitted the Smolnyï Convent, where she finished her days in 1839.

As to Princess Gagarine she preceded her rival to the grave, dying in childbirth in 1805. With the easy indulgence, characteristic of the ideas and the manners of the time, Paul's daughter-in-law, who had become Empress, expressed regret for the favourite in a letter to the Margravine of Baden.

Such was the company in which Paul, who was trying not only to reform but to recreate his vast empire, went out to meet his tragic destiny.

CHAPTER VII

INTERNAL GOVERNMENT: A PROGRAMME
AND ITS FAILURE

I

As regards reforms, Paul when he came to the throne
had, strictly speaking, only one in readiness, and that
was his project of military reorganisation. This scheme
was the fruit of his meditations or of Peter Panine's
suggestions, and though it was neither well conceived
as a whole, nor sufficiently thought out in detail, it was
relatively mature though still rather vague and indefinite.
Paul added to this a much more ambitious programme,
the one precise point in which was that he had made up
his mind *to change everything*. This was enough to make
him undertake the task of a universal reformer. We
shall see how he set about this and what came of it.

The reign of Catherine had been for the country,
which owed to her such a great increase of power and
prestige, a period of realisations. The elements of a new
political and social existence, after the fashion of the
western nations, had been prepared by Alexis, rapidly
developed by his son, and in the reign of Elizabeth had
already been gradually matured. Paul's mother had
made it her principal task to complete this process. She
did not attempt to introduce a profusion of renovating
principles, and indeed on this point she went so far as
to sacrifice her own personal ideas and inclinations.
Thus though in theory she condemned the institution
of serfdom she left it practically intact. She even, in

fact, consolidated it by making the owners of serfs into a ruling class. The reason for this was that apart from them she could not find any material out of which a society in the broad sense of the term could be constructed.

Of course she did not think that this state of things should last for ever. She did her best to create a *tiers état* ; but, on the other hand, she did not believe that in so new a country everything could be done at once. Something was reserved for the future and meanwhile she risked innovation only in small doses—germs as it were which would require a long process of evolution and adaptation to environment. She was a resolute opportunist and, especially in the second half of her reign, she showed a constant anxiety to spare as far as possible the " living flesh " on which she knew herself to be operating. This was why she spread over twenty-one years the process of applying the great administrative reform which she decreed in 1775. The organisation of the fiftieth Government—that of Slonim—forming part of the new districts thus created was not completed until August 8, 1796.

She might have accomplished more and done better things had she not allowed herself to be distracted by her unhappy taste for ostentation, and even more by that passion for adventure to which, however, she owed the beginnings of her prodigious fortunes. It was also her misfortune to reign too long. Towards the end of her life, aged and badly advised, she lost both her sense of balance and her sense of proportion. There was an ever-increasing discrepancy between the scale of the enterprises into which she was incessantly being led and the real resources of the country which, moreover, were squandered and turned aside from the objects for which she intended them to be used. At the same time the administrative apparatus, which had long worked regularly under her hands, began to get out of order from being overtaxed and less expertly manipulated. There were dilapidations and abuses of all sorts at the Ministry of War, whose forces existed only on paper. The Ministry of Marine was completely disorganised and had nothing to show but the skeletons of fleets rotting in the ports. There were more than eleven hundred pieces of business in arrear at the Senate; disorder, arbitrariness and misery were rampant everywhere. And yet, at the time when Zoubof could find no other remedy for the financial troubles of the Empire than to recoin the copper money with an augmentation of its nominal value, his mistress was preparing the expedition to Persia and appeared to be on the point of intervening against the French Revolution !

The Empress was not entirely responsible for this state of things. A great deal was due to deeper causes. Russia had the misfortune to be launched prematurely into modern civilisation and politics without material or moral resources corresponding to her position in the world. The country and its governors succumbed from time to time (as still occasionally happens) under the overwhelming task imposed upon them. Reality avenged itself on their too splendid dreams. Paul was a born idealist and never could understand this : it was his first and most serious mistake.

It would have been excusable if he had merely tried as far as possible to set right the errors of a reign which on the whole was glorious and fruitful. But for him everything was possible. He believed he could do everything and correct everything at once by virtue of the absolute ideal which he carried in his head and which he peremptorily set against all the realities of life. Not content to provide against the difficulties and dangers of the situation in which he found the empire, he proposed by an instantaneous and complete revolution to modify the very foundations of its political and social constitution, the product of long centuries of organic labour.

He set to work in the same spirit as that shown by those who had attempted the same thing in France some years before. He had the same disregard of consequences, the same mixture of ideas partially just and calculations invariably false, the same blind passion—and a temperament such as we have described. The result, as in France, was a catastrophe. A waterspout, an avalanche of laws and decrees—some of them old projects revised, some hasty improvisations put together at the last moment—descended suddenly on his unhappy country like the contents of Pandora's box, without regard for the necessities of transition or the difficulties of administration. Paul, who succeeded one of the greatest artists in government, never suspected that government was an art. It cannot be said that his ideas were unsystematic, but system was not what was lacking in the schemes of the revolutionaries of the day. He was methodical in the very processes of turning everything upside down, and proceeding from unjustifiable destruction to even less reasoned construction he systematically brought his country to the verge of an abyss.

II

Paul took a hand in everything and prided himself on infecting all his helpers with his own feverish energy. His first task was to set in motion the Senate, which was the chief wheel in the mechanism of government. Now, even by multiplying their special sittings apart from those held on the regular days on which they were obliged by ukase to meet, the members of this assembly seemed incapable of disposing of the huge arrears of work which had accumulated. Their business was to do everything, and they had too much to do. They no

longer had the character of a *governing* body, which Peter
the Great had intended to confer upon them; but in
spite of all their vicissitudes they retained a whole mass
of ill-defined, extremely variable but infinitely complex
powers and duties.

Paul seems to have meant to confine them to their
judicial functions, which had been specially developed
by centuries of evolution. He transferred the criminal
business with which the second Division was overwhelmed
to the fourth and fifth Divisions, whose duties had hitherto
been purely administrative. At the same time he created
three provisional Divisions, also with judicial duties,
and he increased the office staff in all. But he failed
here as elsewhere to give his reform a definite shape, or
to carry it out systematically. The senators, while
acting as magistrates and judges, still continued at
haphazard to administer the country. The distribution
of work was always changing, and one duty was taken
away from them only to be replaced by another. For
a short time, for example, they were entrusted with the
management of stud farms! On the other hand, there
were no materials from which to constitute the augmented
permanent staff. A establishment was set up under the
name of the Junkers' School, at which members of the
nobility were to be prepared for this service. Pupils
were so numerous and the military reforms caused so
many to turn to a civil career that Paul soon began to
find disquieting gaps in the ranks. The young men
were ceasing to covet the honour of wearing the epaulette.
" Where the devil are they going ? " asked the Czar.
" To the Junkers' School, sir." " But there should only
be fifty there." " There are four thousand five hundred,
sir." A decree soon dismissed the supernumerary junkers
to the army, but this gave no relief to the Senate, which
groaned under the multiplicity of its functions.

The law's delay, which had been complained of so

bitterly for centuries, was caused by the chaotic state of the legislation of the country. The great enterprise of codification inaugurated by Catherine at her celebrated " Legislative Assembly," and to which she hoped to attach her name, had never even been got into working order. Paul thought he could further the work by changing the name of the body to whom it was entrusted. The " Legislative Commission " became a " Commission for drawing up new laws," and, as might be supposed, matters were little advanced thereby.

In such a matter Paul, who had had no legal education, had no other guide than sentiments which were often right but which could not supply the place of guiding conceptions. Moreover, he had no intention of abdicating his prerogatives. One day some judicial sentence or other showed that the existing law provided the same penalty for offences the gravity of which varied. Immediately he decreed that the reform of this part of the Penal Code was to take precedence of all the rest. The next day, by a note despatched at six o'clock in the morning, he modified this decision by ordering that precedence should be given to a reform of the procedure in use. In the interval his attention had been drawn to the delay which had taken place in settling a trifling case. Another day Obolianmof, the last of his Procurators-General, said to Bezak, the secretary of his office, " We must have some sort of draft law to show to the Emperor within twenty-four hours. . . . It doesn't matter what it is. He is getting bored as he can't have any manœuvres owing to the bad weather. . . . See that it is ready by to-morrow."

Bezak set to work with the aid of Speranski, then an obscure clerk but destined to a great future in the next reign, and of a collection of old French books which had been left in a garret by Gregory Orlof. And at the appointed hour Paul found on his desk a " Commercial

Statute of the Russian Empire." He approved the statute, congratulated the Procurator and generously recompensed his staff. But the law was never put into force or even published.

The Russian Solon, while he made use of their talents, disconcerted his collaborators by certain remarks which strangely enough are held up to our admiration. " Here is your law ! " he observed, striking his chest and addressing one of his entourage who ventured to question one of his orders, respectfully pointing out that it was illegal. It followed that at the end of the reign the " Commission for drawing up new laws," though one of its members was the eminent jurist, Paliénof, had produced very little of any importance, and what they did produce— seventeen chapters on procedure, nine on the law of domains and thirteen on criminal law—was distinguished by the absence of all method or system in the order of topics.

III

Even more ambitiously Paul attacked the two fundamental principles in the political organisation of the Empire. Peter the Great had established a system of class government on a collegiate basis. His great-grandson sought to replace it by a staff of functionaries individually responsible to the Sovereign. The personal element was to govern the upper ranks—the minister being substituted for the college. In the lower the bureaucratic principle was to prevail, and class distinctions were to be eliminated by recruiting the service from all classes of society.

Well conceived and wisely applied this reform would have been timely, and Paul would have found himself beating on an open door. Even in Catherine's time the collegiate system had begun to break up, having been slowly but irresistibly undermined by the growing importance of the heads of certain departments. At the head of the three Colleges of Foreign Affairs, War, and Admiralty the Presidents of these great bodies had all the attributes of Secretaries of State, and left little but the semblance of power to their colleagues. On the other hand, the Senate, as we have seen, was restored more and more to the position of a supreme court of judicature, and justified less and less the title of governing body bestowed upon it by Peter the Great. The Procurator-General, on the contrary, gradually acquired the united functions of a Minister of Justice, of the Interior, and of Finance. All the departments shared the same tendency to develop a predominance of the personal element, and the remaining Colleges of Mines, Manufactures, and Commerce had come to an end, having been abolished by Catherine, who transferred their functions to the Chambers of Finance (*Kazionnyia Palaty*).

In these circumstances Paul was as usual torn between two contradictory desires. He wished to hustle everything and everybody and to accelerate a progress which he considered too slow, and at the same time he wished to undo what his mother had done to further the very movement he was assisting. He obeyed both impulses. On November 19, 1796, he re-established the suppressed colleges. Shortly afterwards the administration of finance was transferred from the Procurator-General to a Treasurer of the Empire, who again was in fact a responsible minister. The idea was good, but unfortunately it clashed with another desire of the Emperor's, which was to compensate the dispossessed Procurator (Békléchof) by giving him as many powers and attributions as possible. Thus while he lost the control of Finance this official was entrusted with the management of the new departments of "State Economy," "Supervision of Foreigners," and "Rural Economy." As if this were not enough he also had the administration of the Junkers'

School, the Geographical Department, and for a short time the Woods and Forests. To enhance the importance of the Procurator the Senate, already fallen from its high estate, was further stripped, and to him were transferred the direction of the codification which had been commenced, and he was directed " to see to the regular despatch of business in all the departments and to the punctual observation of the law in all branches of the administration."

Thus Paul replaced the existing embarrassment of functions by an even greater complication and, practically speaking, decreed chaos. Of the old colleges only the name seemed to survive amid the new and bewildering confusion of authorities and responsibilities which embarrassed and contradicted each other at every turn. Paul's chief idea seemed to be the systematic development of the principle of ministerial responsibility to which he was so much attached. Among the " organic laws " published at his coronation is one creating a new Department of Appanages. This department still provides suitably for the now very numerous members of the Imperial family, and its establishment was certainly a useful measure. Some people regard it as the most important achievement of the reign, though this perhaps does Paul less than justice. Now the Department of Appanages was placed under the control of a *minister*, and in 1800 a *Ministry* of Commerce was also set up, and the question of establishing a *Ministry* of Finance was under consideration. The obviously logical conclusion was the final abolition of all the old collegiate organisations. To this, however, Paul and his advisers could not make up their minds. It would have been to follow in Catherine's footsteps. So in order to give some sort of employment to these bodies who had no longer any *raison d'être* at all, it was decided to make them organs of executive Government! Decisions were to be personal, execution of these decisions collective—this was the result of this part of Paul's reforms !

The centralisation of power which was the natural result of the new principles inevitably tended to destroy the administrative autonomy partially organised by Catherine in the provinces; and the triumph of the bureaucratic system led to the elimination of the social and elective element. The Empress's policy had thrown the administration of justice and police into the hands of the nobility in the districts which she had created. This had grave drawbacks, for it constituted a series of small states within the state in which the agents of the central power had much difficulty in asserting their authority, and where they could not even show themselves without risk. Even the representatives of the local autonomies were bullied by the local potentates, whose creatures they were ; and while Catherine was still on the throne a proprietor in the Government of Voronège had received *with cannon balls* the members of the local tribunal who were seeking to put in an execution on his estates ! Mishandled as they were by those who appointed them, the local magistrates were in no position to offer any effective remedy to the serfs if they happened to quarrel with their masters.

Paul boldly attacked the corporate principle on which this organisation was founded ; but he avoided the only real remedy, which was to enlarge the basis of membership which was too narrowly aristocratic. He was held back both by his predilection for the bureaucratic system, which he wished to extend, and also by the impossibility of finding any assistance of value outside the privileged classes. A people of slaves cannot produce magistrates, and even now, fifty years after the abolition of serfdom, this is still the chief obstacle to the democratic organisation of the *Ziémstvos*. The only remaining course was to abolish the privilege from which these abuses sprang by destroying the very institutions whose beneficiaries made such a bad use of them. Catherine's son inclined to this solution, but never quite made up his mind to carry it out. On September 13, 1798, certain powers exercised by magistracies held by the nobility were transferred to Courts of Justice at Common Law. On May 14, 1800, the members of the inferior district tribunals hitherto elected by the nobility gave place to officials of the Heraldic Department.

The bureaucratic principle was quite consistently extended to the mercantile class and to all the bourgeoisie by the Statute of Corporations (*oustav o tsekhakh*) of November 12, 1799, and the Regulations of September 4, 1800. By these the elective municipalities in all the chief towns of Governments were replaced by officials appointed by the Central Government. The elective system is now again in favour, but Paul's plan is the one still adopted in organising *Ziémstvos* in the Western provinces, where the presence of a Polish element makes elections undesirable. Catherine was not free from this anxiety and took care not to give this part of her Empire the privilege of autonomy which she granted elsewhere. In the countries she annexed she even thought it best to suppress all the independent national institutions. This was so much work done for her successor ; but for him it was enough that it was the work of his hated mother. It was his main object to change or upset all that she had left to him, even if in doing so he contradicted his own programme. The autonomous institution of the old Polish palatinates had an aristocratic corporate basis and were therefore in antagonism with the system he was seeking to establish. He did not hesitate to reconstitute these institutions, nor can it for a moment be contended that having made this exception he did anything elsewhere to abolish once and for all the system of class privilege.

165

IV

It was far from being his intention to declare war on the nobility. They were to be compensated as soldiers for what they had lost as civilians. Under the new Prussian-ised regulations a member of the middle class could not become an officer without having served four years in the ranks. The nobility were to be admitted after serving three months ! Thus Paul maintained the system of class privilege while pretending to abolish it, and to one class he allowed privileges essentially corporate in character though he had condemned this principle !

The nobility were not unnaturally dissatisfied with these measures ; so much so indeed that in the very first year strong measures had to be taken merely to keep up the numbers of the representatives of this class in the service which was to compensate them for what they had lost. On October 5, 1799, a ukase forbade the nobility to put their children into the civil service without the special authorisation of the Sovereign. Other measures of the same kind, suggested by the numerous attempts to evade this provision, soon changed the paradise which Paul had devised for this class of his subjects into a prison, the exit of which was guarded by an angel with a fiery sword.

Paul could never understand their grievance, and to the end of his reign he pursued a policy, which may be called systematic because of the persistency with which it was pursued, but which may well be considered the leading instance of his incoherence. His mother had often said that she liked her nobles to feel their power. Paul thought it best that in his Empire there should be room for nothing but his own omnipotence. His conscious care was to suppress all consciousness, every symbol of social or political power and importance of any kind which was not his own. The Russian proverb has it that " a mass of men is a great man," and the Czar was particularly jealous of groups or collective organisations of any sort, which he regarded as so many rivals. With very few exceptions the law forbade any organised opinion, even for the purpose of promoting a petition. In the spring of 1797 a deputation of Don Cossacks came to St. Petersburg : the sixteen officers composing it were thrown into prison without even being heard. Some months later he ordered the Governor of Riga to investigate the case of some pensioners who complained of being ill-treated by the Commandant, but finding that there were several signatures to their petition he tore it up and returned it as illegal.

From the date of his accession began a series of measures intended to prevent the contamination of the nobility by " unworthy elements." No addition was to be made to the order without a special decision of the Sovereign. A strict heraldic record was instituted and rigorously revised and sifted. In corresponding decrees the nobility are expressly described as the " central column " of the political edifice which Catherine's successor had undertaken to reconstruct and as the natural support of the throne and the State. Was the reformer turning his back on the past and repudiating his own programme ? Not at all ! On January 2, 1797, by another stroke of the pen he abolished Article 15 of the Charter of Nobility of 1785 which conferred immunity from corporal punishment. This was done indirectly, by making a noble forfeit his status when found guilty of a crime punishable by loss of civil rights, and therefore liable to be flogged and branded. For the class interested this was none the less the deprivation of one of their most cherished privileges.

During the Emperor's sojourn in Moscow the Metropolitan Plato interceded for the nobles. He was ill received, and on the following May 4 the nobles were also deprived of the right which they alone retained of presenting collective remonstrances to the Sovereign, the Senate and the Governors of Provinces. At the same time the clergy and the members of mercantile guilds whose status had been recently assimilated to that of the nobility as far as pains and penalties were concerned were also degraded. Paul was resolutely asserting himself as a leveller : everybody was to be under the same law and the same knout. In the course of the year there were six applications of the new provisions, and in one of these a noble lady received a dozen lashes.

Traces of discontent showed themselves, and the Czar took steps to quell the malcontents by all the means in his power. In 1799 the local assemblies of nobles were re-placed by elected magistrates, and the numbers of the electors and the eligible were reduced by a ukase of November 15, 1797, which excluded from all share in the magistracy a noble who had been dismissed from the army. Now such dismissals were very frequent, and on January 14, 1798, the disability was extended to all Court functions.

In 1800 a " Statute of Bankruptcy " pursued the development of this policy in the economic sphere. The powers of the nobles to raise money on their estates were reduced and placed under the control of the State. Paul considered that the financial position of this class was extremely unsatisfactory, and indeed Catherine's reign had disastrously developed in them a taste for excessive luxury and debauchery. But no relief was to be had from the Czar's fiscal policy. The peasants were excused the greater part of their arrears of taxation, but these were mercilessly exacted from their masters, and the nobles, while they lost their right to appoint the district judicature, were nevertheless charged with the upkeep of the courts.

This looked like war to the knife : but when the fighting was at its height a new measure was taken which had no conceivable connection with the question at issue. On December 18, 1797, Paul presided over the " Bank of Assistance for the Nobility," which we have already mentioned and in which, as we have seen, Prince Alexis

Kourakine was to lose much but not his money. The plan of this enterprise, if not devised, had at any rate been countenanced by Mlle. Nélidof's protégé, who could not be suspected of evil intentions towards his own caste; and it is certain that the object was to restore the fortunes of the interested parties by providing them with ready money on conditions most advantageous to them and most likely to deliver them from the servitude of usury.

Loans for twenty-five years at 6 per cent., including interest and the cost of a sinking fund, were granted to the amount of from 40 to 75 roubles per peasant possessed by the borrower, according to the local value of the security hypothecated to the bank. The loan was payable in notes of the bank itself, which themselves produced interest at 5 per cent. and had a forced currency at their face value. Having regard to the condition of credit in the various localities this was almost charity. Did Paul mean to entrap the borrowers and precipitate their ruin? This was destined to be the result, and there were some who foresaw it. But the founder of the establishment had sunk in it too large a part of his own fortune to be inspired by such a calculation.

The bank opened on March 1, 1798, and in a few months distributed notes to the value of 500,000,000 roubles (more than £80,000,000), which, in spite of the forced currency immediately depreciated from 10 to 12 per cent. on exchange, and the aristocratic clientèle of the bank for the most part squandered this debased money like water. But while it made the borrowers poorer than ever, and in fact quite insolvent, it involved the lender (which was the State) in consequences equally disastrous.

Paul had probably been carried away by his fondness for playing the part of a tutelary divinity. Like the worst demagogues of the past—and the present—he was possessed by the chimera of the State as universal providence, and to this he was ready to sacrifice his own predilections

169

and prejudices. His ideas on this, as on other matters, were no doubt rather vague, but it pleased him to distinguish in this way a selected aristocratic body among his servants. From another point of view, however, his vicious and Voltairean nobility, corrupted by Catherine's favours, essentially barbarous under their superficial veneer of elegance, were intensely displeasing to him. Moreover, he thirsted for popularity and had no chance of obtaining it in the surroundings with which the ideas and the associates which he had brought with him to the throne were equally discordant. Finally, he was a disciple of Montesquieu, of Beccaria, and even (though he little thought it) of Rousseau, and it was a necessity of his nature to be in a manner humanitarian, the protector of the weak, the defender of the humble.

There is no doubt that Paul wished to lighten the chains of his innumerable subjects so recently reduced to slavery and so miserable in their servitude. To free them altogether was another matter. Alexis Kourakine might dream of that, because in the Empire of the Czars the difference between a prince and a serf was not great. The philosophers of the Western countries were of course in favour of the enfranchisement of all classes ; they were persons of no account—the natural partisans of democracy. But an Emperor of Russia could not share their ambitions. He might be anti-aristocrat, but democrat—never ! What he wanted was that all classes of his subjects without distinction of origin, condition or function, should prostrate themselves before him, hardly daring to raise their timid and suppliant eyes to the all-powerful master. His ideal was in fact universal serfdom. This was his ideal state, and he banished the thought of reconstruction on any other principle with disgust and horror. After complacently describing the welcome he received in the river villages of the Oka, he added, " If ever, if *ever* . . . there is reform we shall have to go." What he meant is plain

enough.   What then had he to oppose to the rising pressure
in favour of emancipation which suggested to him the idea
that abdication and flight might not be so very far off ?
He did not know ; he went on dreaming and groping in the
darkness, allowing chance to guide his steps.

V

At his accession the peasants were for the first time compelled to take the oath of allegiance to the new sovereign.
This decision appeared to be one of great consequence and
to foreshadow a decisive change.   The peasants were no
longer to be reckoned merely in the inventory of their
masters' fortunes !   They were going to be freed !

Though he had unequivocally condemned the revolt of
Pougatchof, Paul was regarded, by one of these collective
hallucinations which are common in the history of popular
movements, as the champion and the future avenger of the
great mass of serfs who had followed the fortunes of the
false Peter III.   The relations of the " Pretender " with
the freemasons, his rebellious conduct, even the choice of
his associates, kept up the legend, and his first acts after
his accession seemed to confirm it.   On December 10, 1796,
he revoked the extraordinary levy of ten recruits per
thousand recently decreed by Catherine.   On the 10th of
the following November there was a ukase giving a legal
remedy to persons who claimed their liberty.   On December 10 was suppressed the tax in kind on wheat which was
replaced as the peasants desired by a money payment.   At
the same time the new Czar was cold to their lords and
masters and took measures against them of an obviously
hostile character.   There could no longer be any doubt
about it—it was the announcement of a programme of
liberation !

In the provinces, first in the Government of Orel and
then, as the tide of hope and joyous expectation rose

higher, in those of Vologda, Tver, Moscow, Pskov, Novgorod, Penza Kalouga and Novgorod-Siéviérski, the *moujiks* were stirred to the depths. They began to believe that the Emperor not only wished for their freedom but that he had already decreed it, and that this was being concealed by their masters, whose cunning they would baffle. They would obey no one but the Czar : they would not work or pay anything except when ordered by him. Even at St. Petersburg the servants—serfs for the most part—took joint action, and on the parade-ground presented a petition in this sense to the Sovereign.

Paul took fright and was even more alarmed than he need have been. The movement was not very widespread, and though the country clergy was acting as a train to the powder (as they had done in the case of Pougatchof's rising and as they did in the revolutionary outbreak in our own time) there had been no serious disorder. Only in the Government of Orel, on the estates of Stephen Apraxine, had there been any approach to a *jacquerie*, and there all the peasants did was to parade some cannon which they took from a country house and which was fit only for firing salutes.

Paul's humanitarianism did not stand the test. The petitioners on the parade-ground were dispersed with whips, and on the petition which they had dared to present the Czar wrote with his own hand a minute which gave them up to their masters to be punished for their insolence as they deserved. On January 29, 1797, a manifesto recalled the peasants to their duties as defined by the existing laws and customs, and Repnine, with a whole army corps at his disposal, had no trouble in dealing with the " artillery " which was brought against him. Paul on his side emerged from the incident with his ideas even more confused than before.

He did not give up his pretensions to be popular, or even his sincere desire to ameliorate the lot of the miserable creatures whose homage pleased him just because it was so abject. After a confused and not very successful attempt to mitigate the hardships of the *corvée*, he passed a series of measures of the same kind in 1797–1798, which were intended to bring relief to the distressed masses. The price of salt was to be reduced, the allotments to peasants belonging to the Crown were to be increased to 15 diéssatines and they were to have a separate and distinct administrative organisation, and the arrears of the poll tax—amounting to 7,000,000 roubles, one-tenth of the annual expenditure of the country !—were to be remitted. On October 16, 1798, against the opinion of the Senate, which was very energetically expressed, he went further still, and this time struck at the base of the law of serfdom itself. A ukase of this date, which, however, was applicable only to Little Russia, forbade the selling of peasants except with the land which they cultivated. This was a long step towards emancipation, but the kind of transaction which was forbidden in Little Russia was by this very decree implicitly recognised in the other provinces, where it had previously been only tolerated.

On the occasion of the jubilee of the final work of emancipation, which Paul's grandson had the honour of completing, the old order of things, then abolished, found some apologists. They contended that none of the essential characteristics of serfage as found in Occidental countries existed in Russia. This is true from the point of view of strict law, and even of the practice of more recent times, when the institution, evolving itself under the influence of liberal ideas, was already losing some of its most repugnant features. But in Paul's reign in defiance of the law the newspapers of St. Petersburg and Moscow daily published such advertisements as this :

" No. **, ***** Street. A well-behaved girl of sixteen, perfect needlework, embroidery, &c., for Sale at a reasonable price."

This was not merely serfage, but slavery in its worst form. The condition of the Russian peasantry at this time, however, was not uniform. Apart from the three millions and a half of serfs in the hands of private owners, there were almost as many serfs belonging to the Crown, whose lot was much more favourable. They were governed by a special department of State under a system which replaced the *corvée* by a money payment, and which recognised that their legal duties were balanced by rights equally known to the law. Here it was easier for Paul to follow his generous inclinations and he did not fail to do so. He was not content with reducing the burden on these peasants and granting them access to the State forests. He even departed in their favour from his principles of centralised bureaucracy and restored for them the local administrative autonomy which he was destroying everywhere else. In these rural communities he allowed elected magistrates to control the collection of taxes, the police and summary jurisdiction. But this merely aggravated the evils of the ordinary régime, or at least made its defects and miseries more conspicuous by comparison.

These measures may of course have been meant as a prelude to the establishment of a state monopoly of serfage thus mitigated. Paul seems in fact to have for a time favoured this solution of the question, which for a moment tempted his son. He condemned the distribution of lands and peasants, of which Catherine, as is well known, was so prodigal, and in an " instruction " appended to the will which he made in 1787 he declared decisively for a restriction on the rights of private property. Afterwards, however, on this point as on so many others, his ideas went to pieces. Even at Gatchina he became convinced that the State was the master least qualified to keep in order this class of the population, who were turbulent people and needed strict discipline. The agrarian disorders in the first months of his reign confirmed him in this opinion, and he surpassed

Catherine herself in the inroads which he made on the reserves of landed property in the hands of the State. In detail his gifts were not so great. There is only one instance of a grant of as many as 25,000 peasants, which was less than the average given by the Empress to a favourite. This case, too, was that of Bobrinski, in which he was only carrying out one of his mother's last wishes. But if she gave on a great scale, he dispersed in small quantities without measure. According to one calculation his alienations amounted to no less than 550,000 peasants and 5,000,000 diéssiatines.

Nor did he consider what fate was reserved for the peasants whom he thus abandoned. After seeming to recognise the abuses of the authority which he thus substituted for his own, and having even done his best to prevent them, he suddenly turned round and praised its *paternal* character ! He declared it to be excellent in every way, and even proposed to rely upon it in providing for the safety of the State ! As a disciplinary measure a master was authorised to send to Siberia a serf who misbehaved, and serfs deported in this way were counted towards the number of conscripts which the master was bound to supply !

VI

The Czar's robust faith and his deep religious sentiment made him very sensible of the situation of the orthodox clergy whom he was pained to find in very precarious material circumstances, and morally on a very low level. His plan for raising their status was to include them in the hierarchy fixed for his other subjects by the *Table of Ranks*, in which each took precedence according to the services he was presumed to render to the State. This Paul effected indirectly by placing them on an equality with the privileged class of State servants, *i.e.* the nobility. It was for this reason that they were included in the distribution of decorations, though some were not much flattered by this honour and others even refused to accept what was offered. Thus, too, the priests acquired exemption from corporal punishment when the nobles acquired this privilege, and lost it with the nobles a few months later.

The natural effect was to unite the two categories of privileged persons who lost their advantages so soon in a common sentiment of irritation. But the clergy were only at the beginning of their experiences of the instability of the Imperial favour. Though he wished priests to be liable to flogging after having solemnly declared such treatment incompatible with the dignity of their spiritual functions, Paul did not cease to show the greatest possible solicitude for their interests, and this in the most curious ways.

According to the custom of the Orthodox Church, ecclesiastical dignities are entirely reserved for members of the " black " clergy. The " white " clergy had for long been naturally chagrined at this, and the Czar decided, therefore, that half of the available posts should be given to them. He confirmed Catherine's grants of glebes to country churches, and added to them by imposing on the rural communities the obligation to provide for the cultivation of these allotments. Special allocations were attached to episcopal residences, cathedrals and certain churches. Ecclesiastical education being organised on a very defective scale, two theological academies were founded at St. Petersburg and Kasan, and grants were at the same time made to existing institutions of the same kind.

All this was excellent, but another measure was soon announced which interfered in the most cruel and impolitic manner with the domestic life of the clergy. The natural consequence of the marriage of priests, which is not only allowed but is canonically obligatory in the Eastern Churches, is that the priesthood is recruited from its own ranks, though, as clerical families are large, there is no doubt a large margin of persons who must find another career. The problem is not a new one, but Paul's solution was startling. He decreed that all these " useless members " of the ecclesiastical community should, "like the Levites of old," enter the military service of the Empire.

Paul's attitude towards dissenters, and particularly towards those of the Roman Catholic communion, completed the alienation of the Orthodox Church. Tolerance was one of his poses, and he had been more influenced than he liked to own by his interview with Pius VI when he was in Rome. In May 1797 he visited the college which the Jesuits, in spite of the suppression of their Order, had established there. He was delighted with everything he saw, and in conversation with Siestrzencewicz, the Catholic Archbishop, he said he had no wish to imitate the Emperor Joseph, who at Brünn had said to the fathers in his presence, " When are you going away from here ? "

The fathers of Orcha were charmed, less so the Archbishop, who, being in rivalry with the Society of Jesus, viewed them rather from the point of view of the son of Maria Theresa. Moreover, the general interests of Catholicism had not flourished under the treatment accorded to them by Paul since his accession. In January 1797 he had handed them over to a department of public worship attached to the College of Justice, the President of which was Baron Heyking, a Protestant whose first care, as he afterwards admitted in his memoirs, was to lay hands on the property of this section of the religious community. At the same time, as Paul dreaded the jacobinical leanings of the Lutheran pastors who mostly came from German universities, Heyking suggested that the Catholic universities of Vilna, Kiéf and Mokhilof might be used for educating Protestant clergy and become bi-confessional. Paul agreed, but naturally Siestrzencewicz did not, and as the Archbishop was a good diplomatist he carried his point. He gained the Czar's favour by putting the Imperial cypher on his mitre and that of the Empress by celebrating with much pomp the funeral office on the occasion of the death of the Duchess of Würtemberg. The result was the establishment of a separate Catholic department, of which the Archbishop (now *persona gratissima*) was of course made the head.

This concession, which delighted the majority of Catholics though it was less pleasing to the Jesuits, awakened the anxiety of the orthodox, more especially as Paul, who had quarrelled with Plato, Metropolitan of Moscow, was treating Gabriel, Metropolitan of St. Petersburg, with great coldness. At the same time he was warmly welcoming French *émigrés* and even Catholic propagandists of that country. He allowed the Abbé Nicolle to found a school at St. Petersburg, which received pupils from some of the most illustrious families. Numerous conversions were the result, among which were those of Countess Golovine and Countess Tolstoy, both intimate friends of the Grand Duchess Elizabeth.

The Czar's acceptance of the Grand Mastership of the Knights of Malta seemed to make him more resolute than ever in carrying out this policy, and there were sensational rumours which credited him with designs on the Papacy itself! Already, it was said, there were six Cardinals on the banks of the Neva. Others were expected, and Paul, who believed he could command a majority in the Sacred College, meant to proclaim himself the successor of Pius VI and the Apostles!

In 1799 the Jesuits were momentarily in disgrace as the result of a controversy about the bishopric of Kamiéniéts, and they had to leave St. Petersburg. Soon afterwards however, they got the better of Siestrzencewicz, who had held them in check for some time and obtained new advantages, thanks to the celebrated Father Gruber, musician and diplomat, man of science, architect, physician and geometer, who had come from Vienna to introduce to the notice of the Academy of Sciences a new loom of his own invention and who succeeded in gaining the favour of the Czar. It appears that the Society of Jesus were also assisted by one Manucci, son of an Italian spy formerly in the employ of Potemkine. This man was induced by means best known to the fathers to do his best to undermine the credit of Siestrzencewicz, whom he represented as an indolent person, too easy-going to check the spread of freethinking and revolutionary ideas, evils which the Society alone could combat.

Father Gruber availed himself very dexterously of these suggestions, and on August 11, 1800, Paul wrote to Pius VII asking him to revoke the decree of Clement XIV. On March 7, 1800, the Brief *Catholicæ fidei* granted this request so far as Russia was concerned, and the Jesuits obtained permission to establish themselves at St. Petersburg and to set up new colleges in various parts of the Empire. The University of Vilna was handed over to them and they received, by ukase of October 18/29, 1800, the principal Catholic church in the capital, that of S. Catherine, with all its dependencies. Other spoliations soon followed. Father Gruber succeeded in securing the exile of Siestrzencewicz and other bishops insufficiently docile, and it was clear that the Society was to have the control of the Catholic Church throughout the Empire. The subtle Jesuit had now free access to the Emperor, a privilege which he used almost daily, and soon he began to play a part in politics. If one of the defenders of the Society is to be believed the Austrian priest was used by Bonaparte to detach Paul from the Anglo-Austrian coalition.

It is said that in the midst of this triumph an imprudent remark from the new favourite about the progress of the Catholic propaganda among the ranks of the orthodox clergy themselves nearly destroyed his position and that of his Society. The Emperor, much incensed, threatened him

with his cane and with exile to Siberia; but as Father
Gruber was in attendance awaiting his turn for audience on
the very morning of the tragedy of March 11/23, 1801, it is
not probable that there had been any such violent altercation between them so soon before.   Be that as it may, it is
certain that Paul abated nothing of his rigorous attachment to the Orthodox Church and that in his coquetries
with Roman Catholicism in general and the Society of
Jesus in particular he was merely seeking a means of action
against the Revolution.   In this again he was merely
following unconsciously in his mother's footsteps.

VII

In the administrative domain his passion for reform first
showed itself in a rearrangement of the system of Governments, the organisation of which, according to Catherine's
plan of 1775, had only to be completed.   Paul's new system
pretended to be governed by economic necessities, but a
much more obvious desire was to undo the part of the
Empress's work of which she was particularly proud and
which she regarded as the fruit of her own personal exer-
tions.   She was not altogether justified in her predilection
for this among her achievements; for, from the point of
view of delimitation of administrative units, the work was
rather badly done.   It was an entirely mechanical sub-
division, inspired not by ethnographical, economic or other
considerations, but purely by the desire to get from three
to four hundred thousand inhabitants uniformly into each
compartment.   Paul, however, by reducing the number of
the Governments from fifty to forty-one did no better, and in
other respects he did much worse.   Thirty of the new
Governments were to be submitted to the ordinary law.
The remainder were to be administered " according to the
local institutions and privileges."   This was a very imprudent reopening of an old question, which had been

settled twenty years before when the Livonian deputies, petitioning Catherine in this sense, received the reply, " I am not Empress of Livonia ! "

Those who were intended to benefit by the fit of liberalism which Paul believed himself to be displaying on this occasion were not even grateful. The arguments for completing the administrative unification begun by Catherine were very strong. Properly and considerately carried out it would have minimised if not averted that conflict between the struggle for autonomy and the pressure of centralisation which makes its victims sigh for incorporation in the larger system. Had it been strongly organised and consolidated, but at the same time reduced to bold outlines, it would have given sufficient play to the ethnic and historical individualities while attaching the centrifugal components of the Empire sufficiently securely to its capital. But Paul, in his obstinate desire for change, went so far as to sacrifice the key of the positions which Russia had reconquered in the south-west from her secular rival. He separated the department of Kiéf from the three Little Russian Governments in which Alexis had already seen the necessity of incorporating it. By attaching it to the province of Bratslaf he brought it under the domination of Polish influences, which were highly developed in that part of the Empire and have never ceased since to contend with Russian influences for the ancient political and religious capital of the Empire.

In the economic sphere Paul, taught by his apprenticeship at Gatchina and guided by his patriarchal instincts, was better inspired. He was too much occupied with the clothes worn by his subjects, and tried to regulate in too arbitrary a fashion the manner in which they chose to live. But he did not always waste his time so needlessly. A series of decrees confirmed and extended Peter the Great's numerous measures for the provision and reorganisation of corn stores which were to be available in times of scarcity.

The result unfortunately did not correspond to the intention. The peasants were afraid they would never see their grain again, and regarded the attempt to make them store it simply as an additional tax. They were not altogether wrong. The governors of provinces, the heads of districts, and even the State itself habitually drew upon these reserves in order to combat a rise in the price of food by cheap sales, or even in order to make illicit profits; and in fact when the terrible famine of 1810 broke out in the vast province of Arkhangelsk the magazines were found to be empty.

Paul also gave his attention to the problem of forestry, which in our time has become acute owing to the Empire being partially denuded of its fine trees and the consequent lack of necessary fuel in many places. The system of pillage which brought about this result began at the beginning of the eighteenth century, and in order to put an end at any rate to the scandalous depredations in the State forests Paul established a special forestry department attached to the College of Admiralty. Here also he proceeded without tact or discretion, forbidding in 1798 all exportation of wood to foreign countries. This measure, which coincided with the opening of hostilities against France, was dictated, it is true, by political reasons, and was to be extended in the following year to the exportation of cereals. But it meant the ruin of commerce and agriculture in a country which drew its principal revenue from the commodities thus excluded from foreign markets.

More wisely Paul occupied himself with the prevention of fire, the constant scourge of Russian towns and villages, and stimulated the exploitation of peat and coal, regulating the trade in these products and granting rewards for the discovery of new deposits. Stock-breeding also received for the first time a state organisation in his reign, though the chief of the new " expedition " to which it was entrusted was unfortunately no other than Koutaïssof !

The re-establishment of the College of Manufactures was the official outcome of his very sincere desire to develop the industries of the country. This desire was also expressed, though not always so happily, in other enterprises, such as the establishment of a system of canals which was destined to connect the Volga with the Baltic, an energetic repression of the brigandage with which the great artery of river traffic in the country was infested, and a revision of the tariff and the commercial treaties by which England profited and became more and more the mistress of the Russian market and export trade. Subventions and other favours were also granted to various manufacturers, and measures were taken to encourage the production of silk and the distilling trade. Finally, there were laws establishing a system of protection in an ill-conceived and excessive manner, for they were not limited to the taxation of luxuries and stimulated the development of the contraband trade in which Bezborodko set so shameful an example.

The economic position of Russia has recently been made the subject of accounts which, if true, are a terrible indictment of the Sovereign. It is argued that it is only since his reign that there has been the huge interval between the industries of the great Northern Empire and those of the other countries of Europe. Until then Russia had been close behind, if she had not actually surpassed, the most brilliant of her Western rivals. Arzamas, now a very modest town in the Government of Nijni-Novgorod and celebrated only for a literary coterie of the early nineteenth century which bears its name, is said to have then been an industrial centre of an importance rivalled at the time only by Manchester and Birmingham. Moscow, Iaroslavl, and Toula had manufactures such as Arthur Young could not find in France. In each from two to three thousand workmen and more found employment.

It is an established fact that the progress of the industrial and commercial life of Russia in the eighteenth

183

century was relatively rapid, and the causes of the phenomenon did not escape contemporary economists, who liked to emphasise the advantages possessed by the Northern Empire over most other European countries in this respect. These were the absence of the excessive duties or burdens imposed on the industrial activities of other nations by fiscal brigandage and the abuse of privileges, the comparatively restricted development of monopolies, &c. On one point at any rate the comparison is most instructive. English manufacturers at that time had to contribute to a budget which was rapidly attaining the enormous sum of £100,000,000. Catherine's budgets hardly reached the tenth part of that, and a third and sometimes even a half was covered by loans or an issue of paper money. Herein, however, lies the refutation of the too optimistic conjectures which have been hazarded on the intensity of the economic development of Russia at this period.

If the Russian manufacturers and merchants had to pay so little in taxes on a business which equalled or surpassed those of their competitors in the eighteenth century they must have made enormous profits and therefore have amassed large sums of ready money. But the complete absence of great accumulations of capital in Russia is a fact which cannot be denied, and it is not a new fact. There never were any such accumulations, and Catherine always went to the Dutch or English bankers for her loans.

In default of official statistics, which do not exist, those who describe an industrial Russia of the eighteenth century have relied on the descriptions of foreign travellers, who were themselves without any documentary evidence. Such documents as exist do not bear out the glowing accounts of a great development of production. In 1790, for example, imports were 22,500,000 roubles and exports 27,500,000—a modest record. On the eve of the Revolution the commerce of France was four times as great, and the English export trade alone was worth £24,900,000. Similarly, at the end of Catherine's reign the number of industrial establishments in Russia was 3129, employing less than 100,000 men. This will not bear comparison with England, where in 1775 Pitt estimated that there were 80,000 operatives employed in the cotton trade alone. For the year 1802, a study by the conscientious Herrmann inserted in the eighth volume of the *Mémoires de l'Académie des Sciences* makes the number of factories in Russia only 2270 ! One estimate or the other must be wrong. Between the end of Catherine's reign and the accession of Alexander I there was no doubt a depression, but it is difficult to believe that it was so serious as this.

Paul's short reign saw the first beginnings of the commercial relations of Russia and America. Hitherto the two countries had been in contact only intermittently, but since 1784 Gregory Ivanovitch Chélekof, of Rylsk, had been engaged in bold enterprises in the north of the United States. On August 3, 1798, the establishment of the first Russo-American company was confirmed, and on June 9, 1799, the Czar took this body under his special protection and gave them privileges for twenty years. This achievement and that of founding a higher Medical School, the culmination of a series of measures whereby Paul showed his solicitude for the health of his subjects, testify to an activity which accomplished greater things than the organisation of a military household.

The effort which he made, however, was often ill-directed and often rather impetuous than well-regulated, and its results did not correspond to the energy by which it was distinguished, the ambitions by which it was inspired, or even the more modest hopes to which it gave rise. Politically speaking, the principal effect of Paul's reign was to accentuate the bureaucratic character of the governmental machinery which he had set out to reform. Socially, he left untouched and even aggravated the essential problems of Russian life by maintaining the institution of serfage.

Economically, far from averting or even mitigating the ruinous consequences of the previous reign, he committed new imprudences which even more gravely compromised the development of the productive forces of the country.

No doubt the time allowed to him was too short to permit him to achieve more than a sketch or a rough indication of his policy in any direction, but there is enough to show that it was a good thing for Russia that his work was interrupted. The extremely critical financial position which the ambitious reformer inherited was no doubt also a great obstacle in the way of the realisation of this part of his programme, but here again he believed that when he came to the throne he could provide and apply a definite remedy, and he only succeeded in aggravating the ill which he flattered himself he could cure.

VIII

He was ready with his budget, the product of his studies at Gatchina, in which income and expenditure balanced each other at 31,500,000 roubles. But on the calculation of the Department of Finance the upkeep of the army alone *on a peace footing* during 1797 required more than this, and the sum total of the estimated expenditure was no less than 80,000,000 roubles, which exceeded the revenue expected by 40,000,000. There was nothing extraordinary in the discrepancy : the financial history of the whole reign of Catherine made it seem almost normal. Thus after thirty years the national debt had increased to 126,196,556 roubles—a colossal sum for those days. There was more than 157,000,000 roubles' worth of paper money in circulation, and this was from 32 to 39 per cent. below par.

Paul by a vast financial transaction carried out by the firm of Hoop, of Amsterdam, converted the loans contracted there and at Genoa and London into one fund, and decided to borrow no more in future. As to the assignats, this disgraceful expedient also should never be used again and the existing stock should at once be bought up. But how was it to be done ? Paul talked of sending all the Court plate to the Mint. " He would eat off pewter until the paper rouble was at par."

Very little came of all this. Even after reckoning economies, most of which proved impossible to realise, the actual budget for 1797, definitely settled on December 20, 1796, was about double the Czar's estimate. It amounted to 63,673,194 roubles, of which 20,000,000 was for the army and 5,000,000 for the fleet. In July 1797 a readjustment was found necessary, as the distribution of Crown lands had taken away 2,000,000 roubles of revenue from the Treasury. The matter was settled by reducing by this sum the amount assigned to the sinking fund, and in the course of the following year the budgets of Catherine's son were destined to reach and finally to transcend the level of those of the Empress herself.

Paul borrowed as his mother had done before him and with even greater precipitancy. He borrowed at home and abroad. The amount borrowed in Russia itself cannot be calculated even approximately for want of documents, which no investigator has yet been able to discover. His foreign loans began in January 1797, with 88,300,000 florins, and the net result of the financial policy of his reign was to increase the previous accumulations of debt from 43,739,130, to 132,000,000 roubles.

Nor did Paul give up issuing assignats. To the enormous total left by Catherine he added 56,237,420 roubles (14,000,000 a year), whereas the annual increase of this part of the debt during the preceding reign had only been about 6,300,000.

The only point on which the reformer broke with the bad traditions of the past which he had so haughtily repudiated was that of financial organisation, and here he did good work. He freed the Chambers of Finance from irrelevant and extraneous work. On December 4, 1796, he set up a Ministry of the Treasury, and a week later he abolished the Committee on the Debt, and thus, perhaps half-unconsciously, he paved the way for the unity and the autonomy of this branch of the Administration.

He managed, however, to introduce even here all the material disorder in which he used to live while heir to the throne, when, in spite of his great revenues, he was always impecunious. He was as accessible as ever to the wildest suggestions. A Dutch adventurer named Woot, an agent of the firm of Hoop and a protégé of the Kourakines and of Mlle. Nélidof, disputed the confidence of the Emperor with Vassiliéf, the Minister of the Treasury, and led him into the maddest schemes. The country was a happy hunting-ground for charlatans of this kind. Peter the Great himself had asked for the services of Law, and that too in 1721, immediately after the great crash at Paris ! He imagined that the celebrated bankrupt had still large funds at his disposal which he might use in Russia.

The new Law proposed to raise the value of the silver rouble to 140 kopecks of copper, to increase the production of copper from 160,000 to 1,200,000 pouds, and thus to guarantee a new issue of paper to the value of 150,000,000 roubles. This scheme was abandoned owing to the vigorous opposition of Bezborodko, who, however, was won over by the eloquence of the Dutch financier (or, according to Rastoptchine, by a large bribe) and allowed a certain amount of the scheme to be incorporated in the plan of the Bank of Assistance for the Nobility, which in fact was nothing but a huge manufactory of paper money.

It was in vain that the scheme was denounced as illusory and dangerous. The Chancellor had changed his mind, and saw in it a means of securing a net gain of 35,000,000 roubles for the Treasury and of assuring resources to other institutions insufficiently endowed, such as the educational establishments under the direction of the Empress, which alone were to receive from this source an annual subsidy of 400,000 roubles.

The bank stopped payment after existing less than a year, but in the last months of the reign war against France in alliance with England and the war against England in alliance with France, combined with other costly enterprises at home and abroad, were to reduce the Treasury to such penury that Diérjavine Vassiliéf's successor had no alternative but to issue more paper money, an expedient which ended in an even more adventurous undertaking than that suggested by Woot. The plan was to buy up cheaply the enormous stock of goods by which the market was encumbered, owing to the closing of the customs, to stimulate home commerce in this way and to secure a great profit in the increased taxation produced by the artificial movement thus created. The project was submitted for Paul's approval on the eve of his death, at a moment when, according to a contemporary, the total amount of ready money in the Treasury was 14,000 roubles!

IX

The intellectual history of Paul's four years' reign is hardly worth recording. In literature, science, and even in art it was, in spite of the Czar's gallant attentions to Mme. Vigée-Lebrun, a period of eclipse. The police and the censorship stifled the slightest manifestation of independent thought. All activity of this kind was in Paul's eyes doubly criminal as evoking memories of the past reign and of appearing to favour the revolutionary movement of the period. From the moment of his accession the Czar persecuted even the Academy of Science. Even under the presidency of Prince Dachkof the modest studies prosecuted by this body were in no way such as could cause him anxiety, but when Catherine's old friend was deposed and

replaced by the extremely insignificant Bakounine, he
directed his attacks against the society itself, deprived it
of its subsidy and of its house on the Fontanka, and even
went so far as to insist on the removal of the innocent
allegorical symbols on the *jetons de présence* used by the
Academicians.

And yet, as inconsequence was the rule of his nature, he
became the founder of a school for soldiers' orphans, of the
Institute of the Order of St. Catherine, and of the educational establishments which still bear his wife's name. Not
content with this, obscurantist as he was, he established a
new university. This was quite inconsistent with the
measures he had taken to isolate the country intellectually
as by the end of his reign he had isolated it economically.
Since 1798 Russia had been practically closed to foreigners,
and Russians on their side had the greatest difficulty in
crossing the frontiers. Passports were only granted in
exceptional cases and were absolutely refused to all who
asked for them for a scientific purpose. It is true that in
1798 a ukase decreed that a certain number of young
Russians should be sent to foreign seats of learning, but
in the following July another ukase ordered all Russian
subjects studying abroad to return within two months.

The young aristocrats of the Baltic provinces who were
attached to the German schools were deeply affected by this
policy ; and either because he was pleased to remember
that he himself had German blood in his veins or because
he wished to follow the tendency which he had shown
towards re-establishing the autonomy of this part of his
Empire, Paul decided to do something to meet their
complaints. The ukases of April 19, 1798, and May 9,
1799, decreed the foundation at Derpt of " a Protestant
university for the nobility of Courland, Esthonia and
Livonia." This university was even more German than
Protestant. It soon surpassed the scientific attainments
of its rivals at St. Petersburg and Moscow and became a

centre of culture and foreign influence. From a general point of view Russia was the gainer : every manifestation of culture is a benefit. But in the peculiar situation created by Paul, which favoured the spirit of local independence, its natural affinities with German culture and German influence were a certain source of danger to the Empire.

CHAPTER VIII

THE REFORM OF THE ARMY

I

PAUL had nothing of the soldier in him—not even the physical courage. And yet he did more than any sovereign who has reigned in Russia to give the institutions of the country the pronounced character of militarism which they still possess as a legacy from a melancholy past, and which are becoming less and less compatible with the happily modified conditions of to-day. In the Medical School founded by Catherine's son, and soon transformed into a Military Academy, peaceful professors of obstetrics still mount the rostrum with swords by their sides, and generals who have never smelt powder even in a sham fight are to be found in every branch of the civil service, booted, spurred and braided like heroes of a hundred fights.

It does not follow that Paul did much to develop the warlike virtues of his people. The changes he effected produced rather the contrary effect. But while in civil affairs all he achieved was disorder, his military reforms in spite of his incessant changes of mind were of a very different character. In the history of the country they were decisive and had consequences the far-reaching effect of which was unsuspected either by the Czar himself or by his collaborators. He thought little of the military glories of the preceding reign. As a pacifist he disapproved of them. They had been won, he thought, in defiance of the rules of war and the principles of justice. They could

192

not be explained by anything in the material or moral condition of the victorious troops.

It cannot be denied that Catherine's army at the end of her reign displayed all the vices which are apt to be engendered and developed in a heroic age. Heroes easily degenerate into corrupters. Commanders-in-chief of the type of Potemkine, and even Roumiantsof, who themselves exercised dictatorial authority, naturally led their subordinates in their spheres to be equally arbitrary. Colonels held their regiments like fiefs, and used men and money exactly as they thought fit—often for purposes very different from those for which they were intended. Of the 400,000 men nominally with the colours in 1795 no less than 50,000 were non-effective, being attached to the personal service of the officers. Subalterns were compelled to sign false reports by their superiors, who were in collusion with contractors. The soldiers were ill-fed, the hospitals shockingly neglected, and the civil population suffered from all kinds of exactions and excesses on the part of the military. The training of recruits was hardly attempted, and no attention was paid to anything but appearances. If the sheath was polished, the blade might be allowed to rust, and if " a man could see himself " in the barrel of his musket it did not matter about the absence of a lock ! Uniform and equipment were governed by no rule but the fancy of the commander.

As to the Guard, all it retained of its military character was a gala uniform rarely worn. The officers of the " gilded corps " as Paul called it only donned this brilliant costume in order to promenade on the Nevski Prospekt with their hands in comfortable muffs in winter, and followed at all seasons of the year by an orderly who carried their sabres.

This condition of things was quite enough to justify Paul's anger and his projects of reform. He hated above all the work of Potemkine on the one hand and on the

other the privileged regiments which had been the nursery
of so many favourites. But though the ideas of the
reformer were in many respects sound they were vitiated
by a fundamental error. He confounded all the comrades
of the sumptuous Prince of Tauris in one contemptuous
condemnation, and Souvorof among them ! He thought
their successes were unjustified because he could not
understand them. He did not realise the importance of the
boundless force developed and magnified in exceptionally
gifted natures by complete freedom of individual development. With all his faults and all the gaps in his knowledge
of strategy and tactics, Potemkine still commands the
admiration of the best-informed specialists of our day.
And as a leader of men, with his power of infecting them
with something of his chaotic but masterful temperament,
he was, though inferior to Souvorof, a man who awakened
to the utmost the energy of his troops.

Paul, who despised or distrusted all individuality,
proposed to eliminate this characteristic entirely and to
replace it in all ranks of his military service by minute
regulation of everything. This was to be the essential
and the most unhappy feature of the projected reform :
in other respects the measures he took were in many
cases both wise and necessary. The work he did was
ingenious in many of its details and solidly constructed as a
whole, but the absence of all flexibility soon made itself
cruelly felt.

II

It was the Guard, as we have seen, to which he first
turned his attention. Immediately after Paul's accession
it was completely changed in its composition and organisation. Here the merit of the Czar's work was very unequal. He preserved the principle of a privileged corps
recruited on an aristocratic basis; it was therefore a
manifest contradiction to introduce into it *en bloc* the

common rabble of Gatchina. Such a proceeding was comparable to the heroic expedient sometimes resorted to in English Parliamentary crises of creating a batch of peers, and in Paul's case the result was not destined to be fortunate even from the point of view of his own personal safety. The Gatchina element did not conquer the refractory corps into which it was introduced. On the contrary, it was itself partially infected by the vices of its new surroundings and it awakened there a spirit of revolt formerly kept under by idleness and pleasure.

The rearrangement of the units of this corps, augmented as they were by endless creations of new regiments and battalions, need not detain us. It soon gave place to new combinations, which were in their turn replaced by other changes. Throughout the reign the whole army continued to undergo these constant alterations, in which the Czar's peculiar temperament was reflected. He seemed still to be playing with the tin soldiers which had delighted his childhood, and to be arraying them according to his fancy, though he never abandoned certain guiding conceptions formed by him at Gatchina under the imperious inspiration of Peter Panine.

The one exception was the artillery which, under the now predominant influence of Araktchéief, was solidly reorganised. Starting with the celebrated Préobrajenski company of bombardiers, of which Peter the Great had been captain, a new plan precisely thought out and consistently followed was applied to this arm throughout all the army corps, and a complete reorganisation on an autonomous basis was the result. There was complete unity of *personnel* and *matériel*, and each company was a tactically independent unit. It followed that the Russian artillery was easily placed on a war footing, was capable of co-operating with large forces without change in its internal constitution, and had at the same time a much greater manœuvring capacity. In the opinion of good judges it had a marked superiority over most of its European rivals, thongh in point of *matériel* it was still enslaved to the old Prussian pattern, on which decisive improvements had recently been made by Gribeauval in France.

Apart from the interests of the corps itself, for which the Emperor cared nothing, the reform of the Guard wounded many other susceptibilities in almost all classes of society. At the parade of November 8, 1798, Paul published an order requiring all who were nominally on the strength of the Guard but not actually in its ranks to rejoin their respective regiments on pain of exclusion. There were many absentees. In the Préobrajenski alone there were several thousand officers in this category who did not by any means all belong to the nobility. For a financial consideration merchants, civil servants, even the clergy were able to enter their sons, and were glad to do so because it facilitated their promotion even in civil careers. Even unborn children of undetermined sex were registered, and thus very young men became lieutenants with twenty years of fictitious service to their credit. They then exchanged into regiments of the line and took precedence by seniority over officers who had served for many years. Others served at Court as pages, chamberlains or gentlemen-in-waiting, or simply obtained unlimited leave and lived on their estates. Even those officers and soldiers who actually served in the ranks for the most part escaped all military duties.

Paul was perfectly right to abolish all this costly and demoralising system of parasitism. Unfortunately, the parasites who were deprived of the advantages which it brought them or who were packed off to barracks and manoeuvres never forgave him.

THE REFORM OF THE ARMY

III

As regards the army as a whole, three new sets of regulations were published on November 29, 1796, one of which concerned the infantry and two the cavalry. None of the soldiers and none of the statesmen who had distinguished themselves in the previous reign had any part in the composition of this new military code, which was in fact nothing but an extract from the Prussian Regulations and Instructions. The infantry regulations in the Russian version were already four years old and had originally been drawn up for the army of Gatchina. They had been published in 1792 under the modest title of an Essay with the collaboration of Kouchelof, Araktchéief and Rastoptchine himself. They were merely a hasty sketch, a maladroit imitation of what the imitators wrongly believed to be the work of Frederick II, who had never had leisure amid his incessant wars to modify the basis of the military organisation which he inherited. He had been content to leaven it with his genius, and the system of tactics on which his manœuvres were based was even then out of date—a fact which Souvorof did not fail to emphasise.

He called the new regulations " a translation of a manuscript three-quarters eaten by rats, which had been found among the ruins of an old castle," and declared that, never having lost a battle, he had nothing to learn from the King of Prussia. He especially objected to one particular chapter of the new code, which was as it happened quite new, and which set up a system of army inspection to be carried out by officers of all ranks directly appointed by the Sovereign. This, Souvorof complained, was destructive of the whole principle of the military hierarchy. For this Paul cared very little. Even when gained on the field of battle the highest military rank inspired him with no respect. After all the campaigns of Turkey, Sweden and Poland, which had been the glories of her

197

reign, Catherine had left only two field-marshals. In a period of undisturbed peace her son added seven to that number.

In other essential points the Russian imitators deviated from their Prussian model. They aggravated certain penalties and modified the letter or the spirit of many provisions in the direction of greater brutality. Thus the German text forbids a subordinate officer to criticise the orders of his superior " on pain of the severest displeasure of the Sovereign." The Russian version has " on pain of torture."

On the parade-ground, at the price of efforts worthy of a better cause and by dint of revolting brutality, the system gave results which the admirer of the Prussian drill sergeants was inclined to consider satisfactory. Paul learned to his cost what these results were worth in the field, in Holland with Herrmann, in Switzerland with Rimski-Korsakof, and even in Italy with Souvorof himself. In order to gather laurels on the banks of the Po he had to call to his assistance the man who despised his regulations and whose succession of victories was won by defying all convention and laying the Austrian staff under contribution. When the victor of Novi and the Trebbia was deprived of this assistance he was forced to confess that he could not continue the campaign.

IV

The publication of the new regulations was soon followed by a reform of the clothing of the forces. In most regiments of the line Potemkine had introduced a uniform which was simple, loose, adapted to the climate of the country, and more or less in the fashion of the ordinary costume of the people. In one of his letters to Catherine the favourite had written contemptuously of the uselessly ornamental pseudo-martial accoutrements of which most of the armies of Europe have not even yet got rid. " What have soldiers to do with curls and powder and plaits ? They have no valets to dress them ! "

Paul may have been of Cæsar's opinion,* that a man's courage is raised by a brilliant uniform : more probably he merely wished his soldiers to be dressed like those of Frederick II. He got what he wanted, but at what a cost ! The curled and plaited head-dress required many hours of the attentions of the two barbers attached to each squadron. The process, the details of which were disgusting, inflicted cruel torture on the unhappy victims. The method was to impregnate the hair with a mixture of lard and flour, damping it with *kvass*, with which the barrack-room hairdressers filled their mouths before commencing operations. This was accompanied by rubbings and twistings of such violence that young Tourguénief, robust as he was, nearly fainted the first time he experienced them. The " powder " dried into a thick crust which gave the men violent headaches and prevented even the most elementary cleanliness. The uniform itself was not less uncomfortable. Paul insisted on its being so tight that the men could hardly breathe. If they fell they could not get up again without assistance. The gaiters, too, were so narrow that they wounded the legs, and even Germans, in whose country such clothes had gone out of fashion, considered the whole outfit grotesque.

This costume was so inconvenient that it was easily ridiculed, but Paul, who sometimes mixed good with evil, introduced one advantageous change—the fur waistcoat for the cold season. Very wisely also he ordained that the whole of the men's equipment should be issued to them in kind, and not as formerly in money to be distributed at the discretion of the officers. This measure formed part of a general scheme of reform the execution of which was never even commenced. The organisation of army supplies

* Suetonius *Cæsar*, c. lxvii.

was extremely defective, and, for war purposes, practically non-existent. Nothing was done to remedy this, though a few praiseworthy attempts were made at least to mitigate the effects of the inveterate peculation which had been the rule in this department.

Self-contradictory as usual, Paul, while doing his best to develop the military power of his Empire, set out to effect a considerable economy in military expenditure. In 1798, on the eve of joining the coalition against France, he reduced the Imperial forces at one fell swoop by 45,440 men and 12,268 horses! In the same spirit, while he stopped short of no superfluity in the equipment of most of his soldiers he proposed to reduce that of his Guard to what was strictly necessary. There were to be no more of the variegated and richly laced uniforms, of which the plainest cost 120 roubles, no more fashionable mufti to wear in society, no more dress coats or embroidered waistcoats from smart tailors. Silk stockings and buckled shoes were proscribed ; the use of muffs was forbidden under the severest penalties, likewise pelisses, carriages, and a multiplicity of servants. At the cost of 22 roubles an officer of the erstwhile " gilded corps " was to be completely fitted out. He was told he must always wear his reformed uniform and " live modestly."

The curious thing is that the officers concerned were nearly ruined under this very régime by their tailors' bills ! In this, as in all things, the Czar's fancy ran riot. In 1798 Paul signed a treaty with England, and immediately the officers of the regiment of Household Cavalry were ordered to wear the red tunics with blue facings of the Horse Guards. Thanks to the services of Donaldson, formerly tailor to the Prince of Wales, who, as it happened, had established himself at St. Petersburg, Sabloukof* was able to obey the injunction in less than forty-eight hours. But some of his comrades had not yet succeeded in doing

* See *Frazer's Magazine*, September 1865, p. 309.

so before a counterorder was received. Paul had just usurped the office of Grand Master of Malta, and the bright red of the British uniform was to give place to the dark purple of the mantles worn by the great dignitaries of St. John of Jerusalem. A little later the crimson corsages of Princess Gagarine obtained the preference in their turn, and in four years there were no less than nine changes of this kind! At the same time the Emperor compelled every one to wear uniform—even the ordinary copyists in the public offices—without regard to the heavy expense which he thus imposed on these humble and pacific civil servants.

Under Souvorof in Italy and Switzerland these cast-off glories of Prussia shared the fate of the other regulations emanating from the same source. On the forced marches the men vied with each other in getting rid of the more inconvenient articles of this odious equipment, which were replaced by anything that came to hand. Their leader said he cared little how his men were dressed, provided they ran like hares and fought like lions. But Paul, when he heard of this, was very angry. He groaned when he heard that the regulation gaiters had been abandoned between two victories. As for the pikes, which, faithful to the Prussian exemplar, he had introduced in all the infantry corps and which practically disarmed a hundred men in every regiment, they had been used for firewood during the crossing of the Alps. In view of the successes obtained, however, the Czar expressed his willingness to accept the modifications on these points which experience suggested. But he was furious when he saw some of the heroes who had returned from that immortal campaign in the dress in which they had fought. " What! They wish to dress my army in the fashion of Potemkine. Take these men out of my sight and let me never see them again ! "

V

Paul was laudably anxious to develop military education, and this inspired the foundation of a military orphanage in 1798. In this institution a thousand boys and two hundred and fifty girls were maintained in two separate departments, and under the same plan all existing military schools were by a new organisation attached to this establishment. They had been founded by Peter the Great and multiplied by Catherine, and they provided for the needs of about twelve thousand pupils. Paul increased the number of schools to sixty-six and the number of pupils to sixty-four thousand. Thus at the base of the edifice there was considerable progress : the reformer's activities on the higher levels were unfortunately less successful.

It was confined to the establishment at the Winter Palace of a course on tactics, under the direction of Araktchéief, and there even the field-marshals had to attend the lectures of a certain Colonel Kannabich, an old provost-marshal from Weimar. It is easy to imagine the style of instruction given by such a master ! Paul's own acquaintance with military science, according to Tauentzien, Frederick William's envoy at St. Petersburg, was limited to " a superficial acquaintance with the Prussian system and a passion for minute detail." Kannabich was no better ; his ineptitude has become legendary and his prælections have been the laughing-stock of several generations. As to their practical results, Paul was to have some personal experience of them a few months before his death. Ever since the days of the Gatchina army he had tested his soldiers every autumn in a series of exercises analogous to our grand manœuvres—in the course of which he led his troops in battles or sieges. After he became Emperor he carried out this war game on a larger scale, and the Araktchéiefs and the Steinwehrs ended by becoming rather skilful at it. On the last occasion things went badly. The only effect of Kannabich's tactical instructions had been to confuse the brains of his pupils, and their performances were so mediocre that the Emperor addressed them in prophetic words which were destined to re-echo from Austerlitz to Friedland : " Gentlemen, if you go on like this you will always be beaten ! "

The results which Paul obtained, in so far as he secured absolute docility and blind obedience, inflexible rigidity in carrying out the regulations and any order which might be given, were definite and partially satisfactory. Little as he liked the régime to which he found himself subjected, the Duc d'Enghien himself, after some months in Russia with the corps of the Prince de Condé, could not deny the merits of the system from this point of view. " By dint of frightening us they made us attentive and exact in our duties ; even the noble cavalry do more or less what they are told." But the Czar's temperament made him exaggerate even here, so that he lost the benefit of what he had gained by pushing it to an odious and ridiculous extreme.

The obligation to be present on duty, like the obligation of blind obedience, admitted in Paul's eyes of no exception or excuse. In September 1797 he ordered those generals to quit the army who " were in the habit of reporting themselves sick when they were wanted." On June 12, 1799, he decided that "those officers prevented by sickness from following regiments under orders should nevertheless rejoin without further excuse." Organised on this plan, military service is a hell on earth, and it was the officers who suffered the most from his barbarity. In this he was faithful to a general tendency of his mind, which it would be wrong to call democratic, for he acknowledged no principle of supremacy except in himself, but which led him in all things to favour the lower orders at the expense of the rest. The only grievance of the rank and file, therefore, was the concentration of the troops in the large towns, where, in default of proper barrack accommodation, the billeting of the men at the rate of thirty or forty to each house was uncomfortable alike for the lodgers and for the landlords. On the other hand, the new penal system was for the army in general a distinct advance on that which had preceded it. In spite of its aggravated severities it tended in effect to replace the arbitrary sentences of commanding officers by the regular procedure of courts-martial and to give every inferior a legal remedy against his chief.

The chiefs, for their part, found little to gratify them in the new régime. " The military service is stricter than you can possibly imagine," wrote Rogerson to Simon Vorontsof in June 1797. " An officer dare not leave the town without permission even in summer to visit his sister or his family." Even apart from the drills, parades and manœuvres, which were multiplied to such an extent that those who took part in them were constantly overworked, Paul wanted to have his men always on the alert. This perhaps was the reason of the frequent alarms of which Mme. Golovine speaks in her *Souvenirs*, giving as an instance the bugle-call which was wrongly believed to be a signal and put whole regiments in motion. From the general to the sub-lieutenant, every one was continually on the *qui vive*, for the slightest negligence might have the most terrible consequences.

Paul himself did the work of four men, but he was so much occupied with the mechanism of his military machine that he stifled its soul. Even from the point of view of organisation his achievement was very questionable. He deprived the generals of their staffs ; he did nothing to provide or to adapt to the necessities of modern warfare a proper system of supply and commissariat, and thus his armies were always of necessity tied to their Austrian or English ⌐llies. He played, in fact, at being a soldier as he also ן   ed at being a sailor.

VI

The navy contributed nothing to the glory of his reign. And yet Paul, who was very proud of his title of High Admiral, which he retained after his accession, may be said to have done more for this branch of his offensive and defensive forces than for the other, though here also the effects of his self-contradictory mind and character were apparent.

In the previous reign the Russian fleets, commanded by talented mercenaries, had won many and glorious victories under the impulse which Catherine knew how to communicate to the men and things of which she made use. But these fleets had been precipitately constructed and hastily equipped; they had been engaged in incessant fighting and they were worn out. Tchernychof, who was no sailor but a good courtier, directed all his energies to concealing this state of things from the Empress, and Paul himself was ignorant of it until after his accession, when he wished to play with this new toy. The Czar having ordered his fleet out for a cruise, was informed by one of his officers that none of the ten vessels under his command was capable of putting to sea. The ships recently launched were themselves in no better case, owing to the bad quality of the materials used in their construction. One of the frigates sent to the Dutch coast in 1799 had to turn back on the way; she had sprung a dangerous leak! The others had to spend months in the English dockyards before they were even approximately ready for service.

These humiliating experiences, however, produced at least one happy consequence. The Russian detachments who sojourned in English ports and co-operated with British squadrons were trained in the best school, and marked progress in naval science and construction was the result. Paul helped the movement by re-establishing the office of Chief Inspector of Naval Construction which had existed in the time of Peter the Great, and by bringing from Constantinople two French engineers, the brothers Lebrun de Sainte-Catherine, who had rendered great services to the Turkish fleet.

At the same time he restored to their proper destination the fine forests which the founder of the Russian Navy had assigned for its upkeep, and which since his time had been exploited in other ways for the service of the State and even of private persons, being distributed to favourites and pillaged in all manner of ways. They were placed under the care of a special department which was established under the College of Admiralty and which was also charged with the question of reafforestation.

Under the indolent administration of Tchernychof the provisioning and equipment of all the ships had become the prey of a more or less recognised traffic from which the commanding officers derived enormous profits. Catherine bravely made up her mind to put up with it. " I am robbed like everybody," she said, " and that is a good sign, because it shows that there is something to steal ! " Paul did not share this philosophy. He established Boards of Control charged with the periodical inspection of the magazines and the verification of the stores. He wished that the eye of the master should be everywhere, and even the officers' table did not escape his vigilance.

Unfortunately, this minute solicitude was expressed in a new set of *Regulations*, intended to replace the *Statute* of Peter the Great and to extend to the navy the principles and the methods which had already been applied to the army, but the new provisions as a whole gave rise to such practical difficulties that as a matter of fact the old *Statute* remained in force.

On the other hand, as in the case of the army, the Czar's ambition to augment the naval forces of his Empire clashed with a desire for economy which was only too well justified by the state of the finances. Hence there were fluctuations in the naval budget which were incompatible with a consistent programme of progressive development. Catherine had raised her naval expenditure from a modest annual sum of 1,200,000 roubles by successive increments to more than 5,000,000. In the second year of his reign Paul tripled this expenditure, but in the following year again reduced it to 6,707,681 roubles, with a reduced establishment of 33 battleships and 19 frigates. The resources at his disposal were utilised to better purpose, the old units being replaced by a smaller number of greater power and better armed, and thus the reduction was to be compensated. It was none the less a step backward.

In the details of administration Paul continued to give proof of a meritorious activity. He revised the department of justice at the College of Admiralty and organised it on a regular basis for the first time. He undertook at the naval ports many necessary repairs and much new construction. He started several important scientific enterprises, such as the survey of the White Sea, which was commenced in 1797, and the publication in 1800 of an Atlas of Navigation between that sea and the Baltic; he also began a maritime atlas of the whole world, a work unfortunately marred by numerous inaccuracies.

The transference from Kronstadt to St. Petersburg of the Marine Cadet Corps and the allocation to that institution of a supplementary credit of 100,000 roubles did much to raise the level of naval education. New schools of navigation and of naval tactics and construction were established and the Czar was a frequent visitor, as at Kannabich's lectures, following the instruction and taking an interest in the progress of the pupils. His relations with the naval cadets were always of almost familiar intimacy. He distributed scholarships to the poorer of the young men, and in spite of his prejudices he went so far as to send some of them abroad at his own expense. He visited the establishment several times a week and always unannounced, sometimes coming in by one door and sometimes by another, and he once observed to the director: "I never can catch you unprepared! I must ask the Empress to try!"

Paul also gave attention to the mercantile marine, ordered that plans of perfected construction should be laid before him, and gave special facilities to shipbuilders for obtaining material. He wished to encourage the ship-building and fishing industry in North Russian waters, and proposed to inquire into the needs of the various localities, the types of vessel most appropriate to the trade and the best sites for yards. This scheme, however, like so many others, was never carried out. In 1797 the navigation of the Southern Seas was regulated by ukase. "The great navigation," as he called it—that is to say, the voyage under the Russian flag through the Black Sea, the Sea of Marmora, the Archipelago to the Mediterranean —was reserved entirely for vessels built in Russia or belonging either to Russian subjects or to foreigners established in the Empire. The "lesser navigation," which was limited to the Black Sea and the Sea of Marmora as far as the Dardanelles, remained free.

Though he had never been on board a ship before his accession, the High Admiral showed not merely a taste but a perfect passion for naval matters. He took up the reform of the naval uniform as he had that of the uniform of the army, wisely simplifying the officers' dress while equally wisely checking a tendency to slovenliness. But here too he showed the same predilection for puerile and irritating detail. In Catherine's time a certain commander used to appear on the quarter-deck of his frigate, which was cruising off the coast of Spain in the days of the armed neutrality, in a most undistinguished *déshabille*, consisting of "a dressing-gown and slippers, surmounted by a pink cravat and a nightcap"! In Paul's reign a button sewed on crooked meant dismissal.

A navy cannot be improvised, and Catherine's successor

may well be excused for not having accomplished in four years the work of a Colbert. It may, however, be doubted if he would have succeeded better even if he had had ample time at his disposal. When he became Grand Master of Malta Paul requisitioned the best ships in his fleet, six line-of-battle ships, two frigates and various other vessels taken from the Baltic and the Black Sea, to form a special squadron under the flag of the Order. This meant the disorganisation of the naval forces in order to gratify a mere whim.

In the development of Russian power, which in other respects has been so colossal, the solution of the naval problem may perhaps be impossible owing to special geographical and climatic circumstances. Paul was in any case ill-qualified even to prepare for such a solution, because, while his theoretical knowledge was extremely limited and his practical experience altogether wanting, his pretensions were quite unjustifiable. Admiral in name until his accession, he believed that when he became Czar he became admiral in reality, and he announced his intention of taking command of his naval forces the following summer, when he would " conduct a campaign." As he was at peace with all the world the projected campaign came to no more than a cruise across a part of the Baltic, from Kronstadt to Revel. This was to be the equivalent of the annual military manœuvres in the neighbourhood of Gatchina, and Paul formed anew the illusion of really directing a real sea fight.

A yacht designed to carry the flag of the Commander-in-Chief was laid down. It was armed with forty guns and was finally converted into a frigate by special ukase. In this vessel the Emperor and Empress embarked on July 7, 1797. They were accompanied by the two elder Grand Dukes and the inevitable Mlle. Nélidof. Unfortunately, a west wind prevented the fleet from at once setting sail in the direction intended and kept them at anchor.

This did not prevent the Commander-in-Chief from taking his duties very seriously. Even in the middle of a meal he would quit the table in order to go on deck and give orders, without which (so he said) "everything would go wrong." On one of these occasions he noticed a stout volume in the hands of Schischkof, whom he had specially appointed his flag-captain. He questioned the officer, who replied that it contained plans for the formation of the vessels in the forthcoming cruise. Paul's astonishment was only equalled by his anger. "Plans?" he cried. "You have the impudence to make plans when I am here myself!"

Schischkof multiplied his explanations in vain; the Czar would not listen. Fortunately for him, Admiral Kouchelof was on board. When Paul appealed to his experience he was annoyed to find that the admiral was on the side of the flag-captain. He would not be convinced, however, and retired below, furious. "Very well! very well! I shall see how you get on without me . . . !" Mlle. Nélidof had to be called in to calm him. She was entirely successful, and the next day a fair wind enabled the sixty-eight ships to set sail and the Commander-in-Chief could not contain his joy. Always busy and agitated, running from one end of the ship to the other, giving endless orders which were either useless or absurd, he nevertheless chose to play the benevolent monarch. He invited the admirals and the captains to luncheon, and before he sat down the other officers were invited to receive from the Sovereign's hands a glass of brandy accompanied by the traditional *zakouska*.

On the following day, unfortunately, a storm arose. Feeble as were his legs, Paul for a time struggled manfully against sea-sickness, and declared that his responsibilities prevented him from taking rest. He spent the night on deck in full uniform seated on a coil of rope, but after forty-eight hours sea-sickness got the upper hand and, as the motion of the vessel grew no easier, Revel was given up and the fleet put back to Cronstadt.

A journal of the " campaign " was nevertheless composed, with dithyrambic eulogies of the skill of the Commander-in-Chief. The author, who was none other than Schischkof, thus secured his master's pardon for his audacity in drawing up plans which his chief could not understand. He was made aide-de-camp general and received the Order of St. Anne. Paul had shown how well qualified he was to be Peter the Great's continuator. As for his fleet, we shall meet it again in more serious " campaigns," where it did not distinguish itself any more highly.

CHAPTER IX

FOREIGN POLICY

I

THE dramatic events in the history of Europe, then struggling against the French Revolution, which were taking place when Paul ascended the throne will be present to the mind of every reader. On the very day of his accession Bonaparte, who had won the victory of Arcola, was beginning that triumphal march to Vienna which it seemed that nothing could stop. The change of Sovereign which had taken place at St. Petersburg removed the only chance of the allies recovering the upper hand. From the outset of the struggle Catherine had loudly proclaimed her understanding with the defenders of order in Europe, and after the death of Louis XVI she had even taken the lead in demanding the recognition of his legitimate heir. She had always, however, avoided direct intervention, and had never taken any action commensurate with the means at her disposal, so that it even remained doubtful whether she was at war with the Republic or not.

There was little glory in this attitude, but it was justified by very powerful considerations. The community of interests between the great Empire of the North and the belligerents on the side of the anti-French coalition was much more apparent than real. The latter, under cover of the common cause, were pursuing all sorts of private ends; some wanted restoration of territory or compensation for losses, others aggrandisement and new conquests.

212

The only advantage Russia could gain from the confusion was that, while her neighbours were thus fully occupied, she would be left at full liberty to look after her own affairs in Poland and elsewhere. The great Empress, however, was bound by certain obligations of relationship, alliance and monarchical solidarity which she could not decently repudiate, and she applied herself to the task of respecting all the conventions with such infinite dexterity, finesse and tact that the game she played with the Powers was the masterpiece of her diplomacy.

It was not until February 1795, when the "*jacobinière*" of Warsaw had been put sufficiently hors de combat, that Catherine consented to a treaty of joint defence with England against the jacobins of France. Even then she had limited herself to sending a squadron of twelve line-of-battleships and eight frigates under Admiral Khanykof to help the Dutch fleet to blocade the Texel. But at the same time the defection of Prussia, which was consummated by the Treaty of Bâle of April 5, 1795, and the defeats of Austria compelled Pitt himself to enter into negotiations with the Directory.

Catherine at once seized the opportunity of resuming her system of evasions, and it is entirely probable that at the time of her death she had not yet abandoned it, though she was in negotiation with the Court of St. James's for a treaty of subsidies. The exorbitant character of her demands, £120,000 a month and £300,000 for starting the campaign, strongly suggest this ; and the Persian expedition in which she was simultaneously engaged is difficult to reconcile with a more energetic participation in the conflicts of the West. England, on the other hand, showed little eagerness to settle on such ruinous terms, and the British Ambassador at St. Petersburg was entirely opposed to it. Grenville, it is true, sent him powers to accede if necessary to the Empress's excessive demands, but at the same time Pitt sent Malmesbury to Paris, and at Paul's accession Whitworth, who every day encountered new difficulties and defeats, was still waiting for the signature of the agreement.

The strange vicissitudes of this policy in the hands of Catherine's heir are well known. In four years he veered from absolute non-intervention to his Italian and Swiss campaigns at the head of the crusade against the Revolution and back again to an attempt to invade India as the ally of Bonaparte! Various explanations have been given of this extraordinarily erratic conduct, all of them more or less connected with the affair of Malta and all that that implied. Without denying the considerable influence exercised by this factor in the situation on the varying resolutions of the Czar, I believe that the real reason is to be found elsewhere and chiefly in the mind and character of the Emperor himself.

II

His first decisions were distinguished by extraordinary simplicity, which was equalled only by his presumption, but they proceeded from a set of very obvious motives. He wished to contradict his mother here as in all things, and with this was mixed a strain of the idealism which he transmitted to his sons and which so late as 1838 found an echo in the " Summary of the Political Transactions of the Russian Cabinet," prepared by Baron Brunow for the Czaréwitch Alexander Nicolaiévitch. It is there stated that " the means chosen by the Empress Catherine for the execution of her plans are far from consistent with the good faith and straightforwardness which are now the inviolable rules of our policy." Further, Paul had a decided prejudice against the policy of Austria, which he regarded as " Machiavellian " and with which, by a singular misunderstanding, he was accustomed to contrast the *good faith* of the Prussian system. This mistaken idea was supported by illusions which he could not long maintain but which he surrendered most unwillingly. Had he not exchanged oaths of eternal friendship in the presence of Frederick the Great with his nephew and successor, a solemn engagement which was destined to be renewed by Alexander I on the eve of Austerlitz ? Another motive was his love of popularity, which we have already had occasion to notice, and which was inconsistent with a policy the cost of which pressed heavily on the country. Finally, he had neither respect nor love for the order of things which had just been overturned in France. This he was to prove when he treated with Bonaparte and stipulated for a share in the proceeds of new enterprises of destruction. In the meantime, however, what he wanted was peace. There should be no more war, no more conquests, no more interference in Western affairs, which could settle themselves as they liked. The Russians would stay at home and save money.

Immediately after his accession these resolutions were put in practice. The expeditionary corps on its way to Persia was recalled, and at the same time a note from the Chancellor Ostermann informed Whitworth that the negotiations then proceeding for sending a Russian force to Germany would not be carried further. In the following April the auxiliary squadron was also recalled, Paul at the same time protesting that his friendship with England remained unbroken. Grenville in London and Whitworth at St. Petersburg made a show of believing this. They awaited events and contented themselves with a commercial treaty, which was signed on February 7, 1797, and which had in their eyes the great advantage of making it impossible at least to return to the system of armed neutrality which had been so embarrassing to British policy in the previous reign.

Austria showed more annoyance. Cobenzl, the Ambassador, was informed of the new Emperor's intentions by a somewhat dry verbal note, and soon found that he no

215

longer enjoyed the attentions to which he had become accustomed. These were transferred to his Prussian colleague Tauentzien, who, since his arrival in Russia, had been relegated to an obscure position but was now promoted to the front ranks of the diplomatic constellation. The Viennese Court sent a reply in ungracious terms, which curiously enough was not chiefly directed against Russia's defection, but asked the Czar if he would not help his allies at least to restrain Prussia from playing " the dishonourable part of instrument and intermediary of the common enemy." Paul was not moved by this direct allusion to the new relations between the Cabinets of Berlin and Paris, and he was supported in this attitude by Marie Féodorovna.

The Empress had personal motives for hating the Austrians, who were treating her father very badly because he had been compelled by dire necessity to treat with the French invaders. Another grievance was that the reigning Emperor, Francis, had married her younger sister, and on becoming a widower had contracted a new alliance with one of his Neapolitan cousins. The sentimental châtelaine of Pavlovsk could not pardon this " treachery."

Paul condemned not only the principles but the practice of his mother's diplomacy. Had not the success of the negotiations for the marriage of his daughter Alexandrina with the King of Sweden been compromised by a series of " stupid mistakes " ? He would take the matter up himself and they would see. He had already shown great resentment at the rupture of the negotiations, and had even gone so far as to turn his back on the monarch who had refused to become his son-in-law, but he had determined to remember nothing of all this, and when Klingsporr, the Swedish plenipotentiary, arrived he showed that he had forgotten all about it.

It was his diplomatic début and he was determined to

succeed at all costs. He caressed the Ambassador and went to the utmost limit of concession. The religious question remained a difficulty. He promised even that his daughter would ultimately abjure the Orthodox Church if she were not required to do so before marriage. Marie Féodorovna seconded her husband by demonstrations which were in turn practical and romantic. She announced that the dowry would be greatly increased, and gave it to be understood that a new disappointment would probably cause the inconsolable Alexandrina to take the veil. On this the subject of the discussion herself appeared and fell at the feet of her parents, bathed in tears. " Can you doubt any longer, M. l'Ambassadeur, the love she has for the King ? "

Klingsporr showed all the " sensibility " which the circumstances demanded, but he had positive instructions to demand abjuration before marriage, and after exhausting every means of conciliation and seduction Paul could not but see that he had no chance of succeeding where his mother had failed.

III

The first difficulty which Paul's policy encountered was the dumb but resolute opposition of all those whose duty it was to carry it out, in Russia and elsewhere. Ostermann and Bezborodko remained attached to the system of Catherine. In London Vorontsof had become English from head to foot and was under the ascendency of Pitt, as Razoumovski was under that of Thugut at Vienna. In June 1797, Vorontsof on his own responsibility retained the few Russian vessels left in English waters under the command of Makarof which had been ordered back to Revel by the Czar. The mutiny at the Nore at this moment placed the British fleet in a position the peril of which Vorontsof took care to exaggerate. Paul was flattered by the idea that he had saved " the greatest navy in the world," and complimented his ambassador. But the example was contagious. Panine copied Voront-sof at Berlin, and soon began to devote all his energies to promoting ideas and designs which were quite contrary to the instructions he received from Russia.

Thus at the very moment when Paul flattered himself that he was reversing the machinery committed to his charge the controlling mechanism escaped from his grasp. But the Prussian system itself, which he so ingenuously admired, also deceived his expectations. Count Brühl, his old acquaintance, came as Ambassador Extraordinary to his coronation. Paul pushed his simplicity so far as to express surprise that the envoy despatched and received communications in cypher. Was it possible that the " good faith " of the Cabinet of Berlin had anything to conceal ? Bezborodko, in concert with Cobenzl, un-deceived the Czar. The signatories of the Treaty of Bâle had not contented themselves with that agreement ; they had since negotiated another, assuring to France the left bank of the Rhine in exchange for compensations to be given to Prussia out of the ecclesiastical states of Germany.

This was an open secret in all the chancelleries of Europe, but to Paul it was a revelation, and at first he could not believe that it was not a calumny. Very soon, however, seeing that he would soon learn the whole truth, the Cabinet of Berlin itself took the initiative and caused the Czar to be informed in great secrecy of the Convention of August 5, 1796, which had for months been the leading topic of all diplomatic correspondence. The manœuvre did not succeed. Paul was even more indignant that he had been kept in ignorance so long than at the treaty itself. Brühl was overwhelmed with reproaches, and could only say that he had acted according to instructions. The Czar angrily declared that the Convention was contrary to European interests, and addressed to his Minister at Berlin a despatch to be shown to the Prussian Ministers which was couched in terms all but insulting. He recalled his neighbours to their sacred duty of defending the integrity of their common country and said they could have Russia's friendship on no other terms. Prussia had already had her share of Poland and should have no other ambitions. These remonstrances were supported by a military demonstration on the western frontier.

But the Czar did not yet abandon his obstinate attitude of neutrality. Austria was fairly in the grip of the victor of Arcola and Rivoli, and Paul affected to follow the fortunes of the struggle with the air of an unconcerned and even malicious spectator. At the same time he advised England to imitate Austria in treating with France. He did not think that the restoration of the Bourbons should be a condition *sine qua non* of an agreement which was so much to be desired, and he had no objection to the cession of Luxembourg and Maestricht.

But Cobenzl and Whitworth heard very different language at the Department of Foreign Affairs, where Paul was finding himself in the presence of constant and embarrassing opposition. Bezborodko insisted that he should fulfil his obligations under the treaties of 1791 and 1792, by sending to Austria the auxiliary corps of 12,000 men formally promised therein. If Russia intervened in this way and supported her action by a firm declaration it would at least help to moderate the pretensions of France. Paul still resisted. He could not decently appear on the field of battle with a handful of men, nor could he take part in negotiations with a Government which he had not recognised. On April 25 he agreed to a conference between Bezborodko, Cobenzl and Whitworth, only insisting that the Prussian envoy should be present, but he still remained of the same mind and talked of a congress which should be held at Leipzig, in order to effect a general pacification.

Very unexpectedly, at this point the Empress and the Grand Duke Alexander intervened on behalf of Austria.

Cobenzl had persuaded Marie Féodorovna that her father's fate was now in the hands of Austria, and he had very astutely opened up the prospect of possible compensation at Vienna for the unhappy Alexandrina. The Archduke Joseph Palatine of Hungary was seeking a wife. Paul gave way and confidentially informed Dietrichstein, the second Austrian Envoy who came for the coronation, that he would mass six divisions on the frontier and would send a man of weight to Berlin to bring Prussia back to the paths of rectitude. Count Panine, who was young and energetic, would replace the indolent Kalytchof on the banks of the Spree and would be seconded by Marshal Repnine, who would be charged with a special mission and would go from Berlin to Vienna, declaring in both capitals that Russia could not be indifferent to the weakening of Austria and that if Prussia did not induce France to moderate her exigencies, 60,000 Russians would be placed at the disposal of the allies.

Paul was now in the toils, and as his mind was always pursuing some fancy or other and his will constantly vacillated, it was some time before he could free himself. The first departure which he made from his initial programme was all the less justified because in themselves the conditions of Leoben, whether open or secret, had nothing in them to which he could take exception. The integrity of the Empire in which he was interested was expressly stipulated, and this appeared to imply the abandonment by France of the Rhine frontier, as he desired. He had always been indifferent to the cession of the Netherlands to the Republic, and the acquisition of the Venetian littoral by Austria was part of old agreements between Joseph and Catherine to which he did not object. Moreover, as a consequence of a quarrel between Russian subjects and the Venetian Consul at Smyrna he had just forbidden the Venetian envoy all access to his Court.

On the other hand, he had not yet succeeded in discarding

his Prussian infatuation, and was giving ear to suggestions from this quarter which were leading him into courses contrary alike to his first resolutions and his new inclinations. On the eve of taking up arms against the French Republic he was commencing negotiations with Paris through the Cabinet of Berlin which will be described in detail hereafter and which still further confused an already complicated situation.

IV

After the treaty of Campo Formio, Paul took into his own service the corps of the Prince de Condé, which Austria could no longer retain. This was to range himself openly on the side of the adversaries of the victorious Republic. The Prince himself, his son the Duc de Bourbon, and his grandson the Duc d'Enghien, were received with splendid hospitality at St. Petersburg, and their troops were quartered more or less comfortably in Podolia and Volhynia. There was even some talk of a marriage between Alexandrina, who was still without a husband, and the Duc d'Enghien.

This was followed in December 1797 by the installation of Louis XVIII himself in the Castle of Mittau. The King received a pension of 200,000 roubles, and it is easy to imagine how this increased the credit of the whole body of French *émigrés*, who were already so influential on the banks of the Neva. But at the very same time Makarof's squadron was finally recalled to Russia. Grenville talked of the danger of a landing of French troops in England to justify a demand for an auxiliary corps from Russia which had been promised by the treaty of 1795. Paul described these fears as imaginary and, always fantastic, replied by an offer of twelve ships of the line. The Court of St. James's rejoined by proposing a quadruple alliance between England, Russia, Austria and Prussia, a suggestion which, in spite of what has been said to the contrary, was cordially

221

received by Bezborodko. Paul was much less enthusiastic, but was gradually won over to the scheme, which was destined to be carried out by his son in 1813. He became quite eager about it when the Emperor Francis added a request for his mediation in view of an arrangement between Austria and Prussia. Already he saw himself the arbiter of the fate of Europe. Frederick William II had just died; Paul was convinced that his son's conduct would be " more worthy," and was anxious to enlarge the English scheme by taking Denmark into the alliance. He came back to the idea of a congress, which was to meet at Berlin, baffle the intrigues of the Prussian ministers, curb the excesses of Austrian ambition, and bring about a general pacification on a basis acceptable to everybody. All idea of aggrandisement in Germany was to be repudiated by the Powers which had lost nothing in the conflict, to which an end was now to be put, and compensation was only to be given to the real victims of the Revolution, which were the Houses of Orange, Hesse-Cassel and Wurtemberg. Only in this way could the encroachments of France be checked without further fighting.

Events, however, happened in quick succession, which showed how rapid was the progress of revolutionary arrogance and assumption. After Lombardy, Liguria, Holland and Switzerland, Rome in its turn had to endure a republican invasion. At Vienna Bernadotte attracted crowds by displaying the device, " *Liberté, Egalité, Fraternité*," on the balcony of his hotel. Even at Vilna there were traces of a plot for the reconstitution of Poland supported by Bonaparte and connected with an intrigue in which Caillard, the French Minister at Berlin, was said to have tried to involve Prince Henry of Prussia.

Paul was rudely awakened from his dream of peaceful arbitration. He drew up new and very different instructions for Repnine, whose departure, which had several times been postponed, was now finally decided. The

Russian envoy was now to open his mission to Berlin
by the peremptory question, " Was Prussia or was she not
prepared to regard France as the common enemy ? "
At the same time Razoumovski was sent off to Rastadt
from Vienna on a mission of observation.

Unfortunately there was no one at Berlin who could
reply with any frankness to this summons. The new
King, who had been ill-brought up and had been starved
and terrorised by his grand-uncle, was precisely the
timid and feeble creature which such an education might
have been expected to produce. Almost immediately
after his accession he left for a long provincial tour, leaving
foreign affairs in the hands of a trio of councillors who have
left an evil reputation behind them. Of these the first was
Haugwitz, an old pupil of the Moravian brotherhood, a
depraved mystic, " a satyr with the head of Christ," as
Lavater called him, who divided his life between idyllic
domestic happiness and midnight orgies in the lowest
taverns. His talents for affairs were mediocre ; in his
work he was exceedingly pedantic and as frivolous as in his
private life. The next was Lombard, the son of a barber
attached to the French colony " de poudreuse mémoire," as
he said himself. He had formerly acted as copyist of
Frederick's literary manuscripts, but was now a Councillor
of State. He was as evil a liver as Haugwitz, but he had
even less capacity for public affairs and even lower
instincts. Finally, there was Lucchesini, the most gifted
of the three but the most crooked. His chief ambition was
to enrich himself.

All three by taste, interest, or fear of the republican
armies, were like the new King himself, resolute partisans
of the *entente* with France, but were equally determined
not to admit this, either because they were ashamed of
the fact, because they feared Austria, or because they
wished to exploit England.

Repnine reached Berlin early in May 1798, and met the

Prince of Reuss, who had come from Vienna, also as Envoy Extraordinary. Paul's congress was coming to pass. The Russian envoy brought with him a cut-and-dried proposal for a quadruple defensive alliance which, as desired by England, guaranteed the integrity of the possessions of the Powers participating. Repnine had an audience of the young King, who condescended to return in order to receive him. He was told that his Majesty entirely agreed with the Czar and desired to maintain the closest friendship with him, but he could not get any further than that.

Reuss was no more fortunate. Austria began by promising to give up the idea of compensations in Germany if Prussia would imitate her disinterestedness. This was too good to be quite genuine, and the negotiations went to pieces on the suspicion that Austria meant to recover in Italy what she surrendered in Germany. The Emperor Francis made as if to refer the matter to the Czar. "Your Majesty shall be the judge," he wrote to Paul. "I agree in advance to anything your Majesty may suggest." But at the same time in a very different tone Thugut was demanding the immediate despatch of the Russian force of 12,000 men to whose services Austria was entitled under existing treaties.

Paul saw that he had built his fine plans on a quicksand ; he was losing ground and always slipping further in the Austrian direction. Marie Féodorovna, who was still anxious about her family, did all she could to assist this tendency, and two of her brothers, Prince Ferdinand and Prince Alexander, who had come to St. Petersburg via Vienna, helped to play into the hands of Dietrichstein and Whitworth. In the course of the month of May the British Ambassador cleverly made the most of the French armaments, which were being prepared at Toulon. Paul began by promising England ten ships of the line and five frigates to reinforce the Northern Fleet, and ended by discussing the question of a treaty of subsidies, first for the despatch of an auxiliary corps to operate in England, and then for a large army to cross the Austrian frontier from the Prussian side and perhaps even to push as far as the Rhine. The resolute pacifist was growing excited. He was coming back to Catherine's policy and was beginning to wish to take part in the anti-French coalition, not as its tail but as its head. Nothing remained of the consideration which less than two years before had seemed to dictate a prudent reserve. He believed that he had reduced his finances to order, and as for his troops he flattered himself that he had made them invincible. And yet only a few months earlier he had still the intention of treating with the nation against whom he was now making such vigorous preparations.

V

The idea of these negotiations was first formed at the very beginning of Paul's reign. The pacific intentions and Prussian sympathies of the new Sovereign had not escaped the notice of the Directory. Several indirect attempts were made to profit by this, but as early as December 17, 1796, the Directory had sent instructions to Caillard, their Minister at Berlin, to open negotiations with the Russian envoy through Haugwitz. Some days later the same commission was entrusted to Grouvelle, the French Minister at Copenhagen. The latter failed completely to get into touch with his Russian colleague, Baron Krudener, one of the most savage Gallophobes in the Russian diplomatic service, and at the same time the agents of the Republic met with similar rebuffs in several European capitals.

In June 1797, however, Baron Krudener was recalled, and his successor, Katchalof, unexpectedly took the initiative by making advances to Grouvelle and his successor, Désaugiers, who were far from expecting such a demonstration. " Let us get rid of diplomatic subtleties," said Katchalof to Désaugiers : " your Government has proposed a *rapprochement ;* mine desires it. Have you or has M. Grouvelle power to treat ? I know that at Berlin M. de Kalytchof has already been in conversation with M. Caillard on the subject, but he has not the confidence of the Emperor. We are not at war ; therefore there are no conquests to restore. You have only to extend to us the hand of friendship."

At Berlin, in fact, the representatives of the two countries had already got into touch. Talleyrand had succeeded Delacroix at the Ministry of Foreign Affairs, and thought it best to concentrate the negotiations which seemed to promise so well at the Prussian capital. Delacroix had got into difficulties by suggesting that Caillard should treat directly with Kalytchof and send him an official note. On this his subordinate had read him the following lesson in diplomatic deportment. " M. de Kalytchof is a person of small enlightenment, exceedingly timid and circumspect. He would certainly not consent to receive such a document from a Government which his master has not recognised. . . . These questions of form are of course contemptible ; unfortunately, they still bind all Ministers except those of the Republic." On the other hand, the Cabinet of Berlin was determined to keep the negotiations in their own hands. They had taken steps at St. Petersburg which had already produced some effect. Paul had just signed a ukase removing the interdict on wines and other products of French origin. Caillard therefore used the same channel to send to France a note which he had settled with Haugwitz and which was in the following terms : " The undersigned ... is expressly charged by the Executive Directory to communicate to his Majesty's Ministers the desire of the Republic to re-establish peace and the friendly relations which existed before the war between France and Russia, as well as the disposition of the Directory to enter into negotiations on the subject."

The note was sent in February 1797, but the reply was delayed. During the four months which followed Kalytchof, acting under precise orders, reluctantly consented to cease from deliberately avoiding his French colleague, but neither from him nor from St. Petersburg was there any answer to the appeal made by France. It was not until July 3 that Frederick William, who was then at the baths of Pyrmont, was able to inform Sandoz, his chargé d'affaires at Paris, of the Czar's decision, which had at last been communicated to him. It was in the form of a verbal note, not intended for the representative of the French Government but communicated by Bezborodko to Tauentzien, and it gave a wholly unexpected turn to the negotiations. " His Imperial Majesty," it ran, " is much disposed to listen to the overtures which M. Caillard has been instructed to make. . . . His Majesty will welcome with pleasure anything which can have the effect of restoring the former good understanding between Russia and France, especially if this can help the cause of the allies. He will gladly use his good offices to bring the belligerents to an agreement and to re-establish peace, and he is ready to take part directly in a scheme of general pacification on condition that he acts along with his Majesty the King of Prussia and also occupies the position of a mediator."

Whether through misunderstanding or cunning, Paul was turning the tables on the Directory. He had been asked to consent to an arrangement with France by the mediation of Prussia. He was now offering to mediate between France and the coalition ! The French Government could not but regard such a proposal with the greatest distrust, but at Berlin Caillard did not at first grasp its true significance. He was overjoyed at the prospect of at last having in his hands the negotiation which he had so long coveted. Finkenstein, one of the Prussian ministers, asked him to dinner to meet Kalytchof. It seemed that the discussion had begun ! The French envoy accepted the invitation, and highly approved of his Russian colleague's method of doing business. He was easy to please ! Kalytchof could not yet take it upon him to receive a visit from the representative of the Republic, still less could he take it upon himself to visit Caillard. Kalytchof therefore suggested that in order that they might have a private interview they should meet in the Park, now the *Thiergarten*. It was like an assignation !

Caillard meekly gave in to this impertinence, and they met and conversed ; but it was soon clear that there was no chance of an agreement. Very soon, indeed, Talleyrand declared his views on the subject of the Czar's mediation, which of course were that it was absolutely unacceptable. " It would give Russia," he said, " the opportunity of interfering in all the affairs of Germany and of exercising an influence there which would be immense and all the more dangerous because when united with Austria the two Imperial Courts would dispose between them of a force superior to that of Prussia and the Protestant party." The agreement to be negotiated with Russia, therefore, should be limited to the restoration of peace and good understanding between the two Powers and to the renewal of commercial relations on the most favoured nation footing in accordance with the convention of January 11, 1787, and the promise of an ulterior understanding for a new commercial treaty.

Meanwhile Kalytchof had been replaced at Berlin by Panine, who of all people was the least likely to help towards a *rapprochement*. We have already seen what his own sympathies were : his wife, a daughter of Count Vladimir Orlof, accompanied him to Berlin, where she gave proofs of an extravagant Gallophobia. On the other hand, the Courts of London and Vienna had heard of the negotiations in the Park and were most anxious to put an end to them. They were themselves treating with the Republic, the former at Lille, the latter at Mombello and Udine, but they loudly protested that Russia " would dishonour herself " by following their example. The efforts of the French *émigrés* at St. Petersburg, the activity of the Comte de Saint-Priest, whom Louis XVIII had just sent there as his Minister, and the pressing representations of the Prince de Condé himself had the same effect, and the result was visible in the instructions given to Kalytchof's successor.

He was directed to pursue the negotiations with the " regicides," which in his personal opinion were ignominious, but he was also instructed to accept none of the bases which Talleyrand had just indicated. There was to be no return to the old commercial treaty : it was not in the best interests of Russia to admit articles of luxury of French manufacture. Nor could even a re-establishment of diplomatic relations be accepted, as these might serve as a channel for the revolutionary contagion. But what then was left to treat about ? Panine was instructed that none of these negations was to be regarded as absolute ; he was not to be immovable on any question but that of the *émigrés* if the French went so far as to try to prevent Russia from freely exercising the duty of hospitality. Again, he was at once to break off negotiations " if the French Government were insolent enough to propose the restitution of the territories formerly belonging to Poland and now annexed to the Empire."

All this meant nothing, and Bezborodko, to whom Panine's instructions had been dictated by the Czar, saw this quite well. He had nevertheless insisted that the negotiation should be pursued, even though it was deprived of all meaning. Something, he thought, might come of the contact of the parties *in vacuo* which might give substance to the friendly intentions which after all existed. He had no taste for the France of the Revolution, but he thought that an understanding of some kind was the natural consequence of the new state of things created by Bonaparte's victories. Austria and Prussia had successively retired from the contest and England seemed inclined to follow their example. How and why should Russia, who had taken no direct part in the struggle, remain alone engaged ? The imperative logic of the facts must be accepted by both parties and bring them to an agreement.

Panine, however, was very far from sharing this view. He had, in fact, *carte blanche* to follow the personal inclinations which we have already described, and he did not hesitate to make use of it. At the very outset he put Caillard out of court with the question of mediation, which he said was the indispensable point of departure for any serious discussion. Yet he allowed himself to be drawn into the consideration of a draft treaty. He discussed articles, suggested alterations, and ended by accepting a text which he said gave him entire satisfaction. But after the work had been completed at the expense of innumerable conferences and much labour, he declared that he had no power to pledge his sovereign and that all he could do was to send the draft to St. Petersburg.

Poor Caillard had gone to the extreme limit of possible concessions, and perhaps even beyond it. He had not, indeed, gone so far as to permit the Russian Government to be named first in the *French* text. He was a diplomatist by profession and incapable of allowing such a breach of diplomatic etiquette. In order to spare the Czar's susceptibilities he had consented to allow the Executive Directory to figure under its own name as a contracting party instead of the Republic, as was usual. This gave no offence at Paris, but there were other and more serious objections.

The provision relating to the rights of each State over the subjects of the other residing within its borders has been much misrepresented. The actual text of the treaty was as follows : " Members of the two nationalities may freely travel in the respective countries and shall in every case enjoy the protection of the Government, on condition, however, that the said travellers shall in no way meddle in the internal Government or enter into correspondence contrary to public order." Even in this form the provision was considered inadmissible at Paris. " The Executive Directory," wrote Talleyrand, " will never consent to a stipulation so vague and so useless, which would give an arbitrary and capricious Government the opportunity of persecuting Frenchmen in Russia on the slightest pretext and would enable them to set aside our remonstrances."

At St. Petersburg the draft was received even more unfavourably. Bezborodko thought that the stipulations were " perfectly reasonable and proper," but he could get no one to share this view. Paul was becoming more and more amenable to the simultaneous suggestions of Austria and England. He was carrying on the parallel negotiation with the Government of the Republic as a proof of his independence, but he did not take it seriously. He did not regard himself as being at war with France, he said, and he did not wish to become her friend. Also he intended that the conclusion of any agreement between him and that Power should be conditional on the favourable issue of the negotiations then in progress between her and Austria and England. A rescript to Panine had to be drafted in this sense, and as at the same moment the English and French plenipotentiaries left Lille, this meant the rupture of the negotiations with Caillard.

Bezborodko did what he could and merely directed the Russian Minister to suspend the discussion, trying at the same time to maintain a conciliatory attitude with his French colleague. Whitworth attributed this desire to respect the susceptibilities of the Republic to a growing penchant for France. Paul, he thought, was as usual giving way to his fears. " His best friend will always be he whom he most fears." It is easy, however, to imagine what Panine made of his new instructions.

Caillard was astounded when, in the early part of October 1797, the Russian envoy gave him another *rendezvous* in the Park, and told him that " circumstances having changed, the Emperor found it necessary to postpone to a more favourable time the completion of the work which had been commenced." What could have changed in Russia or in Europe in the space of a month? Caillard imagined that they had heard at St. Petersburg of certain Royalist intrigues and had not learned that these had been baffled by the *coup d'état* of the 18th Fructidor (September 4, 1797). But, no : Panine assured his colleague that he had no indication which could justify such a suspicion. At the same time he showed much curiosity about the counterproposals for a treaty which Caillard said he had received from Paris. The Russian Government had not, therefore, abandoned the intention of coming to an agreement. A new request from Panine for an interview some days later seemed to confirm this supposition. Alas, this time the French envoy repaired to the Park on a dismal autumn day only to learn that the Czar was furious. Zagourski, a Russian Consul, had been arrested at Zante by the French authorities in defiance of the law of nations, and Caillard must consider the negotiations as being definitely broken off.

Some weeks later Panine stopped Caillard in the street and told him that if the Directory gave full satisfaction to Russia in the case of Zagourski the conversations might be resumed. Talleyrand of course made no difficulty, but though the conversations were in fact resumed the results were no more favourable than before. Panine boasted of his disregard of his formal instructions to negotiate seriously with the agent of the Republic. He spared no pains to discredit the unfortunate Caillard and to compromise his Government. In this enterprise he showed a gift for intrigue and an absence of scruple which Paul was afterwards to experience to his cost. He declared that he had bribed Caillard's cypher clerk and made use of discoveries which he alleged that he had made in this way in order to implicate the diplomacy of the Republic in an imaginary project for the re-establishment of Poland, in which Prince Henry of Prussia was said to be concerned.

There was no truth in the story, and Paul himself did not believe in Panine's accusations. This drove him back on another expedient. He represented Haugwitz and his colleagues as at variance with their master's policy and as being prepared to negotiate an offensive alliance with Caillard. This was also quite untrue. It was not until May 1798, that is to say, several months after he had altogether ceased to meet his Russian colleague, that Caillard was instructed to obtain from Prussia an agreement on this basis. He failed completely, and that was the cause of his recall and of the substitution for him of Sieyès, of whom the Cabinet of Paris expected better things. Meanwhile, the " peripatetic fancies " of the Czar had developed considerably.

Exasperated by the reports of his envoy at Berlin, he had at first gone so far as to order Panine to upset the Prussian Ministry ! Panine declared that he was in a position to do this, but the means he proposed to use did not commend themselves to his Imperial master. He wished, on the one hand, that Russia should take up a menacing attitude, and on the other that he should be authorised to communicate to the King the deciphered version of Caillard's correspondence. Paul considered the first expedient imprudent and the second dishonourable. But he was disconcerted by the turn which his Envoy was giving to a negotiation on which he had himself no clear idea, and on February 5/16, 1798, he decided definitely to direct that the negotiations entered into with Caillard should be closed.

The Directory on their part did not press the point. The instructions given in May 1798 to the "execrable Sieyès," as Panine called him, did not contain a single word about Russia. They were concerned only with the attempt which was to be made to attach Prussia decisively to the French system in war as well as in peace, and to encourage her to resist the efforts which the Courts of St. Petersburg and Vienna were simultaneously making through Prince Repnine and the Prince of Reuss to throw her, by persuasion or by force, into the coalition in which Paul was himself to be so deeply involved.

VI

Though Whitworth boasted—and sometimes with truth —that the Russian Chancellor was entirely at his service, Bezborodko was sincerely disappointed by the miscarriage of an enterprise which he had striven his utmost to make successful, though he did not much believe that success was possible. Under a genial exterior the Little Russian possessed an incalculable fund of dissimulation, and if he was still attached to the system of alliances adopted by Catherine he did not intend that Russia should play the part of a slave and a dupe.

After the signature of the Treaty of Campo-Formio the Chancellor had strongly objected to the proposal that Russia should support Austria by force in breaking the engagements into which she had entered. His opinion was that an arrangement with France was necessary, and he severely blamed the conduct of Panine. But he was not the master. Paul disdained the experienced wisdom of his minister and allowed himself to be caught in a trap against which he had been repeatedly warned in vain. Prince Ferdinand of Würtemberg adroitly accommodated himself to the Czar's tastes and flattered his weaknesses, and was of the greatest assistance to Whitworth and

Dietrichstein in pushing him into the snare. With military abruptness he spoke of a new campaign against France having been made inevitable by what had passed at Berlin. ". . . Emboldened by success, the Government of the Republic would certainly regard the treatment their representative had received as equivalent to a declaration of war. It was no longer a question whether to fight or not, but how to fight to the best advantage."

As the Emperor still resisted, the Prince, with a melancholy air, observed : " I am already in mourning for all the Sovereigns of Europe. I see that I shall have to mourn also for the Emperor Paul ! "

On July 8, 1798, after a sharp debate, the Czar gave way. Next day he dictated to the Prince the particulars of an army of from sixty to seventy thousand men which was to be employed on the Prussian frontier. Dietrichstein and Whitworth had now the greatest difficulty in restraining him, so eager had he become for the fray !

The Court of Vienna was still quite unprepared for a renewal of hostilities ; it had not even been quite decided whether or not to try the fortune of arms again, and in any case the Viennese Cabinet did not wish to do so before they had quite exhausted all the possibilities of agreement with the Republican Government, whose advances they had urged Paul to repel. The reorganisation of the Austrian forces was not complete, and Thugut distrusted the capacities of those who would be called upon to command them. He had no great confidence in Paul's resolutions; he regarded England as rather too despotic an ally and Prussia as irrevocably sold to France. He had also to reckon with the Congress of Rastadt, where, with the encouragement of the Court of Berlin, the repugnance of Germany to a renewal of the war was making itself strongly felt. For all these reasons he continued to negotiate with the Directory.

Paul understood nothing of all this. He was now as

bellicose as he had formerly been pacific, and spent his time drawing up plans of campaign and drafting proclamations. He ordered his representative at Constantinople to negotiate an alliance with Turkey ; he warmly welcomed an emissary of Montenegro, and flattered himself that he would be able to unite the Crescent and the banners of the Southern Slavs in the war against France ! Since 1767, when one of the numerous pseudo-Peter the Thirds had appeared on the Black Mountains, the relations between Russia and this country had been somewhat strained. Paul was not displeased to have another opportunity of repudiating his mother's policy. But this did not suit Austria. The Montenegrins were already laying claim to Bosnia, which at Vienna was regarded as a counter in the game with France. Catherine's son did not grasp this, and the services of Prince Ferdinand had again to be employed, this time to pour cold water on his exaltation, which went beyond what his friends expected of him !

A firm promise of a Russian corps, which Austria would use at the proper moment in the best interests of the common cause, was for the moment enough. But Paul, thus recalled to realities, fell back into his usual hesitations. He calculated the cost and was afraid. If only England would consent to pay for the maintenance of the troops ! Prince Ferdinand protested. "What ! did you not say that you would not sell your troops, like the Landgrave of Hesse ? You give millions to your favourites and you grudge a few hundred thousand for the safety of Europe !"

This argument had its effect. The Prince insisted on a written engagement, "because in a great man there are always two persons, one who speaks and the other who writes, and it is only the latter who counts." Paul gave his signature on a scrap of paper, but the next morning he seemed to repent of what he had done. The manifest folly of squandering the blood and treasure of his country in a quarrel in which he could not pretend that it was interested came home to him. The Revolution was already losing the character which had made him hate it and was gradually calming down. He had no longer, therefore, any good reason for making war, and it was France herself that, by the capture of Malta, at this moment supplied the motive which determined his decision. This time he was really caught, and he soon became almost entirely docile in the hands of the coalition of foreign interests of which he was to become the slave.

CHAPTER X

IN THE TOILS OF THE COALITION

I

The alliance against France was for Paul a prison from which he was soon to make efforts to escape and in which he felt himself incommoded from the first. He had nothing in common with the companions whom he found there : he was not really of their family. Their ideas and his were different, and even the interests and ambitions which he wished to promote with the help of this alliance encountered rival pretensions of the same kind, and would have been better served by a different alliance.

Thus he came to regard the affair of Malta as the reason why he had to enter the coalition. But the presence of the French at Valetta could not in itself justify the killing of tens of thousands of Russians in Italy and Switzerland. Moreover, the more or less legitimate desires which the Czar proposed to satisfy, being in themselves essentially revolutionary, were scarcely in harmony with his professed object of maintaining order in Europe by means of an anti-revolutionary crusade.

The relations of Russia with the Knights of Malta began about the end of the seventeenth century, when the Field-Marshal Boris Chérémetief, while on a mission from Peter the Great to the Levant, visited the island and received a welcome which inaugurated a period of continuous friendship. Catherine's enterprising policy tended to strengthen these bonds. Bailiffs and commanders of the Order took service in the Russian navy ;

Russian officers went to Malta to finish their nautical education. Diplomatic representatives were exchanged, and Cavalcabo, Catherine's clever agent, strove not unsuccessfully to create a Russian party in the island. In 1770 the Empress went so far as to treat with Ximenes, who was then Grand Master, with a view to common action against the Turks. It was only the opposition of France which prevented these engagements from being carried out. Catherine also favoured the Order in the matter of the Volhynian estate of Ostrog, which the Order was ultimately to inherit, and in 1775 a Grand Priory was established in Poland under the guarantee of the three Courts of St. Petersburg, Vienna and Berlin, with an assured annuity of 120,000 florins.

In 1776 Paul dedicated the Hospital for Naval Pensioners to the Knights of Malta, and caused the Maltese Cross which is still to be seen to be placed on the front of the building. At his accession the Order, having lost most of its property owing to the Revolution, was working for compensation in Russia. It was this that brought the Bailiff Giulio Litta to St. Petersburg, where the presence of his brother, the Nuncio Lorenzo, afterwards Cardinal, assured him of a strong backing. His mission was merely to press the claims of the Order to their inheritance of Ostrog, which had been appropriated by collaterals, but he succeeded beyond his hopes. In January 1797 Paul signed a convention whereby the Volhynian estate was exchanged for an assured annual revenue of 300,000 florins for the maintenance of a Russian Grand Priory. The agreement was ratified in August by Ferdinand de Hompesch, the Grand Master who had just succeeded Emmanuel de Rohan, and the first Grand Prior was the Prince de Condé.

There was nothing in this which could offend anybody, and Cobenzl and Serra-Capriola, the Neapolitan envoy, expressed their approval. But, after spending a few

months at Malta, Litta returned to Russia and presented
Paul with the cross which had been worn by La Valette,
the most illustrious of the Grand Masters, offering him
at the same time the protectorate of the Order. At a
solemn audience, at which all the Court and many dignitaries of the Orthodox Church were present, the Czar
accepted both the gift and the functions proposed to
him.

The Order had already two regularly appointed protectors, who were the Emperor of Germany and the King
of the Two Sicilies. Paul was careful to address to all
the Courts of Europe a declaration in which he disclaimed
all intention of usurping the prerogatives of others.
But the German priories showed some agitation and the
Court of Vienna expressed keen displeasure. For the
moment, however, every one was ready to humour Russia
at all costs, and, no protest being made, the latest
innovation was accepted as an accomplished fact.

II

Things were in this curious position in June 1798
when the capture of Malta by the French produced an
even more singular development. Bonaparte did not
fail to use what had happened at St. Petersburg as a
justification for occupying the island in order to deliver
if from the domination of Russia. He professed to have
found there a treaty whereby Hompesch surrendered
himself to the Czar. This document was no other than
the Convention of 1797 and the retort was ready to hand.
On August 26, 1798 (old style), the Grand Priory of Russia
protested against the surrender of the island, which the
Maltese had already attributed to treachery, though the
state of the defences was such that the Order was incapable
of offering a serious resistance. On September 10 Paul
published a manifesto declaring the deposition of Hompesch

and taking the Order "under his supreme direction," and on October 27 (old style) the junior Priory assumed the right of appointing a new Grand Master and chose the orthodox Sovereign of Russia !

Paul did not hesitate to accept this title; nay, more, he was not content to participate in so audacious a usurpation, which created the strange paradox of a Catholic society under the presidency of the head of another Church. He assigned to the Russian Order an additional annuity of 216,000 roubles for the creation of new commanderies, and he even went so far as to add to the Catholic Priory of Russia an Orthodox Priory, inviting foreign priories at the same time to enter into close relations with these two communities and with St. Petersburg, which was henceforth to be the capital of the Order.

There have been many conjectures as to the Emperor's object in undertaking this extraordinary enterprise. Some have supposed that he wished to acquire a naval base in the Mediterranean. That was probably Catherine's design : but the idea that he could realise it with the complicity of England seems too extravagant even for the heedless folly of her son. The British Government was of course to announce on their undertaking to dislodge the French that they would restore the island to the Knights of St. John of Jerusalem and to their Grand Master, whoever he might be, and this engagement was renewed in the Treaty of Amiens in 1802. But, even in October 1799, Captain Alexander Ball,* when preparing a landing-party in the neighbourhood of Valetta in concert with a Russian squadron, issued a proclamation in which he referred to the protectorate of the King of the Two Sicilies and refused to allow any flag but his to be hoisted on the ground which he proposed to occupy.

Others have connected the Maltese venture with the old

* Afterwards Rear-Admiral Sir Alexander Ball, Bt., Governor of Malta.

chimera of the reunion of the Churches, which even yet haunts some minds. Paul was indeed believed in some quarters to be aiming at the succession of Pius VI, but Malta was too circuitous a route to Rome.

Finally, Baron Brünow wrote in his "Summary of the political transactions of the Cabinet of Russia": "The Emperor Paul regarded this institution (the Order of St. John of Jerusalem established in Russia) as a novitiate from which the nobility of all the countries in Europe might learn lessons of loyalty and honour." Nicolas I wrote on the margin of the original: "For the first time I understand my father's idea." This note shows how uncertain were even those who had the best opportunities of knowing about Paul's intentions. In his vague way he may have had in mind a powerful military organisation opposed no longer to the infidels of the Mussulman world but to all adversaries of religion and monarchy. And yet he set himself to demilitarise the institution and hoped by secularising it and removing the obligation of celibacy to throw it open to the most illustrious representatives of science, art and all the professions. Giulio Litta was thus able to marry, with the new Grand Master's approval, the rich widow Skavronski, a niece of Potemkine. But the net result was that the Catholic Priory of Russia was filled with French refugees, while the Orthodox Priory became the prey of the reigning favourites, and no one could see the vestige of a coherent policy in the Czar's action.

The religious and political world in the Europe of 1798 was equally at a loss. Pius VI began by protesting against Hompesch's deposition and by declining to give the Czar any title remotely resembling that of Grand Master—he declared that he would rather abolish the Order. The representations of the two Littas seem a little later to have modified this attitude, and the Holy Father seems to have been influenced by the hope of a possible *rapproche-*

ment between the two religions. The reports which came to the Vatican from the two Littas in Russia became at one time so seductive that the Pontiff professed himself ready to travel to St. Petersburg to treat in person with Paul. In the meantime, however, he declined to do anything, whether by bull or even by a simple brief, which would imply a recognition by him of the new state of things. Nothing happened during the succeeding months to confirm the illusory hopes which had been instilled into him, and he died without emerging from the perplexity into which he had been thrown.

The Powers engaged in the coalition against France did nothing to diminish the Pope's embarrassment. Apart from the question of the possession of Malta, Protestant England had no interest in the matter. Whitworth, at any rate, in the presence of his Russian friends, did not hesitate to approve of Paul's conduct in " maintaining and honouring ancient institutions." But at Vienna they did not know what to do. Thugut contrived an expedient which it was hoped would at least keep up appearances. He organised a meeting of delegates from various German priories to request the Emperor of Russia to become what he had already made himself, the protector and Supreme Head of the Order. Paul, however, rejected this subterfuge, and in 1797 he had already decided to expel Baron Reuchlin, the Bavarian Minister, on hearing that Bavaria refused to recognise his protectorate. The news turned out to be false and the Baron was provisionally allowed to remain, but a little later the Court of Munich protested in a different fashion. The Elector Maximilian Joseph, being in cruel embarrassment for money, decided to suppress the Bavarian branch of the Order and to confiscate its property. Paul sent for Reuchlin, ordered him to leave within two hours and to tell his master that if this measure was not reversed within a month General Korsakof, who was in the neighbourhood of Bavaria with 50,000 men, would receive orders to lay waste the country. The Minister delayed, owing to the state of his wife's health, to obey this order, so a subordinate officer of police put him in a carriage and conducted him to the frontier.

Paul exaggerated : Korsakof was nowhere near Bavaria. He was never to have so many as 50,000 men at his orders, nor could he ever have used them in this way. But Austria was showing manifest tendencies towards annexation and Bavaria required Russian protection. In July 1799, therefore, a first Russo-Bavarian Convention was signed by Paul as Grand Master of the Order, providing for the re-establishment of the Bavarian priories. Another, dated the following September, provided that Bavaria should furnish an auxiliary corps of 20,000 men against France, while Russia promised to obtain a subsidy from England for their maintenance. At the same time delegates from the German, Anglo-Bavarian and Tcheck priories set out for St. Petersburg, not to discuss the titles of the new Grand Master but to do him homage.

Thus Paul got his way, but his position in the political combination he had adopted was not thereby improved. No doubt the French occupation of Malta to some extent justified his making common cause with the enemies of France. He may have seen in it the beginning of enterprises more directly menacing to the permanent interests of Russia. He had already in fact begun to believe that Bonaparte was on his way to Constantinople. But the Czar disqualified himself as a defender of the peace of Europe by imitating the revolutionaries. After arbitrarily transforming an ancient and respected Order it was odd to find him in the anti-revolutionary coalition, and it soon involved him in inextricable embarrassment and led him inevitably into the other camp.

III

The other reasons by which Paul justified his position in the Anglo-Austrian league were equally unsound. The Polish question was one of them. The Czar's generosity to the Poles was limited to retrospective criticism of the policy of partition, and though the Republican Government, whether out of regard for Prussia or a desire not to close the door altogether on a Russian understanding, had been very reserved on this question, Paul and his fellow partitioners had ground for offence in several incidents for which France was responsible. The policy of the Directory was often very prudent but always very weak. In the treaty of Bâle they had implicitly forbidden themselves all intervention in favour of Polish independence. But in the very next month (May 1795) Joseph Wybiçki, one of the most energetic of the Polish patriots, went to Paris, where he received encouragement, if not promises of assistance, which awakened hopes at Warsaw and suspicions elsewhere which were equally unfounded. Bonaparte went further. During the first campaign of Italy one of his aides-de-camp, Joseph Sulkowski, writing from the headquarters at Legnano, reported that the Commander-in-Chief had used the following words : " Tell your countrymen that I love and honour the Poles, that the partition of Poland is an iniquitous act which cannot be tolerated, and that when I have finished the war in Italy I shall go myself at the head of the French people and compel Russia to restore Poland."

These were idle words, probably exaggerated by the reporter, but such was already the magic power of the words and deeds of the great man that they gave rise to a romantic chapter of military heroism. The " Polish legions " date from about this time; one was formed by Henry Dombrowski at Milan in January 1797, which followed the French armies in their victorious march and covered itself with glory. In January 1798, after the fall of Naples, Championnet sent the Polish General Kniaziewicz to Paris with the captured flags. At this time there were two legions, which in the disasters which followed shrank to 800 men, for they had always been in the forefront of the fight. In February 1800 they were fused into one. But volunteers flocked to the standards, and in March 1801 the two legions reappear, one in Italy, the other on the Rhine.

These exploits naturally led to a revival of agitation in Poland, and Bezborodko was alarmed by its progress on all the south-west frontier of the Empire. The Chancellor feared that if it were favoured by France it might receive a further impetus from the spread of republican ideas and might invade Russian territory, which, he said, " would be the end of all things." But this danger, he considered, was the very reason why Russia should come to an understanding with the Republic. Russia had no ground of quarrel with France except the intervention of the Government of the Republic in Polish affairs, and this interference was entirely due to Russian hostility. Once the cause was destroyed the effect would also disappear and there would be no difficulty in coming to an understanding in the East as well, where there was room enough for the development of the largest ambitions. Overtures in this sense were made to St. Petersburg through the medium of La Harpe by the Directory, who, as Whitworth said, offered " the spoils of the East " in exchange for a mere promise of neutrality.

This was the voice of wisdom, but Paul was by this time under the influence of the third motive, which was pushing him into the arms of England and Austria, and would not hear. It will be remembered that the attempts made in the spring and summer of 1798 by these two Powers to secure his co-operation coincided with the Court intrigue designed to ruin the credit of the Empress and

246

Mlle. de Nélidof. The success of this plot contributed to the success which the Courts of London and Vienna obtained about the same time. Not that the new favourite was of the Austrian party, as some have suspected. She probably hardly knew where the Danube was, and she seems to have been inaccessible to corruption. But Paul had not realised the changes in his wife's family interests which had led her to forsake her old attachment to the Court of Berlin. He had always thought of his wife as a Prussian, and a Prussian she remained for him. In the state of mind produced by the intrigue against her he was easily persuaded that he was asserting his independence by giving way to Austria ! And it was thus that the triumph of Mlle. Lapoukhine in fact assured the triumph of the coalition.

IV

When he returned to St. Petersburg on August 28, 1798, from Campo Formio, whither he had been summoned to help in the struggle with Bonaparte, Cobenzl could see that in this part of the great battle the victory was already more than half won. He had stopped at Berlin from the 7th till the 13th of August in order to make a last effort to obtain the help of Prussia. But the question of compensations still prevented any understanding with Vienna. Paris gained nothing by this, and Sandoz was at this very moment doing his best to prevent Sieyès being sent to the rescue of the ever-unfortunate Caillard. Sieyès did, however, arrive on June 19 to take up his post, and "the unfrocked priest," as he was called at Berlin, was received with coldness and even with discourtesy. He was asked whether he was a civilian or a soldier, a count or a baron. " In France," proudly replied the ex-conventionnel, " we recognise no title but that of citizen, and all our citizens are soldiers."

Still the Court of Berlin refused to accept him as an

Ambassador, and he had to produce new credentials, in which he was described simply as Minister. He awaited in vain the usual courtesies to which, even with this more modest title, he had a right. He was not asked to a single dinner at Court, nor even to one of the King's parties. He had to be content with conferences with his Majesty's Ministers, from whom he got no better satisfaction. Haugwitz was well named " the Minister of adjournments."

But Cobenzl, too, had to leave without gaining anything, and at the same time Repnine quitted Berlin, declaring that " Russia would make war with Prussia, without Prussia, or against Prussia." On July 13 Paul had written to his Envoy Extraordinary that he did not intend to force Prussia to a rupture, but that if she showed any disposition to join hands with France he would be ready to have recourse to extreme measures. On Cobenzl's arrival he displayed much anger against Frederick William. " That man," he cried, thumping a table with his fist, " is not worth that ! " And he was more decided than ever in favour of the Austrian alliance.

Repnine went to Vienna with the news that a Russian corps of 17,000 men under Rosenberg, concentrated with more than 3000 Cossacks at Brest-Litovski, was ready to cross the frontier on the first news of the opening of hostilities. Cobenzl asked, and obtained without difficulty, that these men should be sent immediately to Galicia in order to intimidate France and that they should afterwards move towards the Danube. On this occasion Paul boasted of the efforts he had made to free himself from " the yoke of the jacobins." The Austrian envoy did not appear to understand, so the Emperor explained that he meant " the influence of the Empress and her friends " !

Already, however, in September, before they had struck a single blow, the future comrades-in-arms were beginning to fall out. Rosenberg had quarrelled with Baron Vincent, the Austrian commissary, about some rations of bread due by one party to the other, and Paul had immediately ordered his general not only to stop but to disperse his troops. An old grievance, similar but more serious in character, had been revived between Austria and England. The dispute in this case was about the amount of the subsidies and the method of repayment of loans agreed upon between the allies, and it now became more acute than ever. Paul, always easily excited, became more and more irritated, and arrangements were hastily made at Vienna to satisfy Rosenberg in order to calm him and to secure that the Russian troops should continue their march. The Austrians were, however, in no hurry to test their prowess in battle, for they still cherished the hope that France might be induced to compromise, and the Congress of Rastadt had not said its last word.

V

The entry of the Russians on the scene seemed destined to extricate that assembly from the vicious circle in which it had so long been moving, and in fact, in January 1799, the French plenipotentiaries received instructions to make the announced irruption of Russian troops into the territory of the Empire the subject of an ultimatum. If the Diet of Ratisbon did not effectively oppose it the Congress would be broken up. At the same time, having succeeded in setting on foot the Austro-Russian understanding, Whitworth laboured with redoubled ardour to bring about a similar understanding between Russia and his own country. Following instructions which he had been receiving from London since the beginning of the year, he opened the project which was to be the basis of all the coalitions against France up till 1815. The plan was to form a strict union between Russia, England and Austria, to draw in Prussia and support Naples. The French were to be expelled from Italy, where Austria was to regain Lombardy and keep Venice, and from Holland, to which the Low Countries were to be annexed and which would thus form a barrier against French ambition. This was the grandiose design developed by the mouthpiece of the Court of St. James's. He announced at the same time that Grenville, the brother of the Minister, was to be sent to Berlin to make a decisive effort with Frederick William, and by means of a further remittance of 40,000 roubles he assured himself of the support of Koutaïssof.

This eagerness was impeded by the dilatory tactics of Austria and Prussia, which were unexpectedly seconded by Paul himself, who, in spite of his recent keenness for war, was now given up to other preoccupations. Abandoning state affairs, cutting short religious services, and even neglecting the parade-ground, he had become unapproachable. Mlle. Lapoukhine had appeared on the scene, and the amorous monarch would not allow Bezborodko to do anything but court the favourite and adjust all the rearrangements of position and influence at Court which were the consequence of her romantic change of fortune. The Chancellor, whose strength was waning, was not attracted by this task. He was ill and weary of the enmity of Rastoptchine and Koutaïssof, to which he was constantly exposed. He had therefore asked for leave of absence and was preparing to depart for Moscow. Kotchoubey, the Vice-Chancellor, was also making ready to follow his uncle into retirement, and Whitworth had no one with whom he could talk business.

Paul's energies, however, were reawakened towards the end of the year by the news that fighting had already begun in the south of Italy. On December 17 he informed Vorontsof that he would make an alliance with the King of Naples in order to protect him, and a week later he received Whitworth and declared himself ready to conclude

" a provisional convention " with England for the supply
of 45,000 men on condition of receiving subsidies. He
thought he could overcome the resistance of Prussia by
the offer of all the territory which would be taken from
the French on the left bank of the Rhine with the exception
of the three ecclesiastical electorates, and the troops to
be paid for by England would be used to help the
King of Prussia, " if, as was to be hoped, his Majesty
would display a corresponding energy." Moreover, like
Catherine, Paul demanded enormous subsidies—£900,000
a year or £75,000 a month, in addition to £250,000 for
the initial expenses.

Whitworth was sceptical and Paul again gave way.
On condition that the treaty was to provide for an addition
of territory to Prussia and the re-establishment of the
Stathouderat of the Netherlands he agreed that the 45,000
Russians should be used as England might wish, for the
recapture of Holland or any other purpose. He talked
also of sending another 8000 men to the assistance of the
King of Naples. England had no objection in principle
to the proposed territorial arrangements, and as regards
money Whitworth was lavish. The signatures were
therefore exchanged on December 18/29, before the departure of Bezborodko.*

The same day Paul promised the Neapolitan Government
to send a fleet and an army corps of about 10,000 men to
their assistance. These would at once be sent to Zara in
Dalmatia and would there embark in Neapolitan vessels.
At the same time he negotiated with Sweden, offering
in his turn a subsidy of 300,000 riksdalers in exchange for
a hypothetical promise of co-operation. Forgetful of
his undertaking that Malta should have a mixed garrison
if it were recaptured from the French, he proceeded in

---

* The treaty was immediately afterwards ratified by the British Government,
subject to the relegation to secret articles of the clauses concerning Prussia and
the Netherlands.

anticipation to appoint Prince Dimitri Volkonski to be its Governor.

All this was not to the taste of Austria, whose general, Wallis, was still forbidden to go to the assistance of the Neapolitans. The Emperor did not consider himself obliged to help his father-in-law unless the French took the offensive. As the King had taken the offensive he must abide by the consequences. Paul, however, did not take this view. On December 6, 1798, the Directory had retorted by declaring war, not only on the King of the Two Sicilies but also on the King of Sardinia, and almost immediately afterwards had occupied the capitals of both these Sovereigns. The Czar's relations with Turin had been compromised in 1797 by some impertinent remarks made by the Sardinian chargé d'affaires, Bossi, on the subject of the reform of costume ordered by Catherine's successor. But Paul was now willing to forget this. It was necessary to go with all speed to the rescue of these new victims of revolutionary aggression.

Unfortunately, England and Austria were still quarrelling about subsidies, England alleging that the Court of Vienna had taken her money and wanted more but had not put a single man in motion. The Court of St. James's therefore refused to ratify an agreement concluded at St. Petersburg by Paul's mediation on the subject of subsidies and loans between Whitworth and Cobenzl. Paul was for a moment annoyed with London but soon saw that his abuse was misdirected. On the 20/31 December, therefore, he addressed a characteristic rescript to Razoumovski to the effect that " further hesitation on the part of Austria would awaken suspicion of treachery in her allies. If this attitude were not immediately changed the Russian troops would receive orders to turn back."

Thugut multiplied his excuses. It was their intention, he said, to make war and to prosecute it with the greatest vigour, with the object not merely of turning the French out of Italy but of annihilating them. Thereafter, if Russia would lend 60,000 men, they would invade France from the south, where the population was most hostile to the Directory, under cover of an insurrection which would be fomented in Switzerland. But the season was as yet unsuitable and the long-prepared rupture of the Congress of Rastadt must not be precipitated, nor must the Directory be put on its guard too soon. Razoumovski thought these reasons excellent and did his best to urge them in his despatches. But Cobenzl reported that the Czar's patience would stand no further trial and new proposals were made from Vienna to St. Petersburg.

As war had actually broken out in Italy, would not the Czar consent to use Rosenberg's force there to held the dispossessed Sovereigns whose interests his Majesty had so much at heart ? They would try to do without him on the Rhine, and his troops could be united with those of General Herrmann already intended for Italy—thus forming with the Austrian contingent a powerful army of which the Archduke Joseph would take command. This Prince lacked experience : Thugut therefore suggested to the Czar that Field-Marshal Souvorof, who had already covered himself with glory in company with the Austrians in the last Turkish campaign, should be appointed to assist him.

Paul was at once flattered and embarrassed by the proposal. The Archduke Joseph was already affianced to the unhappy Alexandrina, for whose disappointments this marriage was a slender consolation and who was destined to undergo still further cruel trials. The suggestion therefore seemed to give Russia precisely that commanding position in the coalition which the Czar most ardently desired. His bellicose ardour had moreover been intensified by the treaty of alliance which his envoy had just signed with Turkey, which was soon to receive the adherence of England. This assured the co-operation of these two Powers against France, with imposing forces by land and sea. But Souvorof was in exile and in disgrace, and Paul was still sceptical about the military capacity of a man who did not understand the Prussian regulations.

His pride carried the day. In an autograph letter the Emperor pressed the old soldier whom he had treated so badly to accept the proffered command. But when Cobenzl spoke of the victories which the allies were sure to win under such a leader, Paul shook his head and said, " I wash my hands of it ! " At the same time he wrote to General Herrmann and charged him to keep an eye on " the enterprises in which this old warrior might engage to the prejudice of the troops and the cause which were to be confided to him."

Souvorof accepted, but it could not reasonably be supposed that he would submit to any kind of guardianship, more especially from a general without a military record. But Herrmann was not called upon to try. He was employed elsewhere, and the Archduke, having married Paul's daughter in March, also gave up the idea of winning laurels for himself in Italy. Souvorof therefore retained alone the command for which he was considered so unfit, and he himself was in his turn called upon to assume the duties of mentor. For Paul, with a new inconsequence, sent his younger son Constantine to the war in order that he might serve his apprenticeship under the man whom his father despised.

Thus was prepared the immortal campaign in which the Russian arms were to triumph, though Russia herself was not to win the slightest benefit, and in which at the moment of going to war the allies were quite at variance, alike as to the object to be pursued and the means by which it was to be attained.

VI

Negotiations were still proceeding not only at Rastadt but at Berlin, where Repnine's departure had not terminated the obviously useless pourparlers in which the Emperor had so unsuccessfully intervened. Panine, whose blind and credulous Prussomania Thugut so often denounced, was now becoming practically the master of Russian foreign policy. Bezborodko's departure had left the Department of Foreign Affairs in complete disorder, and the Ministerial crisis which followed coincided with a sort of eclipse of Prussian diplomacy on the banks of the Neva. In 1797 Tauentzien had been replaced by General von Groeben, who on the parade-ground was everything that Paul could desire, but was of no other use whatever.

At Berlin all attempts at an understanding, whether on the side of France or on the other, failed on the question of compensation. Panine and Sieyès, working on parallel lines to obtain a declaration of equal disinterestedness from Prussia and Austria, shared the same discomfiture. The arrival of Thomas Grenville at the end of 1798 merely frightened the Ministry and increased their reserve. Panine thought that Haugwitz and his colleagues were only restrained from joining Austria and England against France by the fear that they might be anticipated by the attack of the Republican armies. He was instructed in the first week of 1799 to take a decisive step with a view to dissipating these fears and the resulting hesitations, and he communicated the Anglo-Russian treaty to the Prussian Court, categorically demanding the adherence of Prussia, and offering a Russian force of 45,000 men under Prince Galitzine, which was to be joined to the Prussian troops, together with a promise of the Czar's energetic support of any suitable compensation which might be asked for the House of Brandenburg and the House of Orange. In case of refusal he was to leave at once for Carlsbad, where his presence was required to prevent a quarrel in the Imperial family, for the wife of the Grand Duke Constantine was at that watering-place, having quarrelled violently with her husband, and threatened to refuse to return to St. Petersburg.

The result might have been foreseen. The King evaded demands for audiences and his ministers cried out that the Russians were trying to compromise them. Panine contented himself with refusing to take part in a masquerade organised by the young Queen and hoped to profit by an apparent tension in the relations between Haugwitz and Sieyès. But the last thing the Government of Frederick William desired was a quarrel with the representative of the Directory. The requisition from St. Petersburg inclined them, no doubt, to effect a *rapprochement* with England, but only in view of an alliance " for the defence of the security of the north of Europe," and this, in their opinion, meant war, not with France but with Russia, from whom they imagined Prussia had reason to fear an attack. Haugwitz said so openly to Thomas Grenville, and later on Panine himself boasted of having prevented an explosion of hostilities between the two countries.

But the Envoy Extraordinary of the Court of St. James's was equally unsuccessful in obtaining what he was instructed to demand. Haugwitz had at first been tempted by the subsidies. The King was for a peremptory refusal, but the Minister insisted that they should at least treat with a man whose hands were full of such persuasive arguments. The English envoy, however, requested a definite answer on March 7, 1799, and received one which cannot have been satisfactory. It was to the effect that " Prussia could not for the moment abandon her position of neutrality, but reserved the right to join Russia and England if the French made any new encroachments."

Austria had practically taken no part in these sterile discussions. But the new Austrian Ambassador at St. Petersburg, Count Dietrichstein, was inclined to take a short way with Prussia and to adopt Paul's formula: " He that is not with me is against me." The Czar, though now under Panine's influence, was eager to apply this maxim to a Court which was abusing his long-suffering kindness and which even refused to second the measures he proposed to put an end to the jacobin ascendency in Hamburg—a refusal which (had Paul but known it) Haugwitz was using to make interest with the " execrable Sieyès." On March 22, 1799 (old style), Groeben was requested to transmit immediately to Berlin a final appeal. Once and for all did Prussia intend to make common cause with Russia, or was it her intention to make common cause with the enemies of that Power? The envoy, much moved, the same day sent off his secretary, Scholtz, who reached his destination on April 2. The result was that four days later a letter, *not even in cypher*, was sent to St. Petersburg *by the ordinary post*, simply saying that for the moment the King had nothing to add to his previous communications. He could not send a more explicit reply before the return of a courier sent to London by Thomas Grenville. In reality this courier had already returned to Berlin, but he had not brought what Haugwitz expected to receive before he would consent to treat with the coalition. That was precisely the same thing that, in 1795, Hardenberg had waited for at Bâle before he broke with France, namely, English gold. In exchange for hard cash Frederick William III, like his predecessor, might be inclined to give the allies fair words. But Pitt refused to give a single sovereign except in exchange for a formal engagement on the part of Prussia to open hostilities against the Republic forthwith. In these circumstances the King and his counsellors thought the best course was to maintain the position they had hitherto occupied and to keep St. Petersburg, and if possible London, uncertain about their real intentions. To do this they did not stick at lying.

On this occasion, so far as the Czar was concerned, the lie was aggravated by impertinence, and it is hard to believe that Paul, in spite of this, allowed Panine to remain at Berlin and pressed Thomas Grenville to stay there too. Yet it was only in June, after the departure of Sieyès, who had been made a member of the Directory, that the Russian envoy decided to leave for Carlsbad. Even then, as the Czar moved his troops stationed in Lithuania nearer the frontier and sent a squadron to cruise off Dantzic, the obstinate Prussomaniac returned once more to still the tempest and make another attempt at a reconciliation.

This return was so unexpected that it seriously alarmed the French chargé d'affaires, who at a later date erroneously supposed that it was only the remonstrances sent by Sandoz from Paris which prevented the Prussian ministers from taking a decision hostile to the Republic against the wishes of the King. Neither Frederick William nor his representatives at Paris required to put himself about. Panine had guaranteed that Prussia ran no serious risk from Russia, so Haugwitz and his colleagues returned zealously to their old plan of doing nothing and committing themselves to nobody, while trying their best to get as much as possible out of all parties.

Paul finally saw that he had nothing to expect either from them or from their master. He was always prone to violent measures, so, when Panine returned to Carlsbad, the chargé d'affaires was ordered to remove the whole staff of the Embassy and even the archives from Berlin. The diplomatic rupture was complete, but that was all. Paul exacted no vengeance for his disappointment and, as was even more strange, he appointed Panine, who was the cause of it, who had mismanaged the negotiations, and had rebelled against carrying out his master's plans, as the successor of Kotchoubey in the post of Vice-Chancellor.

It is true that at this time the Chancelleries had no more to say. It had been vain for Panine, neglecting his instructions, to do his best to support the Cabinet of Berlin in their opposition to the break-up of the Congress of Rastadt. The advance of the Russian troops, which led to a renewal of the French ultimatum, produced a contrary and much more decisive effect. The interruption of the negotiations, the effective opening of the campaign on both sides, alike on the Rhine and in Switzerland, and the sinister intervention of the Austrian *Szeklers,* had put diplomacy and the policy of delay out of court. Violent counsels carried the day, and the clamours which were aroused by the assassination of the French plenipotentiaries had their tragic echo in the news of the defeats of the French army in Italy.

CHAPTER XI

SOUVOROF IN ITALY

I

ATTACKED in Italy and threatened in Germany, France showed a fine courage in again accepting the challenge of the coalition which so constantly revived and to which were now added " the Barbarians of the North." But the energy of her preparations were not equal to the boldness of her defiance. For a year back the Directory had uttered many patriotic sentiments ; but, embarrassed by internal dissensions, disordered finances and the robberies of contractors, the Government had done almost nothing to make the resources of the country fit for the demands which were to be made upon them. And yet it was their intention not only to defend the positions already occupied but to take the offensive almost everywhere on the whole vast line of battle, which extended from the Adriatic to the North Sea.

There was an army of observation in Holland to oppose an anticipated landing of England and Russia, and another and stronger army of observation on the Rhine to cover the left flank of the army operating on the Danube and intended to start from Strasburg and effect the conquest of Swabia and Bavaria. There was a second great Franco-Swiss army, whose task was to secure the possession of the Alps for France, a third which was to roll the Austrians back into Italy beyond the Isonzo, while a corps of observation held Naples and all the south of the Peninsula. Such was the plan of campaign conceived at Paris, for the execution of which they reckoned to put in the field nearly half

260

a million men, according to the calculation of the report left by Schérer for his successor when he left the Ministry of War for the command of the army of Italy. But these forces existed only on paper. The available contingents in reality amounted to exactly one-third of the estimated number. There were 146,417 men in all, of whom 10,000 were Swiss, ill-equipped and for the most part ill-disposed. This was all they had with which to face the formidable onset of the nations, among which Austria alone put forward almost double the number of men in the whole available army of France ! The disproportion of the forces on the one side and on the other was enormous.

Ill-proportioned as they were to its means, the attitude of the French Government, its grandiloquence and the boldness of its designs gave France certain advantages. The coalition was impressed and met audacity with timidity, one consequence of which was the concentration of all the available forces of the allies in Italy. This in a general way diminished the danger which the French had to face, but it made their numerical inferiority at a single point all the more marked.

At the end of April 1799 it was known that the arrival of the Russians in Italy was imminent. Two thousand English troops landed simultaneously at Messina, and, according to Italinski, then Russian Minister at Naples, there was such a panic among the Republicans that they precipitately abandoned most of the territory they occupied and were barely able to hold Naples and Capua. This was a slight if pardonable exaggeration, though the Directory were in fact exceedingly anxious. They had taken the measure of all the other opponents of the Revolution : they knew nothing of these new adversaries. Kosciuszko, who had returned from America and was at Paris as the delegate of Congress, was called upon to supply the deficiency. He drew up a memoir, which was circulated among the French general officers in Italy and which was on the whole encouraging. The Czar's men were tall and strong, disciplined to blind obedience, but incapable of initiative and reduced by barbarous treatment. The officers were brave but very ignorant. The Russian cavalry was rather imposing than really to be dreaded, and the only part of the army which deserved unmixed commendation was the Cossacks, who were most useful for reconnoitring. He passed over in silence the leader of this army, whose presence was destined to have such an important influence on the issue of the battles in which he took part. They had therefore no idea in the French camp that the severest blows of the campaign would come from the warrior who was so little known in Western Europe ; but it must be said that as his colleagues on his own side came to know him better they were equally far from realising his merit.

II

Souvorof's manners and behaviour were disconcerting in their strangeness. As at Kontchanskoïé, he dined at eight o'clock in the morning and remained three hours at table. He then at once went to bed and did not rise until four in the afternoon. This curious practice was in itself sufficient to prevent him from taking part seriously in the military operations which it was his duty to direct. In fact, according to the report of Wickham, the British Agent in Switzerland, Souvorof never took the trouble to visit a post or reconnoitre a position. " All the plans of attack and for marches were made by the Austrian staff officers. . . . The Marshal was rarely present at the execution of them and remained for the most part invisible to the army."

Wickham thought him more than half mad, and this opinion was shared by Whitworth, who a year previously had already represented this to Grenville. The appearance of the great warrior was such that the Austrian people who saw him were also tempted to take this view. On his way to Vienna Souvorof attracted crowds in every town by his innumerable extravagances and absurdities. Half-naked and strangely accoutred, he used to harangue them in a German which was as unintelligible as his French. He entered all the convents and covered himself with scapularies and relics, stopped at every wayside shrine to mutter prayers, and in terms alternately pathetic and grotesque he begged for the benedictions and the prayers of every priest or monk whom he met.

When he arrived at the capital on March 15, 1799, he cried out, " *Vive Joseph !* " at the top of his voice, and when he was checked and reminded that the name of the reigning Sovereign was Francis he displayed the greatest astonishment. " God is my witness that I didn't know ! " He would not stay at the Embassy until all the mirrors, pictures, bronzes, and other objects of comfort or luxury had been removed from the apartments which had been prepared for him, and then he slept in a bare room on a truss of hay.

When he met the leading personages of the Court and of the Aulic Council of War (*Hofkriegsrath*) he refused to communicate to them his plan of campaign. He had none, he said, and must first survey the ground on which he would have to operate. All he did was to hand to each member of the council a little book which, he said, contained the secret of the victories which the allied armies were about to win. It was the study on *The Art of Conquest* which remained unpublished during its author's lifetime and appeared comparatively recently with a commentary by General Dragomirof.* The extraordinary man to whom, in spite of all, Austria decided to commit the fortune of her arms revealed in it something of the transcendant genius which was to triumph over the science and the valour of some of the best French generals. But neither in this small treatise nor elsewhere did Souvorof indicate the chief

* Paris, 1899.

instrument of his triumphs. The secret of these lay in himself, in a spirit and a temper which were strange and, indeed, near akin to madness, but which, even in his declining years, were the source of a great vitality and of his ascendency over others. Even his personal habits, much as they shocked good judges, were not, as was supposed, incompatible with the duties of a commander-in-chief. On the contrary, they had much to do with the remarkable results which he achieved. Souvorof's soldiers, eating and sleeping at the same hours as he, were capable of extremely long and rapid marches. At midnight the Marshal despatched the men who looked after the cooking. Three hours later their comrades started, taking an hour of rest between each stage of seven versts ; and at eight in the morning, having covered five or six leagues, they found their repast ready for them. After eating it, they slept like their general and started again in the same way at 4 P.M., reaching their camp, which was entirely ready beforehand to receive them, at eight or ten in the evening.

During the hot season in Italy this arrangement was particularly agreeable to the Russian troops ; but without the slightest compulsion they would have accepted any other uncomplainingly, so completely were they subdued and fascinated by the strange man who led them. Even at Vienna Souvorof had no difficulty in disarming the distrust and repugnance which his manners naturally aroused. His oddities, originally the product of an impulsive nature with a bent towards a sort of facetious eccentricity, were also to some extent deliberate and calculated. He used them as a kind of screen behind which he hid his real nature, which was a curious mixture of strength and suppleness, of candour and extreme cunning. But he knew how to reveal himself at the right moment, and, no less than his councillors, Francis II was so completely hypnotised by his portentous visitor that the plan of subordinating him to an archduke was immediately abandoned. In order to keep up appearances it was decided to make him an Austrian as well as a Russian marshal, and with that Souvorof took command of the allied armies without having given any one an inkling of how he meant to use them.

The contribution he brought with him was numerically very weak, consisting as it did of barely 17,000 men under Rosenberg, who were already on their way to Italy. Herrmann's corps, now under General Rehbinder, had not yet crossed the Russian frontier. That of Rimski-Korsakof, subsidised by England, and the men under the orders of the Prince de Condé, were still destined to take part in the operations on the Rhine. Moreover, Rosenberg's men had nothing but their muskets, their sabres and a few guns. There was no commissariat, no financial administration, no light artillery, no pontoons, no ammunition, no staff. The Austrians had to provide all that, and Korsakof was on the point of arriving in the same condition. When the Archduke Charles asked him how he would find supplies for his troops, he replied, " I have my Cossacks ! "

Souvorof's chief difficulties were due to his comrades in arms. The *Hofkriegsrath* did not scruple to give orders to the new Commander-in-Chief and at a later stage to intervene in the conduct of operations by imperative directions from Vienna. Souvorof was quite prepared to ignore all these instructions had it not been that the very constitution of his forces made all independence impossible. Two-thirds of the *personnel* of his army (35,000 out of 52,000) were Austrians. In *matériel* the disproportion was even more strongly against the Russians. Thus the plans for marches and the orders for battle were bound to be Austrian, since there was nothing and no one on the Russian side who could furnish these.

From this point of view the choice of Souvorof as Commander-in-Chief must be regarded as a mistake. He had not hitherto made war in Europe and he was quite a stranger to the new methods of warfare which were being evolved in the armies of the West. Though an enemy of the French Revolution, he, too, was a revolutionary in his way, and would have none of the conventions and traditions to which the Austrian generals still clung. He moved in that sphere which is above all art and in which genius, free from methods and principles, draws its force only from personality and inspiration. In this powerful individualism again he had a spiritual affinity with some of the Republican generals, and on this occasion at least he was to prove that he was their master.

Between him and the Viennese camarilla, which, beaten one moment, invariably returned to its stiffness and its routine the next, there was an absolute and irremediable incompatibility of temper. Their military divergences were aggravated by a serious difference of opinion in the political spheres.

When he left St. Petersburg Souvorof had received strict orders to restore the Sardinian States to their legitimate possessor, who had fled to Cagliari and was anxiously following the movements of the coalition. When he left Vienna the Marshal found himself armed with instructions from the Holy Roman Emperor which said nothing of the restoration of the dynasty of Savoy in Piedmont but insisted on the immediate re-establishment of the Imperial authority in Lombardy. The Commander of the Army of Italy was above all things a soldier, and did not allow himself to be embarrassed by the conflict of ideas which thus appeared between the two masters whom he was now to serve. He was in too great a hurry to fight.

III

Before he could reach the front, fortune, from the Rhine to the Apennines, had already turned against France. Masséna had pushed boldly forward into the Grisons, but Jourdan, attacked by the Archduke Charles and weakened

266

by helping Bernadotte, had been pushed back. In Italy
Schérer had won some reputation by his victory of Loano
(November 23, 1795) ; but he was old, worn-out and apoplectic and hated by his troops. The resistance he opposed
to Kray was but feeble, and between March 25 and April 5
he was beaten at Pastrengo and Magnano and compelled
to recross the Mincio and even the Adda. Counting Italians
and Poles the French had in this part of the world barely
30,000 men, maladroitly scattered. But Moreau succeeded
to the command and all was changed. He took measures
for a rapid concentration and summoned Macdonald from
the south.

Souvorof's first thought, and his real plan which he would
not disclose at Vienna, was to prevent him from reuniting
these separated bodies of troops. The allies, especially
the Russians, were pushed forward by forced marches,
covering sometimes as much as sixty-five kilometres a day,
and advanced with such precipitation that the Austrian
staff were nearly driven mad ; but, having left Vienna on
April 4, Souvorof a fortnight later had advanced his main
body more than a hundred leagues. On the 19th he determined to take the offensive, and on the 27th Moreau was
taken by surprise, lost 7000 men at Cassano, and with the
passage of the Adda he left the way to Milan open to the
allies.

The following day Dénissof's Cossacks were the first to
enter the city. Souvorof followed them closely, making his
entry by the same triumphal road that Bonaparte traversed
in 1796. At first sight he made the same sort of impression
as the earlier conqueror. Equally ill-dressed and equally
ill-mounted on a wretched Cossack horse, the Marshal,
like Bonaparte, had nothing of the gigantic and terrible
conqueror expected by the crowd. But Bonaparte had
fascinated or quelled the spectators by his imperious and
tragic countenance, the flame of his eyes, his masterful
gestures. Souvorof's grimaces under the enormous helmet

267

decorated with the Austrian colours which he affected, his little blinking eyes, his grotesque movements, the whip with which he waved benedictions in response to the acclamations of the crowd—all this was merely disconcerting. Meeting General Mélas he seized upon him to embrace him, thereby startling his horse, which threw the general to the ground. Souvorof took no notice but pursued his way to the first church, where he alighted and prostrated himself before the high altar.

Lombardy was conquered and Souvorof stayed three days in the capital to organise a provisional Government. Contrary to what might have been expected he delayed to follow up the advantage he had gained. His further plan was to cut off Moreau from the road to Genoa via Novi across the Bocchetta, and to prevent his junction with Macdonald. But he was already paralysed by the Austrian staff. They alone commanded the sources of information and they reported the junction of the two generals as imminent when one was still separated from the other by three-quarters of the length of Italy. Moreau thus had time to reorganise his force between Valenza and Alessandria, though his position was much more critical than his adversaries imagined. He could not hope to be joined by Macdonald before he was again attacked. There was no possibility of reinforcements from Switzerland or France, and everywhere the country had risen against him. By his mere appearance Souvorof had carried out one of the first obligations imposed on him from Vienna, which was to bring about this rising. The governments set up by France fell to pieces like houses of cards, the Republican authorities vanished, the democrats took to flight. The priests, more popular than ever, preached a holy war, and if Souvorof had not the prestige of Bonaparte, his Russians, fanatical and superstitious in religion exactly like their Italian hosts, became extremely popular. They in their turn passed as liberators.

After too long a hesitation Souvorof at last crossed the Ticino, and Moreau had to fall back again, retreating in the direction of Asti. When he was out of sight the allies marched on Turin, which they occupied without opposition on May 25. The same day Gardane surrendered Alessandria, shutting himself up in the citadel. The French had evacuated the citadel of Milan on the 23rd. In this region they now held only Genoa, Mantua, Coni and the citadels of Alessandria and Tortona. Thanks to the superiority of their forces and the rapidity of their first movements, the allies had in less than two months reconquered the whole of the north of Italy. They had not, however, annihilated Moreau, though for a moment it had been in their power to do so, and therefore what they had achieved, though brilliant, was not at all decisive, and it was soon to be compromised by the combined efforts of the Austrian staff and Viennese diplomacy.

The news of the assassination of the French plenipotentiaries at the Congress of Rastadt (April 28) arrived at this moment. This event discredited the coalition and excited such violent indignation in France as could not fail to re-act on the Italian campaign. At Turin, meanwhile, Souvorof was more and more misled and held in check by his Austrian entourage. He made another triumphal entry, appeared in splendid processions, attended a *Te Deum*, presided over banquets at which his bust was displayed in place of Bonaparte's, and gave audiences at which he surprised the Piedmontese by the vigour of his mind while he astonished them by the strangeness of his language and appearance. In his presence the Austrian generals had the air of corporals. But amid all this pageantry Souvorof was wasting time. Already the rebellion against the French was becoming a revolutionary massacre, and, though they looked like corporals, the Austrian generals were the masters of the situation. Souvorof announced the return of the King; they took possession of the citadel of Turin in the name of the Emperor !

Thugut, on the other hand, now began to reprove the encouragement which had been given to the local insurrections, although in favouring them the Marshal had merely given effect to the orders of Francis II. To encourage sedition, said the Minister, was to play the revolutionary game. He objected equally to the return of the King. Austria meant to keep Piedmont as a hostage until the general pacification. Criticisms and counter-orders now began to fall in an uninterrupted shower from Vienna, making it impossible to carry out any concerted plan.

The situation was like that which arose between Bonaparte and the Directory, but there was a great difference. Souvorof had no resource but to fly into a passion. He did not understand politics, which interested him but little. His business was to fight. But for fighting the favourable hour had passed. Macdonald had succeeded in joining Moreau.

IV

When he was summoned north by Schérer in the month of April, Macdonald had to leave Naples on May 7 at the very moment when the Royalists were again taking the offensive with Cardinal Ruffo at their head, and were driving the French out of Calabria and helping the English to land men from their fleet, which was blockading the town. He left small garrisons at Gaeta, at Capua, and at the Castle of St. Elmo, and therefore could only take about 19,000 men with him. He crossed the Abruzzi, which were already in revolt, and arrived at Rome only to see the Republic crumble before the popular fury. He was reinforced, but again had to weaken his force by leaving garrisons at Rome, Civita-Vecchia, Perugia and Ancona, while an advance guard of 4000 Poles under Dombrowski, which he sent into Tuscany, was overwhelmed by insurrectionary bodies. Still he advanced, and at Florence on May 24 he picked up the corps of Montrichard and Gauthier. Soon afterwards, having got together 24,000 men, he got into touch with Moreau's right, under Victor. His forces were thus raised to 36,000 men, and his plan was to march on Parma and Piacenza via Bologna. Moreau had still 14,000 men, and he on his part would cross the Bocchetta; and, once united, the two generals were certain of a prompt revenge.

This confidence did not spring merely from the heroic exaltation which the Republican armies drew from the revolutionary spirit and from the almost unvarying success which had attended them during the seven previous years. The allies had been constantly reinforced and now had close on 100,000 men in Italy. But they were always ill-informed and the prey of false alarms, and Souvorof, in his endeavour to protect himself on all sides, scattered his forces and made the same mistake as Schérer. Under Turin he had only 20,000 men. It was only at the beginning of June that he divined a concentration of the French towards Genoa. He began to concentrate at Alessandria, but it was Tortona, on the other side of the Apennines at which his opponents were aiming.

On June 11 Macdonald crossed the mountains, crushed an Austrian corps of 5000 men near Modena, marched towards the Po and threatened Souvorof's line of retreat. If Moreau could but join hands with him the game was won. But Moreau, though an incomparable manœuvrer, and though he was much superior to the Austrians in knowledge and inspiration, was after all a man of their generation and quite as deficient as they in prompt and bold initiative. Neither he nor Macdonald had much of the power of rapid decision, of the audacity, the thirst for battle at any risk which made the fortunes of the greater figures in the revolutionary *épopée*. At this critical moment it was Souvorof who displayed just these qualities and turned them against the French.

Leaving Bellegarde with 14,000 men at Alessandria to wait for Moreau and cover the threatened line of retreat, he rushed on Macdonald with 10,000 Austrians under Mélas, Frölich and Lichtenstein, and 14,000 Russians under Chveïkovski, Förster and Rosenberg. He was, or said that he was, convinced that he would prevent the junction with Moreau. He announced to his soldiers that victory was certain, infallible. He taught them to cry out in French, " *Bas les armes !* " and " *Pardon !* " Nevertheless, he strongly fortified a bridge over the Po in case of accidents, though he said nothing of this to his soldiers, whose march he quickened by assurances of an easy victory.

Moreau afterwards described this march as a masterpiece. The allies crossed the Bormida on June 15, on the next day but one they were already on the Tidone—that is to say, they had covered nearly ninety kilometres—and at once, without giving his troops an hour of repose, Souvorof joined battle. The fight took place to the west of the parallel course of the Tidone and the Trebbia, two tributaries of the Po, whose banks have for centuries been the scene of similar combats. On the Trebbia, in 218 B.C., Hannibal measured himself against the Consul Sempronius. On the Tidone, in 1746, a Franco-Spanish army beat the Germans and the Sardinians. Strangely enough, too, it was in this corner of Italy for which the Austrians were fighting the French, that Russians and Poles came to blows for the first time in the war. In a fratricidal struggle Slavonic blood was to flow in a quarrel in which neither Russians nor Poles had any interest !

Macdonald had not expected to be attacked so soon, and the formation of his march (nearly twenty leagues deep) was too much extended. He had only 22,000 men and Moreau was still far off. But the future Marshal put a good face upon the matter and the first day's fighting was indecisive. The heat was intense and greatly incommoded the Russians. Souvorof, clad only in his shirt, surpassed himself. As Wickham points out, he neglected to reconnoitre the positions before the battle, but when the fighting began he was everywhere in person. Towards three o'clock in the afternoon the French were making some progress, but he charged them with a regiment of Cossacks and finally succeeded in thrusting them behind the Tidone.

Next day he had a second bridge built over the Po near Tarpanese, to receive the reinforcements he expected from Kray and to secure his rear. He announced to his soldiers that they had only to pursue a beaten enemy, but he foresaw that the second day would be harder, and he was right. The Poles performed prodigies of valour, and Macdonald now had the divisions of Montrichard and Ollivier. But again Souvorof inspired Russians and Austrians alike with his own spirit and again the day was won. The French were driven back on the right bank of the Trebbia. Their defeat would have been more complete if Mélas had not held back Frölich's division, which had been left in reserve but had been summoned by the Marshal at the last moment.

On the third day the Poles, as usual, were first in the field. Rosenberg and Bagration, Souvorof's favourite aide-de-camp, having driven them back, ventured too far in pursuit, and the situation became so critical for the allies that the Marshal was pressed by his staff to order a retreat. Exhausted with fatigue Souvorof (in his shirt, as usual) was lying on a large stone. " Can you move this rock ? " he answered. It was then announced that the Russian regiments of Chvéïkovski and Förster were themselves on the point of giving way. " If that is so," said the Marshal, " give me my horse." Immediately afterwards he threw himself into the fray as he had done the day before and with the same result. The French had once more to cross the Trebbia.

This result, gained at the price of such efforts and such losses, was in itself by no means brilliant, and it gave rise to bitter quarrels in the camp of the victors. The Russians

reproached the Austrians with having insufficiently supported them on the right, and to excuse himself Mélas
quoted the orders of the *Hofkriegsrath*. On the third day,
in obedience to their orders, he had nearly left the field of
battle. Souvorof nevertheless had secured essentially what
he wanted. Macdonald, much weakened by these three terrible days, decided to retreat without waiting for Moreau, of
whom he had heard nothing. The Marshal profited by this
to advance his columns. On June 20 Mélas was already
at Piacenza, where, in the hospitals, he captured four
French generals and many others of their wounded. The
retreat of the vanquished became a flight. The next
day Moreau debouched into the valley of the Trebbia. He
had been detained at Novi by Bellegarde, whom he had had
to thrust aside. Now his only resource was to manœuvre
so as to dissemble from Souvorof a march which brought
him hurriedly back behind the Apennines towards Genoa.
Meanwhile the citadel of Turin surrendered, and it only
remained for the allies to cross the mountains in their turn
and to finish the work of the campaign on the Riviera.
Unfortunately for them their internal dissensions became
more serious at this very time.

V

From May onwards the idea at Vienna had been to prevent Souvorof from advancing towards the south or in any
other direction before he had solidly occupied all the
northern fortresses. In the political sphere Thugut had
more and more energetically opposed the measures taken
by the Marshal for the restoration of the King of Sardinia
to his dominions. The result was that, after all his energy
and valour, the victor of the Trebbia received a letter full
of reproaches. He was blamed for having retarded the siege
of Mantua. The disposition of his troops was described as
maladroit. The *Hofkriegsrath* absolutely refused to send

reinforcements and claimed to dispose as they pleased of the Austrian corps under Weissmann and even of the Russians under Rehbinder. The successes of the Commander-in-Chief were scarcely mentioned, and the Marshal was congratulated on his " good fortune." This was what wounded the old warrior more than anything.

Souvorof wrote a letter of remonstrance to Razoumovski : " It was my good fortune, says the Holy Roman Emperor. You won and you want troops ! What would you want if you had been beaten ? This fool of a Minister does not know that in order to make use of a victory you want more troops ! They have taken Rehbinder away from me—my one ewe lamb ! That eminent personage, the Archduke Charles, won't even give me what he is ordered to give. . . . My last victories cost me nearly 5000 men. The *Bestimmtsager* are making me lose more than 10,000. . . . Does this silly and timid Cabinet know that a siege can't be carried out without being covered by a corps of observation ? "

But Razoumovski was incapable of establishing this plea and the Austrian staff shared the hostility of the Viennese Council to the Russian general. They even exaggerated the orders they received, and Souvorof, after occupying Piacenza with his victorious troops, was practically reduced to immobility and restricted to superintending the sieges of Alessandria, Mantua and Tortona. He sent three plans to crush the French on the Riviera one after another to Vienna, but they insisted that he should wait for the fall of Mantua, which did not come till July 28. By this time the skill and energy of Moreau had already refashioned an army out of the wreckage which, according to Gouvion-Saint-Cyr, might have been utterly destroyed by an energetic pursuit.

Meanwhile the Directory had been reconstituted, and the events of the 30th Prairial (June 18) had given a fresh impetus to the conduct of the war on the side of the French.

Bernadotte took the Ministry of War. Fortunately for the allies his first act was ill-inspired. He recalled Moreau to the Rhine to command an army which was still to be embodied. Championnet was to command an army of the Alps which was in the same position, while Joubert, one of the rivals of Bonaparte, was to replace Macdonald and Moreau in command of the troops which they had succeeded in reorganising and uniting and which now amounted to 45,000 men.

The new French Commander-in-Chief arrived at the headquarters at Conegliano on August 4. Moreau agreed to remain for a time and assist him with his advice, and both agreed that the force at their disposal was insufficient to confront the allies, who were much superior in numbers and were emboldened by their successes, and that they should not attempt a vigorous offensive until Championnet's army came into action. The two generals were, however, overruled by new instructions from Paris, where the Directory was itself fighting for bare existence and insisted on a military triumph immediately. The generals must have recourse to audacity, must as soon as possible have their revenge for the checks of Cassano and the Trebbia and raise the siege of Mantua. Thus, against the will of Joubert and Moreau, the foolish march on Novi was decided upon.

Mantua had already fallen. Souvorof had made another of his triumphal entries and had added another touch to the legend of his personality by making his faithful Prochka (a servant quite worthy of his master) give him a douche in the principal square of the town in the presence of the astonished population. But in the midst of his quarrels with the Austrians the Marshal did not forget that his new conquest once more left him free to fight. When he heard of the French advance he was overjoyed. Leaving more than 13,000 men at Tortona, he had nearly 60,000 with which to attack his rash enemies, who, being obliged to cover their retreat, could not bring all their forces into battle and would be outnumbered by nearly two to one.

On hearing of the fall of Mantua and of the march of Souvorof, the French Council of War was for retreat while there was yet time, but Joubert could not make up his mind and Moreau was not the man to overcome his irresolution. A day was lost in deliberation and the next day Souvorof was there. Joubert was mortally wounded early in the battle and handed over the command to Moreau. All that the obstinate Breton could do was to dispute the victory (which, in spite of the inequality of the forces, hung in the balance) for more than sixteen hours of sanguinary conflict, which was finally decided in favour of the allies by the arrival of Mélas with fresh Austrian troops from Rivalta.

The French lost 6500 men killed and wounded, and left 4500 prisoners in the hands of the allies, among whom were Generals Pérignon, Grouchy, Colli and Partounaux. But the attack on the heights of Novi, which had had to be several times renewed, had also cost the allies dear, and discord more than ever reigned in their camp. In the opinion of the Austrian staff Souvorof, though victorious, had committed endless mistakes which had nearly led to disaster. He had mistaken the French troops which appeared under Novi for a detachment intended to mask the manœuvres of the main body, and had persisted in attacking with a small part of his force, thus losing the advantage of his superior numbers. Had it not been for Mélas, who came up without orders, the day would have been lost. The Marshal himself very honestly admitted this in a letter to Francis II.

In these circumstances it became difficult for the victors to reap the fruits of their victory. The French fled in disorder to the mountains. They could no longer defend the Riviera, the only territory which now remained in their possession in this part of Italy. Souvorof was now in a position to carry out the plan suggested to St. Petersburg by Vienna, and which, without letting any one know it, the Marshal had adopted for his own. Once Genoa was conquered the way to Paris by the south of France was open before him. The very evening of the battle which, however badly he had managed it, had resulted in a decisive triumph, he was arranging his march for the morrow. Alas! two days later he sent Mélas an order in the following terms : " No further pursuit will take place. The army will reoccupy its former positions."

VI

German historians usually attribute this sudden change of front to instructions received by Souvorof from St. Petersburg, which showed that Paul had cooled towards the coalition, or at least towards Austria. Some such hint may have been given to the Marshal at this time, but it did not compel him to abandon the advantage which had been so dearly bought. Russian historians seem to be nearer the truth in blaming the Austrian staff or the Court of Vienna. Even at Novi Souvorof had had two successive plans for a march on Genoa prepared by General Zach and Colonel Weyrother. The first, which involved all the allied troops, was formally vetoed by the Austrian Staff. Orders from Vienna forbade any operation of this kind. The Commander-in-Chief had himself been directed to detach 10,000 men to pacify Tuscany and Romagna, that is, to conquer them for Austria. Souvorof did not yet abandon his plan. He would march on Genoa with his Russians alone ! But immediately the Austrian transport made difficulties, alleging that they could not provide enough provisions or sufficient pack animals. Souvorof was furious and talked of resignation. He contented himself, however, for the moment with sending a sort of ultimatum to Razoumovski in the following terms : " (1) I must have full

liberty of action in order to sweep the French out of Italy.
(2) The *Hofkriegsrath* must be prevented from interfering
with my plans. (3) From Switzerland I am ready to go
either into Germany or France. Otherwise I have no
business here. I will go home."

The last lines of this message referred to a new plan of
campaign concerted between Vienna and St. Petersburg
under the influence of England, which at this moment was
beginning to exercise a preponderating influence on the
banks of the Neva. Bezborodko had died in April 1799,
struck with apoplexy, after an altercation with Paul, who
had ordered him at eleven o'clock at night to drag the
Prussian Minister out of bed in order to address to him a
new and more menacing summons to his Court to join the
Anglo-Russian alliance ! On the refusal of Vorontsof,
Rastoptchine took the direction of Foreign Affairs, but
the Czar showed his intention of enforcing his personal
wishes in this department, and the news which he was receiving from Italy made him less and less friendly to
Austria. He was much displeased with Razoumovski,
whose chief interests were women and dress, who, in spite
of an enormous fortune, was over head and ears in debt,
and whose chief care was to stand well with Thugut.
Paul thought of replacing him by Kalytchof, but decided to send the latter to superintend the Ambassador
and to intervene in Souvorof's discussions with the *Hofkriegsrath*.

On the other hand, the Court of St. James's, disquieted by
the ambitions which Austria was revealing in Italy, was
beginning to think that the Russians were playing the game
of the Hapsburgs rather too well. In May the English
Government had already demanded that Korsakof's force,
which, by the terms of the contract of subsidies, was at
their disposal, should be used for the deliverance of
Switzerland. At the end of June they formed the plan
of sending Souvorof himself to that country, whence,

reinforced by at least part of Korsakof's men, he could penetrate into France through Franche-Comté.

This was a modified version of the first Austrian plan, but at first the Viennese Cabinet showed themselves by no means disposed to favour it. The Archduke Charles was already in Switzerland with 90,000 men. That was a great many people for such a small country! The fact was that Thugut had spoken of invading France only in order to flatter the Czar. He had no intention of pushing things so far. But Paul's enthusiasm was aroused. After Souvorof's exploits he already believed him to be capable of bringing back Louis XVIII to his capital, and he wished the King to accompany the expedition, the Prince de Condé being placed under Souvorof's orders for the campaign. At this point Pitt raised objections. Once in France Paul's royal guest would have to act as King, and this would prejudice the military operations. Pitt proposed to send the Comte d'Artois instead, but Paul resisted this scheme in language worthy of *le Père Duchesne*. If the British Government were so fond of the brother of Louis XVIII they had only to give him the means of drinking and hunting without seeking to employ him in a situation which required prudence and good conduct.

While the discussion between London and St. Petersburg was proceeding on this point of detail Vienna suddenly gave way on the main issue. Thugut proposed that Rehbinder, originally intended for Naples, should join the army which was to operate in Switzerland and France. He too had begun to think that the Russians were *de trop* in Italy. It only remained to arrange for the combined movement of the Russian and Austrian troops.

The affair of Malta again made it difficult for the two Courts to come to an understanding. Thugut did not directly remonstrate against Paul's usurpation of the Grand Mastership, but he did not prevent Hompesch from issuing virulent protests on the subject from Trieste, where he had taken refuge and where he was acting in all respects as the head of the Order. Cobenzl was severely censured by his chief for having accepted the dignity of Bailiff of the Order, and the Archduke Palatine, when he went to St. Petersburg to be married, was forbidden to accept so much as a cross! In June 1799 Hompesch sent two of his agents to the part of Malta which had risen against the French, and Paul refused to allow Korsakof to move till Austria had made such acts impossible on the part of the ex-Grand Master. Cobenzl, on his own responsibility, agreed, but the news that the " Maltese bauble " had led the Czar to guarantee the integrity of Bavaria roused indignation in Vienna, and Thugut absolutely refused to recognise Paul's intervention in the affairs of the Order in any other capacity than that of protector. In July he gave way, announced Hompesch's resignation, and gave Paul to understand that he might now become Grand Master with the approbation of the Holy Roman Emperor, the Pope, and even the Spaniards. But Paul's annoyance had now been increased by Souvorof's reports and the relations of the two Courts remained strained.

At first Paul had received the Austrian criticisms of his Marshal with a certain satisfaction, but he soon began to feel that the victor of Cassano and the Trebbia was being treated somewhat too cavalierly, and at the end of July he somewhat peremptorily invited Francis II to keep his *Hofkriegsrath* in order. At the same time Razoumovski, accused by Kalytchof of taking part in " culpable intrigues," received a sharp reproof, and a rescript was addressed to Souvorof releasing him from all obedience to Francis II and ordering him to oppose in every way the selfish designs of Austria. If Austria attempted to take possession of the Italian provinces by force, or by means of an understanding with France, the Marshal was to act independently with the Russian forces.

Dated August 11 (new style) the rescript could not reach

Souvorof immediately after the Battle of Novi, nor could it therefore at that time have influenced the decision which we have recorded above. The Commander-in-Chief of the allied forces was simply unable to exercise his functions, and writing to the Czar after the victory of the Trebbia he had already asked for his recall. Paul replied by conferring on his Marshal the hereditary title of Prince of Italy, and by order of the Czar Kotchoubey addressed severe remonstrances to Cobenzl. Razoumovski was ordered to demand an audience of the Emperor and to say that " if this went on " Souvorof would be directed to leave the Austrians and continue the campaign with the English and the Neapolitans alone.

But Paul was still faithful to the cause which he had espoused. In June he had declared war on Spain, had dismissed the Spanish chargé d'affaires, and placed an embargo on Spanish vessels. In August, on account of a political club at Copenhagen, he forbade all Danish subjects to enter the Empire ; and he showed his displeasure with the Margrave of Baden, who had been induced to treat with the Government of the Republic. But in his eyes Austria was betraying that cause in every possible way and especially by enriching herself at the expense of the Sardinian territory, which Russia had helped to wrest from the French.

Charles Emmanuel II had agents both at St. Petersburg and with Souvorof, and had from the first done his utmost, with some success, to maintain and develop this feeling. Austria, on the other hand, claimed that her disinterestedness at the time of the second partition of Poland gave her a right to compensation in Italy. She had no wish to despoil the Sardinian monarch of all his possessions, but she maintained her right at any rate to the territory conquered from the Milanese in the war of the Spanish Succession. Paul, on his side, did not absolutely insist on the immediate return of the King of Sardinia, and did not object to the provisional occupation of Piedmont by the Austrians. He desired, however, that the Government should be administered in the name of the rightful Sovereign. He even assented to the Emperor's reclaiming the Milanese provinces, but he asked that this might be postponed. The first thing, in Rastoptchine's words, was to " exterminate the French."

As a matter of fact, Paul was finding unexpected difficulties in the rôle of protector and arbitrator to the Courts of Italy, and had already reached the stage of disillusion and repentance. Naples, too, was causing more trouble than he had foreseen. Rastoptchine regarded the Marchese di San Gallo, who came to St. Petersburg to help the Duke of Serra Capriola and who spoke of a partition of Italy in his master's interest, as a " charlatan " and an " imbecile." Towards the end of July Souvorof pointed out that the intention of the Court of Vienna to secure the lion's share of the country without the least regard to the general interests of Europe was becoming more and more evident. Paul could contain himself no longer. If they were going on fighting together it must be made clear what they were fighting about. Serra-Capriola and Gallo suggested a congress at St. Petersburg, and the Czar eagerly accepted the proposal.

Austria was alarmed and tried to effect a *rapprochement* with England. But Lord Minto had replaced Sir Morton Eden, whom Thugut had succeeded in rendering docile, and he urged Grenville to adopt the proposal of the Neapolitan diplomatists. The English minister changed his mind to the extent of objecting to the choice of St. Petersburg as a place of meeting, but he was resolutely opposed to any understanding which did not include Russia, the only Power capable of moderating Austrian ambitions. Cobenzl thought that Paul might be appeased if they would be pleased to treat his marshal better at Vienna. The Grand Cross of Maria Theresa or some similar distinction, if granted to the old warrior, might quiet the storm. But Thugut would hear of nothing. He called Souvorof a fool, and thought that Paul's protests against Austria's right to compensate herself in Italy for what she had not taken in Poland were discreditable. If this principle were questioned the partition should be done over again. Blamed by his chief and ill-used by Paul, Cobenzl's position at St. Petersburg was untenable. That of Razoumovski at Vienna was little better. In another devastating rescript Paul invited his envoy not to forget that he represented the Czar. In London, however, Austrian diplomacy was about to obtain a marked advantage against Souvorof, against Russia, and against the interests of the coalition.

VII

The Archduke Charles remained inactive in Switzerland as Paul still delayed to send him Korsakof's corps in accordance with the latest agreement. He possessed a secure superiority of numbers, but he made no use of it. He was, he said, awaiting the Russians. In reality he was obeying his orders, which forbade him to conquer the country for Russia or England. Pitt divined his motive but showed no annoyance. He was absorbed in his new plan of campaign, the scope of which was becoming wider and wider. His scheme was to leave the Austrians to continue the war by themselves beyond the Alps, while the real attacking force, that is the Russians, were used for an invasion of France with the object of restoring the monarchy. Souvorof was to return from Italy with all his men, was to increase his forces to at least 60,000 by the addition of the forces under Korsakof and Condé; he would then crush the French in Switzerland and march on Paris by Franche-Comté, the Austrians supporting this movement from Italy by invading Provence and Swabia and by besieging Huningue and Belfort.

England was to try this manœuvre again, and with better fortune, in 1804 and 1809 : it was finally to succeed in 1814. For the moment Pitt had no great hopes. He even contemplated that the invasion might be a mere demonstration. His chief object was to get the Russians out of Italy for the reason above indicated, and also because Paul's views on Malta and the presence of Russian squadrons in the Mediterranean was causing him anxiety. Austria had already adhered to this plan, but she raised new difficulties about its execution. Yielding to the instances of Colonel Popham, a special envoy from London, Paul had granted to England a new subsidised corps of eighteen battalions for a descent on Holland and an ulterior attempt on the Low Countries. This enterprise had been so far kept secret, but now became known, and according to the Court of Vienna it changed the situation. England and Russia could not be left alone to dispose of the ancient possessions of the House of Austria, perhaps for the benefit of Prussia. Thugut had long thought it would be useful to have a strong army on the Rhine. He now considered this a pressing necessity. As Korsakof had not yet reached Switzerland the Austrian minister considered the season too far advanced for a campaign in France. On the other hand, he was no longer enamoured of the plan already agreed upon to besiege Hunningue and Belfort. He preferred that the Archduke Charles should attack Mayence and then cross into the Low Countries. *In order that there should not be too many troops in Switzerland* the Austrians would evacuate that country as the Russians arrived. The Archduke would take up a position before Mayence with 65,000 men and his right wing would extend to Holland, where he would join hands with the English and the Russians. This was in fact already a military divorce preceding and announcing a diplomatic rupture between Austria and Russia. Perhaps also Thugut had some idea of trying for a separate reconciliation with France which the Directory under the influence of the disasters in Italy might be willing to favour.

Paul knew nothing of this and was by no means distressed at the prospect of the defection of the Austrians in Switzerland. Souvorof he now considered equal to all the Republican forces put together, and with his usual folly he reckoned that after crossing the Alps the Marshal would have 80,000 men at his disposal. Souvorof, on his side, longed for nothing so much as to be free from the *Hofkriegsrath*. He burned to take the road for Paris via Franche-Comté if he could not go via Dauphiné. But he considered the new Austrian plan impracticable in the shape in which it was proposed at Vienna to put it into execution.

Condé's corps had not quitted Vladimir in Volhynia until June 2. Korsakof did not cross the Bavarian frontier until July 26. His advance guard reached Schaffhausen on August 14 or 15, and Masséna, who was left free by the inactivity of the Archduke Charles, attacked the left wing of the Austrians in the mountains, completely defeated it and drove the division of Simpschen and Jellachich back behind the Linth. The Simplon and the St. Gothard were now occupied by the French, who blocked the advance of the Russians from Italy to Switzerland, and the victors, by the possession of these ranges as well as the Haut Valais, the passes of the Grisons, the valleys of the Sihl and the Muota, obtained an extremely strong base for operations in the direction of Zurich. Detachments of French cavalry were already beginning to appear on the outskirts of that town.

Korsakof, on the other hand, did not bring with him into Switzerland the 45,000 men agreed upon in the convention between his Government and Great Britain. Colonel Ramsay, whose duty it was to check the numbers, found that there was such a deficit in the forces actually put in the field that Paul was compelled to agree to a deduction from the stipulated subsidies of 25 per cent. This was an under-estimate. Korsakof had left many of his men on the way and his numbers did not exceed 27,000. Souvorof could not bring more than about 20,000 back from Italy. The Russian generals between them had not, therefore, a force equivalent to that of the Archduke Charles, who, with his 90,000 men, had not been able to make headway against Masséna's offensive. It was at this moment that Francis II directed the Archduke to leave Switzerland without even waiting for Souvorof. Korsakof, supported by the Swiss who were in the pay of England, was to make the best of things by himself. Nothing was to be left to him but the small force under Haddik which would remain between Zurich and Lucerne until relieved by the Marshal.

The written instructions to the Archduke, which were communicated to the Courts of London and Vienna, did not in themselves quite justify the indignation expressed by Souvorof when he heard of them. They were purposely made ambiguous and might be construed to mean that the departure of the Austrians was to depend on their being replaced by a force, Swiss, Russian, or Bavarian, sufficient to replace them. Paul was so completely deceived that he raised no objection. After his recent boasting he could hardly have done so. Had he not declared that the Russians would be 80,000 at the foot of the Alps ? But the letter containing these fatal instructions was accompanied by a verbal commentary which was entrusted to Count Dietrichstein who brought it, and the Archduke was given to understand that at Vienna they wished to see him out of Switzerland as soon as possible. He was only too pleased. He had not succeeded too well in that country, and Wickham conjectured that he was by no means displeased to do a bad turn to the new Prince of Italy, whose successes had excited his jealousy. Without hesitation, therefore, he announced his intention of striking camp and even sent away several regiments.

Korsakof, seeing clearly that if he were abandoned in

this way he would be lost, protested vehemently; he appealed to the Archduke's military honour and was heard. They could not decently part without at least attempting some joint action against the common enemy. Masséna had weakened his left in order to seize the Simplon and the St. Gothard. It was therefore arranged that the allies should cross the Aar an hour's march above its confluence with the Rhine near Oettingen and that a march should be made by Brugg, Aarau and Olten to take the French in the rear. Their retreat being threatened, they would be compelled to evacuate that country, and Masséna himself thought that if the manœuvre had succeeded it might have changed the whole situation.

On August 17, after a march which Wickham described as "really incredible," 7000 Russians joined 32,000 Austrians who had been concentrated for the purpose of this enterprise. But the Austrian officers had not taken proper steps to bridge the Aar : the passage was strongly defended and the attempt had to be abandoned.

Piqued at the failure, the Archduke consented to another attempt, but at this point arrived an unexpected message from Souvorof, who, founding himself on a rescript from the Czar placing Korsakof under his orders, directed that officer to send him 10,000 men immediately for the siege of Genoa ! The Marshal continued to think the plan of campaign in Switzerland in which he was invited to co-operate absurd, and held to his plan of invading France through Dauphiné. Korsakof, supported by Wickham, resisted this order. Souvorof gave way, but several weeks of infinitely precious time had been lost, and after a series of stormy discussions the Archduke definitely decided to continue his march towards Germany, and neither London nor St. Petersburg did anything to stop him.

Korsakof then threatened to quit Switzerland also, and the Archduke finally allowed himself to be persuaded to leave him 22,000 men under Hotze to guard the line from

St. Gothard to Utznach on the Linth, while the Russians replaced the Austrians behind the Limmath between Zurich and the Rhine. The allies were to remain on the defensive until the arrival of Souvorof, who was authorised to bring with him the corps of Rosenberg and now agreed to go to Switzerland to make a stand against Masséna. But Souvorof was still far off, and in Wickham's opinion the task of the Austrians under Hotze was much more to defend the possessions or the pretensions of the House of Hapsburg in the Grisons and the Vorarlberg than to support the Russians against the French.

Thus was prepared the catastrophe which brought Korsakof and Souvorof himself within an ace of annihilation and deprived the coalition of almost all the fruit of its recent victories. At the last moment London and St. Petersburg awoke to a consciousness of the mistakes they had made. Vienna multiplied excuses and counter-orders. It was too late! The Archduke was now directed to replace his left in the positions occupied before August 13 ; to leave in Switzerland enough troops to hold the country till the Russians came ; to abandon the siege of Mayence ; to keep the bulk of the Imperial forces in Swabia so that they might assist Souvorof and Korsakof if necessary. It was too late! When the Archduke received his new instructions he had already been eleven days on the march, and was making haste, as he said, in obedience to pressure from the Courts of London and St. Petersburg. At the end of the month Thugut, who was being overwhelmed with reproaches from these quarters, went further. He accepted the idea that all the Austrian troops should cooperate in Switzerland with the rest ; but already the cannon had thundered at Zurich.

With Hotze the Archduke professed to leave Korsakof at the head of an army of 57,000 men. But this included Strauch's brigade of 4100 odd, posted by Bellinzona and Locarno, and moreover he had rather meanly cheated the

Russian general over the number of efficient soldiers left at his disposal. Their real value was much below the figures which were given. The most trustworthy estimates show that Masséna, with about 80,000 men, outnumbered his adversaries by about 30,000 until the arrival of Souvorof.

Could the Marshal have arrived in time ? The Archduke always maintained that he could. By restricting their line of defence between Coblenz and Sargans, it was open to the allies to remain covered by rivers and lakes, so that the French could not turn their positions on either side, nor could they intervene in sufficient numbers against Souvorof's advance between the Lake of the Four Cantons and the St. Gothard. But the Archduke was not there to inspire his fellow generals. Hotze was a recognised mediocrity, Korsakof was a beginner, " foolish, arrogant, and presumptuous " in the opinion of his subordinate Loewenstein. According to another witness he had told the Archduke that a company of Russians was sufficient to replace an Austrian battalion, and, inspired by ideas of this kind, he extended his troops in a thin cordon which nowhere offered sufficient resistance. This was playing the game of his opponent—an opponent who was " the spoilt child of victory."

CHAPTER XII

THE END OF THE COALITION

I

Souvorof had struggled long and obstinately against leaving Italy, a battlefield on which, having done so well, he hoped to do even better. He had protested his entire obedience to orders, but he had made his departure depend first on the fall of Tortona and secondly on the occupation of Coni and Nice, as well as the western frontier of Piedmont. Thus alone, he thought, could the possession of Italy be assured to the allies, while the Archduke and Korsakof should have time in which to prepare for the invasion of France by Franche-Comté, for which at the proper time he would join them.

The Marshal was right, but his view involved the postponement of the plan until a season in which Switzerland, the chosen base of operations, would be impracticable for the object proposed. Winter was at hand. Souvorof was of course aware of this, but he could not justly be reproached. He had not heard of the new plan till August 25—nearly three weeks after the Archduke had received his instructions. He had then had to wait till September 4 before he was authorised to take Rehbinder with him. Without Rehbinder's co-operation he rightly judged that it would be useless for him to appear in Switzerland. Meanwhile the Austrians had made the crossing of the Alps more difficult by surrendering the passes to the enemy. He was asked to do what was in every respect impossible.

He could not at a day's notice disentangle himself from

the affairs of Italy, where he had innumerable difficulties, both military and political, to contend with. He could not reorganise in a moment his relations with the Austrian staff and transport services; nor could he without deliberation, which required time, form a plan of common action in a country which was entirely unknown to him. These considerations have been left out of account by historians who have accused Souvorof of being too slow. In spite of everything he was to give yet another proof of his prodigious rapidity in conception and in action.

On September 5, twenty-four hours after he was in a position to come to a decision, he sent a circular letter to Korsakof and the Austrian generals in Switzerland, in which he indicated the movements which he would make in order to join them and those which they themselves were to carry out in order to attack the enemy's positions in concert with him. The Marshal meant to cross the Alps by the St. Gothard. On September 17 the brigade under the Austrian General Strauch was to meet him at Airolo at the foot of the mountain. On the 19th the Russians would force the passage and would debouch into the valley of the upper Reuss and the lower Linth. Korsakof, Hotze and Lincken (commanding the Austrian corps at Coire) were to support this movement, the first by crossing the Limmath in order to hold Masséna, whose principal position was between that river and the Reuss, the two others by dislodging the French from the Linth and penetrating between the lakes of Zug and of Zurich. Souvorof would finally advance along the Lake of the Four Cantons, and all would unite on the right bank of the lower Reuss, thus taking the enemy in the rear.

This plan, which was worked out by Zach, the Quartermaster-General of the Austrian army (and not, as has been supposed, by Weyrother, Souvorof's aide-de-camp) has been severely criticised. Clausewitz has characterised the choice of the St. Gothard as his access to Switzerland as " a colossal error," and Jomini has ratified this judgment. Souvorof, however, had his reasons. He had at first thought of the Great St. Bernard and the Rhone Valley, intending perhaps to push on to Berne in the rear of the French. But this was before the Archduke's departure, and his retreat put an end to all action in this direction. There remained the Splugen. By taking this route and reaching the Grisons by the Bernardino Pass the Russians could rejoin the Austrians without striking a blow. To take this route, however, was to contravene the orders of the *Hofkriegsrath*, who desired the Marshal to ‚replace Haddik in the St. Gothard district. Had there been nothing to restrain him but conventional considerations of strategy and tactics, Souvorof would not have hesitated to avail himself of the advantages offered by the Rhine Valley and the Splugenstrasse. He would have had no further to go than he had in order to reach the valley of the Reuss. A week after the Russian army had left Bellinzona, Korsakof and Hotze could have reckoned with certainty on its appearing on the Linth and the Limmath, and even if Masséna attacked them in the meantime they could have retired in the direction of Souvorof and could have even then waited with him in an impregnable position until they received further reinforcements from the *émigrés*, the Bavarians and the troops of Würtemberg.

This, however, was precisely what the Marshal did not want. If the junction was thus effected in peace and security it was to be feared that the Austrians still left in Switzerland would be ordered to follow the Archduke into Germany. He had been officially informed that the *Hofkriegsrath* expected him to relieve not only Haddik but also Hotze, as Korsakof, in the minds of the *Bistimmtsager*, had already relieved the Archduke. He would then be left with less than 50,000 men, safe from all attack it is true, but also quite incapable of undertaking anything. As in Italy, so in Switzerland, his one desire was to fight, to try the fortune of battle at all hazards. It was for this reasons that he gave preference to a plan which was adventurous and rash but which for a few days at least united under his command forces almost equal to those of Masséna, and compelled Hotze, Lincken and Strauch to accept the rendezvous which he gave them on the field of battle.

He did not forget that a mountain range with its defiles, which are so favourable to surprise attacks and turning movements, is as difficult to defend as to attack, and he had good hopes of dealing successfully with Lecourbe. The one weak point in his plan, and the mistake which made its success more than problematical, lay in the complicated system of simultaneous movements which were to agree to a few kilometres and a few hours with a precision which he should have seen to be impossible.

The most recent military history should have warned the Marshal against this miscalculation. What he was attempting was an enveloping movement intended to destroy his adversary similar to that which General Mack had conceived in 1794 for the Battle of Tourcoing, which Carnot had invented for surrounding Cobourg in 1796, Wurmser for destroying Bonaparte, and quite recently Moreau for the conquest of Souvorof himself. The attempt had always resulted in a check and sometimes in a disaster, and the reason had always been the same. In combinations of this kind there is always too much room for unforeseen accidents, and this makes it an easy matter for the enemy to defeat them.

II

Souvorof was the first to be unpunctual to the dates which he had fixed. At the last moment he had been detained by a demonstration made by Moreau towards Tortona, and this made him lose three days. The French general retreated to the mountains and the town capitulated on September 10. The Marshal resumed his march and accelerated it as much as he could. He parted with all his heavy artillery, which was to rejoin him via Milan, Chiavenna and the Engadine, and even with his luggage, which he despatched to Schaffhausen by way of the Tyrol. He retained only twenty-five pieces of small calibre, which he had borrowed from the Piedmontese stores, and on September 15 his troops were already at Taverna at the foot of Mont-Cenere. He himself reached Bellinzona before them and hoped to find there the pack-mules which he had requisitioned from the Austrian transport service. Alas! On the very day of his arrival he wrote to Rastoptchine: " I have reached Bellinzona, but there are no mules, no horses, nothing but Thugut, mountains and precipices."

This time Thugut was not to blame, and Mélas, when asked to give up his own pack animals, may be excused for not complying. He promised to do all he could to provide others, but 1350 mules—the number demanded by Souvorof—cannot be found at a moment's notice. Souvorof finally hit upon the idea of using the horses belonging to his cossacks, but in the meantime five more days had been lost and the attack on the mountains was postponed from the 19th till the 24th of September.

This had its advantages. Masséna had planned a general attack for the 25th and had prescribed movements to Lecourbe denuding the passes, which were already more than his 12,000 men could effectively supervise. There were only a few battalions under Loison on the line of the Reuss, and Lecourbe was not there in person. Neither he nor Masséna expected Souvorof's arrival, at least so soon, and when they heard that the Russians had appeared before Airolo both thought that it was a mere demonstration. This simplified the task of the assailants.

The tourist who now visits the monument erected to Souvorof between Andermatt and Fluelen at the bend of the narrow gorge where the troubled stream of the Reuss roars among rocks and giddy precipices, rarely fails to express his astonishment. " What ! Did he pass through here with his army ! " And the memory of Thermopylæ suggests comparisons humiliating to Lecourbe and his men to the spectator who knows that there were many more than 300 Frenchmen to bar the passage of the modern Xerxes. But Souvorof did not pass there with his whole army, or even with a quarter of it. He never even thought of engaging his whole force in the defile of the St. Gothard. On September 21, 6000 men under Rosenberg had set out by Donigo and Santa Maria for Disentis, in the valley of the Upper Rhine, to strike at the Oberalp and take in the rear the French positions on the range. At the same time Lincken had sent General Auffenberg's detachment from Coire to Disentis, with instructions to make for Amsteg and so turn the defence of the valley of the Reuss. These measures having been taken, Souvorof again divided what remained of his forces into three columns, one of which, alone under his personal command, ascended the valley of the Ticino and crossing the Gap of Uri and the Devil's Bridge took the St. Gothard from the front. The other two, under Bagration and Derfelden, were to carry out simultaneously on the right and left turning movements with a very large radius, so as to surprise the enemy in every direction and keep him everywhere between two fires. In these conditions, far from hampering the assailants, the mountain enabled them to utilise to the utmost their very great numerical superiority.

The incidents of the struggle which never, in point of fact, made very serious demands on the Russians, have been embellished by tradition. Souvorof's soldiers are said to have recoiled from the task, and it is reported that he could only restrain them by ordering them to dig his grave in the ground which they were abandoning. The fact was that Souvorof, alert and confident as ever, had rather to restrain the enthusiasm of his men. He himself found it hard to await the result of the manœuvres intended to break the resistance of his adversaries. But Bagration, leading his detachment behind Airolo on the left of the French, soon opened the south of the pass. At the Devil's Bridge Loison did his best, but found himself taken in the rear by Rosenberg, and at midday on September 26 the Russians with little loss were at Altorf, where Souvorof hoped to be in touch at least with Lincken, if not with Korsakof and Hotze.

He made one of his sensational entries into the little town, but there was no news of Lincken and his comrades, and the march to Lucerne in two separated columns must have seemed to him impossible. The Marshal thought that Lincken, not being able to get further, was awaiting him in the valley of the Muota, and on the following day he determined to join him. Surprise has been expressed that he did not try to reach the upper waters of the Linth by the defile of Klausen : this route, which is quite easy, offered him the certainty of meeting Lincken. It has been supposed that he was influenced in the course he took by the Grand Duke Constantine. Paul's younger son had, in fact, added to the difficulties of the expedition by his presence. He had followed the final phases of the campaign of Italy without distinguishing himself, and he was to intervene in Switzerland at a later stage with even less glory. But his opinions, though expressed in a tone of command, were usually inspired by a timidity which on this occasion was unlikely to suggest the course taken by the Marshal.

In the Muotathal the Marshal did not know what awaited him, and the road to it was much more trying. It led by the Schächenthal to the foot of the Ruosalp, and after that there were only the shepherd's tracks through the steep Kinzig Pass. In order to reach the top and gain the valley beyond the Russians had to expend much more courage and energy than on the St. Gothard, and when they reached the end of their journey they found the news of the disaster at Zurich awaiting them.

III

As Korsakof and Hotze scattered their forces between Zurich and the Oberland, Masséna had simultaneously concentrated his troops. His army had been weakened by contingents which he had had to send to the Rhine, besides the 12,000 men under Lecourbe, the 9000 men under Turreau in the Haut Valais, and a reserve of 7000 with Klein and Humbert in the Frickthal near Bâle. Still, with Soult, Mortier and Lorge he had at his disposal about 40,000 men all massed on the upper Reuss, the lower Linth and the left bank of the Lake of Zurich. He heard vaguely of the arrival of Souvorof. He was pressed by the Directory " to do something," as Joubert had been before Novi, and was threatened with the loss of part of his forces, so he was awaiting his opportunity. At the end of the month, on the news of the fall of Bernadotte, whom he hated and who hated him, he came to his decision. By a series of rapid manœuvres he anticipated the movement which Souvorof had prescribed to the Austro-Russian forces. It was he who was the first to cross the Linth and the Limmath. Thrusting aside Hotze, who lost his life in the fighting, he drove the wreck of his force back on the Rhine and confronted Korsakof near Zurich. That presumptuous general was routed at the first shock, lost 5000 men, a hundred cannon, all his material, the treasury of the army and all his papers. According to Wickham he proved his complete incompetence, before, during, and after the battle. He had scorned the advice of the Swiss officers as to the positions to occupy, and when the fighting began he was incapable of giving a single order. It appears that he even refused to listen to Pichegru, who from the Archduke's headquarters offered his assistance and his advice. With the correspondence was revealed to the French the whole secret of the intrigue of Barras which appeared from documents recently sent from St. Petersburg and Mittau.

Thus, thinking he would find Lincken on the Muota or at Schwytz, Souvorof learned when he was setting out for this town that Masséna had just entered it with 20,000 Frenchmen! At the same time Lecourbe returned to the positions he had temporarily abandoned and attacked the Marshal's rearguard at Altorf. The position of the Russians became more than critical. Any other than Souvorof would probably have considered it desperate. At Muotathal, on September 30, it appeared that he had now only 16,584 combatants, of whom 2852 were cavalry. The passage of the St. Gothard, and still more that of the Kinzig Pass, had carried off the rest.

Far, however, from thinking of surrender, Souvorof would not even hear of a retreat. The Grand Duke Constantine objected to an attempt of Schwytz, which would really have been folly, so the Marshal resolved to make for Glaris, sweeping out of his way Molitor's weak brigade of 4000 men, which was the only force at this point and was already fighting Lincken. He would then reunite the shattered remnants of the forces of Korsakof and Hotze and would try to get his revenge.

Even this was much to ask of fortune and too much to require of the vigour of an army which had already suffered so much. Masséna mistook the direction taken by the Russians and had joined Lecourbe at Altorf in order to pursue them into the Schächenthal; but immediately afterwards he used the flotilla on the lake in order to return by Brunnen to Schwytz. He gave repeated orders to "close the mousetrap" in which he believed Souvorof to be now hopelessly imprisoned. It would probably have been so for any other man than the victor of Novi. But there were numerous ways out of the mousetrap, and the French generals showed neither their customary daring nor even the confidence which the position of their adversary and their recent victory should have given them. The bravest and most skilful among them, Mortier and Molitor himself,

299

showed hesitation and anxiety. They should have thought of nothing but barring the passage of the handful of men who were at their mercy, and we find them preoccupied most about assuring their retreat in case of a check ! They were visibly terrified by the renown which the conqueror of Macdonald, Moreau and Joubert had brought back with him from Italy.

Their first contact with his army, which was now so much enfeebled, justified their apprehensions. In the valley of the Muota Masséna attacked the Russian rearguard with 10,000 men and received a severe check. Mortier, in spite of his orders, disappeared, and Molitor allowed himself to be overwhelmed in the Kloen Valley, and Souvorof succeeded in reaching Glaris. A rapid march by Mollis and the Kerenzerberg on Sargans would now put him in a position to obtain, if not the revenge which he had too ambitiously foreshadowed, at least a prompt junction with the Austrian forces of Lincken, Jellaschich, and Petrasch. But a new obstacle arose which was not due to the French.

Souvorof's plan was energetically supported at the council of war, by the Austrian General Auffenberg, the Swiss officers, and Colonel Clinton, the English commissary. The Grand Duke Constantine alone opposed it with a formal veto. The route which had been chosen was, in his opinion, too much exposed to the enemy's attacks, and in the end he succeeded in getting another adopted. This was a more circuitous road by Ilanz, Coire and Maienfeld. It protected the army from all attack, but it was undoubtedly a retreat, though Souvorof still refused to admit it. Moreover, it was to expose the fugitives to new trials which were severe enough to overcome their endurance and their courage and to which under another chief they would certainly have succumbed.

The Col du Panix, which had to be crossed, was already covered with snow on October 7. Its height is 2400 metres, it is surrounded with precipices, and the passage was not only difficult but perilous. The horses slipped and the Marshal was more than once on the point of being hurled into the abyss. The old soldier, always intrepid, struggled in the hands of the cossacks who offered him violence in order to protect him. And yet both for the leader and for the army which he had commanded in happier days, this march forms the strongest claim on the admiration of posterity. It deserves a place of honour in the military history of all time.

IV

At Ilanz, Souvorof was already in a position to carry out the re-concentration and the re-provisioning of his troops. When he arrived at Feldkirch he was at first more inclined than ever to take the offensive once again. This course was now no longer rash. Since September 28 the Archduke had suspended his march and had to some extent retraced his steps. Korsakof had again got into touch with him and had re-occupied his first camp at Doerflingen, near Schaffhausen. On his right Nauendorf, with 8000 Austrians, covered the Rhine from Waldshut to Schaffhausen. On his left Colonel Titof, with a regiment which had escaped the disaster at Zurich, held the approaches to the Lake of Constance. Condé's corps, some Swiss battalions which were being organised, and certain Bavarian contingents already on the march promised reinforcements which would soon make good the losses which had been sustained. But the general who had been conquered at Zurich was prostrated. His former vain-glory had been replaced by complete discouragement, and the Archduke was by no means disposed to renew the attempt at common action. He had at first decided to wait for Souvorof, and had thus allowed Masséna to recover from the alarm into which he had been thrown by the Marshal's arrival in Switzerland. Souvorof having escaped him, the French general threw himself upon Korsakof, whom he compelled

301

to abandon all the left bank of the Rhine. But the victor of Novi was soon himself to pass through the most curious alternations of warlike ardour, which seemed to be merely intensified by his recent trials, and a depression of spirit which had even less foundation.

He began a letter to Rastoptchine with a proud announcement that he was preparing to join hands with Korsakof " in order to repair the evil," but continued after a few days' interval by representing his situation, and those of the Archduke and of his lieutenant, as such that there was no hope of continuing the war. " The victorious army," he wrote, " is reduced to 10,000 men. The infantry is barefoot and without clothes ; provisions are insufficient ; there are so few cartridges that I have to avoid fighting. Korsakof is without tents, without cloaks and without money ! " He exaggerated his losses and the distress of the army. The Archduke, he said, was keeping 18,000 men in Switzerland, but he was putting them in garrison. Thugut was thinking only of making peace with the Directory. The Marshal had heard of the presence at Vienna of two French diplomatic agents who had been secretly sent there, and he concluded by saying, " I have no hope of being able to act ! "

What had happened between the beginning and the end of this letter ? Wickham, the English agent, had done his best to initiate and to help negotiations to secure an understanding between the Marshal and the Archduke, with a view to concerted operations. The Archduke seemed inclined to agree, and Souvorof hastened to make Weyrother draw up a detailed plan. But Count Colloredo, an aide-de-camp of the Archduke who arrived at Feldkirch on October 12, made objections. The Austrian Commander-in-Chief thought the plan too complicated. On the other hand Wickham, who accompanied Colloredo to Feldkirch, also changed his mind. He had become convinced, contrary to Weyrother's opinion, that, even with the corps of Korsakof and Condé, Souvorof had at most only about 30,000 men who were fit to be put in the field. He had, moreover, a very poor opinion of these troops, who, he said, were brave enough, but who, since their sojourn in Italy, had lost all discipline, and were led by officers who, apart from their regimental duties, knew nothing of war. He had dined with the Marshal, and though he had been warned to expect, and had expected, eccentricity, he had formed the opinion that he was quite incapable of command. The hero who had filled Europe with the noise of his exploits had all the appearance of an imbecile ; he walked about the room dangling his arms, wagging his head and talking insanely. Wickham spoke to him of a plan of campaign proposed by the Archduke. Souvorof lifted his eyes ecstatically and said that he had had a vision in the night which forbade him to enter into any engagements of this kind. The very next moment he surprised his interlocutor by delivering a series of appreciations of the Austrian army which were marked by reflection and sound judgment, and for two hours he talked on all sorts of subjects with the most complete lucidity and a great deal of intelligence. But when Wickham tried to bring him back to the actual military situation the Marshal again began to wander, and Wickham withdrew without being able to make anything of him. A further interview led only to Souvorof's making the following confession, which, if more intelligible, was equally disconcerting :

" I will have nothing to do with your Swiss or your Bavarians. What I want is what I had this year, that is, an Austrian army. I have been most unjustly deprived of this, and without it I can do nothing, for my Russians, though in many ways the best troops in the world, are not fit to act by themselves. . . . Secondly, I want to go back to Italy. . . . I want to enter France by Dauphiné, the Archduke, helped by the Bavarians and the Swiss, seconding me in Switzerland and Franche-Comté."

Wickham was to carry these declarations to the Austrian headquarters, but, without waiting for an answer, Souvorof left the next day with his army for Lindau, in Swabia, which brought him no nearer to Italy. At Lindau, however, the negotiations continued, through Wickham's mediation, and Souvorof even showed some impatience for their completion. With the débris of Korsakof's corps he had now united Condé's contingent as well as the Bavarian and Swiss detachments under Roverea. He had received a rescript from Paul couched in very flattering terms and leaving him full liberty of action. The Court of Vienna, moreover, yielding to Cobenzl's instances, had at last decided to send him and also to the Grand Duke Constantine the Grand Cross of St. Theresa. This comforted the Marshal, but he stuck to his plan, which was to leave the Alps for the Apennines. Paul helped to confirm Souvorof in this resolution by constantly talking of sending Louis XVIII into France, though his opinion of his royal guest at Mittau was hardly more favourable than that which he had expressed about the Comte d'Artois. " He is a very learned Prince," the Czar observed about the elder brother, " but his character is by no means frank, and in spite of all that has happened to him he has preserved his taste for giving orders before he is on the throne. . . . He is moreover often misled by his intimate friend and favourite, the Comte d'Avaray, a restless and pushing person." As regards the *émigrés* of Condé's corps, the Czar strongly advised the Marshal not to take them into France : " They would carry fire and sword everywhere and would cause the best disposed people to revolt."

And yet, after having again announced to Simon Vorontsof that with the Archduke's help he had every hope of repairing the damage done by the defeat at Zurich, Souvorof, having been rejoined by his heavy artillery, started off again a few days later for Augsburg, with the intention of encamping his troops between the Lech and the Iller. He had strong and pressing reasons for leaving Switzerland and its immediate neighbourhood. The attitude of the population of that country to the Russians was becoming such that Wickham anticipated a general rising against the foreigners who had so recently been received there as liberators.

As to the reasons for these changes of attitude, one certain fact dominates the controversy which has arisen regarding them. The separation between the Russians and the Austrians, which had been half completed since Souvorof's departure for Switzerland, had had the inevitable consequence that the Marshal could not provide for the subsistence of his troops in the regular way. In default of a proper commissariat of its own his army were now reduced to living on the inhabitants, and that meant plunder—not the organised plunder of the revolutionary armies, but robbery pure and simple, which was much worse. Even in Italy the incompatibility of temper between the allies, which had appeared from the first, had produced an insufficiency of provisions, and this had led to occasional and accidental outbreaks of pillaging on the part of the Russians. Hence the laxity of discipline observed by Wickham. In Switzerland the accident had become the rule. The English agent reported that the heroes of the Trebbia and of Novi arrived at Feldkirch laden with spoils which they had collected in the Cantons of Uri, Schwytz and Glaris, where, however, they had been very well received. Wherever they went they spread destruction, ravaging even the vineyards and cultivated land of all kinds. The French system of enforced contributions in money, however onerous to the country, was, said Wickham, " a blessing in comparison." The officers allowed their soldiers to have their way and often took part in their excesses. Souvorof shut his eyes, conscious that he could not feed his men otherwise, and also careful to maintain his popularity in view of the pretensions of the Grand Duke Constantine to the chief command.

These assertions were corroborated by other witnesses and, as we shall see, they received the most striking confirmation from Souvorof himself. But violence and pillage were not the only annoyances which the unhappy Swiss had to endure. On the arrival of Korsakof, La Harpe, the old tutor of the Grand Dukes Alexander and Constantine, was a member of the Directory of the Swiss Republic. He had been expelled from Russia, but he bore no malice to any one but Catherine, and lost no opportunity of praising her son, " our unfortunate and misunderstood Prince." At the same time, however, he applauded the successes of " the excellent Masséna," and in July 1799 he was simple enough to write to the Czar begging him to interest himself in the freedom of Switzerland as he had himself, in 1793 and 1794, supported to the utmost of his power the interests of the rightful heir to the throne of Russia. Paul's answer was to order Korsakof to arrest the insolent Director and to send him under escort to St. Petersburg, whence he would be sent to Siberia !

" The excellent Masséna " prevented this order from being carried out and La Harpe stuck to his illusions. " Knowing the heart of the Russian Sovereign as he did," he declared that he had nothing to fear even if his arrest was carried out, and he persevered in this opinion even after Paul, having no other way of wreaking his vengeance, had taken away his pension.

When the master set such an example, it is easy to imagine how his subjects behaved to the compatriots of the illustrious Vaudois, and to understand Souvorof's haste to seek more hospitable winter quarters elsewhere. He did not, however, give up his plan of using his troops in the service of the coalition, or of again commanding an Austro-Russian army. More and more, however, the idea of arriving at an understanding with the Archduke for this purpose became repugnant to him. He evaded the meeting which the Prince proposed, though he still continued to urge him to co-operate in a short winter campaign, in the course of which " there would be no difficulty about beating their Championnets and Bonapartes." But he immediately relapsed into the wanderings which were now habitual, and his correspondent found little to encourage him to answer.

Now at this very time Paul, under the impression made upon him by the disaster of Zurich, was becoming much averse from the prolongation of his association with Austria in war and even in politics. In the first transport of his fury he even decided on a complete rupture. On October 15/26 he wrote to the King of England to announce that " the perfidy of the Court of Vienna " compelled him to order Souvorof to " occupy himself with the arrangements necessary for the repatriation of his troops." " While we thought that we were three against France, we were in fact only two," he wrote, and he enclosed with this message a copy of a letter which he had addressed to the Austrian Emperor in the following terms :

" Seeing my troops abandoned and delivered up to the enemy by the ally on whom I counted most ; seeing that his policy is contrary to my views, and that the safety of Europe is being sacrificed to plans for the aggrandisement of your Monarchy ; having besides every reason to be displeased by the ambiguous and crafty conduct of your Minister—whose motives, out of respect for your Imperial Majesty's rank, I wish to ignore—I hereby declare with the same loyalty which made me fly to your assistance and aid the success of your arms, that from this moment I abandon your interests in order to devote myself entirely to my own and those of my allies, and that in order that the bad cause may not prevail I cease to make common cause with your Majesty. . . ."

It might seem that after this there was nothing more to be said on either side. The essential knot of the coalition seemed to be cut and the combination against France seemed finally at an end. Paul was not yet contemplating

the possibility of an arrangement with the Government of
the Republic, but in his letter to George III he expressed
the opinion that " the time appointed by Providence for
the fall of the revolutionary régime was not yet come."
Meanwhile he proposed to the King a closer alliance, in
which he thought it would be possible to include Sweden,
Denmark, and even Prussia. He stipulated, however,
that it should be directed against Austria, " the power
which at the present moment is most dangerous."

But the Czar was not yet done with his perfidious ally,
and through her the coalition was still to hold him captive
for a time. But he was already on the way to freedom
and all the more inclined to take it as his armed alliance
with England had already ceased to charm him.

V

The Anglo-Russian Convention, which was signed on
June 11/22, 1799, at St. Petersburg, in view of an expedition to Holland, required Paul to assemble at Revel 17,593
men who were to be embarked in a fleet half English and
half Russian. To these George III promised to add 13,000
men from his own army and further bound himself to pay
£88,000 for the upkeep of the Czar's forces at the beginning
of the campaign and £44,000 a month as long as it lasted.
No difficulties had arisen except on the question of the
command. Paul objected to the appointment of the Duke
of York, whose military reputation was in fact none too
brilliant. But as he also took up the position that General
Hermann, who was to be second in command of his
soldiers, should not serve under any one who was not of
the blood royal, the choice of the Duke was confirmed.

The plan of inducing Sweden to co-operate had had to be
abandoned in view of the exorbitant subsidies claimed by
the Court of Stockholm—1,000,000 riksdollars in advance
for 8000 men and an annual payment of 1,500,000. The

enterprise, however, seemed to offer the fairest prospects of success. In effecting a landing in the Netherlands the allies could afford to neglect the Dutch army of 25,000 regular troops, who were slow to mobilise and who were thought to be disaffected. The Dutch fleet, with its crew of 14,000, was more imposing, but it was hostile to the new régime and devoted to the House of Orange. The French army of occupation, which amounted to 17,000 men under General Brune, was therefore to all intents and purposes reduced to its own resources, and the allies, who had a superiority of numbers of nearly two to one, should have easily prevailed. It is well known how this anticipation was falsified.

The Russians and the English disembarked about the middle of September 1799, but were unable to agree on a combined plan of action. The Duke of York had already proved his absolute incompetence in similar expeditions, and Whitworth states that Paul had chosen Hermann, as he had chosen Korsakof, against all advice. On September 19 the Russians for the first time got into touch with the enemy at Bergen. They were badly led and feebly supported by their allies, and they were completely defeated. Hermann was taken prisoner and Jerebtsof, the best of his lieutenants, was mortally wounded. Other engagements equally unsuccessful soon completed the demoralisation of the vanquished, and on October 18 a capitulation was signed obliging them to restore their prisoners and leave the country on the 30th of the same month.

The English had the satisfaction of retaining the Dutch fleet, which they had captured in the Texel. The Russians had only the humiliation of the check which they had encountered and, in accordance with the British Constitution, they were ingloriously relegated to quarters in the islands of Jersey and Guernsey. Vorontsof congratulated himself on this, as he felt that the presence of these troops nearer London would shed little glory on his country!

The effect of these events on Paul's mind may be imagined. Even on the sea his co-operation with " the most powerful navy in the world " was bringing him no great successes, and by the intervention of Austria was even to expose him to a most mortifying affront. Faithful to his promise, he had placed his fleets at the disposal of England. From Kronstadt a squadron of fifteen sail of the line, four frigates and a transport had set out under the command of Admiral Makarof to join Duncan at Yarmouth, but of these one division did not reach its destination until November, and was then in such a condition that none of the vessels were fit for service. One of them, which carried Kartsof in command of the detachment, had foundered. It was not until the following spring that, after refitting in English ports, three Russian line-of-battle ships and one frigate in all were in a condition to put to sea. They were sent to the Mediterranean to reinforce another auxiliary squadron under Ouchakof which had been borrowed from the Black Sea Fleet and was intended for concerted action with the Turks. A third squadron under Tchitchagof, consisting of six sail of the line, five frigates and four transports, had embarked part of the Russian forces intended for the expedition to Holland and had taken part in the capture of the Dutch fleet.

Ouchakof's squadron of six line-of-battle ships, three frigates and three brigs, with 1700 troops, joined a Turkish squadron of four line-of-battle ships, six frigates and ten gunboats in the Dardanelles in August 1798, and these vessels were transferred to the command of the Russian admiral. At this time, since the Battle of the Nile (August 1, 1798), the English controlled the Mediterranean, blockading Alexandria and Malta and protecting the Kings of Sardinia and the Two Sicilies, who had respectively taken refuge at Cagliari and Palermo.

Ouchakof's mission was to drive the French out of the Ionian Islands, and thereafter to help the English to restore the sovereignty of the Pope and the Kings of Sardinia and Naples. The genius of Pitt had succeeded in effecting one of the strangest and most surprising combinations in history. United with the soldiers of the successor of Mahomet, the troops of the Orthodox Czar were to help in restoring to the Head of Catholic Christendom the dominion which had been taken from him by the eldest daughter of his Church!

Ouchakof discharged the first part of his task with complete success. Cerigo, Zante, and Sainte Maure were taken between September 28 and November 5, 1798, to the great joy of Paul, who lavished honours and rewards on the conquerors. After a more obstinate resistance, Corfu also surrendered on February 19, 1799. But when the Russian admiral endeavoured to support in the south of Italy the action which Souvorof had begun so brilliantly in the north he encountered the ill-will of Austria.

Having directed Rehbinder's corps on Naples, the Marshal invited Ouchakof to blocade Ancona, from which the French were in a position to harass the Austrian transports crossing the Adriatic. On his side the King of Naples sent to Corfu to ask for help. Ouchakof told off two detachments, one of which, under Captain Sorokine, left for the coast of Otranto, while the other, commanded by Admiral Poustochkine, made its landing further north near Ancona.

When Sorokine approached Brindisi the French garrison took to flight. The effect of Souvorof's first successes was already making itself felt. The captain landed 600 men and six cannon and sailed north in triumph, while the small force which he had disembarked carried Foggia with ease and pushed straight on to Naples, where they made their entry on June 9 at the head of Cardinal Ruffo's militia. But shortly afterwards Nelson arrived in the harbour with seventeen sail, bringing back the King from

Sicily, and the Russians thereafter played a part too subordinate for Paul's vanity.

In September 1799 it was even worse. Ouchakof himself appeared off Palermo and proposed to attack Malta, in accordance with peremptory orders received from St. Petersburg. The English opposed this, allowing it to be seen that the presence of the Russian admiral in the Mediterranean was as distasteful to them as Souvorof's prolonged sojourn in the north of Italy was to the Austrians. Ouchakof generously offered his help towards the capture of Rome and rapidly sent off in this direction a portion of his landing-party. The English, however, were before them at Civita Vecchia, and having, on September 27, brought about the capitulation of the French garrison they remained in occupation of the place. The Neapolitans had Rome as their share of the spoil. The Russians got nothing.

Meanwhile Poustochkine, having no troops to land at Ancona, had been reduced to blockading the town, which was occupied by 3000 French and Cisalpine troops under Monnier. It was not until October that the arrival of Fröhlich with 8000 Imperial troops brought him the necessary reinforcements. The Austrian general, however, immediately claimed the chief command, completely evicted the Russian admiral, and on November 13 (new style) he negotiated with Monnier a capitulation which surrendered the town to the Austrians alone, and refused to allow the Russians and the Turks even to enter!

The French commander had insisted on the insertion of this clause on the ground that a violation of the law of nations had been recently committed at the capture of Fano, to the north of Ancona, by Count Voïnovitch, an officer of the Russo-Turkish forces. Both the Russians and the Turks protested and hoisted their flags beside the Austrian colours on the ten French vessels which had been captured in the harbour. Fröhlich ordered them to be removed, by force if necessary, and did the same with the posts which the allies introduced into the town. In all material particulars the Russian and the Austrian reports of this incident are in agreement.

This gave the tottering coalition a blow from which it never recovered. At St. Petersburg, Panine vainly endeavoured to help Cobenzl to neutralise its effects. The minister's credit was already shaken and that of the ambassador was almost gone. Cobenzl was indeed almost in quarantine. According to the report of his Bavarian colleague, " he was suffering from a loathsome disease which had so intensified his natural ugliness that he became even physically a hideous and revolting object." For this reason he had been obliged to forego the honour of marrying by proxy the Grand Duchess Alexandrina, and when the Czar received the news of what had passed at Ancona he forbade the Ambassador to come to his Court until Russia had received suitable reparation.

The Court of Vienna could not and did not refuse this, but as usual complied with an ill grace and after much delay. In December they were still trying Paul's patience, and by this time things were going badly with the coalition; and the English, despairing of taking Valetta by themselves, were actually inviting Ouchakof to join them in Maltese waters. It was too late. The Czar had had enough of the bonds which, in spite of his impetuous temper, he had found so hard to break, and he was now on the point of leaving his prison for ever. The summons to Ouchakof from the English camp crossed an order from St. Petersburg directing the admiral to return to Russia, and at the same time the negotiations which were still proceeding for the maintenance of Austro-Russian co-operation ended definitely in a rupture.

VI

After Zurich and the letter he had written to Francis II the Czar had made as if to set aside Austria altogether. About the middle of October 1799, Kotchoubey communicated to the Corps Diplomatique assembled at Gatchina a circular note inviting the " German Princes " to unite under the Russian flag, failing which the Czar would leave the coalition. Rastoptchine, in conversation with Whitworth, went so far as to contemplate " quite calmly " the idea of a *rapprochement* with France, and desired to know the opinion of the British Cabinet on this point. In Panine, who soon afterwards succeeded Kotchoubey, the coalition gained, it is true, a resolute partisan, but the new Vice-Chancellor had to reckon with the dominant influence of Rastoptchine, and moreover he was devoted to Prussia and was inclined, as far as Austria was concerned, to take up an unconciliatory attitude on the subject of compensations.

Cobenzl built his hopes on the approaching arrival of the Archduke Palatine, who was to submit a project which it was thought at Vienna might bring back Paul by appealing to his greed. It suggested the annexation of Bavaria to Austria in exchange for the Netherlands, the erection of Piedmont into an independent sovereignty for the Archduke Antony, the son of the Emperor, who would marry the Grand Duchess Anne, and the constitution of the three legations as an appanage for the fiancé of the Grand Duchess Alexandrina. The Archduke Palatine was no diplomatist, so Thugut thought proper to give him as a colleague Count Dietrichstein, who had already gained Paul's favour when he attended his coronation, and who had married a Russian wife.

But Dietrichstein, in spite of his marriage with a Chouvalof, was no longer a *persona grata*. He had intervened, as we have seen, in the quarrels between Korsakof and the Archduke Charles and Paul regarded him as responsible for the premature retreat of the Austrian forces. Moreover, the Czar, having examined the Austrian proposal, took no great fancy to it, perhaps because the Grand Duchess Anne was only four years old. Inspired by Panine, he turned his back on Austria and again took up the idea of a league of the Northern Powers. On October 29, 1799, he signed at Gatchina a treaty of alliance with Sweden and warmly welcomed the Danish envoy Baron Blome, who, after a sojourn at Copenhagen, reappeared at St. Petersburg offering the adhesion of Denmark to the league in return for a guarantee of the Danish possessions. Finally, forgetting his recent experiences at Berlin, he wrote to Frederick William proposing a renewal of the old alliance and addressing him as " the first sovereign of Germany." This letter may never have been sent, as has been supposed, but Baron Krudener, who was appointed to succeed Panine on the banks of the Spree, was directed to concert with Prussia " the best means of setting limits to the insatiable ambition of the House of Hapsburg."

The Court of Berlin showed no more readiness than before to abandon the policy of neutrality, and the Czar was, on the other hand, urged from London to sacrifice to the common cause his grievances against Austria, however legitimate they might be. Paul, however, continued to oscillate unsteadily between two policies. On the eve of his daughter's marriage (October 30–November 11, 1799) he forbade Count Dietrichstein to be present, as " he had no liking for intriguers." The next day he was pacified, but some days later a report from Souvorof, dated at Feldkirch on October 14 (new style) and filled with invectives against Austria, threw him again into a passion and he had the document published in the *Official Gazette* !

The envoys of Naples and Sardinia diligently poured oil on the flames. The Duke of Serra-Capriola had himself married a Russian and had for long been in high favour,

which he had recently increased by doing homage to the
new Grand 'Master of the Knights of Malta in the name of
the three Priories of Capua, Barletta and Messina. He
now declared that he feared for his country less because of
the necessarily temporary domination of the French than
because the Austrians wished to reduce it to permanent
slavery. His henchman the Marquis di Gallo was more
enterprising, and indeed spoiled the game by revealing
extravagant pretensions which led to his being dismissed
without a farewell audience.   Nevertheless, under the influence of the Duke and his Sardinian colleague, of Rastoptchine
and of Whitworth himself, who rather imprudently also
denounced the " perfidy " of the Court of Vienna, Paul
became more and more anti-Austrian and therefore more
and more ready to leave the coalition. At the end of
November Whitworth saw that he had gone too far and
tried to repair the mischief by presenting new proposals.
He offered subsidies for 60,000 Russians, England engaging
to harass the coasts of France and Holland with her own
forces. Rastoptchine drily refused to discuss this and
Souvorof at the same time received orders to bring his
forces back to Russia.

This appeared to be the end of all things. Paul was
resuming his liberty. The next day, November 18/29,
1799, Panine in vain tried a last effort. He wrote a letter
to the Czar, after which, if he was not listened to, he could
only " expect to receive his dismissal in cruel and ignominious terms." He was surprised to receive no answer at all.
His message, passing in ordinary course through the hands
of Rastoptchine, had never reached its destination. Paul
had, however, not yet ceased to hesitate. On December 2
(old style) a new rescript enjoined Souvorof to remain
where he was and to be ready to take the offensive.

This was simply another *coup de théâtre* without the
slightest change of circumstances to warrant it. It simply
meant that Paul was moved by his separation from the

Grand Duchess Alexandrina and had had a return of tenderness for the house into which his favourite daughter had married. On the eve of his departure the Archduke Palatine had thought proper to communicate to the Grand Duke Alexander the correspondence which had passed between the Archduke Charles and Souvorof, and from it the Czar got the impression that all the faults had not been on the side of the former, as he had supposed. A letter from Francis II in very kindly terms confirmed this impression, and Austria and the coalition seemed to have carried the day.

But the victory had no consequences. Paul, having given himself again, immediately tried to draw back. Even if Souvorof stayed in Germany that did not involve his subsequent participation in the war. Very soon Paul made that depend on the reception of a kind of ultimatum which he had addressed to Vienna and which required the dismissal of Thugut, the repudiation by Austria of all designs of aggrandisement and her consent to the re-establishment in Italy of the state of things which had existed there in 1798. Furthermore, Paul confided to Whitworth that he felt that the presence of his troops in Germany would be chiefly useful in that it would prevent Austria from seizing half the peninsula ! He repudiated all idea of further co-operation with the Austrian troops and would fight France with no other ally but England. The Marquis de Vioménil would take command of the Russian forces which were wintering at Jersey and Guernsey, and with seventeen Russian line-of-battle ships would join the English land and sea forces for a descent on France between Bordeaux and Sables d'Olonne.

Now, at this very moment they were considering at Vienna whether it would not be a good thing to get rid of Souvorof and his Russians at any price. Austria was then on the best of terms with England and hoped to obtain her help in securing the Milanese territories as they had been before the war of the Spanish succession—that is to say, including Novara and the fortresses. Minto himself seemed favourably disposed, and on November 19 Thugut sent to St. Petersburg an " *aperçu* " which he had drawn up in this sense. This document arrived some days after the *coup de théâtre* of December 2 and produced a new reaction. Kalytchof definitely replaced Razoumovski at Vienna and was directed to inform the Emperor and his Ministers that " if they persisted in this course " the Czar would recall his troops. Things were moving towards a diplomatic rupture which Souvorof's new quarrels with the *Hofkriegsrath* in the military sphere were rapidly making inevitable.

VII

Germany had been no more hospitable to the Marshal than Switzerland, and for the same reasons. Things soon were so bad that Derfelden, one of the Russian divisional commanders, and the only one who, in Wickham's opinion, had any merit, handed in his resignation, " not wishing to serve in an army of brigands." And on November 2/13, 1799, even before he received the Czar's orders, Souvorof had to announce to Francis II that he was under the painful necessity of taking his troops back to Russia. This decision had been foreseen and was expected without regret at Vienna, but it was feared that the departure of the Russians would make the French bolder and more difficult to deal with. They therefore still tried to temporise, but Souvorof would not wait.

He set out on November 28, at the very time when at St. Petersburg a change of resolution was imminent which would bring him to a standstill. He stayed for a short time in Bohemia, but this was merely due to difficulties of transport, and he was surprised at Prague by the Czar's new orders. He at once wrote to Francis II, requiring winter quarters and assuring him that his army was ready to take the field at a moment's notice. But Thugut was also averse from further co-operation, and in the very presence of Kalytchof he protested violently against a suggestion made by Minto that the Russian forces should be increased to 80,000 men. Germany could not support so many ! A small auxiliary corps, just sufficient to alarm the French, was all he asked of Russia. After a long discussion he accepted the principle of joint action on a greater scale, but on the basis that the two armies would act separately, the Russians on the north and the Austrians on the south of the Main and the Neckar.

Souvorof's reply when this proposal was presented to him was such as might have been expected from the recent declarations of the victor of Novi. He held to his idea of penetrating into France through Dauphiné at the head of an Austro-Russian army. He would fight on the Neckar if that was insisted on but only under the same conditions. With a frankness which was to prove fatal to him he did not fear to confess to Paul himself the reason for this, which was, as we know, that he could not do without the equipment, the staff, the commissariat, the ambulances and the siege train which the Austrians had furnished to his army in Italy.

If he could be satisfied on this point he promised a certain victory, whatever ground was chosen for battle. He was charmed with Francis II, whose name he never pronounced without touching the ground with his fingers, after the fashion of Russian moujiks ; with Minto, who, however, wrote to his wife that he had never seen " such a madman or such a contemptible creature." " What he says," added the Ambassador, " is absolutely incomprehensible and what he writes is the same. . . ." Count Bernstorff, a Prussian diplomatist, when passing through Prague, had an interview with the Marshal which produced a similar impression on his mind.

But, on the other hand, Souvorof's hosts could not fail

to be struck with the aspect of the Russian camp at Prague, the exterior of which was really imposing, though the Grand Duke Constantine with his brilliant suite was no longer there. He had already returned to Russia, not without leaving painful memories behind him, especially in Swabia, where he had distinguished himself by acts of revolting savagery. In default of the Grand Duke, however, Souvorof behaved more like a sovereign than a mere prince. He held a Court, gave audience to distinguished persons, military and civil, who came from every corner of Europe. Nelson wrote to him from Palermo a letter in which he lavished upon him the most flattering expressions. He discovered a physical resemblance between the Marshal and himself, and the former replied with compliments mixed with epigrams and anagrams.

As at Feldkirch, these strange frivolities were still occasionally illumined with flashes of real insight and dignity, as when he declared proudly to the assembled Austrians and English who had a moment before been surprised and disgusted by his absurdity : " Gentlemen, it is not the gold of England, nor the bayonets of Russia, not the cavalry nor the tactics of Austria, nor Souvorof himself that will restore order, win victories or obtain the desired results. Nothing can do that but justice and disinterestedness in politics, honesty and good faith and loyalty of conduct which will win the hearts of the people."

Very seriously, too, he was considering the prospect of soon taking the field again. But on January 8, 1800, Paul sent him definite and this time final orders to bring back his troops to Russia.

This was not, as has been generally supposed, or at any rate it was not entirely, the result of the affair of Ancona. At this time the Czar still expected to receive full satisfaction for the insult to his flag ; but the military divorce between the Russians and the Austrians was bearing bitter fruit. Count Peter Tolstoy had just arrived in St. Petersburg from Souvorof's camp, and when pressed with questions had admitted that under Souvorof's command the army of Novi and La Trebbia was now nothing but a collection of bandits, as Derfelden had said—as brave as ever but incapable of holding their own against European troops. On hearing this report Paul was nearly suffocated with rage. With his usual inconsequence he decreed the degradation of the too truthful officer, but he at once made it clear that he believed what he had said.

Souvorof, however, even before he received the message which recalled him to Russia, had set out in that direction. Thugut had absolutely refused to give the Marshal any troops, even the few thousand Austrians, without whom Souvorof said he could not appear on the battlefield; and he had also no less peremptorily required the Russians to evacuate Austrian territory, where their presence gave rise to unanimous complaints. All hope of an understanding in this quarter was at an end.

Only Condé's corps remained before Linz and they were negotiating for a transfer to the service of England. The Duc d'Enghien, in particular, was very unwilling to resume the obscure " life of a colonel of Russian dragoons in a cantonment of Volhynia." Souvorof made no objection, and Grenville proposed to the Czar that this corps should be sent to Trieste, whence it would join in England the troops intended for the descent on France. But favourably as he had recently been disposed to the Court of St. James's, Paul had already changed his mind. London was showing too much friendship for Vienna. The Prince de Condé therefore had a long time to wait before he learned the result of the overtures made to St. Petersburg ; and when, in March 1800, he regretfully decided to set out for Russia, he was abruptly informed by Prince Gortchakof, the Russian commissary who accompanied him, that he was no longer in the service of the Czar. Paul, yielding to a moment of anger, had sent orders to the Marshal to disband this corps, and at St. Petersburg at the same day's parade he made several French officers at St. Petersburg lay down their arms.

Souvorof was at the same time blamed for having approved of the Prince's plans, and reproaches and ill-treatment were showered upon him. Paul's conduct to his illustrious soldier, however, though it was entirely unjustifiable, was not inspired by such puerile motives as is commonly believed. It is said that Souvorof's only offences were having abandoned the Prussian uniform, having permanently employed a " *général de service*," and other breaches of the regulations. Paul was quite capable of absurdly exaggerating the importance of such things ; but the information given by Tolstoy about the condition of the army which he had just left furnished a much more serious reason for the resentment shown by the Emperor, who found confirmation of Tolstoy's account in Souvorof's own letter admitting that he cou d not take the field without the Austrians ! The Czar was the author of a military reform which deprived the Russian generals of their staffs without providing them with a commissariat ; but he was incapable of admitting that he was partly to blame for the inevitable result. He replied to Souvorof by reproducing word for word the humiliating admissions contained in his letter, drawing the conclusion that as it was considered that the Austrians alone were in a position to carry on the war they had better do it by themselves. Thereafter he continued to give the Prince of Italy more and more manifest intimations of his displeasure.

Souvorof spent the end of the winter on his estate at Kobryn, where, though he felt more and more, both mentally and physically, the strain of his recent experiences, he preserved his customary ideas and his usual habits. He still played with the village children, still sang in church, still made plans for the invasion of France. In April Paul was remorseful and pressed the Marshal to come to St. Petersburg. He now referred to him as " the hero of all the centuries," and quite unexpectedly assigned to him luxuriously furnished apartments in the Winter Palace, ordered a triumphal arch at the entrance to the capital and arranged for processions and music to honour his arrival. But at the last moment all these preparations were countermanded ; the wind had changed again, and it is believed that this was due to Koutaïssof.

The ex-barber went to meet Souvorof by order of the Czar, and the Marshal is said to have pretended not to recognise him, and to have questioned him with a feigned simplicity about his origin and the services which had been rewarded by so brilliant an advancement. He then turned to his valet, who has already been mentioned, and said : " Prochka ! As I tell you every day, you should give up drinking and stealing ! You won't pay any attention. But look at this gentleman : he was once what you are now, but as he was neither a drunkard nor a thief you see he is his Majesty's Master of the Horse, a Count and Knight of all the Orders in Russia."

Either because of this outburst or for some other reason which has remained undiscovered, " the hero of all the centuries " arrived at St. Petersburg on the evening of April 20, 1800 (old style) without any kind of pomp, and went quietly to the house of Count Khvostof, his nephew, where he had to go to bed at once. On March 6, after repeated attacks of fainting fits, he succumbed, and Paul did not even follow the body of the illustrious general to the Cathedral of St. Alexander Nevski, where he found his last resting-place.

VIII

With this man, who, in spite of everything, still dreamed of fighting at the head of an Austro-Russian army, the last chance of a return to the past disappeared. The Court of Vienna had now, very tardily and with a very ill grace,

entered upon the inevitable course of concession and reparation. General Fröhlich was court-martialled. An
Ambassador Extraordinary was appointed to carry excuses
to St. Petersburg. But at the same time Paul's irritation
was revived by the news which he was receiving about his
daughter Alexandrina. It appeared that she was being
ill-treated, and indeed suffering what amounted to persecution at the hands of a jealous sister-in-law, Maria Theresa
of Naples, the second wife of the Emperor Francis. Everything the young wife did was imputed to her as a crime —
even the brilliancy of her diamonds, which eclipsed those
of the Empress, was an offence! At Buda-Pesth the
Grand Duchess charmed the Hungarians by her grace and
beauty. She won their hearts by adopting the national
dress, but also fell under the suspicion of encouraging
separatist tendencies, which her presence seems in fact to
have excited. Hence a supervision which was so close and
irksome that, in order to enable poor Alexandrina to par-
take of a favourite national dish, her chaplain Samborski
had to go to market himself to buy the necessary fish,
which he concealed under his cloak!

When in March 1801 her sister-in-law died in childbirth,
it was said that Maria Theresa had something to do with
it and that the most necessary medical treatment had been
withheld!

On the other hand, Rastoptchine was prevailing more
and more over Panine, and this combined with Paul's
growing disgust for the coalition to bring back the Czar to
the programme with which he had begun his reign. The
future defender of the old capital against the French was
now showing that in spite of his cosmopolitan education he
possessed the old Muscovite spirit, which was hostile to all
contact with the rest of Europe. Russia in his view had
nothing to do with external conflicts to which Russia was
no party and to which she was sacrificing her own interests,
especially in Poland. This was Catherine's idea, with which,

however, both Paul himself and his favourite counsellor mixed a vague and very contradictory desire for a *rapprochement* with France. The events of the 18th Brumaire enhanced the impression produced by the disappointments of the Austrian alliance, and, according to Whitworth, "the virtues of Bonaparte" were becoming a favourite subject of conversation among the Czar's entourage. The Duke of Serra-Capriola declared that between Thugut and Bonaparte the comparison was all in favour of the latter, and Paul began to feel the fascination of the hero of Arcole and the Pyramids. Disgusted as he was with his partnership with Austria, he had contracted in her company a taste for adventure which henceforth left him no rest.

The coalition was supported, however, by the whole clan of *émigrés*, among whom had lately become prominent a man whose military reputation seemed capable of exercising a powerful fascination upon the Czar. Dumouriez, with the approval of Louis XVIII, had asked permission to come to St. Petersburg in order to communicate a plan which, as he affirmed, promised a certain triumph to the common cause and great glory for the Emperor of All the Russias. Paul for a long time left the general's letters unanswered, but in December 1799 he yielded to the instances of Panine and decided to receive him. But when Dumouriez arrived on January 9, 1800, he found a new change of humour and a much colder welcome than he expected. He had reckoned on having to deal with Panine, but found himself face to face with Rastoptchine, who asked him to return at once with a purse of a thousand ducats which the Czar offered as travelling expenses. The general, however, insisted on at least one personal interview with the Sovereign. Six weeks passed, and yet, in spite of all the efforts of Panine and Whitworth, this request was not granted, and meanwhile at Copenhagen and Berlin pourparlers with the representatives of the Republic were already in progress.

At last, on March 5, 1800, a note from Rastoptchine invited the traveller to present himself on parade on the following morning. He went in full uniform and on horseback, but again he was disappointed. The Emperor did not appear. Whitworth and Panine, however, scored a temporary triumph about this time, and two days later the much-wished-for interview took place. Paul was very gracious to the emissary of the *émigration,* and declared his unchangeable resolve to defend the cause of legitimate monarchy and the rights of Louis XVIII. If we may believe Dumouriez, he even added, " You should be the Monk of France ! " But at the same time he did not conceal his admiration for the First Consul ; and when Dumouriez expressed doubts as to whether the *coup d'état* of Brumaire could serve as the foundation of a durable government the Czar replied sharply, " Authority concentrated in a single person constitutes a government ! "

Not as yet disconcerted, the hero of Valmy developed his great plan, which consisted simply in securing for the coalition the assistance of Denmark in return for subsidies to be paid by England, and in attempting a descent on Normandy. Paul asked for a detailed memorandum on this subject and Dumouriez thought the game was won. He was already discussing the details of execution of the plan with the Danish and English envoys, Blome and Whitworth. But after receiving the memorandum the Czar demanded another about what might be attempted in the south of France, and obstinately avoided a second interview. Dumouriez was several times allowed to meet the Emperor on parade, but in the intervals between the evolutions Paul would talk of nothing but military technicalities, and on March 20 even these short meetings came to an end. On April 15, 1800, Rastoptchine peremptorily repeated the order to leave Russia, as the Emperor did not think the time was ripe for carrying out his projects.

At this time an answer from London on the subject of

Malta was being awaited at St. Petersburg. There the resistance of the French was nearly exhausted, and Paul wished to be assured that the rights of the Grand Master of the Order to the possession of the island would be respected. He proposed that it should be garrisoned by a detachment of Russian troops concurrently with those of England and Naples until a definite arrangement could be arrived at. On this point Whitworth had always given the Czar the most explicit assurances, expressing his own conviction in his letters to the Foreign Office that the ambitious monarch had no intention of personally acquiring the island. Paul, however, was still distrustful, and began to show a certain sourness in his dealings with the British Ambassador, for which there were several reasons. The chief of these was Whitworth's refusal to wear the insignia of the Order after having received the honour of being made a Knight. The representative of the Court of St. James's would have been very glad to satisfy the new Grand Master on this point. Personally, indeed, he was much in need of Paul's good graces. He wished to marry the widow of the Duke of Dorset and was trying to get a peerage. In order to have a lord at his Court, Paul had consented to support this request. But in London they were in no hurry to fulfil Whitworth's ambitions, and they explicitly forbade their envoy to assume the outward signs of membership of the Society of St. John of Jerusalem.

Further, Paul was not pleased with the Convention of El Arich of January 24, 1800, which was negotiated by Sydney Smith and assured the repatriation of the French army of Egypt with their arms and baggage. The sojourn of the Russian troops at Jersey and Guernsey was another source of friction. A young English girl was abducted and violated, and General Essen, Herrmann's successor, refused to deliver up to justice two of his soldiers who had been guilty of the crime. The result was a riot in the island and a storm in London itself. Vorontsof cut the matter short by accepting British jurisdiction ; but immediately afterwards new differences arose on the subject of the subsidies promised by the Court of St. James's for the maintenance of the Russian troops.

Dumouriez's reception had suffered from all these circumstances. In vain the general begged in very humble terms for a farewell audience. With still less dignity but with no more success he asked for a share in the distribution of lands which was made to the *émigrés*. He had to content himself with the thousand ducats which he had been promised ; but he did not despair. He dined with Moraviof, the Russian Minister, as he passed through Hamburg, and said that he was convinced that the Czar would never abandon Louis XVIII. But after the rupture with Austria a rupture with England was soon to follow.

Until April 1800 the British Cabinet was still rather naïvely revolving new and vast projects, based on the co-operation of Russia, for the forthcoming campaign. In spite of Vorontsof's hints they were tactless enough to insist on the addition of 30,000 Austrians to the Russian forces under Souvorof's command, according to the expressed desire of the Marshal. Pitt wished to retain at any rate the Russian troops which had fought in Holland and to employ these in Italy, " where the two Powers would guarantee each other the possessions they might retain in that country on the conclusion of peace." In order to retain the Czar's co-operation he went so far as to waive the susceptibilities aroused by the presence of the Russian flag in the Mediterranean. He said nothing of Malta, but he hoped to be able to divert Paul's ambitions to another object by suggesting the possibility of a conquest of Majorca. In November he had already decided to send Popham* back to St. Petersburg to offer a new treaty of subsidies and a plan for a general pacification on the follow-

* Afterwards Rear-Admiral Sir Home Riggs Popham, K.C.B.

ing basis. The restoration of the French Monarchy was to be considered as desirable but not as a condition *sine qua non*. The integrity of the ancient territory of France was to be recognised. The *status quo ante bellum* was to be maintained in Malta and the Adriatic islands. No arrangement was to be considered which would leave France in possession of the Netherlands or in a position to dominate Switzerland, or whose object was to exchange Bavaria for the Italian provinces coveted by Austria. The King of Sardinia was to be restored on condition of retroceding Novara in exchange for Genoa. Any conditions which would leave Austria Venetia and part of the Legations were to be considered acceptable. For the rest there was to be a return to the *status quo ante* subject to suitable compensation for Naples. For herself, England would be content with the colonial acquisitions she had already made, and if Majorca was taken by the Russians there would be no objection to their retaining that island.

Even in November 1799 there was little chance that these proposals would be favourably received at St. Petersburg. Popham was much delayed by bad weather and did not reach the Russian coast till the end of March 1800. By this time it was impossible for him even to enter into conference on the object of his mission. After a quarantine of a fortnight he was allowed to travel to the capital, but he asked in vain to see Rastoptchine, who left his notes unanswered. He then, in more urgent terms, asked for an audience of the Czar, "in order to communicate to his Majesty important messages with which he was charged, after which he was to return to England." Then, and not until then, he received an answer, which was to the effect that " Captain Popham might return when he pleased."

Whitworth at the same time was treated no better. He was refused passports for a courier whom he wished to send to England, and, when he inquired the reason of this unusual procedure, was informed that the Czar owed him no account of his actions. As he insisted, Panine had the mortification of having to inform him that Paul was dissatisfied with his conduct as Ambassador and had asked for his recall. It was true. As early as February, Vorontsof had received from his Sovereign a rescript to the following effect : " For some time I have been displeased with the conduct of Sir Charles Whitworth. Circumstances require that Ministers should be exact and candid in their utterances, and he should therefore be recalled and replaced by some one else."

The Duchess of Dorset's fiancé had seen the storm coming. He suspected that one of his cyphered letters had been intercepted, and had even thought of giving out, " in order to avoid scandal," that he had obtained several months' leave. Meanwhile he ceased to use his cypher except to lavish praises on the Czar and for the essential parts of his despatches he had recourse to other cryptographic methods. He broke through his habitual reserve on the subject of the Czar's private life and went into ecstasies over the magnanimity of Mlle. Lapoukhine's protector in giving her the husband of her choice. In sympathetic ink, however, he added his first sincere expression of opinion about Paul. " *The fact is, and I speak it with regret, that the Emperor is literally not in his senses. This truth has been for many years known to those nearest to him, and I have myself had frequent opportunities of observing it. But since he has come to the throne his disorder has gradually increased.*" Perhaps Paul himself read these lines, for they " had a remedy for everything " in the " black cabinet." Whitworth, however, flattered himself that the storm would pass. Rastoptchine was to blame for it, but he could not long remain in power. At all costs England must retain the Russian alliance ; but this was not a reason for attempting to cajole the Imperial lunatic. " *The more he is courted, the more difficult it is to manage him,*" wrote the Ambassador. The British envoy was informed by Panine of the negotiations which had begun between St. Petersburg and Paris, but he did not believe they could succeed.

In London, Vorontsof shared this optimistic view. He had already received orders to arrange for the repatriation of the Russian troops in Jersey and Guernsey; but on Panine's advice he had taken advantage of the fact that they were neither precise nor peremptory, and did not hasten to execute them. On the contrary, he continued to send suggestions to St. Petersburg for the employment of this force for a descent on France. The two ambassadors were soon to be cruelly disillusioned.

On April 13, 1800, Vorontsof was directed to leave England temporarily, " to take the waters on the Continent." Three days later this was followed by a rescript, signed by Panine himself, in the following terms : " His Majesty, finding in your reports propositions contrary to his wishes, directs me to say that if you find it irksome to carry out these wishes it is open to you to resign." " You see what I am obliged to sign," added the Minister in a note attached to the official message. " I wet your hands with my tears. . . . There is no help for it ! "

Vorontsof resigned, but asked and obtained permission to reside in England, his second fatherland, as a private individual. He chose to live at Southampton and handed over the affairs of the Embassy to Lizakiévitch, the counsellor of the Legation. He did not present letters of recall, for the disorder of the Department of Foreign Affairs, for the control of which Panine and Rastoptchine were fighting, was such that no one seems to have thought of taking the necessary steps to fulfil this formality.

The Court of St. James's asked that a successor might be sent, and Paul again replied that " Sovereigns were not obliged to account for their actions." The King of England need not replace Whitworth unless he liked. Whitworth had received his letters of recall in June, and presented as chargé d'affaires his Counsellor of Legation Casamajor. But soon afterwards, when Hailes, the English envoy, was leaving his post at Stockholm he either forgot, or neglected, or deliberately omitted to call on his Russian colleague, and immediately, in spite of the representations of Panine and of Rastoptchine himself, Paul sent orders to Whitworth that he must withdraw his whole staff. At that moment 18,000 of the Czar's troops and fifteen line-of-battle ships flying his flag remained in the hands of the English!

This did not prevent him from acting as if he was deliberately provoking not merely a diplomatic rupture, but a war to the death against his ally of yesterday. In August, in fact, on receiving news that some merchant ships under convoy of a Danish frigate had been detained by one of the English admirals, he actually opened hostilities by placing an embargo on the ships, country houses and funds belonging to Englishmen then in Russia. Stephen Shairp, the English Consul-General, was himself sentenced to expulsion, a decision which was conveyed to him in no gentle terms, and numerous English sailors were thrown into prison and afterwards sent into the interior of the country in bitter weather.

This meant war. In October Lizakiévitch was appointed Minister at Copenhagen and quitted London in his turn, leaving some of the staff and the archives of the Legation to the care of the Chaplain Smirnof, who is the only example in the history of Russian diplomacy of an ecclesiastic having been entrusted with such functions. Still, however, there was no fighting. England was passionately absorbed in her struggle with France, and received all this provocation with an admirable if phlegmatic determination not to take offence. She hastened to give satisfaction to Denmark, and thus obtained, in September 1800, the withdrawal of the measures taken against her nationals in Russia. But in the following month things again went wrong. The Maltese question cropped up again and Paul was exasperated to a pitch of fury which was practically madness.

On September 7 the island fell into the hands of the English, and Rastoptchine, not without effrontery, requested that a Russian corps might be landed at Valetta in accordance with the previous conventions. As he did not at once receive a reply which satisfied him, the measures of August were reimposed with aggravations. English merchandise in Russian warehouses was sequestrated, all payments to British subjects were suspended ; a commission was appointed for the liquidation of accounts between Russian and British merchants.

In addition to all this, Russia in December entered into treaties with Prussia, Sweden and Denmark, which renewed and extended the system of armed neutrality of 1780, which was always regarded by the British Cabinet as peculiarly inimical to British interests, and this time, though with much regret, Pitt had to abandon the conciliatory methods which he had carried to such lengths. In his turn he placed an embargo on the vessels and the goods of the neutrals (though from this he still made an exception in favour of Prussia), and as they on their part forbade English vessels access to the Baltic a fight appeared to be imminent.

Paul became more and more bellicose. In January 1801 he directed Saltykof, the Governor of Moscow, to place strong posts in all the houses in the town which belonged to Englishmen. At the same time Rastoptchine directed Smirnof to leave at once for Hamburg and to take with him not only the remainder of the staff of the Legation but all the Russian officers and all the workmen belonging to the Czar's navy who were then in England ! He seems to have thought that this order could be carried out in spite of his almost insulting reply to a recent and courteous communication from Grenville. " Nothing," he had said, " would be done to alter the measures which were being taken against England so long as she continued to usurp the rights of the Order at Malta." Moreover, as the tone of the last letters addressed to St. Petersburg by the British minister had displeased the Czar, he had directed that they should be returned.

Poor Smirnof escaped from the embarrassment into which he had fallen. While he was consulting Vorontsof about the course he should pursue, a despatch from Count Pahlen announced the accession of Alexander I and the return of the former ambassador to the post from which Paul had deposed him. Meanwhile the winter season alone had prevented England and Russia from exchanging shots. Prussian troops were preparing to occupy Hanover; Danish troops were taking possession of Hamburg and Lubeck, where British goods were confiscated. Paul was hurriedly fitting out what remained of his fleet and was concentrating an army corps on the shores of the Baltic. He was in no position to give any help to his allies. At the time of his death, Denmark and Sweden, in spite of his warnings, had neglected to cover sufficiently the passage of the Sound, and in March 1801, when the Russian fleet was imprisoned in the ice, seventeen English line-of-battle ships and thirty frigates under Parker and Nelson had arrived without hindrance under the walls of Copenhagen. They promptly reduced the defences of the town and forced Denmark if not to abandon her allies, at any rate to sign a truce of fourteen weeks. After this, Nelson entered the Baltic, where Sweden and Russia were in their turn threatened by this formidable adversary.

Paul was not in the least alarmed. He was then engaged in a series of negotiations, to be related in the next chapter, the purpose of which was an alliance with France against England, an object which he was now pursuing with as much ardour and as little reflection as he had shown in embracing the cause of the coalition.

CHAPTER XIII

PAUL I AND BONAPARTE

I

IF Paul had entered the coalition without any good reason he had from the very first several excellent ones for quitting it. The events of the 18th of Brumaire and the Battle of Marengo supplied him with an even stronger motive for doing so. It cannot be said that the Czar's decision was exactly determined by these events, for his acts were never either well reasoned or reasonable. Both of them, however, doubtless had their share in hastening a process which detached him from Austria and England and inevitably pushed him towards France.

He was attracted to the new ally both by reason of the disappointments he had experienced and the ambitions he had formed in the company of his former friends. It had been his vocation as an absolute sovereign, no less than his pleasure, to defend the principle of authority. But the title by which he held his own crown was by no means so irreproachable as to make him an unbending legitimist. He had championed Louis XVIII because he appeared to be the only possible representative of peace and order in France. But now the jacobins had an adversary and a master by the side of whom his royal guest at Mittau made but a poor appearance. Further, when he joined Austria Paul thought he was fighting for justice ; but he found that his companions-in-arms were using their own forces and his entirely for their own advantage. Against them and their greedy usurpations Bonaparte at this time seemed to be the true defender of the rights of Europe, and as justice had changed sides should not her partisans follow her example?

In this, as in all other matters, the confused brain and weak will of the Czar were governed by anything rather than the logic of the situation. A much more cogent influence may have been the valet who was then in guilty relations with the wife of a more or less converted jacobin. Mme. Chevalier may well have played a part, like other adventurers and adventuresses, in this chapter of history. But she did not create the double current which was drawing together the two nations still hot from the savage combat in which they had been engaged. In France this movement had origins equally obscure, of older standing and hardly less questionable.

When Bonaparte came into power he took the initiative in seeking a *rapprochement* with that enemy of the Republic who had struck her the most deadly blows. There was nothing new in this policy; but if, as has been said, Bonaparte found the substance of it in the papers of the Directory, he must also have recognised that much of what he found there was of little use. Since the beginning of 1799 the French Government had been overwhelmed with projects either for conquering Russia or for disarming her hostility. Of the numerous citizens who came forward with plans, one Guttin, formerly Inspector-General of Manufactures in Russia was the most enterprising. In a series of memoirs presented between April and November 1799 he developed a system based on the dismemberment of the Turkish possessions in Europe and the reconstitution of the Kingdom of Poland. The acquisition by France of her natural frontiers, besides the Ionian Islands, Crete, Cyprus, Sicily and Egypt; the annexation of Constantinople and the Balkan provinces to Russia; the aggrandisement of Prussia by the addition of Austrian Silesia, Mecklenburg, Hanover, Hamburg, Bremen and Lubeck; the secularisation of Germany; the diminution of Austria, which was to become a mere auxiliary, was to be expelled from Italy, and was to receive no compensation except to a small extent on the Lower Danube—such were the subsidiary features of his scheme. Starting from their Asian possessions on the shores of the Caspian, the Russians were to resume their march on Persia and were to join hands with a French army which, from Egypt, would threaten the British colossus in Bengal.

Guttin was a visionary, but it is not unlikely that the future negotiator of Tilsit owed something to his tumultuous imagination. Talleyrand, however, reported unfavourably on his memoirs on October 25, 1799, and no doubt all that the First Consul at first remembered of this romantic literature was a hint given to the Foreign Minister in August by Otto, the French chargé d'affaires at Berlin. "I am surprised that you have not yet tried to win him (Paul) over. He is a kind of Don Quixote, very inconsequent and very obstinate, whose only desire is to satisfy his vanity." At that time the hero of the first campaign of Italy saw the Czar and his Empire only through the eyes of the Polish legions, so that there is no indication in the instructions given to Beurnonville, who succeeded Sieyês at Berlin towards the end of 1799, of any idea of a reconcilation with Russia. So late even as January 27, 1800, the First Consul, writing to Talleyrand, asks his opinion merely on the best means of persuading Prussia to put herself at the head of a league of Northern Powers against her Eastern neighbour.

A Russian historian has attributed to the future Prince of Benevento the merit of having rectified the ideas of his chief on this point by suggesting to him the possibility of using the good offices of Prussia as a means towards a reconciliation with the Czar, as well as of employing for this purpose at St. Petersburg the services of the Comte de Choiseul-Gouffier, whose hopes, like those of some other *émigrés*, were already turning towards the sun which was rising in France. But for all Talleyrand's ingenuity and his gifts of political clairvoyance, the Franco-Russian *rapprochement* of 1800–1801 came about in a different way.

II

In January 1800, Bignon, who preceded Beurnonville as chargé d'affaires at Berlin, and Baron Krudener, the new Russian envoy, chanced to be staying at the same hotel, the Soleil d'Or. A Jew named Ephraïm, who was a disreputable agent of the Prussian Government, drew the French diplomatist's attention to the coincidence, at the same time speaking of the desire of Prussia to improve her own relations with Russia.

Krudener was still without any official status, and had been presented to ministers by the British chargé d'affaires simply as " a traveller." He had instructions, however, to sound Haugwitz about a defensive alliance which the state of Europe seemed to require. If assurances were required on the subject of compensations, Krudener was to " flatter their cupidity " but to promise nothing definite. The Court of Berlin received these overtures with enthusiasm, but thought it best that Russia should first make peace with France, to which end she offered her good offices. Hence Ephraïm's hints.

Talleyrand was prompt to see the advantage of following this up by conciliatory expressions, and persuaded the First Consul to allow him to make a pronouncement in this sense to Sandoz, the Prussian chargé d'affaires at Paris. On January 20 Beurnonville arrived at the Hôtel de Russie at Berlin, where he met Baron de Krudener, who happened quite by chance to have changed his hotel. This time Haugwitz himself came on the scene with more explicit declarations. Prussia would be delighted to serve as an intermediary between St. Petersburg and Paris, and if France were prepared to make a sacrifice in the Mediterranean it would, *especially if disagreeable to Austria,* assure the success of her intervention. Meanwhile Beurnonville, as a former Knight of St. Louis and a servant of the old monarchy, was loaded with attentions, which contrasted with the treatment received by Sieyès. Though he was a middle-class person, he was accepted as a gentleman of the *ancien régime* temporarily disguised as a republican, and the future Marquis of the Restoration was invited both to the large and the small receptions at Court. Being very vain and a novice in diplomacy he was greatly pleased, and believed himself on the way to play a great part in history.

It was clear enough what was meant by the " sacrifice in the Mediterranean," and an evasive answer was soon dictated from Paris to the representative of the Republic : " France would willingly recognise the Czar as Grand Master of the Order of St. John of Jerusalem, a title which could be established as well at Rhodes or St. Petersburg as at Malta." Haugwitz seemed satisfied, and on his side the First Consul authorised Beurnonville to continue the negotiations.

It remained to ascertain the views of Russia. The Court of Berlin seemed ready to guarantee that she was equally ready to come to terms. But Baron Krudener's attitude revealed nothing of this. He had been told, so Haugwitz said, of the friendly dispositions of his French colleagues, but he still did nothing which showed the faintest desire to respond. He even ostentatiously avoided them, and seemed to fear even their civility. Beurnonville expressed his surprise to King Frederick-William, who observed : " What can you expect ? One of your civilities might send him to Siberia ! " He added, however, that the negotiations should go on. They must first reach an agreement. Civility would come later.

The Russian postponed his reply until he had consulted

St. Petersburg, and when his courier returned he declined in the most abrupt and peremptory manner to have anything to do, directly or indirectly, with the French envoy. At the same time, while they still held out hopes of an agreement with Russia, Haugwitz and his colleagues became much more reserved. Beurnonville could not understand it, and thought he was being trifled with; and even Talleyrand could make nothing of the situation, especially as the Cabinet of Berlin, which was well informed as to the real situation in Russia, was extremely reticent on this subject. What had happened at St. Petersburg was this. Krudener reported the French overtures on January 16/28, 1800. Early in February (new style) Paul wrote in the margin : " As to a *rapprochement* with France, I should be glad of it, especially if she came to me as a counterweight to Austria." Panine, however, ventured to add his own commentary to his master's, and wrote : " I could never carry out this without acting against my conscience." And the instructions he sent to Krudener were in the sense of a letter he wrote to Vorontsof, in which he says : " *His Majesty ordered me to answer* that he would listen to no proposals from the Corsican usurper. . . . The follies of the Haugwitzian policy were not likely to shake the principles of our august master."

His hatred of the Republic and of the power of France was irreconcilable. It was his ambition to play the part of a second Pitt at the other end of Europe—younger and less prudent, but equally ardent and indomitable. It is true that he added a confidential note to his despatch to Krudener from which may be divined the situation in which the despatch was written. " I do not conceal from you that things are growing worse and worse, and that tyranny and insanity are at their height." Krudener, however, was not the man to take such a hint. He was devoted to the Vice-Chancellor and shared his views, and, as Kotchoubey said, " he looked upon the Republic not with the eyes of a Russian diplomatist but with those of an *émigré.*"

The Prussian Cabinet had no desire to clear up the situation. They sincerely desired that an agreement should be reached. But they wished to keep the negotiations in their own hands and therefore took no trouble to indicate ways and means. Moreover, they expected to receive a commission for their intervention, and they had hoped that Beurnonville would at once open up the question of a general peace and the advantages which would accrue to Prussia. The representative of the First Consul had nothing to say on this interesting subject until the end of February, and then all he could do was to utter a " profession of disinterestedness," which was not by any means what the Prussians wanted.

Like his predecessor, Bonaparte refused on principle to be a " *marchand de peuples.*" " France," he said, " desired to keep the Rhine frontier, but that was a settled thing, provided for in the treaties of Berlin and Campio Formio, consecrated even at Rastadt, and therefore irrevocably introduced into the public law of Europe. As France, therefore, asked nothing but what she already possessed, the Government of the Republic hoped that the other Powers would follow her example and refrain from producing new claims." When it was answered that Prussia in the Treaty of Berlin had been faithfully promised compensation for what she had abandoned on the left bank and that it was popularly supposed that secret articles in the Treaty of Campio Formio provided that the new French frontier should respect the Prussian enclaves, Beurnonville was silent.

Haugwitz's zeal for a Franco-Russian understanding promptly cooled, and in the course of the following weeks, as the military situation seemed to turn to the disadvantage of France, he gradually raised his terms. Besides giving up the left bank of the German river, France must also evacuate Holland and Switzerland and recognise the independence of these countries. A *rapprochement* with Russia could be had on no other terms. He communicated nothing of all this to St. Petersburg but boldly represented it as concerted with the Russian Cabinet, hoping thus to bring the French Government to terms.

But at this very time Bonaparte and Talleyrand were already receiving very different news from another quarter. Bourgoing, their representative at the Hanseatic courts, reported that he had it from a sure source that the moment was extremely favourable for approaching Paul with offers of peace. The " sure source " was, it is true, apparently of little value. Bourgoing's information came from a certain ci-devant Marquis de Bellegarde, an *émigré* who had made useful friendships in Russia, notably with Rastoptchine. According to him Rastoptchine, Koutaïssof, and Mme. Chevalier were on the point of triumphing over Panine. M. de Bellegarde was not in himself a very credible witness, but Bourgoing found confirmation of his testimony in the attitude of Mouraviof, the Russian Minister at Hamburg, professedly still an enemy of France, who, however, in his cups was in the habit of violently abusing England and Austria.

Even when he was drunk Mouraviof knew what he was about, and Bourgoing was not mistaken. Amid the conflicting influences to which he was exposed Paul still hesitated. He agreed at this very time to receive M. de Caraman at St. Petersburg as the official representative of the King of France. With more wisdom he decided that he must await the result of the Italian campaign, where the First Consul's fortunes were in the balance. But there could be no doubt that Bonaparte and France attracted him. Talleyrand, with his sure instinct, clearly divined this, but he could not yet see how to get to close quarters with this impotent despot, who was betrayed and buffeted by his servants.

As Berlin gave him no help he decided to have recourse to Hamburg, and Bourgoing, on June 23, 1800, the day after Marengo, was able to give him a piece of advice, the importance of which he was no doubt far from foreseeing and which has hitherto been buried in the French archives. It is right that the credit of the idea should be restored to the obscure diplomatist who originated it, for, when interpreted by the First Consul with the amplitude which he knew how to impart to everything, it changed the face of the diplomatic campaign, which had begun so badly, and assured its success. No doubt Marengo had also its due share in securing this result.

Bourgoing wrote : " I have again been considering the means of effecting a *rapprochement* with Russia. My friends still think that this can best be done by the intervention of the Court of Berlin, but they are also of opinion that it might also be managed by cajoling Paul I. For this it would be enough to act in the spirit for some time displayed by our official journals. But in addition some steps should be taken to show our consideration for the Russian people and above all for their soldiers. It would be well to show kindness to such as are prisoners of war—perhaps even to allow them to return to their country."

III

On July 20, 1800, a letter from Talleyrand to Panine was sent by courier to Bourgoing. It contained the announcement that the First Consul had decided to send back all the Russian prisoners of war in his hands without exchange. It seems that Bonaparte, from motives which he explained to no one, had already accorded special privileges to the subjects of the Czar who had fallen into captivity. The officers were allowed to carry arms, and he had taken care that the men were well fed. He now offered to send them all back to Russia with the honours of war, with their standards, their weapons, and with new clothes. The message was to be given in exchange for a receipt to the Russian Minister at Hamburg, who was to be asked to forward it to St. Petersburg by special courier. Here the perspicacity of Bonaparte and Talleyrand failed them, and French diplomacy, on the eve of one of its most brilliant triumphs (and after Marengo!), was to experience a cruel humiliation.

Bourgoing wrote to M. Mouraviof to ask for an interview on a matter of importance to both governments, but could not find at the Russian Minister's house so much as a servant who was willing to take in the letter! He sent it by post and got no reply. Mouraviof was imitating Krudener. A representative of Louis XIV, or even of Louis XVI, would no doubt have forborne to press the matter further. But the ministers of the Republic had had both time and occasion to get rid of this kind of susceptibility. Bourgoing therefore renewed his application three times, equally without success. At last, in a fourth letter he revealed the object of the correspondence, pointing out to his colleague that the responsibility of refusing to transmit so important a communication was perhaps greater than that of receiving it. Bourgoing went on to suggest that an answer might be sent to the address of a M. de la Croix, from which it should be fetched in the strictest secrecy. This time a reply did come, in the shape of an unsigned note to the effect that the writer "could not communicate with M. de la Croix without express permission and still less undertake to charge himself with a letter, no matter what the contents."

Bourgoing thought of sending Talleyrand's letter to Panine by the ordinary post, but changed his mind. After all, Mouraviof now knew of the First Consul's intentions and could not fail to communicate them to his master. It would therefore be best to await the effect of this indirect communication. This reasoning was justified by the event. Paul was made awaie of what was offered; but already his dispositions and those of his entourage, with the exception of Panine, had been modified in a sense much more favourable to France. Mouraviof might be deaf at Hamburg. At St. Petersburg the echoes of the thunder of Marengo were not unheard.

Already, in spite of his colleague's opposition, Rastoptchine had secured that Baron Krudener should be directed to cease to avoid the representative of the Republic. The Czar was in accord with the Berlin Cabinet in wishing to raise the question of a general pacification in connection with this resumption of diplomatic relations; but his views on this subject were by no means those which had been expressed on his behalf by the Prussian ministers. Baron Krudener's new instructions said nothing about Malta, and as to the Rhine frontier merely expressed the hope that the acquisitions of France might be reduced as far as possible. Paul's chief care was the fate of the Italian sovereigns, the Elector of Bavaria, and the King of Portugal, whom he wished to see maintained in their possessions. If the King of Sardinia could not be reinstated in Savoy and in the other parts of his dominions annexed to France he desired that his Majesty might receive compensation in the Cisalpine territories. There was not a word about Prussia or the compensations which she represented as being supported by the Czar.

This was communicated by the Bavarian Minister, Baron Posch, to Beurnonville, who rightly concluded that he need no longer count on the co-operation of Frederick-William and his Ministers in bringing about a Franco-Russian *rapprochement*. He thought that he would soon be able to do without it, but another disappointment awaited him. The last post had brought Baron Krudener a despatch which Panine had again been able to edit; he cancelled an interview which had been arranged, and ended by declaring that no conversation with the French

Minister would be of any use, as he had no orders to discuss anything with him.

Beurnonville was in despair, but his troubles were nearly over. The step which the First Consul had taken on Bourgoing's advice was having its effect. The Czar was deeply touched by his courtesy, though for a time Panine succeeded in preventing him from replying as he wished. Talleyrand, however, was by this time trying to get his communication to St. Petersburg in another way—by sending back Major Serguiéief, one of the captive Russians, and even by writing a letter in which he allowed it to be understood that the First Consul would be very accommodating on the subject of Malta, being ready for " any sacrifice that might be necessary rather than let the island fall into the hands of the English."

This was not yet the abandonment of the island, though it has been so represented, or even the recognition of Paul as Grand Master. For this reason the letter cannot have been accompanied by the gift of a sword formerly presented by a Pope to one of the Grand Masters of the Order, La Valette or Villiers de l'Isle Adam, according to varying versions of the story. The two countries were still at war, and the possession of Malta and the Grand Mastership were two of the most important points in the negotiation for peace. To send such a gift would have prejudged the intentions of the Republican Government, and neither Bonaparte nor Talleyrand was capable of such folly.

Even Major Serguiéief had some difficulty in transmitting the two letters entrusted to him to their destination. Krudener kept him at Berlin, refused passports, and undertook himself to forward them. This was designed to enable Panine to make what use of them he pleased. But the inspiration of the First Consul carried the day, and Krudener was categorically ordered to enter into negotiations with Beurnonville. On September 12, accordingly, the two diplomatists met in conference in the gardens of

Haugwitz's house after a dinner arranged for the purpose of the meeting. The tradition of the furtive meetings of 1797 was maintained : the Cabinet of Berlin retained the means of figuring as a third in the negotiations and Krudener was complaisant enough to forward their design.

IV

This first conversation led to no positive result. Beurnonville had no powers to treat, and Krudener on his side was not authorised to commit himself deeply. He listened amiably to the condition imposed by the First Consul on the return of the Russian prisoners, saying that the Czar accepted them in advance. He confirmed the expression of his Sovereign's views on the question of a general pacification given above, adding only a request that the possessions of the Duke of Würtemberg might be guaranteed. At St. Petersburg the struggle between Panine and Rastoptchine still continued. It was not until September 26 (old style) that the former refused to become the interpreter of the new resolutions of his master or even to answer Talleyrand. The latter therefore took up the pen and wrote the celebrated note which has been the subject of so much discussion. Rastoptchine said :

" His Imperial Majesty of All the Russias, having taken cognisance of the letters addressed to his Vice-Chancellor, Count Panine, directs me to acquaint the First Consul that a harmonious agreement with his Majesty can only be secured by the accomplishment of his Majesty's desires as already signified to General Beurnonville : (1) The surrender of the island of Malta and its dependencies to the Order of St. John of Jerusalem, of which the Emperor is Grand Master ; (2) the re-establishment of the King of Sardinia in his dominions as they were before the entry of the French into Italy ; (3) the maintenance of the integrity of the dominions of the King of the Two Sicilies; (4) of those of the Elector of Bavaria; and (5) of those of the Duke of Würtemberg." At the same time the President of the College of Foreign Affairs announced that General Baron Sprengtporten would be sent to France to receive the Russian prisoners.

Apart from the stiffness of its style, which could scarcely have surprised the French Government after their recent experiences of Russian diplomacy, this note added nothing to the previous communications from the Cabinet of St. Petersburg. It merely changed into a definitely formulated demand the suggestions which had previously been made by the Cabinet of Berlin in the form of advice. As Baron Krudener had hitherto been silent on the subject of Malta, Haugwitz found himself, on this topic at least, the authorised interpreter of the Czar. This fact had its importance and was destined to exercise much influence on the subsequent course of the negotiations.

Meanwhile the exact nature of the mission to be entrusted to Sprengtporten* had not yet been settled. Panine, who could not prevent it, reduced it to the simple task of bringing back the prisoners set at liberty by the First Consul who were now assembled on the eastern frontier of France; the envoy was not even to show himself in Paris, where there was nothing for him to do. But it was Rastoptchine who gave Sprengtporten his instructions, in which he was charged " to express to the First Consul his Imperial Majesty's gratitude and his desire to reciprocate the courtesy, and to bring together two Powers which were destined by their position to live at peace, and whose union might have a decisive influence on the tranquillity of the rest of Europe."

---

* Panine is said to have objected strongly to the choice of Sprengtporten, who was a native of Finland and after having been a strong partisan of Gustavus III had deserted the cause of Sweden and had exerted himself with equal zeal in preparing the union of his native country with Russia. Paul is said to have replied : " Well, could I do better than to send a traitor to treat with a usurper ? "

Rastoptchine continued : " The Emperor authorises General Sprengtporten to declare to the ministers with whom he may have to treat [sic] that his Majesty did not for a moment hesitate to withdraw his troops from the coalition as soon as he perceived that the views of the allied Powers involved aggrandisements which his disinterested good faith could not permit. As owing to their separation France and Russia could never be in a position to injure each other they might well unite, and by the constant maintenance of harmony between themselves prevent their interests from being injured by the aggression of other Powers."

On the other hand, Panine had his way so far as to forbid the general to treat with any one about anything but the repatriation of the Russian soldiers. To this contradiction Paul added a supreme aberration, and enlarged in another direction the mandate thus limited. He desired Sprengtporten, after fulfilling the purely military object of his mission, to go straight to Malta and take possession of the island in his Majesty's name ! Nothing was yet settled ; it was by no means certain that anything would be settled. But before an agreement was reached, for which he had no power even to negotiate, Sprengtporten was to act as if the most controversial of all the clauses had been setttled in favour of Russia ! Moreover, the situation had already changed : since September 5 Malta had ceased to be in the possession of France. The surrender of the island had now to be demanded from England, and a courier was sent after Sprengtporten, who had already started, with the news. This, for the moment at least, deprived the negotiations between France and Russia, as Paul conceived them, of any apparent object. The Czar's other demands were all concerned with the problem of a general pacification, and war was still raging !

In his instructions to Beurnonville Talleyrand was careful to take account of the new situation. The event of September 5 had eliminated the only one of the Czar's demands which could interfere with or condition the separate accord which the two Powers had in view. The best plan therefore was first of all to bring about their reconciliation and then in a spirit of mutual benevolence to consider the general questions raised by the Czar. Prussia had nothing to do with this negotiation, and Beurnonville was to prevent her from interfering on any pretext whatever. The conferences should take place alternately at the residences of the two negotiators. If Baron Krudener insisted, the first conference might be at his house. All this was excellent, but was far from being what Paul and his counsellors had hoped, and poor Beurnonville was soon made to feel this.

He politely offered to call on Krudener and met with an icy reception. The Russian envoy was by no means inclined to treat on the basis of these instructions. A week later he informed his French colleague that he had received despatches and curtly told him to come again. It is clear that the callow diplomatist had allowed the Russian to conclude that he might treat the representatives of the Republic as he pleased. The event justified the assumption. Beurnonville, in spite of his instructions, responded in the most docile manner and attended as he was bidden, only to be told that St. Petersburg would listen to nothing outside Rastoptchine's note.

At the same time Haugwitz made it clear that he was determined not to be set aside. The laborious negotiations of the last eight months between Berlin and St. Petersburg had at last borne fruit. By a treaty signed at Peterhof on July 16/28, 1800—Panine's final triumph—the two Powers had resumed their former alliance. Though it was purely defensive—" inoffensive " the wags called it—and allowed Frederick-William to maintain for the time the expectant neutrality to which he was so much attached, this event marked none the less a return to the traditions of a diplomatic intimacy which, it was thought at Berlin, would prevent either Power from conducting separate negotiations with third parties.

Rastoptchine thought differently, and had intended to remove the negotiations with France to Copenhagen or Hamburg, where Mouraviof, who had suddenly relented, was trying to get into touch with Bourgoing. But so much annoyance was immediately manifested on the banks of the Spree that the idea had to be abandoned. Baron Krudener therefore remained accredited to treat with Beurnonville, and Haugwitz posed more deliberately than ever as the recognised mouthpiece of the Cabinet of St. Petersburg. According to him, Rastoptchine's note of September 26 had passed through his hands, and Talleyrand in his turn had charged the Prussian Minister with his reply.

This was one of the tricks of legerdemain which are part of a familiar tradition of Prussian diplomacy, piously preserved down to the present day. The fact was that Rastoptchine's note had been sent to Paris through Krudener, who had communicated the contents to Haugwitz, thus enabling the Prussian Minister to mystify Beurnonville. Talleyrand's reply is a historical curiosity. Krudener received it in the shape of a *verbal note* from Haugwitz and sent it on to St. Petersburg on November 8/20. It passed there as an official version of the views of the French Government, but there are strong reasons for thinking that Talleyrand knew nothing about it and had nothing whatever to do with its composition.

At this very time in every one of his despatches he was urging Beurnonville to keep Prussia out of the negotiations. Why, then, should he himself have brought in Haugwitz ? Again, Rastoptchine's note was official : why should the reply have been semi-official ? Further, the substance of the note, which was as follows, suggests anything but a French origin. There was a demand that Russia should recognise the Rhine frontier, an offer to guarantee jointly the possessions of the Elector of Bavaria on the left bank and the dominions of the Duke of Würtemberg, a promise to preserve the integrity of the kingdom of Naples and to assign proper limits to the temporal power of the Pope. France engaged to re-establish the King of Sardinia in all his possessions but Novara, and suggested that suitable compensations might be arranged by means of secularisations for the Powers which had lost territory and *in particular for Prussia.*

Some of these stipulations manifestly contradict the declared policy of the Consular Government, which had just categorically affirmed the principle of reciprocal disinterestedness as the basis of all future arrangements and had not less peremptorily refused to discuss the question of the Rhine frontier. The decisive argument, however, against this questionable document is that there is no trace of it in the archives of the Quai d'Orsay. On the other hand, there is there the minute of an *official* answer sent by Talleyrand to the note of September 26. It is dated December 21, a month later than that which he is said to have sent semi-officially through Haugwitz. It contains no reference to this verbal communication and is in contradiction with its substance. It is as follows : " The undersigned has submitted to the First Consul the note dated September 26 which was addressed to him by his Excellency Count Rastoptchine. The undersigned is directed to reply that the principles laid down in his Excellency's note seem right and proper in every way and that the First Consul adopts them."

That is all. There is nothing about Prussia or the Rhine frontier or secularisations. This communication, which shows the hand of Bonaparte, was clearly not adopted by Talleyrand in concert with Haugwitz. It is out of keeping with Beurnonville's previous instructions. It is a new fact, a dramatic surprise, which can be explained only by the circumstances out of which it arose.

By December 21 negotiations for peace had been com-

menced with Austria. In spite of Hohenlinden, the Court
of Vienna was contesting every inch of the ground and was
threatening to break off the discussion. At this moment
Sprengtporten arrived in Paris, and Bonaparte divined
from his conversation with him that the Czar was only
waiting for a sign in order to throw his sword into the
balance on the side of France, when Austria would be at his
mercy. He was convinced that ordinary diplomatic
methods were out of place with the Russian " Don
Quixote." It would always be possible to take back in
detail what he conceded *en bloc*. Malta being out of the
discussion the rest mattered little, and the victor of
Marengo resolved on one of the bold strokes with which, in
diplomacy as in war, he was wont to disconcert his adversaries, and he replied by simply accepting all the Imperial
demands. Six weeks before this there was no reason why he
should give way so easily, and even then he was by no means
disposed to admit the Prussian pretensions. What, then,
are we to say of the earlier " answer " of Talleyrand to
Rastoptchine, in which these pretensions were so much
favoured ? It has been accepted as a historical document
by the best-informed authorities, but it is neither more nor
less than a diplomatic forgery.

Prussian diplomacy availed itself of its position as for
the moment the intermediary between St. Petersburg and
Paris to press its own claims and seek its own advantages.
It kept up appearances so adroitly by sufficiently close
approximations to the truth that the truth has only now
been discovered. The appearance of Sprengtporten in
1800, however, was destined to derange this design not a
little.

V

The general reached Berlin early in November, and at
once Beurnonville and Krudener found themselves practically out of the game. The Finnish adventurer was

himself a trickster, and took advantage of the vagueness of his commission to magnify his office. In a mysterious but all the more impressive manner he gave out that he held in his hands the destinies not only of Russia and France, but of all Europe. At this moment Krudener heard the news of the fall of Panine, who was dismissed from his post as Vice-Chancellor and shortly afterwards exiled to his estates near Moscow. All the news from St. Petersburg seemed to show that the recent ministerial crisis corresponded to a change of policy of which Sprengtporten might perhaps be the accredited representative.

On October 1, 1800 (old style), on receipt of the news of the capture of Malta by the English, the President of the College of Foreign Affairs presented to the Czar a memoir which showed marked traces of excitement. Rastoptchine began with an examination of the part played by Russia in the coalition and came to the general conclusion that it had ended in failure. He went on to sketch an entirely new policy which coincided curiously with Guttin's* scheme and may have owed something to a suggestion from this quarter. The basis of this policy was a partition of Turkey in concert with Prussia, Austria and France. A Greek Republic was to be established under the protection of Russia and the three associated Powers, and at the same time the new league was to put an end to the domination of England by a renewal of the scheme of armed neutrality as conceived and organised by Catherine. The execution of this plan would be a glory to Russia, for it would unite on one head the crowns of Peter and Constantine. Russia's share in the projected partition was in fact to be Roumania, Bulgaria, Moldavia, and Constantinople. The whole scheme was in fact the grand design of the preceding reign in a slightly different form. In conversation with his friend the Georgian Prince Zizianof, who was in command of an army corps in his native country, Rastoptchine went

* See above p. 336.

354

so far as to sketch the plan of an expedition which would attack the power of England at its source in India.

Paul annotated the margin of Rastoptchine's original manuscript in his own hand, and showed that he was delighted with his Minister's ideas and quite ready to agree. Rastoptchine wrote : " France, even when weakest, has always taken up the attitude of dictating laws to Europe. Her present ruler is too selfish, too successful and too ambitious of glory not to desire peace. He will profit by internal peace to prepare for war against England, whose jealousy, whose trickery and whose wealth will always make her, not the rival but the implacable enemy of France. Bonaparte has nothing to fear from her on the Continent. . . . He has exhausted Austria. Prussia is at his orders. It is Russia only that he fears, and his conduct towards your Imperial Majesty is an evident proof of this. . . . Austria is persevering in the disastrous war which has continued for eight years and is losing sight of Prussia, a Power which it is one of the essential objects of her policy to keep under constant observation. . . ." Paul's note in the margin is : " What can one expect of a blind people ? "

" Prussia, having wisely given up the war, has an alliance with France. . . . England also has need of peace. She has profited by the time during which the Powers of Central Europe in which they engaged only at her instigation. . . ." Paul observes : " Like us miserable sinners ! "

" In order to seize the commerce of the world she has had the audacity to invade Egypt and Malta. Russia, alike by her position and her inexhaustible resources, is and ought to be the first Power in the world. . . . Bonaparte is trying to gain our friendship. . . ." Paul's note is : " He may succeed."

" Prussia is flattering us in order to gain our consent to compensation for herself when peace is made. Austria crawls before us. . . . England, thinking that no *rapprochement* is possible between us and France, will perhaps have the insolence to show her flag in the Baltic. . . . When peace is made all these Powers, with the exception of Austria, will have gained great advantages. . . . Russia alone, after losing 23,000 men, will be without compensation. . . . Your Majesty has given history the incontestable right to say that Paul began a war without cause and ended it without gaining his object. . . ." Note by Paul : " I am to blame."

Then followed the scheme of partition, Russia's share in which was indicated above. Austria was to have Bosnia, Servia and Walachia. " Is not this too much ? " asked Paul. To Prussia Rastoptchine gave Hanover, as well as the bishoprics of Paderborn and Münster. France's share was to be Egypt. The future Greek Republic, though placed under the protection of the four Powers, would in fact place the Hellenes under the Russian sceptre. The Czar agreed that Bonaparte should be " the centre of the plan." He was intoxicated with the sensations of a man who leaves the blackness of a dungeon for the light of day. Rastoptchine felt that Sprengtporten was but a sorry instrument with which to carry out so grandiose an undertaking. He therefore offered to go himself to Berlin, Vienna and Paris, and imagined all sorts of stratagems to ensure the secrecy of his mission. He would pass for being in disgrace and exiled, with orders to travel abroad. The Emperor sensibly objected : " This is to confound what is useful with what is futile." But none the less he attached a final note of approval to the memorandum : " I approve of your plan and desire you to carry it out. God grant that it may succeed."

On reflection, however, the Czar and his Minister thought that things were moving somewhat too fast. Sprengtporten was already on his way to France, and it was best to wait for news of his reception there. But the general, if he was not acquainted with the wonderful scheme, had some inkling of the effervescence of new ideas in which it had originated, and this increased his natural tendency to magnify his own importance. Paul and Rastoptchine decided to accelerate his arrival at his destination, though they did not think fit to define more precisely the object of his mission, and accordingly, on November 21, the envoy resumed his journey.

At Berlin, Beurnonville and Krudener, who were much embarrassed and puzzled, resumed their interrupted conversations—but without more success than before. Contrary to expectation, the Russian envoy's attitude was unaffected by the change which Sprengtporten's language had seemed to indicate. The representative of France was still to wait in vain for a visit from his Russian colleague. One day, on the pretext of evading the curiosity of Haugwitz and his police, Krudener would propose (as in 1797) a rendezvous in the park where the wintry weather secured a discreet solitude. But at the last moment the Minister was confined to his room by illness, and Beurnonville, always obliging, hastened to his bedside. Alas! even when they met the two augurs found nothing to say to each other. Haugwitz himself now indicated Sprengtporten as more qualified than any one to reveal the intentions of his master : he had taken care to send Lucchesini to Paris beforehand to watch the progress of the Franco-Russian negotiation, which, as it now seemed, was likely to be settled there.

Panine's departure had now put an end to the antagonism which had divided the direction of foreign affairs in Russia into two conflicting currents, but Rastoptchine occupied himself with his master in pursuing chimeras, and the disorder of the department was aggravated. The instructions given to the various agents had been contradictory before. They now became quite unintelligible. Sprengtporten had left St. Petersburg uncertain of what was expected of him. He had not received any further light on the subject ; but he did not mind. He was glad to have a free hand. He was an adventurer in pursuit of adventures.

VI

In France there was of course equal uncertainty as to the character and object of this mission. General Clarke was sent at Beurnonville's suggestion to meet Sprengtporten at Brussels and was disappointed to find that he had power only to take over the prisoners and to give friendly assurances. Still, he allowed it to be supposed that he would soon receive a more extended commission, and posed as a man who was in the special confidence of the Czar. He severely criticised the conduct of Baron Krudener, who, if he had been better advised, might have been allowed to treat with Beurnonville. He said he had represented this to his Government and expected himself to be appointed to negotiate the peace. To these promising announcements he added some remarks which were less pleasing. Paul I was, he said, a just and honourable sovereign, but his confidence was often abused. " If an enemy speaks against you, you may in a moment lose your position and your office. I might myself lose the confidence which the Emperor has reposed in me. I hope that it will not be so, but it is not impossible."

Clarke was at the same time unfavourably impressed by the attempts of this singular negotiator to take advantage of him by talking English and German by turns, only coming to French—with which he was more familiar— when he found that Clarke knew the other two languages better than he. In spite of everything, however, he was courteously received and treated with great distinction. At Paris he displayed great enthusiasm for France, and even a liking for the institutions she had adopted, going so far as to use the Republican calendar in dating his correspondence.

More than ever he assumed all the air of an Ambassador. He conferred with Talleyrand, who was then absorbed in preparing the Treaty of Lunéville, with Cobenzl, who was doing his best to recover at the council board the ground which had been lost on the battlefield, and with Lucchesini, who was now reduced to the rôle of an anxious spectator of the progress of the negotiations. He saw the First Consul, and as his assurance did not fail him even in the presence of the great man, he began to be taken seriously. Talleyrand addressed a note to him, the object of which was to induce Russia to intervene between France and Austria. The Emperor Francis II agreed to treat without England and to concede the Rhine frontier to the Republic, but he demanded the line of the Oglio as a boundary in Italy, which made it impossible to reinstate the King of Sardinia in all his dominions. In Germany he proposed arrangements which would equally prevent the provision of compensation for Bavaria and Würtemberg. For these reasons it was necessary that a Russian plenipotentiary should be sent to Lunéville.

At the same time Talleyrand replied to Rastoptchine as we know, and on the same day, December 21 (for the *first* time, in spite of all that has been said to the contrary), the First Consul himself sent a personal appeal to the Czar, in which Cæsar addressing Don Quixote made good use of the information he had been able to collect about the character of his eccentric correspondent. Talleyrand's reply and the message of his chief are complementary. Bonaparte said : " I have had the pleasure of seeing General Sprengtporten. I have charged him to inform your Majesty that, from considerations of policy as well as from my esteem for you, I desire to see the two most powerful nations in the world promptly and irrevocably united. . . . If your Imperial Majesty will charge some plenipotentiary possessing your full confidence to treat, there will be peace on sea and land in twenty-four hours. For when England, the Emperor of Germany, and the other Powers are convinced that the wills and the powers of our two great nations are directed to the same end, their arms will fall from their hands and mankind will bless your Majesty for delivering them from the horrors of war and the discord of factions."

He offered, in fact, the position of arbiter of the world's destinies to Paul, and continuing in the same key he evoked a vision of their forces united to crush England, to recapture the Mediterranean and partition Asia. But above all his aim was to intimidate Austria, to disarm the coalition once for all, and to place Don Quixote at Cæsar's service.

If Paul had lived he might have succeeded. Sprengtporten never received the powers which he was, or said he was, expecting. Rastoptchine, when he heard what was going on at Paris, was much annoyed. The impertinent pretender was poaching on his preserves. He therefore hastened to send him the following laconic note : " His Majesty directs me to acquaint you that the prisoners of war are your sole concern and that you are to return to Russia with all speed when your mission is concluded." Thus called to order, Sprengtporten confined himself to signing with Clarke a convention which restored to Russia 6732 men, of whom 134 were generals and superior officers. Rastoptchine, however, was not to have the pleasure of substituting himself for his too enterprising agent. Paul intended to direct the negotiations himself. The First Consul lost nothing by this. Even before he knew what the flattering propositions were which were being addressed to him, Don Quixote rushed into the path which he was expected to take with an ardour beyond the most sanguine calculations.

VII

Following the suggestions of his minister, Paul proceeded to provoke England by the League of Neutrality which was reconstituted at this juncture. This was already in a manner to ally himself with France ; but even in this manœuvre he did not fail to show his customary folly and inconsequence. In spite of the sentimental objections of Marie Féodorovna, he invited Gustavus IV, one of the Leaguers, to come to St. Petersburg for the ratification of the new agreement. " Ah ! " groaned the Empress, " every room here will remind him of the promises he gave to poor Alexandrina ! " Paul paid no attention to this, but no sooner had the King come than there was a quarrel, and not content with rudely dismissing his royal guest, the irascible autocrat tried to starve him *en route* by recalling the commissariat officers attached to his service.

On December 16 he had treated with Denmark for the same purpose. Four days later he took offence at the interpretation which the Danish Minister, Rosenkranz, put upon the engagements he had taken, and dismissed him from his Court, recalling from Copenhagen his own Minister, Lizakiévitch, who had only just arrived. He made arrangements, nevertheless, to repel an attack by the English, and was erecting batteries at Kronstadt for this purpose which were at this time hardly begun and for whose construction whole years were needed. At the same time he was giving France the best possible proof of his conversion.

He had royally entertained Louis XVIII at Mittau and had obliged the Court of Vienna to send Madame Royale back there, writing to her uncle in these terms : " Sir, my Brother,—The Princess will be restored to you or I am not Paul I." Again in May 1799 he had interested himself keenly in the fantastic enterprise of La Maisonfort and Barras, who aimed at restoring the monarchy, and had charged Vorontsof to demand the energetic assistance of England. The essential feature of the plan was an invasion of France through Franche-Comté, which was given up because Barras asked no less than ten million livres on the conclusion of the Restoration and one and a half million for preliminary expenses! Now, on December 18, 1800, M. de Caraman received a sudden order to leave St. Petersburg. Mme. de Bonnoeil probably had something to do with his disgrace. This adventuress had already been all over Europe and had tried her talents of seduction and intrigue at the Court of Berlin. She boasted of her "tender friendship" with Rastoptchine and insinuated that she had other relationships which had enabled her to exercise in even higher quarters an influence favourable to the French cause. She had been for some time at Mittau, and while at Madrid had been intimate with the Duc d'Havré, who revealed to her the secrets of his correspondence. She was thus in a position to give the Czar some information of a character which gravely compromised Louis XVIII's agents at St. Petersburg. Paul had the correspondence of M. de Caraman intercepted and deciphered and found therein the proof of a treasonable understanding between Panine and the Court of Mittau.

The result was in every way very alarming for Louis XVIII. He immediately appealed in very humble terms to the Czar's indulgence and asked permission to send another minister to St. Petersburg. All he gained was an answer signed by a mere secretary which suggested that worse was to follow. " His Majesty should not intervene on behalf of M. de Caraman, who is an intriguing person. . . . The Emperor desires to be master in his own house. He regrets to remind the King that hospitality is a virtue and not a duty."

Paul no longer condescended to correspond personally with his royal guest; but on this very date, December

18/30, he decided, before he had received the First Consul's letter, to take the initiative in writing to the " usurper." He held his head high in making this advance, but it was an advance all the same. " The duty of those," he wrote, " to whom God has entrusted power to govern nations is to devote themselves to the well-being of their subjects. I will not discuss the principles which each country has adopted. Let us try to restore that peace and quiet to the world which are so much needed and which seem to conform so closely to the immutable laws of the Almighty. I am ready to hear what you have to say and to converse with you."

For this conversation Paul needed an intermediary, but he did not choose Rastoptchine, whose presence was indispensable at St. Petersburg and whose docility was doubtful. Paul wanted an insignificant representative, and it was no doubt for this reason that he appointed Kalytchof, who a short time before had been recalled from Vienna to replace Panine. Meanwhile the Czar replied himself to the First Consul's letter, which he had now received, and in much more amiable terms. The same day, Count Fersen, the military governor of Mitau, submitted to Louis XVIII an order in the following terms which he had just received. " You will notify to the King that the Emperor advises him to rejoin his wife at Kiel as soon as possible and to establish himself there."

Some weeks later, after having returned unopened a letter from the unhappy Prince, who had obeyed the Imperial injunction without protest, Paul withdrew the pension of 200,000 roubles which had hitherto been paid to him and on which he relied for the maintenance of his followers. The Czar was passing over bag and baggage to the side of the French Republic : so at least it appeared.

VIII

His real plan, so far as he had one, was different, and appears in the secret part of Kalytchof's instructions. Kalytchof was the purest type of a Muscovite *grand seigneur*. He detested the Austrians and had been sent to Vienna to'replace Razoumovski, who was accused of liking them too much. But Kalytchof hated the French equally and had a horror of the Republic.

His instructions were dated November 19, 1800 (old style), and revealed nothing of Rastoptchine's great scheme. That was to be developed by Paul in more direct communications. In their official part they did no more than expand the five articles of the imperious note of September 25. Paul recognised the Rhine as the frontier of France. He promised less formally to open his dominions to French commerce and allowed the First Consul full liberty to settle with England as he pleased, provided he ultimately joined the League of Northern Powers. In return Bonaparte was to evacuate the other territories occupied by him in Italy and elsewhere. He was to restore Egypt* to the Porte and not only guarantee the possession of Malta to the new Grand Master of the Order of St. John of Jerusalem, but to invite his allies to facilitate his access thereto. Paul further required the restoration of the new Pope, Pius VII, to his dominions. He expressed a desire to humble the House of Austria, and permitted Bonaparte to take a portion of its hereditary domains, which had been so obstinately defended by Thugut, for the purpose of indemnifying the German Sovereigns and the King of Sardinia. But he refused even to discuss the question of Poland.

The secret portion of Kalytchof's instructions was more

---

* It will be remembered that according to Rastoptchine's plan Egypt was to be given to France and Turkey was to be sacrificed or rather destroyed. No doubt the Czar and his minister were not particularly careful to harmonise the successive versions of their scheme.

novel. Paul began by requiring as an indispensable condition of any understanding with France the recognition by Spain of the new Grand Master of the Order of St. John of Jerusalem. Next, in view of the eventuality of war with England, Paul called upon the First Consul to carry out the descent on the English coast which he had been for so long announcing. In return for this the Emperor promised an advantageous commercial treaty.

In the domain of chimeras fancies of all kinds come together and genius is the near neighbour of insanity. Paul may thus have had a vision of the camp of Boulogne. He also foresaw the Empire. After insisting on the obligation of the regular Government of France to suppress the clubs, the Polish committees, and in general all democratic propaganda, Kalytchof was to hint to the First Consul the advisability of taking the title of king and making the crown hereditary in his family. Paul went on to explain his motives as follows: " Do not forget that my intention is to restore the peace of Europe, and that, in recognising France as a Republic and Bonaparte as its Sovereign, my desire is to prevent Austria, England and Prussia from succeeding in their plan of aggrandisement, which is as injurious to the general well-being as the principles of the French Revolution—perhaps even more injurious. I prefer letting one hydra exist to tolerating the birth and growth of several."

At bottom, then, the Czar continued to regard the France of the Revolution as a monster, agreement with which was preferable only to a greater evil. And he persisted in making Malta the pivot of his foreign policy. Krudener had instructions to sound Beurnonville on the subject ; and if he could induce him to promise to co-operate in the recovery of the island from England, and not to make peace with that country except on the condition of the restoration of the island, the Russian envoy had orders to sign on the spot a treaty of peace in the form desired by the French Cabinet.

The diplomatic machinery set in motion to secure the *rapprochement* with France had now become extremely complicated, and, like Krudener at Berlin, Kalytchof at Paris was the last man in the world who was likely to clarify or facilitate the negotiations. He was a narrow-minded pedant, who carried to his new post all the out-of-date ideas and prejudices from which Paul and Rastoptchine were at least partially trying to free themselves. For him peace with the Republic might perhaps be tolerated—an alliance was in the highest degree improper. Paul thought him docile because he was narrow: in reality he was excessively obstinate, and had made up his mind to do nothing to overcome the difficulties which he was certain to meet in the discharge of his task. In this he found a discreet but resolute auxiliary in the Marquis de Lucchesini, whose mission also was to prevent a peace and an alliance, from which Prussia despaired of getting any advantage.

Moreover, Paul's representative travelled with such majestic deliberation that he did not reach his destination until February 10, the day after the Peace of Lunéville was signed. This event considerably altered the situation—Cæsar had no longer the same motive for throwing himself at the head of Don Quixote. Austria was *hors de combat* and Bonaparte was safe on the Continent. On the sea, England for the moment was not threatening him so much as Russia and her allies. The respective positions being changed, the rôles were changed as well, and Paul, who so lately had referred scornfully to Bonaparte as a " usurper," now wrote two further letters in rapid succession, pressing him in almost suppliant terms to do something against " the common enemy "—in other words, against England. But he in his turn had to wait for an answer. It was not until February 27 that the First Consul wrote, and then in the style of a general order he acceded to the Czar's wish, sketched a plan for a descent on England, but at the same time dictated his terms. The Black Sea fleet was to join the French and Spanish squadrons in Sicilian waters. A Russian or Prussian army corps was to be sent to Hanover, "to make sure that the Elbe and the Weser were closed." Before the alliance was concluded he was already taking the command. Furthermore, he intimated the presence of Murat and his division on the Neapolitan frontier, and invited Paul to take measures in this quarter to secure that Ferdinand IV " behaved himself "—that is, closed his ports to the English. He showed no intention of sparing Paul's protégé, and his envoy, the Marquis de Gallo, was met by a firm resolution to keep him out of the negotiations. He was told that Italian affairs should be settled in Italy, and that it was the business of Murat and d'Alquier, the French plenipotentiaries, to settle those of Naples—pacifically or otherwise.

All this was far from meeting the views of Paul or his Ambassador, and Kalytchof began with a somewhat acrimonious protest against the treatment offered to his Sicilian Majesty and his representative. He conferred with Talleyrand, however, but immediately found himself at variance with him even as to the scope of the discussion. Like Krudener and Panine before him, Kalytchof wished to conjoin the negotiations for peace between France and Russia with those affecting the general pacification. These France wished to keep separate. The Russian also desired to introduce into the terms of the treaty a clause obliging the two countries to place social order " under an inviolable safeguard," and to " forbid propaganda inconsistent with their respective institutions." Talleyrand now accepted this on condition that a similar clause was inserted in all treaties subsequently negotiated by the two countries with other Powers. Kalytchof drew back. He had no instructions to assent to such an extension. When they fell back on the problem of the general pacification the conversation took the same turn. Talleyrand accepted the demand that the restitution of Malta should be a *sine qua non* of any treaty between France and England, but on condition that the Russian fleet acted with the French in recovering the island from England. Again Kalytchof had no orders. He *had* orders, however, to demand the evacuation of Egypt, and at this point the First Consul intervened and declared that "what had been acquired at the price of the purest blood of France could not be abandoned."

The negotiation was thus stagnating, and Paul, in his feverish humour, would no doubt have taken some means of expediting matters ; but the unhappy monarch had now but a few days to live, and in the confusion caused by his death Kalytchof was left free to pursue his course of obstruction and delay. He was offended by the society of the swashbucklers, the parvenus, the unfrocked priests and the sans-culottes among whom he found himself, and the descendant of the boyars was not in the least placated by the almost royal honours with which he was surrounded. He condescended to admit that in the First Consul he had to do with a great man, but he wrote to Rastoptchine of the French that he could see nothing but what was "false and insidious in their conduct : much talk and civility but no readiness to do what we want." He got on better with the remnants of the old aristocracy which was in course of reconstitution, and this led to a stiffness in his relations with the official world, which was all but insolent, and led to a severe but well-merited rebuke from Talleyrand.

This, however, belongs to the history of the reign of Alexander I. By the middle of April 1801 Paul was dead, and the First Consul had decided to send a confidential agent to St. Petersburg, who was to lay before the new Sovereign the conduct of the Ambassador who had been so unfortunately chosen by his predecessor. By this time, too, Bonaparte had settled without Russia's help several of the questions at issue in the negotiations which had advanced so slowly. The Marquis de Gallo, for instance, had been sent back to Italy and had been compelled to sign a treaty at Florence in which Naples gave way on all points.

The confidential agent who was sent by Bonaparte to complain of Kalytchof was Duroc, who has usually been represented as having concerted with Paul an expedition against India. But at the date of his leaving for Russia it was already known at Paris that Paul was dead ! Was there, then, at an earlier date some correspondence between the Czar and the First Consul apart from the sterile discussions between Kalytchof and Talleyrand ? The explanatory memorandum on the law approving of the Treaty of October 8, 1801, refers to a " direct correspondence " which it had been decided to conduct between the Sovereigns, and which " by producing the frankest and fullest communications on both sides would soon have smoothed all difficulties and led to the most gratifying results."

All that is preserved in the archives has already been placed before the reader and it is far from fulfilling so flattering an expectation. There *may* have been some further communications between the Governments of the two countries of which the secret has been so well kept that no documentary evidence survives; but Paul's conduct during the last months of his life does not bear out the theory that it was intended to establish or lead up to an agreement.

At some date subsequent to the peace of Lunéville, Rastoptchine drew up with his own hands and submitted to the Czar a second memorandum, full of great schemes for the partition, not this time of Turkey, but of Prussia. Russia was to have " all Western Prussia with all the country beyond up to the Vistula." As compensation Frederick-William was to receive the Electorate of Hanover or the Duchy of Brunswick, as he preferred, together with the Principality of Hildesheim and the Harz Mines. Rastoptchine calculated that Bonaparte, wholly absorbed in the annihilation of the power of England, would agree to everything, and " in a few years Russia would be the dominant power on sea and land. Mistress of the finest shores of the Baltic . . . she would dominate Prussia, Denmark and Sweden. Austria would not dare to move. Italy would enjoy a peace which she owed to the Emperor, who would look on at the death struggle between France and England and would alone regulate the destinies of all the power of Europe."

There is nothing to show, however, that this plan formed the subject of a communication addressed to the First Consul, who, when Kalytchof was dining with him on March 28, 1801, used language which seems to exclude the supposition of any understanding, actual or contemplated, between himself and the Czar. " If," said Bonaparte, " I could have some conversation with him we should very soon agree on joint action." Now at this date Paul was dead and had done nothing to facilitate such an interchange of views.

No doubt he decreed and put in execution an expedition to India. Was this in concert with Bonaparte ? A plan of campaign has been produced which is said to have been sent from St. Petersburg to Paris and returned with annotations by the First Consul requesting further information, which was supplied by Paul. This and other documents of the same kind might have passed without the knowledge of Kalytchof and Sprengtporten, leaving no trace in the official papers. But who could have carried the plan to St. Petersburg ? It could not have been Duroc, as is alleged by the publishers of the document, as his instructions are dated April 24, a month after Paul's death. But several Russian agents circulated between St. Petersburg and Paris between January and March 1801. In February, Major Tiesenhausen brought a letter from the Czar to the First Consul, and Levachof, the Grand Veneur, arrived at Paris during the negotiations for the Peace of Lunéville to plead the cause of the King of Naples. There may have been others who are unknown. The difficulty is to place historically the alleged concert which they are said to have helped to bring about, and it seems insurmountable.

IX

Bonaparte certainly had such an expedition in his mind and did not require Paul's suggestions. Every one about him was thinking of it, and the question had engaged attention in France much earlier. In 1776 Necker had refused supplies for an attempt of this kind. In 1782 Louis XVI had adopted the plan of a campaign the object of which was the destruction of Bombay. So recently as 1799 the Alsatian Nagel, an old comrade of Suffren who had married the governess of two Russian Grand Duchesses, had presented to Talleyrand a plan " for striking a mortal blow at the English power in India."

Bonaparte certainly knew of these papers, and in accepting the suggestions which they contained he doubtless did not fail to take account of the possibilities opened in this direction by the Franco-Russian *rapprochement*. That *rapprochement* had still to become an accomplished fact. The great man was himself subject to outbursts. Did he then anticipate the slow progress of the negotiations which were being conducted by Kalytchof ? At St. Helena he said so to O'Meara in a manner which seems peremptory : " If Paul I had lived you would already have lost India ; we had formed a joint plan for its invasion." But what is this testimony worth ? And even if Napoleon's words were correctly reported, of what value are they compared with the irrefragable evidence of the facts ?

At the end of February 1801 Lucchesini believed that the First Consul was studying the subject. So far, however, as studies and plans went, there was no mystery and no occasion for anxiety to any one. All the chancelleries of Europe knew of it and England herself was not in the least alarmed. And why ? Because these projects in the form which they were now taking at Paris depended on a condition which did not seem in the least likely to be realised. On this particular point the Franco-Russian Concert was already out of the question. At Paris at the end of February Bonaparte was still collecting information, consulting maps and making calculations. As early as January 12 (old style) Paul had sent orders from St. Petersburg to the *ataman* Orlof, the officer who was in command of the Don Cossacks, to concentrate his troops at Orenburg and march *at once*, via Khiva and Bokhara, on the Indus in order to attack the English establishments. Was this done with the assent of the First Consul and according to a plan concerted with him ?

The date of the event is enough to negative this supposition. It was previous to the exchange of the first messages which passed between the heads of the two states. But in addition to this Bonaparte was not mad, and the character of the expedition thus decreed was such that it is impossible to suppose that he had any part in its preparation. It was in fact not prepared at all ! Orlof was sent off without any previous attempt to secure an undertaking with the Asiatic Sovereigns through whose dominions he would have to pass, without any consideration of the resources which would be at his disposal in these countries, with no commissariat, no camping material, no ambulances, no money, and even no maps ! Such maps as he had went no further than Khiva ! And yet Paul ordered this officer to press on to the Ganges after strongly occupying Bokhara as he passed, " in order to prevent its falling into the hands of the Chinese " ! He was already in imagination handling the wealth of Bengal. Bonaparte's imagination did not work in this way.

PAUL I AND BONAPARTE

As his orders were precise, Orlof started, and probably the First Consul was not even informed of the fact. The *ataman's* force amounted to 22,507 men, whose artillery equipment was twelve mortars and twelve cannon. He alone knew the object of this mobilisation, which the cossack women thought was a form of exile or punishment which was being inflicted on them. They wished to accompany their husbands and to take their children with them. The winter of that year was severe, and the sufferings of all who took part in the expedition were terrible. Half a regiment were nearly drowned crossing the Volga, and by the time he reached the Irghiz on the Asiatic side Orlof had lost a large part of his horses and had not a kopeck left. Paul's death, which occurred at this moment, saved him. The first care of Alexander I was to recall the wretched cossacks, who were far not only from Bengal but from Bokhara.

Until very recently the same project of invading India continued to haunt the minds of those in Paul's position. In 1801 it was not concerted with France and no commencement even was made to carry it out in earnest. Paul was no longer in a condition to think or act seriously. He gave absurd orders, signed insane decrees, prepared to go to war in company with Bonaparte with armies which existed only on paper, and practised on the map of the world the game of redistribution which he had learned from Rastoptchine. At the end of March Bonaparte, weary of Kalytchof's evasions, had recourse to his favourite tactics ; he suddenly addressed himself to Sprengtporten, declaring that, except for Egypt, he accepted all the Czar's conditions. All that he asked in exchange was Paul's active assistance in an attack on England through Belgium, a demonstration on the Irish coast, and an attempt on India, which clearly had not yet been concerted. The First Consul thought of attempting it by way of Egypt. But the proposal was not made in time to reach Paul, and we may doubt whether he would have agreed to it. Before he died the Czar, following a suggestion from Berlin, had conceived a new project of partition, and he had it in mind to make it the subject of an ultimatum to the man whose alliance he was seeking !

He was to give Bavaria Salzburg, Bamberg and Berchtesgaden. Würtemberg was to have the Lower Palatinate, Münster and Hildesheim ; Denmark would receive Hamburg, and Prussia Hanover on condition of immediately occupying the Duchy. On March 3/15, 1801, couriers were sent to Paris and Berlin notifying this decision. Next day it was necessary to send new ones. The Czar had forgotten Sweden, to whom he now proposed to give Lübeck, the Duke Bishop receiving either Bonn or the Principality of Werden in exchange. The Cabinet of Berlin were required to give their consent at once. As this was not forthcoming, Krudener was directed to leave his post if in twenty-four hours Hanover was not occupied by Prussia, and Kalytchof was directed to invite the First Consul to proceed to effect the occupation.

Paul's delirium was no longer manifest merely in the discreet seclusion of the chancelleries. It was published abroad in the fierce light of the periodical press, and to the astonishment of his contemporaries the most convincing proof of the growing disorder of his faculties came from the Czar himself.

X

Before he brought himself to consent to divide the world with Bonaparte he had led those about him to believe that he was seriously thinking of challenging " the Corsican usurper " to single combat. He had chosen the scene of the meeting and had appointed his seconds. He now gave the widest publicity to another challenge of the same kind, addressed, this time, to his old comrades in arms. As most of the apologists have supposed, this was no doubt merely a pleasantry, the point of which, however, seemed to be turned against himself.

The account of this incident, which is due to Kotzebue, presents obscurities and contains several errors of detail which throw some doubt on the *ensemble* of the facts as presented by the German author. The substance of his account is, however, confirmed by other witnesses and is beyond question. Kotzebue had just returned from Siberia, where he had been sent as we have seen. On December 16, 1800 (old style), he was sent for in all haste by Count Pahlen, the Military Governor of St. Petersburg. He thought he was about to be sent back to the neighbourhood of Tobolsk, if no worse befell him, and his wife fainted. But the couple were promptly reassured. With an enigmatic smile Pahlen explained that the Emperor had decided to defy all the Sovereigns of Europe and their ministers to single combat in a sort of tournament. He had chosen Kotzebue to draw up the challenge, which was to be published in the newspapers. Thugut was to be specially aimed at, and General Golenichtchef-Koutousof and Pahlen himself were to be named as the Czar's seconds. His Majesty was impatiently awaiting the text, which therefore had to be produced on the spot.

Reassured, but much embarrassed, Kotzebue did what was asked of him, but his work was not approved of. Its tone was not " stiff " enough. He tried again, and this time was summoned to the presence of the Emperor, who explained to him his intentions. " You know the world too well not to follow the events of current politics. You know what part I have played. I have often done foolish things, and (with a smile) it is just that I should be punished. I have therefore imposed a penance on myself and I wish this to be inserted in the *Gazette de Hambourg* and other newspapers."

Paul had himself drafted a paragraph in French to the following effect : " We learn from St. Petersburg that the

Emperor of Russia, seeing that the Powers of Europe cannot agree among themselves and desiring to put an end to the war which has devastated them for eleven years, means to select a place to which he will invite all the Sovereigns of Europe to fight in single combat. They will each be attended by their most enlightened ministers and their ablest generals, such as Thugut, Pitt, Bernstorff. The Czar himself proposes to take with him Generals Pahlen and Koutousof. We do not know whether this is true, but it does not appear to be altogether without foundation, bearing as it does the imprint of that with which he has been so often taunted." As he read the last words Paul laughed heartily. He asked Kotzebue for a German translation of the *communiqué* and discussed at great length the exact rendering of the words " with which he has been so often taunted."

Next day the translator received a snuff box set with diamonds, and Pahlen sent the German text to a Hamburg merchant, who, by producing a letter from the Military Governor of St. Petersburg, succeeded in persuading the local paper (which at first refused) to insert it. It appeared on January 16 (old style), and next month on February 19 and 27 (old style) the *Nouvelles de Saint-Pétersbourg* (No. 16) and the *Nouvelles de Moscou* (No. 17) published the following :

" The mystery of the news published in the *Nouvelles de Saint-Pétersbourg*, Nos. 24 and 34, on December 30 last, is at last cleared up. No one understood the paragraph which was extracted from a letter addressed by Rosenkranz, formerly Danish envoy at St. Petersburg, to Copenhagen, in which he stated that the Emperor had said at table : ' It would be a good thing if rulers would settle their differences by single combat like the ancients.' It is on these words that the Danish envoy founded the story which he sent to Copenhagen. The letter was intercepted and the Emperor ordered an extract to be published in the

Nouvelles de Saint-Pétersbourg and forwarded to ministers at all foreign Courts. At the same time his Majesty ordered the Danish Minister to leave St. Petersburg."

The incriminated matter had never appeared in the *Nouvelles de Saint-Pétersbourg* on December 30 or on any other day. Paul regretted and was ashamed of the practical joke which had exposed him to the derision of Europe. He was now awkwardly trying to put matters right, and not less awkwardly he brought in the Danish Minister to justify his dismissal from Russia.

There was now nothing but unreason in all that he said or did. Of all the acts to which he lent his name during this period of his life there is but one which has some show of intelligent purpose. By a manifesto of January 18, 1801 (new style), he proclaimed the reunion of the Georgian Provinces to Russia. This measure was declared to be necessary owing to the discord which desolated the country, divided the reigning family itself, and made national defence impossible. It was justified by the desperate appeals made by the Czar George for the intervention of the Russian Government. In Poland and elsewhere Catherine had set up similar reasons or pretexts, and the Persian expedition which she ordered was itself a reply to the desire of the Georgians to be assisted against their neighbours. On his accession Paul had hastened to recall the troops under Valerian Zoubof; but in Georgia, as in Persia, events had followed their natural course and annexation became inevitable. It was another entanglement, and perhaps it would have been better for Russia not to engage in external adventures the resources which she might have more usefully employed within her own borders. But though he disapproved of the policy which Catherine favoured he none the less maintained it.

He assured the Georgians that their rights, privileges and property would be respected. This guarantee was common form in the relations of Russia with conquered peoples.   Paul kept to the tradition, but generally speaking in his relations with the outer world his intellect and will in the last days of his life were giving way completely and were sinking rapidly into the abyss.   The crisis had been expected from the first by the more perspicacious observers; it came less soon than they expected; but it was inevitable in itself as well as in its tragic close.

PART III: THE CATASTROPHE

CHAPTER XIV

THE FINAL CRISIS

I

PAUL's challenge to the Sovereigns of Europe was merely an unmannerly jest, but the Czar was defying England in good earnest at a time when he had in the Baltic a fleet of forty-seven ships, of which barely fifteen were fit to put to sea. True, the French alliance and the League of Neutrality enabled him to unite against this formidable adversary all the maritime Powers but Turkey. But the alliance was hardly made before he was doing his best to destroy the League by his provocative insolence. Prussia would not move; Denmark was hesitating; Sweden was impotent for lack of money. Russia was in fact isolated for all practical purposes, and in the Baltic, as everywhere else, the terrible Armada which bore the British flag—205 ships of the line and 284 frigates, with a crew of 139,000 men—had no serious resistance to fear.

" The Emperor is literally mad," Whitworth wrote when on the point of leaving St. Petersburg. He was not alone in expressing this opinion. It was re-echoed by thousands of voices all over Europe. Some were alarmed and some amused, but all were more and more astounded. In Russia Rogerson, a good judge as he was both a Court physician and a political confidant, held this view, and it was shared by Simon Vorontsof in England. " Everybody," says Prince Czartoryski in his memoirs, was more or less convinced that the Emperor was subject to fits of mental alienation. Even Madame Vigée-Lebrun, who had always been well-treated by Paul and was consequently on his side, deplored the caprices of the " all-powerful lunatic," which were becoming a public scandal.

The general impression that Paul was mad was modified by the course of the Italian Campaign. Souvorof's victories threw a mantle of glory over the aberrations of his insane master. But these triumphs were ephemeral. Zurich promptly effaced the renown of Novi. Moreover, in Russia as elsewhere, every one clearly saw that the country had no real interest in the triumphs for which it paid so dear. The general opinion of Paul's mental condition which was previously entertained therefore became stronger and clearer between 1800 and 1801. If we may believe O'Meara, that opinion was shared by Bonaparte at the very time when he was seeking Paul for an ally. " Yes," he is said to have said at St. Helena, " I think he had partly lost his reason."

Was it only partly ? It has still to be determined how far the disease in its final phase had gone. Was it merely an aggravation of eccentricities of mind and character, in spite of which Paul in the course of a fairly long life had been able as Prince and Emperor to discharge the duties of his position, not indeed without frequent failures but sometimes with a certain distinction ? Was he, on the other hand, as the conspirators of 1801 asserted, a raving lunatic, fit only to be restrained or to be destroyed like a mad dog ?

II

According to Esquirol's classical definition madness is " a cerebral affection usually chronic, unaccompanied by fever and characterised by disorders of the senses, the intelligence and the will." On this definition Paul had become fit for a lunatic asylum long before the last years of his life. " There is no one," wrote Marie Féodorovna to Plechtchéief in 1794, " who does not every day remark the disorder of his faculties." Catherine noticed it like everyone else. But when she tried to keep her son from the throne, why did she not have recourse to medical advice ? She seems to have regarded the " disorder " as due to a hereditary taint, and if Paul was in fact the son of Peter III the source of the mischief was clear, even apart from his descent from the House of Holstein, in which Catherine found three cases of insanity in the course of fifteen years. These were Ivan, brother of Peter the Great, who was a congenital imbecile; Alexis, the son of the reformer, a nervous and weak-minded subject; Peter II, an erotic neuropath, worn out at fifteen, and his daughter Elizabeth, who was violent, capricious and unbalanced, sensual even to licentiousness, and yet given to pietistic mysticism and, towards the end of her life, afflicted with nervous troubles and perhaps even paroxysms of hysteria.

But on this side Paul's heredity is uncertain, and mental alienation, when it does not spring from congenital imbecility, which was not the case with Paul, is supposed to be invariably accompanied by certain physical disturbances — characteristic changes in the gastric channels, in the pulse, in the movements of the body. Dimsdale found nothing of this, and the history of epileptic attacks from which Paul is said to have suffered appears to be unfounded. When he was past forty Paul seems to have enjoyed the usual health of average persons of that age, and he was to all appearances robust and capable of supporting fatigue. In insanity the memory is usually the first faculty to be attacked, whereas Paul to the end of his days was exceptionally gifted in this respect. Physically, most lunatics become stout : Paul, on the contrary, remained thin.

One might be tempted to class him in the category of abnormal persons which has been established and popularised by Lombroso—men who are neither mad nor weak-minded; who occasionally are even of more than average intelligence, but whose faculties are subject to innumerable functional disorders. In such a case a man's faculties, however powerful, remain useless, because he has not the faculty of directing or co-ordinating them. His thoughts and his actions are in perpetual antithesis. The man of yesterday is not the man of to-morrow. He is wanting in logic and coherence; his sentiments and inclinations are not under control and the result is that his most impeccable reasoning ends in the most preposterous conclusions. He becomes the sport of passion and impulse, and, though his thoughts may be wise and his intentions excellent, he has all the appearance of unreason and immorality.

Is not this the very portrait of Paul? But again, if closely examined, does not Lombroso's formula seem to express little more than his perplexity in the presence of certain phenomena, which one of his rivals, perhaps with reason, has preferred to place " on the borderland of madness," a vague territory which it is difficult to define? In this indefinite and indefinable region we find a great number of people " who are not like other folks," but whom no one thinks of shutting up. They live the common life, manage their affairs often with much wisdom; sometimes they discharge difficult duties with intelligence and sustain their views with sufficient reasonableness to pass muster. This conception, however wanting in precision, must suffice us provisionally. In physique Paul corresponded to it very closely, with his low, receding forehead, his projecting jaw, his premature wrinkles and baldness. Similarly in the moral sphere, his liability to obsessions and hallucinations recall the stigmata of the type.

There were also, however, indications of a contrary character. Without being sterile, degenerates, as we may term those beings who dwell in the region intermediate between sanity and insanity, are not usually accounted prolific. If they have children these usually show more or less trace of their tainted origin. Now, Paul had many children, both in and out of wedlock, and among his legitimate descendents physical and mental vigour, or at least an apparently well-balanced mind, was the rule.

Moreover, the hallucinations to which he himself alleged that he was subject are not established beyond doubt. It is not impossible that the Czar was playing upon Mme. d'Oberkirch's credulity when he told her the story of his walk by night on the quays of the Neva with the ghost of Peter the Great. And in any case we may be sure that the story has lost nothing in the telling. But, besides these morbid conditions, there are forms of partial mania which are known to medical science, among which is a particular form of megalomania which Lascasagne, following Maurice Beaujeu, has termed *Cæsaritis.* The tendency to this malady may appear very early, even before the patient is ten years old, and we have seen in Paul's case striking instances of his predisposition to such symptoms.

Phrenologists pretend to locate in the front part of the skull the seat of the " centre of associations." All the portraits of Paul show a deformity of this part of his head. The characteristic feature of the cerebral anomalies which may be the consequence of this appears in the continual contrast between impressions and ideas resulting from defective action of the centralising organ. Now, Paul was above all things a man full of violent contradictions and oppositions, which he exhibited with complete composure, as when he combined the mystic aspirations of a mediæval knight with the coarse brutality of a Prussian corporal, or donned the insignia of the Order of St. John of Jerusalem when he went to call on Mme. Chevalier!

But when all is said and done the fundamental problem remains unsolved. How did this aberration, whether it be called degeneracy or partial insanity, come to develop to such an extent in a man whom Dimsdale declared to be of normal constitution ? Did the mischief in the end become sufficiently grave to justify us in describing the victim as a lunatic in any real or dangerous sense ? The surroundings of the unhappy Prince, his education and the conditions of his life supply us with the explanation. There was a poison in them more noxious than opium or any other drug, and the most active ingredient in it was the mortal contagion of the restlessness of the time in which he lived. It was that which in fact produced the final phase of his disease.

Other sovereigns before and after Paul, some of them much less well endowed than he, have exercised in the same country the same absolute power without abusing it as he did, or using it to revolutionise the interior organisation, the foreign policy of the Empire, or the public and private lives of their subjects. Paul wished to reform everything more completely even than Peter the Great dreamed of attempting. If he conceived this mad ambition, was it not because he was in intellectual communion with the contemporary revolutionaries in France and elsewhere, because he was attacked by the same fever, obsessed by the same chimeras, and because like them he sought to secure the happiness of mankind by dint of tyrannical decrees ?

In this sense it seems to be a historic fact that he was mad, and it remains to show how this fact, thus defined, reacted on the events with which he came in contact. This is a new problem and one equally hard to solve.

III

Prince Kotchoubey, on his recall from exile after the accession of Alexander I, wrote, in August 1801, to Simon Vorontsof : " No one who did not see the last years of Paul's reign, and who therefore is not in a position to know at first hand all the disorder, the disorganisation, the utter chaos they have produced, will ever understand our position or will realise the trouble it will be to put things right again." These are expressive words, but, coming from one whom Paul had disgraced, they may not carry conviction. The English Consul, Shairp, for similar reasons may not be accepted as a credible witness. In a report to Grenville in February 1801 he says : " It is impossible to describe the horror which the public has of the present Government. . . . The ukases and the explanations of ukases are so numerous and at the same time so ambiguous that to send you copies would merely be to embarrass you unnecessarily." Duroc may perhaps be considered more impartial. He arrived in St. Petersburg soon after Paul's death and was well aware what a mortal blow that event dealt to the hopes of the French Government. Yet the envoy of the First Consul does not hesitate to declare that the régime which ended with the Czar's tragic death was " intolerable." Paul was making a desert of his capital. " Nothing could come into it, or indeed into the Empire. The prisons were full. Men were mutilated and exiled on the slightest pretext."

One of these statements is confirmed by statistics. The records of 1800–1801 show a marked diminution in the population of St. Petersburg and a corresponding fall in rents. Many houses were standing empty, and the emigration to foreign countries reached proportions hitherto unknown. In spite of the difficulty of getting passports there was among certain classes a general exodus.

A few months after the accession of Catherine's son foreign observers were already perceiving symptoms of the spirit which produced this flight. Count Brühl, the Prussian envoy, was not deceived by the acclamations which saluted the new Sovereign at Moscow during the coronation festivities. " Discontent is general," he wrote, " even in the provinces and the army. . . . The whole edifice, splendid as it seems, is in a very precarious condition. The Emperor, in his desire to correct the faults of the old Government, is upsetting everything, introducing a new régime which is unpopular, which is not properly thought out, and which is being put into operation so precipitately that no one has had time to understand it."

Two years later Kotchoubey, who was still in office, wrote to Simon Vorontsof : " The internal administration could not be worse. No one thinks of anything but feathering his own nest. A man comes into office with the idea that he may be dismissed within a week. He says to himself, ' I must secure a grant of peasants to-morrow.' The peasants are granted and he is dismissed. He comes into office again and gets more peasants. This game is played every day. Troops have just been sent to Finland—no one knows why. . . . Think what all this costs ! There is no economy and can be none, and no one dares to remonstrate."

Two years later still a French *émigré*, collecting information about the causes of Paul's death, repeats the self-same complaint. According to him these causes were " the perpetual variations which threw him (Paul) from one extreme to another : the uncertainty in which all public servants, from the Field-Marshal down to the humblest sub-lieutenant, had to live. To-day one had a place ; to-morrow one might be in disgrace ; the day after in one's place again ; the next day in fear of Siberia. The Russian Empire is very productive, but it was on the verge of ruin for it has no industry,* and can only maintain its place in the European community by its exports, which were annihilated by prohibitive laws. Another set of causes were the petty vexations of the elaborate rules about dress, which the Czar changed as he felt inclined, and the innumerable other trifling annoyances to which all classes of his subjects were exposed."

The same note is heard even in the bosom of the Imperial family, and its insistence shows better than any other

* See above, p. 183.

testimony the disorder which the Emperor spread about him. The abyss gaped in the very household of the despot, and his own son was one of the first to dig it !

Alexander at twenty was physically a charming young man, quite unlike his father. He was tall and slender and had his mother's blue eyes, her rosy complexion and her ingenuous smile. Catherine saw in his character what the public also saw—an angelic and beautiful nature, full of true and noble impulses. He did not take after his grandmother, and she certainly did not attempt to fashion him in her own image. She wished him to be different and better, feeling that he at least would not have to win a throne for himself or to defend it against bitter competition. Thus the most exalted hopes were founded on his accession, and after his death, in spite of bitter experience, his widow remained attached to this illusion, for illusion it was. When he is studied more closely he appears in a different light. His soul is full of tortuous convolutions and dark shadows. He appears indifferent to all the temptations of ambition. A cottage in Switzerland is his ideal of happiness. Yet he was ready to conspire to dethrone his father, and while awaiting that event he could write secretly to César de la Harpe as follows :

" My father, when he ascended the throne, wished to reform everything. He began brilliantly, but the sequel has not maintained the promise of the first days. Everything was turned upside down. . . . It would be impossible to tell you all the mad things which have been done. . . . There was severity without justice, much sentiment and complete inexperience of affairs. Employment goes by favour ; merit has nothing to do with it. . . . The farmers are burdened : commerce impeded, individual liberty and comfort are at an end ; that is the picture of Russia ! "

And the writer did not stop at criticism. He sought a remedy for the evil and saw it in a *coup d'état* which was to be prepared by revolutionary propaganda! He too was attacked by the nervous disorder of the time. He had thought of flight, but, after consulting his friends, he had decided to remain, being persuaded that he could do better work in Russia forwarding " the best kind of revolution." His friends were the members of the Secret Committee which he formally constituted after his accession and which he was fond of calling his Committee of Public Safety. This body was already taking shape. It contained Paul Stroganof, who gained his political education at Geneva and Paris, Nicolas Novossiltsof, who was completing his in London in the intimacy of Fox, and Adam Czartoryski, whose only thought was for Poland. This was their common plan of action : " Our idea is during the present reign to have as many useful books as possible translated into Russian. We shall only publish such as can be authorised, reserving the others for the future. . . . When my turn comes we must work, of course little by little, to create a representative body which will, under our directions, work out a free constitution. My power will then cease absolutely, and if Providence seconds my endeavours I shall retire to some corner and live contented and happy. . . . Heaven grant we may succeed in freeing Russia and making her safe from the attacks of despotism and tyranny."

" When my turn comes———." At the date of this letter Paul was only forty-three. Did Alexander intend that Russia, groaning under the yoke of a demented tyrant, should await the natural end of a life which was then perhaps only half over ? That is hardly probable. In the very first year of his father's reign, during the coronation festivities, Alexander made Adam Czartoryski draft a manifesto for his own accession, setting out all the defects of his father's Government and all the advantages promised by his own. It will be remembered that Paul had taken a similar precaution during Catherine's lifetime.

Alexander no doubt knew this, and such examples are contagious. But he went further. Paul had been content to attack his mother's Government. His son organised a revolutionary propaganda and sought to gain over the Chancellor of the Empire in person. Through Victor Kotchoubey, one of his young friends, Alexander asked Bezborodko to draw up a scheme of constitutional reform. Bezborodko obeyed, out of respect for the heir, but his work did not answer to expectations, for the Chancellor declared himself a partisan of absolute power and contented himself with expressing the hope that the *samodiér-javié* maintained in its integrity would impose, not the caprice of a single master but a respect for the law.

The genesis of the tragedy of March 11/23, 1801, is clearly apparent in this more or less conscious and more or less deliberate progression of ideas. Of course, the Grand Duke in the autumn of 1797 had no fixed date in mind for the event which was to hasten his succession. Probably he never had any precise idea on the subject. But less than a year after his father's accession he had in mind the necessity of modifying the regular course of devolution of the Crown and of organising the country in a revolutionary manner.

His talk of retiring to a Swiss farm once the work was done is common form in the programmes of all men of great ambition. Was not Bonaparte to announce after Arçola and Rivoli that he meant to rejoin the ranks " as an ordinary citizen " ?

But had the young Grand Duke, like the other malcontents, personal reason to complain of the reigning Sovereign and the Government which he directed ? And was the discontent of all the categories of Paul's subjects above mentioned well founded ?

IV

At twenty years of age, at the time when he was most virulently attacking his father's Government, Alexander was first Military Governor of St. Petersburg, head of one of the regiments of the Guard (the Siémionovski), commander of the military division of the capital, Inspector of Cavalry in this division and in that of Finland, President of the Commission for the food supply of the capital, housing and police. From 1798 he was also at the head of the War Department, and from the following year onwards he had a seat in the Senate and in the Council of the Empire. Paul did not wish his heir to be treated as he had been treated himself. He inflicted on his sons, as on every one, civil and military tasks which were painful, for the most part useless, and often absurd. But the young Princes did not find them so very oppressive. On board of the *Emmanuel* during the famous cruise of 1797 the two Grand Dukes, Alexander and Constantine, spent hours on deck performing the manual exercise. This was not from obedience to their father or from a desire to please him. Twenty years later, after he had become Emperor, the eldest brother with Nicolas and Michael did exactly the same thing before the crew of a ship which was being inspected in the harbour of Cronstadt.

Alexander was shy and short-sighted ; he was deaf in one ear and had a slight limp—infirmities contracted in the course of manœuvres. He had consequently some difficulty in satisfying so exacting a master as Paul, and like every one else he was sometimes overworked and more or less rudely reprimanded. But he affected not to notice these trials and passes them over in silence in his letter to La Harpe ; his only preoccupation seemed then to be the misfortunes of his country. Were these misfortunes so serious as he said ?

As regards this, Alexander was influenced by suggestions

the source of which is easy to discover. Everywhere about him in the services, functionaries and officers of all ranks were undoubtedly suffering both from the ill-usage to which Paul's capricious humour every day exposed them and from the perpetual insecurity in which as a consequence they had to live. The prætorians of the Guard all resented keenly, and some of them furiously, the loss of their ancient privileges and the indulgences to which they were accustomed. The nobility was humiliated and degraded. The nobles were embarrassed in the use of the discretionary powers which they had usurped over the serfs. Ultimately they were ruined by the Czar's economic policy and the consequences of his quarrels with England. According to Shairp's report for 1801 a third of the produce of the country found no buyers.

This and this alone was the reason why the Russian aristocracy was hostile to the French alliance against England. It was equally hostile some years later when a similar treaty was concluded by Alexander, and in this sentiment there was no admixture, as has been supposed, of preference for English ideas or English manners. The " boyard " of 1801 who is described as regarding an English lord as " the arbiter of elegance, the model of high life, the supreme embodiment of good form, elegant luxury and feudal pride," exists only in the imagination of a historian* whose ingenuity is superior in this instance to his information. He is an anachronism in 1801 and is even now an exception to the general rule. It is also contrary to the facts of history to attribute to the Russian nobility of the day contempt or distaste for French culture as represented on the banks of the Neva by the melancholy band of *émigrés,* " needy, beggars reduced to the parasitic trades . . . always pirouetting like a dancing-master or drawing themselves up like a *maître d'armes.*" † This also is a

---

* Sorel, *L'Europe et la Révolution,* vol. vi, 119–20.
† *Ibid.*

sentiment of recent growth.   In the days which followed
the Revolution those who were perhaps responsible for the
catastrophe, and who certainly were its victims, were very
differently regarded in Russia.   Even in poverty and exile
they retained some of the qualities which went to make
up their prestige and their charm, their misfortunes gave
them a new dignity and a title to compassion ; even their
vices and their absurdities seemed, at least to the aristocracy of the country which entertained them, to be merely
a distinctive mark of the civilisation borrowed by Russia
from the West.   This being so they were still in high favour
at St. Petersburg, where the France of the *ancien régime*
was very popular.   England, with her hauteur and her
rudeness, attracted nobody, but, as Sorel says, this time
with perfect truth, " the fortunes of the boyards were in
the cash boxes of the City."

Alexander was in touch only with the few who were
acquainted with the secrets of home and foreign policy
and who saw with anger and with terror the perils to which
the incapacity or insanity of the Czar was exposing the
country.   For the Grand Duke this narrow circle was " all
Russia " ; but the mass of his future subjects was outside
this and they had none of these more or less legitimate
causes for discontent.   They knew nothing of the exhaustion of the finances or the disorder of the administration
or the threats of England ; and to them on the whole
Paul's Government gave every cause for satisfaction.

Even in the Guard the soldiers had not, or did not believe
themselves to have, any serious cause for complaint.   They
were beaten, it is true, but on the whole less than in the
previous reign, and between two floggings they received
regular distributions of brandy and small coins—a novelty
which they greatly appreciated.   As Paul was equally
prodigal of thrashings and of brandy they were inclined to
regard him as the best of monarchs.   Besides, they were
not alone in receiving blows and insults.   The officers had

392

their share in the common lot, and this appealed to the levelling instinct which is so powerfully developed in the Russian people and which Paul did his very best to encourage. Implacable as a judge, Paul preferred to strike at the head. " A cornet," writes Sabloukof, " might without fear bring a charge against his colonel . . . and be certain that his complaint would be impartially examined."

In the civil services the Czar's policy was similar, and led to similar results. His visible anxiety to protect the weak against the strong gained him a real popularity, especially at the commencement of his reign. The following is a contemporary comment on the changes which then took place: "A general upheaval deprived many people of their livelihood by taking from them the means of battening on the sweat of their neighbours, and by keeping every one at their peril within the limits of fair dealing."

It is certain that Paul's tragic end was not wholly or even chiefly due to his errors and his excesses. On the contrary, he owed his ruin to his most meritorious endeavours, which united against him a coalition of the basest interests and passions. The spirit of the age was slavish in the extreme even in the highest classes, and this tyrant, like so many others, might have been excused the grossest cruelty had he only attacked the dignity of this part of his subjects. But he took the bread out of their mouths and not only wounded their vanity but interfered with their pleasures. That could not be tolerated. He repressed the abuses of the administration of the Imperial Palaces and thus exasperated the whole band of gilded and greedy idlers whom Catherine had tolerated because their presence gave a colourable excuse to her own debauchery. It was from among them that the instruments of her son's assassination were recruited. The ruling spirit had a higher origin.

Paul's Government was detestable and the ruin and

disaster which he caused was destined to be felt in the very
heart of the masses whom he flattered, but for a time it
was natural that he should pass for a beneficent sovereign,
and out of the thirty-six millions of his subjects thirty-three
at least fully believed that they had every reason to bless his
name.   Among the upper classes discontent and a spirit of
revolt were excited and fostered by the liberal propaganda
to which Alexander and his friends made a show of de-
voting themselves.   The propagandists were few in number
and their influence was very much restricted.   When
Czartoryski says that *everybody* believed Paul to be insane
he explains that he means " the upper classes, the high
officials, generals, officers, civil servants, which in Russia
means all the nation that thinks and acts."   We should
now say in Russia, " all the *intelligentsia*," which means
very much the same thing.   The mass of the people on
which Paul was foolish enough to rely was, in the contemptuous English phrase, " nobody."   They had no
political or social value ; they were not a force which could
be utilised.   In our time also the attempts which have
been made to bring this element into play have failed and
the hopes which have been founded on its assistance have
been deceived.   Thus the foundations which Paul tried to
lay were insecure and the edifice which he reared upon
them crumbled at the first shock.

The catastrophe was inevitable, but it seems to have been
precipitated by an act which, had it been properly carried
out, might have conciliated many of his adversaries.
On November 1, 1800, the Czar decreed a general amnesty.
All the public servants and officers who had been exiled
or dismissed during the previous four years were to be
recalled to St. Petersburg and to their duties.   They were
to present themselves as soon as possible before the Czar
and receive from his lips the confirmation of his clemency.
In a few days the roads leading to the capital were covered
with a procession of " *revenants* " hastening to respond to

this call. Some came in their coaches and six, some in ordinary *kibitkas*; others, for whom disgrace had meant utter ruin, came on foot.

Paul was charming to the first-comers, but he soon grew weary. There were not places enough for so many. Most of those who came did not even have the honour of seeing their Sovereign, and those who came last were arrested at the gates of the city. It is said that Pahlen perfidiously suggested the amnesty in order to put the Czar in a difficulty. But Paul was quite capable of imagining it for himself, and in his attempt to strike an attitude of generosity he had only succeeded in concentrating around his palace a mass of anger and hatred like a heap of explosives, in which the vengeance which was now close upon him would find its most suitable material.

But the explosion had been long prepared. Immediately after his accession Mme. Vigée-Lebrun was in great fear because, as she said, there was a general belief that a rising against the new Sovereign was imminent. The Grand Duchess Elizabeth, wife of the heir-apparent, writing to her mother on August 4/16, 1797, gives a long description of two singular incidents which had caused alarm at Pavlovsk where the Inperial family were then gathered. Countess Golovine also mentions a sudden movement on the palace of various troops constituting the garrison of the Imperial residence without any apparent cause. " I wager my head," writes the Grand Duchess, " and so would many others, that some of the troops have something *im Sinn*, or that at least they hope to bring about something by gathering together in this way. . . . O, if only they had some one to lead them ! Oh, mamma, he really is a tyrant ! "

Thus only nine months after Paul ascended the throne his entourage were convinced that the troops whose duty it was to guard him were meditating treachery, and in his own family the possibility of this eventuality was causing not fear but joyous expectation ! Perhaps his undutiful daughter-in-law was mortified that her husband was too timid and indolent to put himself at their head, and perhaps too the troubles which distracted Alexander's household began in this terrible source of discord.

But these disquieting incidents, which perhaps were merely accidental, did not recur, and in the two following years Paul, distracted by great affairs and deceived by the apparent docility of every one, forgot his terrors amid his feverish if sterile activities. About the middle of 1800, however, he had fresh reason for anxiety. Heaps of ruins had accumulated about him and the sky was dark. His domestic happiness was destroyed, his ambitions were deceived ; he had himself given the lie to all his ideals of public and private life. Was this not enough to affect his mind ? He was depressed and melancholy, he lost his appetite and rarely smiled. He was awaiting with feverish impatience the day when he could leave all the residences which hitherto had taken his fancy. He could no longer rest or feel secure in any of them. What he wanted was a fortress—a citadel with walls of granite, surrounded with deep moats, each access protected by a drawbridge; and so with wild haste the construction of the Michael Palace was pressed forward by dint of ukases at the cost of millions.

V

Besides being an impregnable fortress, the new residence was to be a magnificent palace. Paul had soon given up his preference for rustic simplicity under the influence of his impressions of the French Court and the tastes of Marie Féodorovna, who, like all the German Princesses of the period, worshipped only the sun which rose at Versailles. In spite of the simplicity of Étupes, she adored pomp and ceremony, and we have seen how the shepherdess of Pavlovsk had developed by the time she was crowned at

Moscow. The Court of the Semiramis of the North was accounted the most brilliant and sumptuous in Europe; but Paul considered that the Empress did not preserve with sufficient strictness the respect due to the majesty of the supreme rank. He determined to introduce a discipline as severe as that of his regiments, and combined Versailles with Potsdam, not without a reminiscence of the Asiatic ceremonial which until very recently was customary in the old Kremlin. Even the ladies had to kneel when they kissed his hand, and the regulations governing this act of homage prescribed a series of gestures, courtesies and pirouettes which was very difficult to execute. If a young *freiline* made a mistake she was brutally turned out and was called *doura* (stupid) to her face. Nevertheless she had to present herself on the following day, often only to be told by the usher, " To-day you are not fit to appear before his Majesty ! "

The lives of the members of the Imperial family and their suites were determined down to the smallest detail by regulations of military precision. The Emperor rose between four and five and worked in his cabinet until nine, receiving reports and giving audiences. He then rode out with one of his sons, usually the Grand Duke Alexander, to inspect some establishment or some work in progress. From eleven till twelve there was parade, and then work again till dinner, which was served precisely at one. The table was laid for eight only, twice or three times that number being present at supper. After a short siesta there were further visits of inspection and more work from four till seven, then a Court, where the Czar often kept every one waiting but did not allow any one else to be late. When he arrived the list of persons to be presented was handed to him, and he marked on it in pencil the names of those whom he wished to be asked to supper. Sometimes as he walked round the circle he spoke to a few people, but those present were forbidden to talk to each other.

PAUL THE FIRST

On the stroke of nine the dining-room was thrown open. The Emperor entered first, giving his arm sometimes, but not always, to the Empress. Casting about him glances always severe and often angry, he would brusquely hand his hat and gloves to the page whose duty it was to receive them, and would take his place in the centre of the table with the Empress on his right hand and his eldest son on his left. Silence was now no longer enforced, but no one dared to use the privilege of speech except to answer the Emperor, who as a rule talked only to his son or to Count Stroganof. The rest of the party remained mute. Very often he contented himself with glancing round the table in the intervals of eating, scrutinising his guests' faces and noting their attitudes. To a lady who had kept on her gloves from caprice or forgetfulness he sent a page with the command, "Ask her if she has the itch!" After supper, if he was in a good humour, Paul was fond of throwing the dessert from the table all over the room and making the pages scramble for the choice morsels. At ten the day was over and the Emperor went to bed.

In Catherine's time the staff had been extremely numerous. It was now much reduced. From September 1, 1800, the officers of the garrison of Gatchina ceased to have the entry to the theatre and the church of the Palace. Paul had discovered suspicious faces among them. Even in his restricted sphere the Czar allowed no intimacy. There were no charming evenings like those at the Hermitage when Catherine, banishing etiquette, rested from the fatigues of power and parade. He kept up these parties, but always " with the glittering crowd of civil and military officers who under the eye of the master maintained all the stiffness of a battalion under arms."

Here as elsewhere everywhere, costume, gesture, attitude and words were according to regulation. At the blessing of the waters, a ceremony which takes place in January in twenty degrees of frost, the rules required those present to appear without pelisses, in silk stockings and Court shoes. One year Prince Adam Czartoryski was struck down by an attack of congestion. Many others had to go to bed as soon as they returned home. Paul was unmoved. In the evening, when the report of these accidents was presented, he was merely surprised. " I felt hot myself," he observed. Even in the country no relaxation of the code was allowed, the sole exception being when the Emperor occasionally condescended to play with his youngest children, when the nurse with the baby on her knee was actually permitted to remain seated in his presence !

Ceremonial observances did not stop at the walls of the Imperial palaces ; it extended to the streets. In the neighbourhood of the Imperial residences it was the rule for the passers-by to uncover, whatever the weather, and as the custom of the country compels the coachmen to hold the reins in both hands they had to hold their caps in their teeth. Paul, without any prompting from his police, who have sometimes been made responsible for these rules, would compel ladies of the highest rank and advanced age to alight from their carriages in order to salute him when they met him, at the risk of plunging into mud or snow in their ball slippers. If the rule was broken the carriage was confiscated, and the coachman, the footmen and sometimes their masters were corporally punished. Men had to remove their pelisses and come to attention.

All this was very different from Versailles, and there were several reasons for his divergence from the model which was held up for him to imitate. One of these was his desire to imitate Frederick II. With all his extravagance the son of the prodigal Catherine had pretentions to economy and simplicity. He proudly showed Prince Czartoryski a hat the braid of which was much worn ; winter or summer he wore the same cloak, changing only the lining according to the season. When he travelled in the provinces he affected to lodge in the peasants' houses, and forbade under the severest penalties that any preparations should be made for his reception.

And yet his shortest journeys recalled the movements of a caravan. They required no less than a hundred and thirty-five horses. There was nothing brilliant or elegant about the train, but there were a great many people in a great many carriages, most of which were mere carts with wretched horses. This company devoured in its passage enough to victual a small town. This is what was required for each meal prepared by the Czar's travelling kitchen : Several *pouds* of beef, a calf, two goats, a sheep, two sucking pigs, two turkeys, four fat hens, two capons, six or ten fowls, four pairs of chickens, two brace of blackcock, four brace of partridges, four brace of woodcock, three *pouds* and a half of the best flour, ten pounds of fresh butter and a similar quantity of salt, a hundred eggs, ten bottles of thick cream, as many of milk, a *viedro* of cabbage, fifty large crayfish, four pounds of meal, two dishes of fish on ordinary days and twelve on fast days, not to mention cucumbers, mushrooms, lemons, vegetables, &c. &c. &c.

It is not much, considering the number to be fed ! and Louis XIV's unaided appetite demanded more copious ménus. But the inferiority of Gatchina to Versailles was even more apparent in the moral sphere. The *roi soleil* reflected in his superhuman personality the splendour of a whole constellation of stars of varying magnitude, who all contributed to the glory of the central figure. Apart from himself Paul would not allow anything to exist but a dust of obscure and inert atoms. He alone could draw them from the nothingness to which next moment he would again consign them. " You have to learn, sir, that in my Empire no man is great except the man to whom I speak, while I am speaking to him." If this remark was not in fact uttered by Paul, there is at any rate no doubt that it faithfully represents his point of view. He was completely convinced not only of his own greatness but of his goodness and virtue. As the representative of God on earth, was it not natural that he should participate in His perfection? In this conviction he never ceased " to pose for his own admiration," as the Grand Duchess Elizabeth said, and he arranged his Court entirely with a view to making it a theatre for this sort of display.

But so conceived and produced, the spectacle became intolerable for the other actors, and after reigning for three years Paul began to feel the stage collapsing under the gorgeous scenery. Then with all the haste of those who are afraid he thought of nothing but flight, of changing his abode for an inviolable sanctuary. He was going out to meet his fate.

VI

He had been born in the Summer Palace, a vast erection of wood dating from the reign of Elizabeth. Shortly after his birth there were rumours that a soldier on duty before the Imperial residence had had a vision of the Archangel Michael. Paul's mystic temperament seized eagerly on the legend, and it was decided that the old palace, now uninhabited, should receive the name of the Michael Palace and should be replaced by a more sumptuous building of hewn stone. Starting with this, there was gradually evolved under the influence of mysticism, terror, reminiscences of Versailles and mediæval fantasy, the vision of a romantically magnificent Bastille, which Ivan Bajénof, freemason and architect, was charged to build. This artist fell ill, and his plans were remodelled by Brenna, a simple master builder who had been brought from Italy by a great lord of Poland. The work suffered by the change; the style affected was that of the Italian Renaissance, degraded to the level of a builder's labourer. The expenses of construction and interior decoration in three years were officially stated as nearly two million roubles, and in reality amounted to much more.*

Brenna made a considerable fortune, for the materials were not of the best. Granite was only used for the lower parts of the edifice. Above these the walls were in common masonry hideously plastered with the colours of the favourite. Paul gave many orders as to details, and is even believed to have contributed sketches of what he wanted. The result was a hideous and discordant mixture of forms and colours, a strange mixture of luxury and squalor, absolutely without harmony or artistic taste. The Czar's great anxiety was to instal himself as soon as possible in this unattractive residence, and on November 1, 1800, consumed with impatience, he returned to St. Petersburg, earlier than usual. The fortress palace was not ready to receive him. The walls had not had time to dry. With all speed they were covered with panelling, which hid the dampness for a time. Soon, however, the panels sweated at the joints and the paintings laid on new plaster were already fading to such an extent that Kotzebue says that he could not make out the design. Pictures, furniture and carpets deteriorated to such an extent that soon after the Emperor's death they had to be removed in order to save them from complete destruction. A thick mist filled the rooms, so that, in spite of the abundance of the lights, people could not recognise each other. The place was uninhabitable, and those whom Paul condemned to live there with him felt that they ran the risk of suffocation. Everybody kept repeating, " The Emperor is mad ! " " This cannot go on ! " The spirit of revolt spread through the whole Court, from the chamberlains to the domestics, and when he insisted on them taking up their quarters in this dismal abode he made his whole entourage the accomplices of those who were already seeking an opportunity of getting rid of him.

* Kotzebue, who no doubt exaggerates, puts them at 15 or 18 millions.

THE FINAL CRISIS

He did not heed them, and on February 1, 1801, he was already sleeping in the room in which, six weeks later, he met his death. The next day he gave a ball in the new palace, which, though in the centre of the city, was officially described as " suburban " and governed like a fortress. There was a considerable garrison. Armed posts occupied all the issues and kept watch on all the approaches to the *castle*, as Paul directed his house should be styled. There was a *castellan*, Brisgalof, who twenty years later was still wearing the grotesque uniform assigned to him. Twice a day the drawbridges were lowered to give passage to the " service of correspondence with the city," which was organised in the German fashion, and brought in the letters with a great noise of horns and cracking of postillions' whips.

Paul found much amusement in all this, but his chief pleasure was the illusion that he was at last in safety. He had multiplied his precautions and had even gone so far as to arrange a small kitchen near his own apartments, where he no doubt intended to have his meals prepared by a confidential servant in case he was alarmed by some attempt to poison him. He hoped, however, to live happy and at ease in his retreat, which was so well defended.

Princess Gagarine established herself in a suite of apartments communicating with those of the Emperor by a secret staircase, and it was rumoured that he was on the point of repudiating his wife in order to marry his mistress, whose divorce he was about to secure. It was asserted that he had already obtained the approval of the new Archbishop of St. Petersburg, whose sudden elevation to the rank of Metropolitan was thus explained. Others, however, believed, or pretended to believe, that Mme. Chevalier had already the *entrée* at the new palace by night and that the actress was supplanting the great lady. There were many other even more scandalous stories, for the conspirators, whose plot was already in train, did their best to spread rumours which were likely to make the unfortunate Czar odious to his subjects. Paul's own conduct unfortunately made their task easy.

VII

With occasional returns of affection and politeness which were witnessed by very few, Paul treated his wife in public with increasing rudeness, and behaved similarly to his two eldest sons, reserving his affection ostensibly for the two youngest, Nicolas and Michael. Alexander used all his stock of supple dissimulation (which was considerable) to disarm the distrust and anger of his father, but in vain. He lived with his wife in solitude, surrounded himself with servants who were devoted to the Emperor, and never spoke to a foreign minister or a great officer of State except in his father's presence. Paul was not appeased. He had no idea of his son's real feelings, but in spite of the security of the Michael Palace he could not give up his habit of distrusting and suspecting everybody, and he had the folly to let this be seen.

Always on the alert, he spied upon the slightest movements of his heir, and tried to take him by surprise by coming unexpectedly into his room. It is said that one day he found there Voltaire's *Brutus* open at the page on which occurs the verse :

Rome est libre, il suffit, rendons grâces aux dieux,

and that the Czar, returning to his own apartments without saying a word, ordered Koutaïssof to carry to Alexander *The History of Peter the Great* open at the page containing the account of the death of the Czarevitch Alexis, executed by his father's orders. No better way could be found to make Alexander shake off his timidity and indolence and thrust him into the arms of those who were offering to save him and also the Empire. In fact, the

young Grand Duke was already gravitating in that direction, and at the Michael Palace a new and strong reason
arose why he should let himself go.

On February 6, 1801, a nephew of Marie Féodorovna,
Prince Eugene of Würtemberg, who was destined to command a Russian corps in the campaigns of 1812–1814,
arrived at St. Petersburg. He was at this time a boy of
thirteen and when Paul invited him to stay with his aunt
in Russia it was only an instance of the occasional fits of
kindness which alternated with the brutality with which
he treated the Empress. But the Czar's fancy, which had
become more and more unmanageable, was soon more
deeply engaged.

The boy presented himself before the Emperor in a
Russian dragoon uniform, in boots which were so large
that when he tried to kneel before the monarch he overbalanced himself and fell on the floor. But he found
favour in the eyes of Paul, who raised him himself,
placed him in a chair and lavished on him so many
caresses that he attracted universal attention. General
Diebitsch, the young Prince's mentor, could not refrain
after this interview from embracing him on the stairs with
such vehemence that he lost his wig ! Hardly had the new
favourite got home when he received the Cross of Malta
and found a crowd of visitors at his door. Not long afterwards he alarmed his entourage by getting a young maid-
of-honour of his own age into serious trouble, and at a
Court dinner he entangled his spurs in the tablecloth, nearly
upset the table, and measured his length on the ground
in the presence of the Czar. Paul's kindness, however,
seemed undiminished, and on his expressing astonishment
at the increasing deference shown him the young prince
was told by General Diebitsch that the Sovereign had
decided to marry him to his daughter Catherine and make
him his heir. In a note which he afterwards wrote,
Eugene showed that he firmly believed that Paul seriously

intended this, and even asserts that the Czar was on the point of shutting up his wife and all his family but Catherine in a convent, if indeed he did not put Marie Féodorovna to death !

These rumours were spread abroad by Diebitsch or others and were generally believed. Paul's behaviour lent probability to the most bizarre conjectures. Princess Gagarine was said to have heard him say, " Soon I shall be compelled to behead some people of whom I used to be fond ! " or " I have a plan in my mind which will make me seventeen years younger "—an allusion to the age of the Grand Duke Nicolas, who was the same number of years younger than his brother Constantine. Neither is likely to have repeated these remarks to Pahlen, from whom Bennigsen is said to have heard them. But Paul was believed by everybody to be capable of anything. He sowed terror and alarm about him, and that feeling of the imminence of some startling but not undesirable event which is the most fruitful source of dire catastrophes.

In spite of the care which was taken to keep him ignorant of the rumours of the streets, Eugene could not fail to notice the perpetual irritation of the Czar and the " grimaces " which the Emperor made at all the members of his family. Sometimes Paul seemed to be intoxicated, but though the young Prince, deceived by his manner, professed to have seen the Sovereign drinking freely at a Court party, it does not appear that Catherine's son ever forsook his customary sobriety. The intoxication which was affecting his reason is not to be found at the bottom of a glass.

Princess Lieven never for a moment believed that Paul wished to marry Mme. Chevalier. " Follies were attributed to him," she says, " which never entered his mind." But she says it is certain that the despatch of Orlof and his men on the way to India was due to a deliberate design of the Emperor's to destroy the Don Cossacks, because he detested the constitutional form of the government of their tribe. Her husband was then Minister of War and had charge of this expedition, or at least transmitted the order by which it was governed ! In the last days of the reign Mme. Lieven must often have heard the words, " This cannot go on ! "

Meanwhile, in the gloomy palace, there was a succession of balls and parties, and the foreign envoys, who had to be careful what they put in their despatches, declared that " there was an unceasing round of gaiety." Prince Eugene, however, saw everywhere anxious looks and faces convulsed with terror. The police redoubled their severity. The capital was practically in a state of siege : " At nine o'clock . . . barriers were erect ed in the larger streets and only doctors and accoucheurs were allowed to pass." The weather, always gloomy in winter in this latitude, was this year even more dismal than usual. " For weeks," writes another contemporary, " we never saw the sun. No one wished to go out ; it was dangerous. It seemed as if God himself had abandoned us."

There was tragedy in the air, and though the number of those who were preparing the catastrophe was very small, every one was art and part in the conspiracy. "Everybody felt it coming," wrote Prince Czartoryski, " wished for it, feared it, was sure of it. Every one spoke of it under his breath, constantly expected it without knowing when it would come. There was a vague but unanimous presentiment of an inevitable change. . . . It was the fashion among the young men about the Court to talk in the most reckless manner on this subject, to amuse themselves with epigrams on Paul's absurdity and injustice, and by imagining the most grotesque devices for ridding themselves of his tyranny. . . . The aversion which they imprudently flaunted was a State secret known to all and betrayed by none under the most dreaded and suspicious of Sovereigns."

In spite of every precaution to prevent him from hearing ugly things, Prince Eugene also heard among the whisperings the fatal words, " This cannot go on ! " or " The Emperor is mad ! " The belief that the Sovereign was suffering from a malady which was destroying his reason and making it impossible for him to remain on the throne was now general. In the previous spring Rogerson had already noted the progress made by the alarming symptoms of the patient and by the view taken of the case by his subjects. " The cloud is darkening," he wrote to Simon Vorontsof, " the incoherence of his movements increases and becomes more manifest from day to day. . . . Every one about him is at a loss what to do. Even the favourite (Koutaïssof) is becoming very anxious, and I can see that they are all inclined to come back to the Grand Duke." He advises the Ambassador to " procrastinate." In February 1801 Vorontsof in his turn wrote, in sympathetic ink, to Novossiltsof, who was also in England, comparing Russia to a ship whose captain had gone mad in the midst of a storm, and he described a scheme of rescue in which he asked his young friend to participate.

" The second-in-command is a sensible, quiet young man in whom the crew have confidence. I beg you to return on deck and to represent to the young man and to the sailors that their duty is to save the ship, and that it is absurd to be afraid of being killed by their lunatic of a captain when in a very short time the madman will drown them all." The writer being subject to sea sickness, was unable himself to risk a long voyage in order to succour the distressed ship, and as Novossiltsof declined to do as he was exhorted Vorontsof was in despair.

But at this very moment an understanding had already been reached between the young lieutenant and some of the crew. If it had not yet been settled how the demented captain was to be deprived of the command, it was at least decided that the helm must somehow be wrested from his frenzied hands. Now, in his fortress palace Paul had deprived himself of his best means of defence by successively banishing the few men who were genuinely devoted to him. Araktchéief and Lindener had been in exile since October 1799, and in February 1801 Rastoptchine himself followed them. He was replaced by Pahlen. Paul was surrendering himself to his executioners.

CHAPTER XV

THE PLOT

I

HAD he been left to his own resources or those of his revolutionary committee Alexander would probably not have gone very far. He would probably have " waited his turn " without doing anything to hasten it. Moreover, two members of the triumvirate, Czartoryski and Novossiltsof, had left Russia, and Stroganof the third was anything but a man of action. But even among the men with whom Paul surrounded his son there were malcontents of a very different stamp, and the young Grand Duke was to be solicited by them, for without him it was impossible to imagine any change of government in Russia, and Alexander was probably alone in imagining that they could do without a monarch.

The idea of a conspiracy for Paul's overthrow had been slowly maturing since the commencement of the reign. It began as an inclination, a vague scheme or merely a passionate if passive longing entertained in the most various quarters and even in the bosom of the Imperial Family. It appears to have taken definite shape at the end of 1799. Since October in that year Count Panine had occupied the post of Vice-Chancellor, but had found himself excluded from all effective participation in the direction of foreign affairs by the growing favour and the all-pervading influence of Rastoptchine. He was twenty-eight and full of vigour ; his past was already brilliant, and in the future he hoped for even greater things. His family traditions and his personal pride alike forbade him to accept such a situation. Moreover, his absolute faith in his own judgment and his sincere patriotism led him to identify his ambitions with the interests of his country. The advice given by Rastoptchine to Paul, and Paul's habit of listening to no other counsellor, were certain, he thought, to lead to the ruin of the country and that catastrophe must at any cost be prevented.

This soon led to the ruin of the young diplomatist himself, for a sharp conflict with the Emperor became inevitable. Panine had been brought up in the house of his uncle, Nikita Petrovitch, and could not rid himself of an offensive habit of treating the Emperor as he had seen his imperious uncle treat the Czarevitch. The Czar, on his side, retained in his relations with the nephew something of the deference which he had used towards his former mentor, and when provoked beyond measure he would stride away from the young Panine in order not to give way to the anger which was suffocating him.

Panine, with all his coldness, was a dreamer, fond of mystery and occultism, and attached to all kinds of fantasy. In the latter half of his life he was destined to become a passionate votary of magnetic science. It was probably his taste for intrigue, full of the shadows and thrills of tragedy, which inspired him to take part in the plot, for he was too much of an idealist and too little of a man of action to fill the part of arch-conspirator. He used to attend the meetings of his accomplices with a dagger concealed under his waistcoat, but, left to himself, he would probably never have menaced Paul's life or even his throne. Yet he took to conspiring quite naturally, and in order to pass from dreaming to action he sought the help of men whose minds and temperament were very different from his own.

When he returned to St. Petersburg he had renewed a

friendship which can only be explained on the theory of the identity of contraries or the connection of extremes. The son of a Spanish gentleman in the Neapolitan service, called Don Miguele Ribas y Baions, or more probably of an Italian porter answering to the name of Ruobono, Admiral Joseph Ribas was nothing but an adventurer with the soul of a bandit—in fact, the precise type of conspirator for the enterprise. He was born at Naples in 1749 and was at Leghorn in 1774 when Alexis Orlof was in the roadstead with a Russian squadron, and after having annihilated the Turkish fleet in the Bay of Tchesmé turned his attention to the abduction of the famous Princess Tarkanof. Young Ribas seems to have helped Orlof in the latter and less glorious exploit, and this gave him an unexpected chance of a career in Russia. In 1776 he married Anastasia Sokolof, a protégée of Potemkine's, and this enabled him to make his way. In spite of these associations he contrived to keep his place even after Paul's accession, and in 1798 he was a member of the College of Admiralty. In the following year he was made Admiral and head of the Department of Forests. Hitherto he had every reason to be satisfied, but early in 1800 he was dismissed for shameless peculation, and though he soon recovered the Imperial favour and became the Deputy Vice-President of the College of Admiralty, he had lost, on Rastoptchine's estimate "the chance of stealing half a million roubles a year." This he could not forgive, and he was quite ready to give a very favourable reception to the overtures of Panine.

The two men used to meet at the house of the fair Olga Jerebtsof, sister of the Zoubofs, and Whitworth's mistress. Some are of opinion that the first suggestion of the plot came from this dissolute woman, who was in the pay of England. Others—a large number—believed that it was directly instigated by King George's Ambassador. Mme. Jerebtsof had her own reasons for hating

Paul, who had exiled her brothers and sequestrated their property. She also showed a strong liking for English guineas, which appear to have helped her at a later period to acquire one of the finest estates of the Demidof family. This money, however, seems to have been gained in a different way ; it was the proceeds of a sojourn in England after Paul's death, during which she was so fortunate as to gain the favour of the Prince of Wales. She returned to Russia with a son who, under the name of Nord, founded a family which in recent years still had a distinguished representative in Russia. This adventure, however, had no conceivable connection with the conspiracy of 1800, and there was nothing in the personality of Olga Alexandrovna to suggest that she was of the stuff of which female arch-conspirators are made.

As to Whitworth, it is out of the question that he can have been the initiator. Everything we now know goes to show that the origin of the plot dates back to the last months of 1799 or the first months of 1800. At that time the Ambassador had no reason for desiring the death or dethronement of Paul on public grounds, and he had one very serious private reason for wishing to keep him in power. He was taking an active part in Russia in the negotiations whereby the Court of St. James's still hoped to bind the Czar to the English alliance, and, thanks to the Czar's support, he was on the point of realising his own personal ambition. In March 1800 he was made an Irish peer by the title of Baron Whitworth of Newport Pratt, but he left Russia before receiving his patent.

If he had not shared the illusions of Pitt and Grenville he would not have failed to inform his chiefs of the highly dangerous expedient which he thought necessary in order to avert the consequences of their mistake. Now, there is not the least trace of this in his despatches, and the last of the series—even that of February 1800—in which he reveals the fact of Paul's insanity, are concerned only with the best means of turning it to advantage. As Mme. Jerebtsof's lover he must have known of the plot; he may have shown some sympathy with it, and in the last moments of his stay at St. Petersburg he may even have given it some discreet encouragement. It is impossible that he can have done more. At the time of his departure from Russia in May 1800 the conspiracy was still in the clouds, and it is notorious that Whitworth, after leaving Russia, was quite absorbed by his own affairs and entirely ceased to interest himself in Russian questions.

It is easy to explain the legend which has arisen in Russia that he and English gold were the chief instruments of the crime. It was said that piles of rouleaux were seen at Count Pahlen's house, that Valerian Zoubof and his wife handled heaps of glittering guineas, and that Mme. Jerebtsof brought back millions from England with which to pay the conspirators. If she had done so, she would certainly have kept them for herself, but, as a matter of fact, most of the gold then in circulation in Russia was foreign, and chiefly English, owing to the British subsidies which were being paid to the Czar's troops. Whitworth's correspondence shows no expenditure for this purpose from the secret funds entrusted to him.* It is entirely unlikely that the British Government, even if they had been willing to reward Paul's assassins *after the event,* would have entrusted millions to Mme. Jerebtsof for that purpose. That lady, moreover, had other means of gaining adherents to the causes in which she was interested, and in plotting the death of their Sovereign

---

* It has been supposed that apart from his despatches which I have consulted at the Record Office there is another and inaccessible part of his correspondence. It is possible, though it is difficult to imagine why he did not reserve for these ultra-confidential reports certain passages of those now open to our curiosity in which, using sympathetic ink, he spared neither Russia nor the Czar.

some at least of the conspirators had other and nobler motives than greed. Public opinion in Russia disapproved of the crime, but it is not necessarily in Russia's interest to insist on proving that its motives were so vile. For, if the story of a bribe is to be accepted, it must be remembered that if the money was offered by the English it was taken by Russians. There is nothing, however, which obliges or even allows us to accept the story.

When Panine and Ribas commenced the intrigue they could depend with certainty on the co-operation of Mme. Jerebtsof and the probable assistance at the last moment of her lover. By themselves, however, they could not accomplish anything very serious. Panine lacked the nerve and Ribas the capacity. The former not being a soldier was without resources ; the latter, being a notorious rascal, did not inspire confidence. They agreed therefore to add a third to their number. Like all conspirators, they aimed at securing the help of armed force, and Pahlen, who was a general of some reputation and had been Military Governor of St. Petersburg since 1798, was a natural choice.

II

According to certain Russian authorities, Pahlen had nothing to do with what is called the *first* plot, that which was started by Panine and which, having miscarried, had no direct connection with the second, which was destined to succeed. The facts of the case do not bear out this version of what happened. Pahlen was certainly associated in the initial phase of the enterprise with Panine, who remained in touch with subsequent developments even after he had relinquished the command of the affair. At first, no doubt, his participation was of the slightest, but how did he come to be engaged at all ? There was nothing either in his career or in his character which would have led one to expect him to do such a thing.

During the first months of Paul's reign the series of his successes had been somewhat interrupted. But though he had been dismissed from his post as Governor of Riga he had been called in the following year to other and higher functions, and he was in the habit of jesting about his misadventure. He used to compare himself to " these dolls which you may upset and place head downwards, but which always stand up again." He had been a cornet in the Guard in 1760 at the age of seventeen, and had been one of the heroes of the Prussian campaign of 1759. He was wounded at the siege of Bender in 1770, and had been a major-general since 1787. His brilliant services had been recompensed while Catherine still reigned by the gift of the fine estate of Eckau in Courland, and his appointment as Military Governor of the capital seemed to open the most flattering prospects.

He was a tall, broad-shouldered man, with a very high forehead, and according to Mme. de Lieven he had the " most honest and jovial " face in the world. He was " very witty, original, and genial " and " was the very embodiment of rectitude, gaiety, and carelessness." He took life lightly, and lived in an atmosphere of health and joy. Marie Féodorovna shared this impression. " It is impossible to know this good old man and not to love him," she wrote to Plechtchéief on September 9, 1798.

The two ladies, and almost all the world besides, were deceived in him. The bonhomie, the joviality, the carelessness, the rectitude, were but a mask under which " the good old man " had for nearly sixty years concealed a very different person who was only now about to be revealed. There was indeed, under that attractive exterior, an abyss of perfidy and ferocity, an iron will, and a reckless audacity at the service of an ambition as boundless as it was unscrupulous. His acquirements were very limited, and he had no proved capacities to recommend him for important civil or military posts. In 1812 public opinion indicated him as the most suitable Commander-in-Chief against Napoleon, but this was on the strength of the services he had rendered before Paul's reign, for he did not afterwards serve in the army. In this he was fortunate, and with Paul his gifts as a courtier, his unfailing flexibility, his unchanging good humour, his ever ready wit, and his imperturbable *aplomb*, all contributed to assure his fortunes.

He made good use of his resources. To his new post he soon added those of Civil Governor of the three Baltic provinces, of Military Governor of Riga, and of Inspector of Cavalry and Infantry in the Livonian division. He continued to rise, and the day seemed to be at hand when he would triumph over all rivals and reach the summit of power.

And yet in the midst of this uninterrupted ascension he lent an ear to Panine! Was it because he distrusted the unmerited favour of which he had become the object and that he thought it best to anticipate a possible reaction by revolt. It may be so. Paul loaded him with benefits, but left him no rest. One day he took offence at a letter in which Kotzebue from the depths of Siberia begged for the intercession of Pahlen, who was half his compatriot. " They seem to think you can do anything," complained the Czar. Next day he dismissed Mme. Pahlen from the Court in the most outrageous manner because her husband had concealed from the Emperor a duel of which his favourite, Princess Gagarine, had been the cause. It may well be that Pahlen longed to be free of the constant fear of a fall which at every moment threatened him like the other ephemeral favourites.

At this time, however, he only half surrendered himself

to the conspiracy. No doubt his eminently practical and fundamentally brutal nature could ill brook the presence of Panine at the head of so dangerous an undertaking. Moreover, even if Pahlen's help could be entirely depended on, it was not by itself sufficient. Panine did not desire Paul's death. He thought of setting up a regency on the pattern of those which the mental alienation of King Christian VII in Denmark and King George III in England had made necessary in these two countries. In Russia, as there, the regency would fall to the Heir Apparent, and it was therefore necessary to secure the consent of Alexander. The young Prince was highly popular. The favour with which he was regarded grew as the hatred of his father increased. It was said that when Alexander threw himself at the Czar's feet imploring mercy for the ever more numerous victims of his anger, Paul repulsed him and kicked him in the face! It was said, too, that Alexander had had a telescope set up at one of the windows of his apartment so that he could watch the unhappy men who were sent to Siberia from the parade ground. When one of the sinister troikas bearing a victim into exile appeared a confidential servant was sent off at a gallop to meet him at the gates of the city and give him money from the Grand Duke.

Panine did not hesitate to take Alexander into his confidence. Pahlen, who stuck at nothing, had arranged an interview between the Prince and the Vice-Chancellor, which took place in great secrecy at a public bath. Panine described in eloquent terms the critical condition of his Empire and laboured to convince his hearer that what he proposed was compatible with filial sentiment in accordance with the precedents of England and Denmark, Paul could be deprived of the government without any violence. He would be relieved only of the cares of his rank, and would be deprived of none of the pleasures of life, while he would be relieved of the terrors which now poisoned his every hour.

Alexander did not allow himself to be convinced, but he seems to have shown no indignation. Panine's ideas probably agreed with his own and the proposed *coup d'état* was no doubt what he himself secretly desired. He did not accept the proposal, but he kept the secret, and remained in touch with Panine, exchanging letters with him through Pahlen. He, too, may have considered the idealistic Panine an unsuitable leader for such an enterprise, more especially as the Vice-Chancellor himself appeared to hesitate. He had not yet given up all hope of victory in the struggle with Rastoptchine.

The affair thus remained in suspense. In August 1800 Pahlen was appointed to command one of the fictitious armies which Paul ordered to be organised, and gave up the governorship of the capital. This spoiled the chances of the plot which depended on the co-operation of the garrison. Panine therefore, in the following month, tried a decisive stroke not against Paul, but against Rastoptchine.

He drew up two notes which, as he thought, could not fail to open the Emperor's eyes to the difficulties and dangers of the policy in which the President of the College of Foreign Affairs was involving Russia. Panine put forward a plan for the general pacification of Europe, and proposed himself as the negotiator of a scheme which he thought would commend itself to all the Courts of Europe. It was a naïve manœuvre. The notes had to pass through the hands of Rastoptchine, and Panine knew from experience that they had no chance of reaching their destination. His rival simply used them in the composition of the famous memorandum in which he offered to negotiate the partition of the world on equal terms between Russia and France, and thus for the moment completed his conquest of his Sovereign. But this check also had the effect of finally tearing Panine away from his uncertainties and his illusions.

Putting aside his usual custom of " never visiting any one for fear of compromising his dignity," Panine went to General Swetchine, Pahlen's successor as Military Governor, and asked him to come to see him. He came, and was received in an empty house lit by a single candle. Panine was fond of this childish *mise en scène*, but when he revealed his design the general absolutely refused to help him and the danger of the game became extreme, for Swetchine had an established reputation for loyalty and chivalry and no one knew what he might not do. Ribas was consulted, and renewed the negotiation with much skill. Swetchine was unmovable, so Ribas embraced him, saying, " You are the most honest of mankind. . . . Long may you remain faithful to your duty." Some days later, however, Swetchine was dismissed and replaced by Pahlen. This was the last success of the Vice-Chancellor and his associate. On November 15 (old style) Panine lost his place ; a month later he was exiled to his estates and had to leave St. Petersburg. On December 2 Ribas died. The plot seemed ruined, but, in fact, it only now began to succeed, for it now had a chief who was capable of organising success—Pahlen himself.

In November the general amnesty produced more favourable conditions for recruiting the conspiracy. It brought back the Zoubofs to St. Petersburg, a result which Mme. Jerebtsof afterwards attributed to her having given Koutaïssof 200,000 ducats. More probably the ex-barber had been won over by the hope which was held out to him that his daughter might become a Princess Zoubof.

The last of Catherine's lovers maintained his reputation as a rake of the first water, and during his recent sojourn in Germany his adventures had formed abundant material for the *chronique scandaleuse* of that country. The two younger Zoubofs, Plato and Valerian, were made commanders of the First and Second Cadet Corps, while Nicolas, the eldest, received the rank of Grand Equerry. Paul saw them often and treated them well, but he delayed the restoration of their estates, which they did not get until a few days before the Czar's death. All three were living in the meantime on money advanced to them by Leveau, the French banker at Berlin, and they were therefore impatient. Pahlen easily secured the doubtful advantage of their support. Nicolas was married to a daughter of the great Souvorof, and derived some prestige from this union. He was a wild bull of a man, who was capable of bravery when drunk; when sober, he was the terror of his fellow-conspirators, for he went about the streets muttering to himself in a state of visible disquietude, and it was feared that he had confided the secret to his wife, who was nicknamed the *Souvorotchka*, and was so silly and talkative that she was capable of proclaiming it on the housetops. Of the two other brothers, Valerian was a dreamer and Plato an idler, perhaps neither such a fool nor such a coward as he has been represented, but a man of a nonchalance made up of scepticism, disgust, and depravity, out of which nothing could shake him.

At the last moment Pahlen was more fortunate. In February Rastoptchine's disgrace concentrated almost all power in his hands. He kept the military command of St. Petersburg, took the post office, and shared the direction of foreign affairs with Prince Kourakine. He was thus enabled to work more at his ease, and he put his hand on Bennigsen. Bennigsen had been a page to the Empress Elizabeth at the age of ten, ensign of the Guard at fourteen, and afterwards a general. He had accounts of his own to settle with Paul. He had several times been dismissed and restored to his rank since 1797, and had finally found himself living forgotten on one of his estates in Lithuania. The amnesty found him in this retreat, but did not tempt him to leave it. In February 1801, however, he received pressing letters from Pahlen urging him to return to St. Petersburg and promising him the best possible reception. Paul did, in fact, receive him very kindly, but immediately afterwards turned his back on him. Bennigsen was furious and wanted to return to Lithuania, but Pahlen persuaded him to stay.

Bennigsen was a Hanoverian, and as the Czar was threatening his country with a French or Prussian occupation, it was easy to convince him that the safety of Russia depended on Russia changing her master. He was about the same age as Pahlen and, like him, he was tall. In other respects he was his living antithesis. He was dry, stiff, and serious, " like the statue of the Commendatore," as Mme. de Lieven put it. Among the hair-brained young men who formed the majority of the conspirators he was a valuable element of prudence. His natural coolness did not desert him at the critical moment, and perhaps it was he who assured the success of the enterprise.

Meanwhile Pahlen was still the intermediary for the correspondence between Panine and Alexander. He supported the representations of the ex-Vice-Chancellor by direct advances, and he succeeded in clinching the negotiation. The Grand Duke had weakened even before Panine's departure. He sighed as he listened to what was said to him ; he did not say no, but he did not say yes, and at each interview he became more involved in the plan. In February, if not sooner, he had definitely thrown in his lot with the conspirators.

III

There is a whole mass of quite conclusive and consistent evidence that Alexander did finally assent to the plan. His confidences to Czartoryski would alone be sufficient to prove this, and, if their authenticity is questioned, all the circumstances of the tragedy of March seem to prove that he was, at least morally, an accomplice. " If you had been here," Alexander is said to have told his friend, " I should never have been led on as I was." This confession was followed by an account of the Emperor's death, in the course of which the face of the narrator assumed " an expression of inexpressible grief and remorse." Czartoryski also shows that Pahlen's account of the Grand Duke's participation in the event of March, as given by Langeron, is entirely true.

A letter from Panine to Marie Féodorovna dated either 1801 or 1804, the draft of which has been preserved, also appears very conclusive. It is not known whether it was actually sent, but it is sufficient that it was written to the Empress. It is at the same time a vigorous defence and a deliberate accusation :

" You cannot accuse me without repudiating your own flesh and blood. My conduct, the motives of my action, can and should displease Paul's consort, but they were those which influence any public man. . . . I desired to save the Empire from certain ruin. I wished to place the regency in the hands of your august son. I thought that if he himself directed the carrying out of so delicate a matter he would eliminate undesirables. . . . If the Emperor* committed to unfaithful hands the plan which I presented to him for the safety of the State is it I, madam, who should be blamed ? . . . The Emperor's own letters would be enough to show you that my conduct

* Alexander.

423

in this affair were such as to merit his esteem and confidence."

In a later memoir, probably written in the reign of Nicolas, the ex-Vice-Chancellor is even more explicit. " I possess an autograph paper which proves to demonstration that all that I meditated and proposed for the safety of the State for some months before the Emperor's death *had the sanction of his son*."

Only one point in these assertions requires correction. It seems certain that Alexander did not give the direction of the conspiracy into the hands of any one, but held the threads himself until the last moment, while he took care that he should not appear. In disreputable affairs it was afterwards his invariable practice to put forward the instruments while hiding the hand which made them work. It is possible that on this occasion the tool, to some extent, betrayed the workman, and that the young Prince was " led on," as he afterwards complained to Czartoryski. Pahlen knew Paul and probably foresaw that "they would not make the omelette without breaking eggs," an expression which he is said to have used at the final moment, and no doubt he kept this to himself until the final moment had come. Panine's plans on paper excluded all violence and, at a distance, may have seemed to him to be realisable. Between these two collaborators, whose natural impulse was never to look things in the face, Alexander, who had a great gift for reticence and evasion, probably succeeded in deluding his own conscience. Perhaps he brought himself to think sincerely that Paul would resign himself without a struggle to his deposition, and would easily accept the compensations which were being prepared. His son would enlarge and embellish the Michael Palace for him ; he would build there for the ex-Sovereign a splendid theatre and a superb riding school, and on this ingenious compromise every one would live together in happiness and contentment.

THE PLOT

And yet should not Alexander have taken precautions against the accidents inseparable from such a dangerous undertaking ? Should he not have tied the hands of Panine and Pahlen by strict orders and precise engagements ? He is said to have done so, but this is more than doubtful. If he had Pahlen would not have failed after the event, when the "accident" had happened, to give himself at least the air of a man who had been overwhelmed and betrayed by faithless associates. Alexander, on the other hand, would have shown a just anger against the traitors. Neither thought of doing anything of the kind. Furthermore, it is well known that Prince Peter Volonski, the Grand Duke's own favourite aide-de-camp, took part in the attack on the Michael Palace on the fatal night. It is most unlikely that he did so without the sanction of his chief, and the manner in which Alexander treated him afterwards seems to be conclusive evidence of his real attitude to the affair. At his coronation Paul's successor raised this officer to the rank of aide-de-camp general, attached him even more closely to his person, and never again separated himself from him. Later he was made Field Marshal, Chief of the Staff, Member of the Council of the Empire, Minister of the Court and Domains, and Chancellor of all the Russian Orders. After following the new Emperor in all his campaigns and all his journeys, the man who was notoriously one of the father's murderers attended the son in his turn when he came to die !

Alexander *of his own motion* never punished any of those who took part in Paul's assassination. One refuses to believe that he wished for his father's death. He wished that "the demented tyrant" should cease to reign and to torture everybody, more especially those nearest to him. How could this be managed ? His son did not know, and did not wish to know. He shut his eyes and allowed it to happen.

Panine's absence moreover necessarily gave the conspiracy a new character, and made it deviate from the original programme. No doubt the ex-Vice-Chancellor would hardly have succeeded in eliminating all chance of a fatality from the undertaking. With Ribas he had introduced an element of the very worst augury. But Panine was a man of character, and when he was sent away it was men like Ribas who were the masters and the character of the work was altered. Swetchine says that in the course of Ribas's attempts to seduce him from his allegiance, he received an assurance that Paul's life would be respected. But the Italian did not speak of a regency or of a pleasant retirement for the Sovereign. He personally thought an abdication would be necessary, and would have to be followed by internment in a fortress. To this he added some even more disquieting provisions. " In order to conduct the dethroned monarch to his prison it would be necessary to cross the Neva, and, as the river was full of ice driven by the current, it would be impossible to be sure that an accident might not happen." Perhaps Alexander had himself heard such reservations made.

IV

Between February and March the number of conspirators rapidly increased, but, it appears, never exceeded sixty. Pahlen took care to secure the Guard, that traditional instrument of a Palace Revolution. The recent infusion of the Gatchina element into this corps made this a difficult and perilous undertaking. The commanders of the Hussar regiments and of the Ismailovski* regiment were content with things as they were. Dépréradovitch, who commanded the Siémionovski, was

* In the Guard the heads of regiments had the rank of general and the squadrons were commanded by colonels.

regarded as untrustworthy, but he joined, and along with him Talysine, in command of the Préobrajenski, and many others, among whom were Prince Iachvill of the Horse Guards, whom Paul is said to have struck with his cane and who was therefore nothing loth.

The civil element was very poorly represented on the list, which contained only one administrator of note, Trochtchinski, formerly secretary to Catherine. Few of the names belonged to the old aristocracy. Kotzebue is alone in citing a Dolgoroukof, who was probably Prince Peter Petrovitch, then a very young aide-de-camp, and afterwards destined to have the celebrated interview with Napoleon on the eve of Austerlitz. Sabloukof mentions an Alexis Zakharovitch Khitrovo, a colonel on half pay, at whose house, quite near the Michael Palace, the conspirators are said to have often met.

Talysine was a very valuable recruit. He had been brought up at Stuttgart, where he had attended the school founded by Duke Charles. His education was brilliant according to the standard of the time, and he was a mystic and a freemason. He owed the command of the Préobrajenski to Panine, who had no doubt his own views in securing this favour for him. Young, rich, and unmarried, he gave supper parties which lasted far into the night; he was extremely popular in his regiment, and his house was a valuable centre for the party.

The same was true of the Servian Dépréradovitch, who lived very generously and arranged frequent councils under cover of dinners and suppers. He was married to a Gortchakof, the sister of the grandmother of Leo Tolstoy, the illustrious author, and controlled a very important connection. He had always conducted himself with gallantry in the Polish and Turkish campaigns, and he enjoyed Paul's particular confidence. His adherence to the plot was attributed to a feminine influence of the same character as that which, in later days, was to ruin his fine military career.

The feminine element in various ways exercised a determining influence on the conspiracy. Colonel Nicolas Borozdine joined because of six weeks' detention in a fortress to which he was sentenced because he had been so unlucky as to attract the attention of Princess Gagarine, and he was about to marry one of the daughters of Mme. Jerebtsof, whose daughter-in-law, the favourite's sister, kept the plotters informed of Paul's slightest doings.

In defiance of the Czar's decrees against luxury, the fair Olga Jerebtsof dispensed a sumptuous hospitality. She attracted all the gourmets of St. Petersburg to her elegant suppers, after which she went to Pahlen disguised as a beggar. Her liaisons and her manœuvres did not escape the notice of the police, but the police again were under Pahlen's control, and Koutaïssof and Mme. Chevalier, who had been bought or won over, did their best on their part to disarm the vigilance of the authorities.

But in this dark intrigue all was not corruption. Panine was not the only one who was inspired by more generous sentiments. Valerian Zoubof maintained that he was carrying out Catherine's orders, she having enjoined him and his brother Plato to regard Alexander after herself as their sole legitimate Sovereign. Other ambitions also manifested themselves in the revolutionary movement and gained the sympathy if not the co-operation of some who were actually in the inner circle surrounding Marie Féodorovna. The Kourakines were inclined to think that in the end Paul would not be able to retain the supreme power, in which case his wife would be designated as his successor in view of Alexander's youth and timidity. The Empress herself certainly never thought of dispossessing her husband, but she was always much preoccupied about her personal popularity and had been particularly so since her relations with her husband had entered on so unpleasant a phase. She never went out without trying to provoke some incident or to furnish material for an anecdote bringing out her merits, which were real enough. Bernhardi goes so far as to think that she knew of the plot, and it is not impossible that, between the insults to her dignity and her affection, and the threats of which she and those nearest and dearest to her were becoming the objects, she had resigned herself to choosing the lesser of two evils, believing more sincerely than her son that the affair would be carried out peacefully.

The plotters, however, had their own troubles and were far from having won over all the Guard. Apart from the soldiers, whom they did not even try to approach, a large number of officers remained refractory. There was General Kologrivof, the representative of an old family, a good rider, but a stupid man whose insignificance had saved him from the disgrace which overtook his more gifted comrades. He had been rapidly promoted and had just been granted 15,000 diéssiatines of land in the Government of Tambof, and was quite satisfied with the government to whom he owed these advantages.

The Commandant of the Michael Palace, Nicolas Kotloubitski, or *Nikolka* as Paul familiarly called him when, as often happened, he gave him some confidential mission, had also the best of reasons for not desiring a change. The son of a humble Government clerk, he owed to his service at Gatchina his promotion at the age of twenty-two to be aide-de-camp general of the Emperor. He was even more stupid than Kologrivof and equally faithful.

Another recalcitrant was Nicolas Sabloukof, the author of the memoirs so often quoted in this book, who was then in command of a squadron of the Horse Guards. He was no courtier, and had not come from Gatchina,

429

but he was one of the few privileged persons who were spared by Paul's caprice and anger. He was impeccable as a soldier and a man of unblemished honour. The Czar liked him and respected him for the deferential frankness of his address.

The strange thing is that none of these men informed their master of the danger which they knew to be threatening him.

V

The fact was that, though the plot itself was hatched in a comparatively narrow circle, it was associated with a conspiracy of silence which had a very much wider range. A fortnight before the event happened it was being talked about in the streets where Paul vainly flattered himself that he had ears. Several people who knew all about the proposed attempt and rejected with horror all idea of taking part in it, found good reasons for not divulging what they had heard. Count, afterwards Prince, Christopher de Lieven, Minister of War, was initiated at the last moment and congratulated himself that he was ill, which prevented Pahlen from asking his assistance. Had he done so, said Lieven after the event, his only course would have been to blow out his brains. He could not denounce the conspiracy, for " that would have meant the ruin of all that was best in Russia." The more scrupulous deliberated what they would do if they were asked to join. Sabloukof consulted Salvator Tonci, Secretary to the ex-King of Poland, a painter of historical subjects and portraits, and author of a system of philosophy the object of which was " to bring men face to face with God." By his advice Sabloukof decided, after careful consideration, simply to observe so strict a reserve that no one would think of coming to him.

On the night of March 11/23 Sanglène, an official of the Department of Police, was coming home in a cab and was asked by the driver : " Is it true that they are going to kill the Czar ? What a crime ! " " What is the matter with you ? You are losing your head ! For heaven's sake don't say such things ! " " But, sir, we are talking of nothing else among ourselves ; every one keeps saying, ' This is the end ! ' " Some hours later, about midnight, at the moment when the tragedy was being consummated, the guests at supper in several houses were consulting their watches and demanding champagne " to drink the new Emperor's health."

Thus the precise instant of the execution of the conspiracy was known even by those who took no part in it, and Paul knew nothing—nothing, that is, which enabled him to take effective precautions. No doubt he had suspicions and apprehensions, but these had been his daily bread for many years, and this was in itself enough to blind him. He had passed through so many unreal dangers and had lived so long amid nightmares produced by his own imagination which had always passed off without his coming to any harm that he had ended by becoming comparatively confident of safety. This was based on the belief, carefully encouraged by Pahlen, that by striking out at hazard as he had always done he would always triumph over his enemies, as, in his own opinion, he had always hitherto succeeded in doing. Alas ! Hitherto he had never fought with anything but phantoms.

According to Pahlen's account, which is no doubt much distorted and possibly entirely invented, he, the chief contriver of the plot, a few days before its execution revealed its existence to the victim in highly disconcerting circumstances, without however in any way compromising its success. Paul's character was such, however, that there may well be some truth in it. On March 9 he went to the Emperor at seven o'clock in the morning and, to his alarm, found him grave and preoccupied.

Paul shut the door of his cabinet as soon as Pahlen entered, stared at him silently for two long minutes, and then said:

" You were here in 1762 ? "

" Yes, sir, but what does your Majesty mean ? "

" You had a share in the conspiracy which deprived my father of the throne ? "

" Sir, I was a witness, but not an actor in the *coup d'état*. I was too young, a mere subaltern in a cavalry regiment. But, sir, why do you ask me this question ? "

" Because . . . because they want to do again what was done then ! " *

Pahlen was for a moment overwhelmed, but soon recovered his coolness and said, with complete calm :

" Yes, sir, I know that. I know the conspirators — and I am one of them."

" What ! "

" It is quite true."

And the cunning Courlander explained that he was pretending to participate in the plot in order to be in a better position to watch its progress and to hold all the threads in his own hand. He then tried to reassure the Czar.

" Do not seek to compare your position with that of your unfortunate father. He was a foreigner and you are a Russian. He hated, despised, and alienated from him the natives of this country; you love them and are loved by them. He irritated and exasperated the Guard which is devoted to you. He persecuted the clergy; you honour them. There was then no police in St. Petersburg; now it is so perfect that no one can say a word or stir a step without my knowing it. . . ."

" All this is quite true, but we must not go to sleep."

" Doubtless, sir, but in order to avert all risk I should

* Heyking and Locatelli assert that Paul had been warned by the Procurator-General Obolianinof.

require powers so wide that I fear to ask you for them. Here is a list of the conspirators——"

" Arrest them, clap them in irons, and put them in a fortress, or send them to hard labour in Siberia ! "

" It would have been done already, sir, but . . . I fear to wound you as a husband and a father. . . . Read the names, those of the Empress and two of your sons are the first ! "

This conversation is said to have ended, after some demonstrations of emotion, in Paul's signing orders for the arrest of Marie Féodorovna and the two elder Grand Dukes. Pahlen was authorised to use them when he thought the time fitting, but he took care not to execute any of them, using them only to conquer the final scruples of Alexander while the alarm caused by the incident made him hasten to precipitate the dénouement of the tragedy.

Pahlen in this account probably yielded to the temptation to colour somewhat highly the skill and coolness with which he handled the situation. On another day he states that Paul in a playful mood took a fancy to search his Minister's pockets. " I want to see what you are hiding there—love letters, is it ? " It happened that in one pocket was a message from the Grand Duke Alexander which Panine had just sent to his accomplice and which he had not had time to destroy. Without flinching, Pahlen held the Sovereign's hand. " What are you doing, sir ! Leave me alone. You cannot endure snuff and I am constantly taking it. My handkerchief is impregnated with the smell of it and you will be poisoned ! " Paul started back with the exclamation, " Disgusting ! "

Bennigsen and Plato Zoubof both describe the scene of March 9 and both aver that there was no question whatever of a plot. Pahlen was presenting to the Emperor a police report as he did every morning, which he crammed with anecdotes, mostly invented, for his Majesty's amusement. Very foolishly he had placed with this document a list of the conspirators, and Paul, who playfully put his hand in the pocket containing the two papers, very nearly became possessed of the compromising one. Pahlen, however, had enough presence of mind to retain it, knowing it by the fact that it was thicker than the other. The Czar pulled out only the report, which he read with much amusement, not observing Pahlen's agitation.

Be this as it may, Paul appears to have suspected something in the first days of March. His apprehensions must have been very vague, for he would not have hesitated to strike down the guilty ones whoever they were, and Pahlen was not indispensable. In his eyes one man was as good as another. " Here every man is a Bezborodko ! "

Nevertheless he began to distrust the Courlander, for without his knowledge he decided to recall to St. Petersburg Araktchéief and Lindener, whom he had so foolishly sent away. One was on his estate of Grouzino and the other at Kalouga. It was folly to imagine that the messages which he sent would escape the notice of the Military Governor of St. Petersburg. Pahlen intercepted them and pretended to think they were forged, as the Emperor did not know of their despatch. Not without some confusion, Paul was forced to avow what he had sought to conceal. The messages were sent off again, but this time Pahlen gave orders that the recipients should be detained at the gates of the city.

Paul had mismanaged things, and now had no one about him but traitors or fools. " If we had had the least suspicion," said Koutaïssof to Kotzebue at a later date, " a breath would have destroyed all these plans." With all the means of being well informed the ex-barber knew nothing. According to a well-known story he received a letter on the eve of the crime which gave full details of the plot, but neglected to read it in time or was prevented from making use of it because Prince Zoubof, whom he hoped to have for a son-in-law, was indicated as one of the chief conspirators. Kotzebue thinks the story is founded on a letter which was found in his apartments when he was arrested after Paul's death, and which he had not opened because Mme. de Lieven's servant, who brought it, had told him the contents, which were of no importance. Readers of Montaigne will be tempted to seek the origin of the story in Chapter IV (Book II) of the Essays, where numerous cases of similar negligence leading to fatal consequences are recorded.

Others, notably Andrew Razoumovski, who returned in February from a fourteen months' exile in Siberia, Count Golovine, and even Princess Gagarine herself, are said, more or less probably, to have had warnings. But, however widely the knowledge was spread, there were some at the Michael Palace and its neighbourhood to whom it was unknown. Paul's own doings during the last days of his life, which can be followed almost hour by hour, also prove to demonstration that though his suspicions were awakened they had not up to the last taken any precise form. His humour showed no trace of any keener anxiety than usual. On the contrary, on the eve of his death he was unusually affable. On the morning of the fatal day he visited his wife before she rose, addressed her affectionately, and brought her a present which he knew would please her more than the most costly jewel—a pair of stockings worked by the young ladies of the Smolnyï. After this he played with the younger children in her presence. In his palace fortress surrounded by people who trembled if he looked at them Paul thought he could defy all his enemies. His mother had said : " You are a stupid savage if you do not know that you cannot fight ideas with cannon." He had tried and, after reigning four years, he liked to recall this remark, adding : " I wonder which of us now is, I won't say savage, but stupid ! " His attitude, his words and, above all, his decision to recall Araktchéief and Lindener no doubt made Pahlen hasten the moment of execution.

The attempt had at first been postponed until after Easter, which in this year fell on March 24. It was afterwards fixed for March 15, either because the conspirators had more faith in the regiment which was to be on duty at the Michael Palace on that day or because they wished their attempt to coincide with the Ides of March and the anniversary of the death of Cæsar. Finally they decided to gain another four days. Pahlen affirmed afterwards that this was done on the advice of Alexander, who pointed out that the third battalion of the Siémio- novski, which would form the principal part of the Guard on March 11, was more manageable than any other. It seems that a note from him in this sense, which conclusively proved the Grand Duke's complicity, has actually been preserved.* But there were already abundant proofs that he was with the conspirators, and it was probably the arrival of Araktchéief, who was expected on the night of the 11th, which determined the choice of the conspirators. It was arranged that they should go to the Michael Palace about midnight. The officers of the Guard who had joined them would at the same time march several battalions there. Paul was to be surprised in his sleep and hear sentence of deposition. After that they would see.

* The author cannot indicate the source of this piece of information, but it is absolutely trustworthy.

CHAPTER XVI

THE NIGHT OF MARCH 11/23

I

MARCH 10/22, 1801, was a Sunday, and there was a concert and a supper at the Castle. Mme. Chevalier sang but Paul did not appear to enjoy her *roulades*. That evening he wore the expression of his worst days. The Empress seemed anxious, and the Grand Duke Alexander and his wife visibly shared her disquiet. Between the concert and supper the Emperor went away as usual, but it was observed that his absence was longer than usual. When he returned he stopped before the Empress, crossed his arms, and stared at her with a sinister smile, drawing in his breath noisily, as he always did when angry, and repeating the whole performance in front of his two elder sons. Immediately afterwards he accosted Pahlen, said some words in his ear and passed into the dining-room. Prince Eugene of Würtemberg was alarmed, and asked Mme. de Lieven: "What does this mean." "It concerns neither you nor me," she replied drily. At table there was a deathlike silence. After the meal was over the Empress and the Grand Dukes went to thank the Czar in the Russian manner. He repulsed them and hurried back to his own apartments. The Empress wept, and the party broke up in great agitation.

Early next day Father Gruber was in attendance at the door of the Emperor's cabinet awaiting his turn for an audience. He had been coming every morning for some time, but not, as has been supposed, in order to discuss a plan for the reunion of the Catholic and Orthodox Churches. More probably the subject of the conversation was the First Consul, and the preparation for common action with France. Pahlen, however, had reached his Majesty's presence before the Jesuit, and he was not desirous that Paul should receive Gruber that day : the reverend Father was too much interested in the continuance of a régime under which he enjoyed such high favour. The Minister's audience, therefore, was unusually prolonged. Pahlen had brought a bulky portfolio from which he drew report after report. The hour of parade approached before he was finished, and Paul impatiently asked : " Is that all ? " " Yes, but Father Gruber is here again." " I have not time to see him." And the Jesuit was sent away.

At parade it was noticed that the Grand Dukes Alexander and Constantine were absent. The Emperor was still gloomy, but he did not punish any one, though all the officers of the Guard were ordered to meet Pahlen after parade, and he told them that Paul was much dissatisfied with the manner in which they performed their duties. " I am commanded to tell you," he concluded, " that if you do not entirely alter your conduct the Emperor will send you all to a place where it will be impossible to find your bones. . . ."

The last phrase is quite in Paul's manner, but it is probable that in order to create in his hearers a state of mind favourable to the execution of the design which he had in view, Pahlen was putting words in his master's mouth without having received any special mandate. Paul did not as a rule depute to others the task of scolding and frightening his subordinates, which was so much to his own taste, and there is nothing to show that at this moment he had the intention ascribed to him. The parade had passed off without his showing the slightest sign of annoyance, and while his minister was storming in his name the Sovereign was very peaceably taking his usual ride with Koutaïssof. When he came back to dinner it even seemed as if the fury of the previous day had altogether subsided; he was quite calm again, and in every way well disposed. Meeting Kotzebue in the vestibule of the palace, he asked him to draw up a description of his new abode, and spoke of a statue of Cleopatra, a copy of the original in the Vatican, which he had ordered for the grand staircase. The author was agreeably surprised by his kindliness and good spirits.

Dinner passed also without any renewal of the outbreaks of the night before, and there was no trace of them for the rest of the day. The Empress went to pay a visit to the Smolnyï and the Emperor went to see his son Nicolas, with whom he showed himself in a very playful humour. "Why do they call you Paul I?" asked the child. "Because before me there was no other Emperor of that name." "Then shall I be Nicolas I?" "Yes, if you come to the throne." On this the father looked long and thoughtfully at his son, pressed him to his bosom, and left the room without a word.

There was obviously, as always with him, some *arrière pensée* which disturbed him, but equally obviously he was not troubled by any thought or apprehension of immediate danger. A few minutes later he was with his architects discussing a plan he had formed for the embellishment of the summer garden. Next he busied himself with the despatch of two couriers. One of these was to carry to Baron Krudener at Berlin an autograph letter in French to the following effect: "You are to inform the King that if he will not make up his mind to occupy Hanover you will be obliged to leave his Court within twenty-four hours." The second message was for Kalytchof, and instructed him to urge the First Consul to substitute

439

himself at once for Prussia in case the latter refused to do what was asked.

These letters were not reasonable either in form or substance, but they were quite in Paul's usual vein at this point in his history. By some historians, even in France, it is believed that Pahlen wrote the following warning at the bottom of the first letter: " The Emperor is not well to-day; his illness may become serious." The original has been found among the archives of the Russian Embassy at Berlin and shows no trace of this, but perhaps the note was sent separately in a private and confidential letter.

II

The absence of the two Grand Dukes is said to have been due to some measure of severity which Paul had taken against them, the precise nature of which is now hard to ascertain, so confused and contradictory is the evidence. By the express orders of the Grand Duke Constantine Sabloukof was on this day designated out of his turn as colonel on duty. This was contrary to the regulations, as it was his squadron which was on guard at the Michael Palace. This is the first enigma, but it seems that the Grand Duke had reasons for wishing the whole regiment on that day to be in the hands of this particular officer.

Sabloukof's duty was to present himself at the Palace at eight o'clock in the evening to present the usual report. A lackey barred his progress at the entrance with the question: " Where are you going ? " " To the Grand Duke Constantine." " Do not do so, for I have orders to inform the Emperor at once." " You do your duty and I will do mine." In the antechamber the Grand Duke's servant Roudkovski again stopped the colonel. " What is your business here ? " he asked. " I think

you are all mad to-day ; I have come with the report."
" Enter ! "

The Grand Duke seemed much agitated. While
Sabloukof was reading the report, Alexander entered
in a furtive manner, " like a startled hare," says the
colonel in his memoirs. At the same moment Paul
himself, booted and spurred, entered by the opposite
door with his hat in one hand and his cane in the other,
and advanced with measured steps as if he were on
parade. The elder of the two Grand Dukes at once
hurried back to his apartments ; Constantine remained
transfixed with terror, " like an unarmed man meeting
a bear," as Sabloukof says a little further on. Turning
lightly on his heels the colonel presented his report to
the Emperor, who merely remarked, " Ah, you are on
duty," and with a gracious wave of his hand to the officer
he left as he had come.

At this moment Alexander peered through the door-
way by which he had just fled, waited till the sound of
another door closing behind the Czar showed that the
coast was clear, and then entered on tiptoe. Constantine
turned to him, gaily : " Well, brother, what do you think
of my idea ? I told you that he (pointing to Sabloukof)
would not be afraid." Alexander looked at the colonel
with admiration : " What ? You are not afraid of the
Emperor ? " " Afraid ? Why should I be afraid ? " I
am on duty ; out of turn it is true, but still I am on duty."
" Then you don't know that we are both under arrest ? "
Sabloukof burst out laughing. " Why do you laugh ? "
" Because you have long desired this honour." " Yes,
but not on the present conditions. Obolianinof has just
taken us to church to take the oath." " I have no need
to be made to take the oath. I am loyal. . . ." Constantine cut him short : " Very good. Go back, be on
your guard and keep a good look-out ! "

While Roudkovski was helping Sabloukof to resume

his pelisse in the antechamber, Constantine called his valet and asked him for a glass of water. As he was filling the glass Roudkovski noticed a fragment of a feather in it. He removed it with his fingers, observing : " It floats to-day, to-morrow it will sink."

This account by Sabloukof of what passed has all the appearance of sincerity, but there are serious objections. The fact that the Grand Duke Constantine was then under arrest is confirmed by other witnesses. This, however, is attributed to some trifling negligence on duty and cannot have any connection with suspicions which led Paul to require his two elder sons to renew their oath of allegiance. The Czar would not have contented himself with so mild a measure, and above all he would not have left one suspected of treachery in the exercise of an important command and in a position to communicate with officers under his orders. The two Grand Dukes were not even confined to their apartments, for their presence at his Majesty's table on this very day is chronicled by the *Court Journal.* Sabloukof's veracity is above suspicion, but we have only an English version of his memoirs, the Russian original of which remains unknown to us. Moreover, the memoirs as published in *Fraser's Magazine* are presented merely as an extract " from the papers of a deceased Russian general officer."

At supper the table was laid for nineteen, and the two Grand Dukes were present. The Emperor was quite different from what he had been on the previous day. He was extremely gay and exceptionally talkative, though he was preoccupied with a bad dream which he had had on the previous night, when it had seemed to him that he was being forced into a garment which was too tight for him, and that he was being suffocated. This detail may very well have been invented afterwards. Alexander remained so silent and sullen in spite of the numerous remarks addressed to him by his father that Paul

at last said : " What is the matter with you to-day ? "
Alexander said he was indisposed, and Paul urged him
to consult his doctor and to take care of himself. " You
should always deal with indispositions at once, in order
to prevent them from becoming serious illnesses."

Many have seen a double meaning in this remark,
but it is not unusual to find that under the influence
of preconceived ideas people will give very far-fetched
interpretations to the most ordinary facts and phrases.
It is also said that the Grand Duke having sneezed, Paul
said ironically : " To the accomplishment of all your
wishes, Monseigneur ! " But according to another
witness the Emperor merely used the customary formula :
" God bless you ! " which is much more probable, for
Paul was not by any means in a tragic humour. On
the contrary, he was radiant with childish pleasure in
a new service of porcelain which was used for the first
time that evening and was decorated with views of the
Michael Palace ; he chaffed Prince Youssoupof, the
President of the College of Manufactures, about the bad
quality of the mirrors in one of the saloons which distorted the reflection of his face. But he showed no
displeasure, though when he retired about ten he is said
to have again become thoughtful and to have said :
" What must come will come ! " Prophecies however, as
is well known, are usually posterior to the events which
they are reputed to predict.

III

Paul went to bed later than usual that night. Gay
as he was he was full of cares. As he rose from
table he sent order to Sabloukof to come to him at
once to the Palace. Cornet Andréievski, who brought
the order, reassured the colonel, who was alarmed by
such an unusual summons. All was well, and as he

passed the post held by the Horse Guards, which he had done three times, the Emperor had saluted them in the most affable manner. Sabloukof knew the caprices of his Sovereign and troubled no more about it.

His men were posted in the room adjoining the Emperor's cabinet. At a quarter-past ten the soldier on guard called the post to attention. Paul came out of his cabinet, preceded by his favourite dog Spitz and followed by General Ouvarof, the aide-de-camp on duty. Ouvarof's name appears in the list of conspirators, but why Princess Lapoukhine's lover should have been among them it is difficult to conjecture, for he was loaded with favours. Spitz ran straight to Sabloukof, whom he had never seen before and fawned on him till the Czar struck him with his hat. The dog then drew back a few steps, sat down, and stared obstinately at the officer, while Paul said to him brusquely in French : " You are jacobins ! " Sabloukof was so disconcerted by a remark so unexpected that he mechanically replied : " Yes, sir." Paul smiled. " Not you, but the regiment." The colonel at once recovered his presence of mind. " I may be a jacobin, sir, but you are mistaken about the regiment ! " Paul shook his head : " I know better ; send away the post." Cornet Andréievski took the men back to their quarters. Spitz did not move, and still continued to stare at Sabloukof, while behind the Emperor's back Ouvarof smiled. The colonel, who understood nothing of all this, remained at attention awaiting an explanation, which was soon given. The Czar was displeased with the regiment and had decided to send it to the provinces. He added graciously that, as a favour, Sabloukof's squadron would be in garrison at Tsarskoïé-Sélo, but he desired that all the squadrons should be ready with arms and baggage to set out at four in the morning. Having given this order he signed to two footmen who were standing near and, pointing to the place which the

post had just quitted, he said : " You will stay there."
He then went back to his room and thence he passed into
the apartments of Princess Gagarine.

Sabloukof's regiment, with very few exceptions, was
as free from jacobinism as he was himself. It may
therefore be supposed that Pahlen had taken care to
awaken distrust of them in the Czar's mind. Hence the
arrest of the Grand Duke Constantine and the disgrace inflicted on the whole corps. Sabloukof's imagination or that
of his English interpreter may have embroidered on this
theme, but it is certain that at this moment Paul had no
suspicion that any danger was imminent or he would
not have dreamed of replacing a post of thirty well-
armed men by two footmen who, though they were
called " *hussars*," owing to the pattern of their livery,
had no arms of any kind.

While with Princess Gagarine Paul continued his
correspondence. He was writing to Prince Plato Zoubof,
but on subjects which had no connection with his personal
safety, about which for the moment he felt no anxiety.
He asked for some young pupils of the Cadet Corps to
act as his pages, and inquired after Baron Diebitsch,
the Governor of the Prince of Würtemberg, who had
just been appointed Commandant of the First Division
of that corps. Catherine's ex-favourite was spending the
evening with General Klinger, a poet of reputation and
a native of Frankfort. Plato, more indolent than
cowardly, was enjoying himself, engaged in general
conversation, and allowed no one to divine anything of
the terrible drama in which he was so soon to be taking
part. Perhaps he, too, imagined that the affair would
pass off quietly. He sent the pages required, and as to
Diebitsch replied : " The general does neither well nor
ill, he lacks the knowledge to do well and the power to
do ill."

At eleven o'clock, still with Princess Gagarine, Paul

wrote yet another letter to Lieven. It was the last he
ever wrote, and it gives the measure of his intelligence
and good feeling. The War Minister had been ill for
some time, and the Czar had determined to replace him
by the husband of his mistress, a young man without
the slightest military education or experience, and apart
from his poetical talent a complete nonentity. Paul
announced his decision in the following terms :

" Your indisposition lasts too long, and as public
affairs cannot be regulated by the state of your inside
you will have to surrender the portfolio of war to Prince
Gagarine."

The apologists of Paul and his reign will do well to
meditate on this document, which may be regarded as
the moral and political testament of the son of Catherine.

IV

While Paul was writing it the final preparations were
being made for the attempt which it was decided to make
that night. During the day Dépréradovitch, the Commander of the Siémionovski, had sent for an ensign in
his regiment, a youth of sixteen or seventeen, on whose
docility and discretion he apparently thought he could
rely.

" Have you a carriage ? "

" Yes, Excellency."

" Are you going to send it away in the course of the
day ? "

" I shall do as you tell me."

" Very good ; go to the treasurer of the regiment
and get a box of cartridges. You can put it under the
seat of your carriage. Leave it there till nine o'clock
in the evening, keeping the carriage within call, and
then bring it to me."

" At your orders, Excellency."

" Go. I have no more to say. Be careful. We shall have a new Emperor to-night."

The young man was punctual at the rendezvous, and when he arrived received these further orders :

" Go to headquarters, where you will find a battalion under arms. Go along the ranks yourself and hand each man a packet of cartridges just as you find them in the box."

An hour later the general followed the ensign. He inspected the battalion minutely, man by man, examining both arms and faces. Then placing himself in the midst he gave the order in a very low voice : " Fix bayonets ! The battalion will attack ! Charge ! " During the manœuvre he constantly repeated, " Softly, as softly as possible." Finally, with infinite precautions, he gave the order : " Battalion ! March," and they set out with stealthy tread without a word or the clatter of arms towards the Michael Palace. The officers kept silence themselves and imposed it on the men.

The same thing happened with the Préobrajenski, with perhaps fewer precautions. Few officers—not more than six or seven per battalion—accompanied either regiment. They had been recruited to the conspiracy at the last moment and in some cases had not been initiated at all. The men were all ignorant of the reason for this nocturnal expedition. Some, who showed anxiety, were told that they were going to defend the Emperor, and they were satisfied with that explanation. Dépréradovitch marched so softly that he did not arrive till all was over. He was always late, but perhaps this time his lateness was intentional. As a matter of fact, at the moment when they were about to enter the Michael Palace, the conspirators had at their disposal only one battalion of the Préobrajenski.

In order not to attract attention they supped at different houses, where they drank to excess in order to give themselves courage. It was not till nearly eleven

447

that they assembled at General Talysine's in an annexe of the Winter Palace, where the first battalion of the Préobrajenski was always quartered. They were about sixty in number, and most of them were drunk. Pahlen did not come till half-past eleven, and while they waited for him his accomplices emptied many more bottles of champagne. At this moment a discussion seems to have arisen on the subject of the end to be pursued in the projected enterprise as well as of the best methods to employ. It is easy to imagine what this debate was like, conducted as it was in the excitement of such a moment amid the fumes of wine by men who were for the most unintelligent and less capable than usual of coherent thought. A plan for a constitution was ventilated. Plato Zoubof had several in his pocket. Some pronounced audaciously for the deposition of the whole Imperial family. But failing the Romanofs where would they find a Sovereign? In that aristocratic group there were no republicans. The meeting proceeded amid vociferations and hiccups. It was degenerating into an orgie and no conclusion had been reached. All that was clear was that they were not agreed about anything, and that they knew neither what they wanted to do nor what they would do.

The gathering became very noisy, and there were witnesses. The conspirators were still drinking and servants came and went with fresh supplies of liquor. One of these could easily have given the alarm at the Palace. Nobody thought of such a thing—no doubt because Paul's fortress was reputed unapproachable. Behind its ditches, its drawbridges, and its guards Paul had become inaccessible to any one who might have been tempted to save him by opening his eyes to the danger.

Trochtchinski, the only penman at the gathering at the Winter Palace, finally secured the adoption of a draft manifesto announcing that the Czar being attacked by a serious illness appointed the Grand Duke Alexander as his co-regent. Panine's programme had carried the day with the tacit corollary not foreseen by the ex-Vice-Chancellor that the patient should be interned at Schlüsselburg. But what if Paul resisted ? That was the crucial point. Panine had said nothing of that, but the question had now to be faced ! Even if the Czar allowed himself to be carried to his destined prison they were not done with him. He would still have his partisans, who would no doubt try to rescue him, as had been done in the case of the unfortunate Ivan VI, who had been imprisoned in the same place. And it was not quite certain that such an enterprise would be equally unsuccessful. The terrible spectre of a victorious counter-revolution followed by inevitable reprisals rose before the eyes of the men whose lives were at stake. Was it not better to anticipate such a risk ? They were inflamed by these reflections and cries of death were heard.

But Pahlen arrived. He at least had not drunk anything, and he had made Bennigsen observe a like sobriety. The others were all the better for their potations, for without a stimulant some of them were capable of drawing back at the last moment. Already, in the course of the discussion, Prince Zoubof had shown that he was hesitating. Pahlen, however, would allow no more discussion. The hour of action had come. They would see what they would do if Paul resisted. It was at this moment that the head of the conspiracy is said to have used the famous phrase : " You cannot make an omelette without breaking eggs." Thereafter he called for a glass and invited the company to drink "the health of the new Emperor." This being done he cut short indiscreet questions by giving the signal for departure.

They were to separate into two groups, one of which

was to be led by Pahlen himself, the other by Zoubof and Bennigsen. Catherine's ex-favourite could not be passed over as a leader because of his title and the high position he had occupied and still kept, and because his uniform glittering with decorations ensured respect from every one. He was accompanied by his brother Nicolas, whose vast height dominated the other conspirators and gave them confidence, Bennigsen would do the rest. Valerian Zoubof had lost a leg in the Polish wars, and so was not of much use, but being the most respectable of the three brothers he served as a hostage for the others, and Pahlen took him with him. The night was dark and cold, and it was raining.

V

The chief post at the entrance to the Michael Palace was furnished in turn by all the regiments of the Guard. That evening it was composed of a company of the Siémionovski, under the command of Captain Paiker, one of the Gatchina officers whose stupidity was legendary. The men occupied a vast guardroom on the ground floor in front of the grand staircase. Paiker was incapable of betraying Paul, but the conspirators relied on his two lieutenants, whom they had won over, and who, they thought, would easily circumvent their chief.

In the interior of the Palace a little further on, in another great room on the ground-floor, there was always another and lesser post, consisting of but thirty men, who were always furnished by a privileged battalion of the Préobrajenski, whom Paul had constituted a separate corps under the name of the Body Guard (*Leibkompania*). This second post was commanded by Lieutenant Marine, who had purposely filled it, as to one-third with old grenadiers attached to Catherine's memory, and as to the rest with members of the Guard who had been disbanded and absorbed into the Préobrajenski, and no doubt regretted their old regiment.

Paul's apartments were on the first floor, and were reached by the Gallery of Apollo, so called because of the copies of Raphael's cartoons with which the walls were covered. A vestibule adorned with six pictures of the legend of St. Gregory by Van Loo led to a white saloon with a fine ceiling by Tiepolo representing the history of Antony and Cleopatra. The third room contained the Czar's private library, and immediately preceded the Imperial bed-chamber which he used also as a study in accordance with a tradition in the family of Catherine which was followed until recently.

Once there the conspirators, in the absence of the guard whom Paul had dismissed, had no further serious resistance to fear. They were spared the trouble of overcoming even the intermediate obstacles. Pahlen had undertaken to make a frontal attack on the Palace with the small company under his orders, forcing the main entrance if necessary. But, like Dépréradovitch, he loitered on the way. He even seems to have manœuvred in such a way as not to arrive until after the issue of the attempt, whatever it might be, leaving the honour and the danger to the detachment led by Plato Zoubof and Bennigsen. It has been thought probable by many that he was seeking to reserve to himself the means of pretending to have helped to avert the blow if the plot failed.

Zoubof and his companions, on the other hand, presented themselves at a small door which still exists on the side towards Sadovaïa Street. This door gave on a back staircase, which led more directly to the Emperor's apartments. There, too, there was a moat to cross and a drawbridge to pass, but the difficulties of the assailants was solved by the presence among them of Peter Vassilié-vitch Argamakof, who was equerry-in-waiting at the

Palace, and whose duty it was to inform the Sovereign
forthwith of any unusual event, such as a fire or a riot
in the capital. The drawbridge was, therefore, lowered,

PLAN OF THE EMPEROR'S APARTMENTS

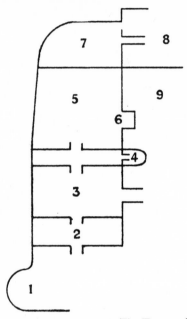

1. Back Stairs
2. White Saloon
3. Library
4. Staircase to Princess Gagarine's
   apartments
5. The Emperor's Bedroom
6. Cabinet (no exit)
7. Room separating the apartments
   of the Emperor and Empress
8, 9. The Empress's Apartments

and at the same time Talysine surrounded the Palace
with the Préobrajenski battalion, who came in through
the upper garden. Every night in this garden there
was a great gathering of crows and rooks, which screamed
at the disturbance. This alone should have given the
alarm, but it seems to have startled no one but Talysine's
soldiers, who crossed themselves and spoke in low tones
of the evil omen.

There were two doors leading from the library to the
bed-chamber. Between them there was a sort of ante-

chamber contrived in the thickness of the wall, which was great at this point. This contained on one side a recess in which one of the Emperor's body-servants slept, and

PLAN OF THE EMPEROR'S BEDROOM

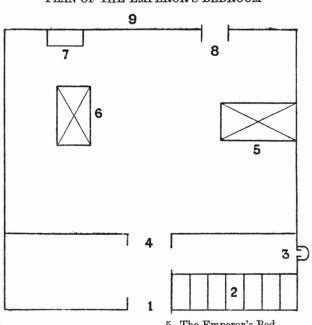

1. Door
2. Cabinet
3. Access to the Staircase leading to the Apartments of Princess Gagarine and Koutaïssof
4. Door

5. The Emperor's Bed
6. Table
7. Fireplace
8. Door
9. Room giving access to the apartments of the Empress

on the other the staircase leading to the apartments of Princess Gagarine and Koutaïssof.

The Czar's bedroom was very large and lofty. The walls were panelled in white wood and adorned with landscapes by Vernet, Wouverman, and Van der Meer. On the right was a small camp bed, above which was the portrait of a knight of St. John of Jerusalem which was very highly valued by Paul. A poor portrait of Frederick II and a bad statuette representing the Prussian

453

monarch on horseback completed the decoration of the room. On the left was a piece of furniture made of mahogany, supported by ivory columns with brass bases and capitals, which the Czar used as a desk.

In the library the two servants whom Paul had substituted for the dismissed guard were sleeping heavily. Argamakof woke them and ordered them to open the door numbered 1 on the plan. According to some accounts he told them that he had come to announce a fire; others say that he pretended that it was five o'clock in the morning and that he had come to report as usual. One of the men, however, guessed that they were being deceived and called for help. He was cut down with the stroke of a sabre. His name was Komilof, and in after years he was attached to the service of Marie Féodorovna and rceived a house and a pension as further compensation. The other footman obeyed, and introduced the conspirators into the antechamber actually adjoining the Czar's room. The valet who slept in the closet marked 2 disappeared, either abandoning his master to his fate or intending to rush to the nearest post to give the alarm. Paul was thus cut off from the staircase marked 3, by which he might have fled. There should have been another issue open to him by the door marked 8, which led to the room between his apartments and those of the Empress. There was here a post of thirty men of the Siémionovski, commanded by Lieutenant Alexander Volkof, a cousin of Sabloukof's. This officer was personally known to Maria Féodorovna, and a protégé of hers, and would probably have done his duty. But a few days previously, under the influence of suspicions which he had himself conceived or which had been suggested to him by Pahlen, Paul had had this door barricaded. Thus he was trapped hopelessly.

VI

In spite of, or perhaps because of, the abundance of witnesses the final scene of the drama cannot be reconstituted with certainty. The conspirators entered the bedroom in comparatively small numbers, having either forced the door marked 4 on the plan, or having succeeded in getting it opened to them on some pretence. More than half of them remained behind, either on purpose or because they had lost their way in Brenna's labyrinth of staircases and corridors. Awakened by the noise Paul tried instinctively to hide himself behind the screen which during the day concealed his bed, or according to other accounts in the fireplace, which was very deep and entirely concealed him from his assailants. For a moment they thought they had missed him and, struck with fright, they were already thinking of flight themselves. "The bird is flown!" exclaimed one of their number. But another at that very moment caught sight of the Czar's feet, and the refuge of the unfortunate man was discovered. Plato Zoubof and Bennigsen advanced upon him with drawn swords, and one or the other announced to him that he was under arrest.

Paul, as we know, was not courageous; and a braver man than he might perhaps have failed to conquer the paralysing sensation produced by so unforeseen an attack. He was in his night garments, unarmed and in the presence of these men who had all the appearance of bandits, and it appears that he was almost inarticulate. "Arrested!" he is said to have muttered. "What do you mean by arrested?" According to Bennigsen he added: "What have I done?" These were his last words.

This version is the same as that which Lord St. Helens heard on his arrival at St. Petersburg, but he does not mention the source of his information. He reports that

Paul immediately lost his presence of mind and merely stammered a few words of reproach. He was at once struck down and thrown on the ground by one of the meaner conspirators, who finished his work by strangling him in his sash.

Other accounts, however, have it that Plato Zoubof had a prolonged conversation with the Czar, and invited him to resign his power for the good of his country and to sign the manifesto which had been drawn up by Trochtchinski. The unhappy Emperor was surrounded by the conspirators, who hustled him towards his desk, on which one of them had placed the document. In spite of his terror Paul then made an attempt to intimidate his aggressors, and not succeeding, he called for help and attempted to push his way through them, when Bennigsen stopped him with the point of his sword. According to this account the dénouement was accidentally precipitated by a panic which at this moment seized those of Bennigsen's companions with whom the Czar was engaged. While he was struggling in their midst a noise of steps and voices was heard in the antechamber. It was the late comers who had arrived; but their accomplices thought that Paul's cries had been heard and that they were coming to the rescue. Already, indeed, the alarm had been given from one end of the palace to the other. Below Paiker called his men to arms. He was held back by his lieutenants, as had been foreseen by the conspirators, who persuaded him to write a report! An hour later he was still writing! At the other post on the ground-floor Marine had more difficulty with some of his soldiers. They had come from Gatchina, and they wished to fly to the rescue of their Sovereign, who had promised them fifteen diéssiatines of land in the Government of Saratof. It was in vain that their young lieutenant, pistol in hand, shouted: " This is none of your business ! " (*Nié vaché diélo.*) They paid no attention.

At last he called upon the old grenadiers who had served Catherine and ordered them to leave the ranks and bayonet the Gatchina dogs if they moved an inch.

The Gatchina men did not move, and Paul was left to his fate. But the murderers knew nothing of this, and all but four or five of them gave themselves up for lost and started to fly in good earnest by the way they had come, not thinking that this was the way by which the Czar's presumed defenders must be advancing. Charging Plato Zoubof or Prince Iachvil to look after the prisoner, Bennigsen rushed behind the fugitives to bring them back. This, at least, is his own account of what passed. When he came back Paul had ceased to breathe. He had at first been thrown down by Nicolas Zoubof, who is said to have felled him with a blow on the temple delivered with a heavy gold snuff-box. According to another account, he fell accidentally and wounded his head on a sharp corner of his desk. As he got up and struggled desperately, and cried more and more loudly, he was strangled by Iachvil, Tatarinof, or Skariatine with a scarf which may have belonged to one of the assassins or may have been his own, which lay near together with his sword.

Bennigsen, who naturally wished to minimise his responsibility by denying that he took any direct part in the assassination, has himself given varying accounts on these points of detail. As his momentary absence did not appear to be fully explained by the alleged panic of the murderers—which could only have been momentary as the two detachments immediately met and recognised each other in the antechamber—he gave a second explanation of it. The bedroom, which was the scene of the tragedy, was illuminated only by a night-light, which was placed on the Emperor's desk. It was upset by Paul himself or one of the conspirators, and Bennigsen had therefore to go and fetch another light. But is it possible that the assailants were not furnished with torches ?

One fact is certain. There was a tumultuous rush of a band of drunken men on a defenceless victim ; a horrible struggle, a rain of blows from fists, spurred heels, and even sabres—culminating in the strangling of the victim. Paul was vigorous in spite of his diminutive stature, and his death agony was long as he struggled to loosen the fatal knot from his neck. It was said that, as he still struggled, a French servant of Prince Zoubof undertook to " expel his soul from his body " by jumping on the prostrate form of the fallen Sovereign. But even the death of the " tyrant " does not seem to have ended these hideous barbarities. Excited by their horrible work, and infuriated by the resistance which they had encountered, the executioners fell upon the corpse. The English doctor Greeve, who superintended the embalming of the body, told Kotzebue that he observed a broad contused area round the neck, another on one temple, a red patch on the side, two red patches on the thighs which appeared to be due to violent pressure, further bruises on the knees, and traces all over the body of blows probably inflicted after death. He saw no trace of any wound produced by a cutting instrument.

The last observation has not, however, escaped contradiction. Among Paul's pages at this time was a certain Prince Khilkof. He was admitted with his comrades to see the Sovereign lying-in-state, and was allowed to kiss his hand. A family tradition has it that he observed, while performing this pious duty, that two fingers of the glove to which he pressed his lips were empty.*

Some years later, when the name of Nicolas Bolgovski, a captain in the Ismaïlovski and one of the participators

* I owe this piece of information to Mme. Nélidof, born Princess Khilkof, the widow of the late Russian Ambassador at Paris.

in the crime, was mentioned in the presence of Alexander I,
he said to one of his intimates :

" Do you know what this man did ? He took my
father's head by the hair after he was dead and dashed
it against the floor, crying, ' So much for the tyrant ! ' "

Other horrible details are given in the contemporary
accounts. It is said that as one of those who were
strangling him wore the red uniform of the Horse Guards,
Paul thought it was the head of the regiment, the Grand
Duke Constantine himself, and cried : " Mercy, Monseigneur, mercy ! For pity's sake, air ! air ! "

During the killing, according to their story, Bennigsen
simply took up the attitude of one unconcerned in what
was happening. He went into the next room and
occupied himself with the pictures, while Plato Zoubof
turned his back and drummed on a window with his
fingers, nervously exclaiming : " Good God, how that
man screams ; it is horrid ! "

Both men in after years affirmed frequently that the
Czar was killed, not only without their participation, but
against their wishes. But even on this point their
testimony varied according to their hearers. In the
memoirs of Countess Potocka we find the following :
" Bennigsen felt no embarrassment in speaking of this
scene of horror. . . . He looked upon himself as a latter-
day Brutus."

On the other hand, Lord St. Helens records in one of his
despatches a detail which, while it contradicts the apolo-
getic asserverations of the two accomplices, surpasses in
atrocity all the others already given. Paul, it was said,
escaped alive from the hands of his assailants. One of
the Court doctors was summoned to lay out the body,
and discovered that the Emperor still breathed. Then,
after all the tumult was over, it was deliberately decided
in cold blood to finish him. The Ambassador on this
occasion also, however, fails to give the source of his

information, which was perhaps only one of the innumerable falsehoods then current.

VII

According to the positive testimony of Czartoryski, which is above suspicion, Alexander was awake that night or had taken precautions to be at hand when required. According to the account given by a servant of the Grand Duchess, afterwards the Empress, Elizabeth Pahlen came to see the Grand Duke at six in the evening, and this is confirmed by the Grand Duchess's maid, who adds several significant details. This woman was no ordinary servant. Her name was Prascovia Hessler; she was of English extraction, and was greatly esteemed and loved by all the Imperial Family for her high qualities of mind and character.

Alexander came in to his wife's room at ten. The Grand Duchess was already in bed. He called the maid and asked her to help him to take off his boots and his uniform. He then took off his cravat and lay down, saying to Hessler : " Please remain in the antechamber to-night till Count Pahlen comes. When he does, come into this room and waken me if I am asleep."

It is more doubtful whether Constantine knew what was being done. According to several witnesses at the time when the crime was being committed he was sleeping as one sleeps at twenty. But Hessler relates that Alexander, too, slept profoundly while he awaited the arrival of Pahlen, slept indeed as he was to sleep in 1814 under the walls of Paris when about to give audience to the deputation from the city who brought him the capitulation. It is possible that, knowing his younger brother's frivolity of temperament, Alexander did not take him into his confidence. Sabloukof, however, says that he received an order in Constantine's handwriting *a few minutes after one o'clock in the morning* to place the regiment under arms, but *without baggage*. This direction, therefore, was not given in order to carry out the instructions previously given by Paul. Moreover, the bearer of the message added a verbal communication from the Grand Duke, to the effect that the Michael Palace was surrounded by troops, and that muskets and pistols should be loaded with ball.* This message can only have been sent while the tragedy was at its height, before the death of Paul and the accession of Alexander; for then the investment of the Palace by the troops which had been won over to the conspiracy naturally came to an end. Further, it must have been sent with the connivance of the officers commanding these troops. It could not otherwise have got through. In any case it is clear that Constantine was *not* asleep at the moment of the crime, though he may have been awakened by the noise.

If Alexander was in a deep sleep at the time of his father's death, it is a proof of a truly terrible insensibility. But it is extremely difficult to be certain on this point. Various persons have been indicated as having been the first to convey to the Grand Duke the fatal news. Prince Czartoryski says it was the elder Zoubof who came " dishevelled, his face flushed with wine and murder," to announce to the heir that " all was over." Alexander, either hearing imperfectly or pretending not to understand, asked : " What is over ? "

Constantine Poltoratski, however, claimed for himself the honour of having before any one else saluted the new Sovereign with the title of " Majesty." The account of the Grand Duchess's maid is still the most probable : " At half-past one in the morning Count Pahlen entered the antechamber of their Imperial Highnesses' bedroom and said : ' Is the Grand Duke asleep ? ' ' Yes.' ' Go in and tell him that I am here.' The Grand Duke was

* *Fraser's Magazine,* 1865, p. 316.

sound asleep, and near him the Grand Duchess was sitting on the bed weeping and sobbing. When she saw me she said, in a terrified manner : ' What ? Have they come for him already ? ' "

The two women with difficulty wakened the sleeper, and when he at last got up and dressed and went to Pahlen in the antechamber, the maid noticed that the Military Governor called him " Your Majesty." Pahlen may have been accompanied or followed by Nicolas Zoubof and some other actors in the drama, among whom was no doubt Poltoratski. The attitude of the heir was thoroughly disconcerting. He was urged to show himself to the troops, and this was indeed a matter of the most pressing importance. Paiker was still writing his report, but his men were murmuring. An even more alarming movement of revolt was threatening among the Préobrajentsy of the other post. They had been told that they were there to defend the Czar ; now they were informed that the Czar was dead. They had become distrustful and were demanding to see the body, and it was impossible to satisfy them.

Alexander, however, was far from taking on himself any responsibility of sovereignty. The first impulse of his evasive nature was to shirk the accomplished fact, however great his own responsibility for it had been. He said over and over again that he could not and would not accept the crown. According to Poltoratski, when Pahlen told him what had happened he fainted. Others say that, having been dragged down to the vestibule of the Palace, he had to be hurriedly led, or rather carried, back to his room owing to an attack of nervous convulsions by which he was overtaken. There he was found shortly afterwards by Rogerson sitting in a corner in his wife's arms. Both were weeping so bitterly that they did not see him come in.

The bulk of the evidence seems to show that Elizabeth

Aléxiéievna had also been in the secret. It will be remembered that three years previously she was already longing for the overthrow of the tyrant, and even if she did not know what was going to happen on this occasion, as Mme. Golovine avers, the invasion of the Palace must have reminded her of the disturbances at Pavlovsk in the early days which had thrilled her with such joyous expectation. Mme. Golovine says also that she threw herself on her knees, praying that " whatever happened might be for the good of Russia ! " It may be. But other witnesses say that she did not content herself with prayers. She used all her energies to restore her husband's courage, and with the aid of Pahlen, who roughly shook the young master and told him " not to be a baby ! " she at last induced him to appear before the post of the Préobrajenski.

Alexander, however, was still on the verge of collapse, and found nothing to say to the soldiers who, for the most part, were visibly hostile. His silence and his air of being overwhelmed by what had happened perplexed them still more. What were they to think ? What was being hidden from them ? Was Paul really dead ? Would he not reappear in a moment with angry face and uplifted cane as on the parade ground ? In vain Marine cried : " Long live the Czar Alexander Pavlovitch ! " There was no response. The Zoubofs came forward and harangued the sullen troops : it was in vain !

Pahlen, pushing Alexander before him, hurried on to the men of the Siémionovski. There the new Czar was more at ease. Though he was in command of the whole Guard, this regiment was regarded as peculiarly his own. He was warned in no gentle tones by his escort : " You are ruining yourself and us, too ! " and he succeeded in stammering the few words which were put in his mouth: " Paul had died of an attack of apoplexy. His son would follow in the footsteps of Catherine the Great." The

463

effect of this was what might have been expected. There was an outburst of enthusiastic cheering, and Pahlen breathed again. But Marine's Préobrajenski were still on the defensive, and there was great danger of a conflict which might have had incalculable consequences. Alexander's one idea was to fly from the gloomy Palace filled with horror, from the bloody corpse which accused him, and from its too faithful guardians who were threatening him. On Pahlen's advice he decided to hand over the command of the Michael Palace to Bennigsen and to go himself to the Winter Palace.

A wretched carriage with a pair of horses was in waiting. It has been supposed that it was intended to take Paul to Schlüsselbourg, and it may be that Pahlen, in order to give colour to his pretended intention, had actually ordered it. Alexander entered this vehicle with Constantine, while Nicolas Zoubof and Ouvarof got up behind. The following account is given by a contemporary :

" The carriage left the Palace ; it was stopped, but one of the servants called out, ' It is the Grand Duke ! ' The other said, ' It is the Emperor Alexander ! ' A cry of ' Long live the Emperor ! ' spontaneously arose, and the battalion followed the carriage at the double to the Winter Palace, where the new Czar alighted." *

Alexander would have wished to take his wife with him. Their relations had become more cordial during the crisis, and his cowardly nature yearned for the support of her courage. There was however an obstacle to this, " an additional embarrassment " as he called it, thus giving the measure of his character and of the delicacy of feeling which he habitually showed. He was leaving without

* This is taken from the unpublished memoirs of Baron de Damas, an *émigré* then sixteen years of age and sub-lieutenant in the first battalion of the Siémionovski. He was afterwards a Minister of State under the Restoration. I am indebted to his grandson the Comte de Damas, who is preparing a volume of his Souvenirs, for permission to publish the above extract.

having seen his mother, without troubling to ask what had become of her, without the slightest feeling that he should show her some sign of affection, were it only a word of sympathy and condolence! Was it forgetfulness, indifference, or another unconscious manifestation of his monstrous selfishness? No doubt it was all these, but it was also cowardice again, an instinctive recoil from the terrible moment when his eyes would meet those of the desolate woman whom he had helped to make a widow.

But Marie Féodorovna was not the sort of person to allow herself to be forgotten. When she heard what had happened she thought she had a chance of playing a leading part, and, thinking as little about her son as he did about her, she ranged tumultuously through the sombre Palace which he had decided to forsake. She was devoted to her husband, in spite of his ill-usage and his threats; she had neither contrived nor wished for his death, but she was not disposed to accept the position of a mere dowager. In the days when she and the Czar had been close allies he had always spoken of entrusting her with the Empire if anything were to happen to him. By this he meant merely that she should be regent during the minority of their son, who was then only ten years old. But in such matters the female mind is apt to be confused, and to her Alexander with his timidity and weakness seemed to be still a child. She was nothing of a politician; but she was of an arbitrary and ambitious temper, and under the influence of grief and dismay she entirely lost her head.

She was informed of what had taken place by the Dowager Countess Lieven. Without waiting to dress she rushed towards the chamber in which Paul had breathed his last, but they were unwilling to show her the disfigured corpse. She was therefore stopped in her way and this completely deprived her of her self-control. Why should she wait? Was the Emperor really dead?

Dead or alive they had no right to prevent her from showing her love for him. With the greatest respect the commander of the post, who had Pahlen's orders to let no one pass, barred her passage, and neither her threats nor her entreaties availed against the crossed bayonets which stopped the way. Half naked, with a fur cloak about her shoulders, she wandered through the Palace seeking another entrance, but at the same time trying to secure her recognition as reigning Sovereign. She proclaimed her rights aloud and harangued the soldiers: " If there is no Emperor I alone am your Empress! I alone am your legitimate Sovereign. Defend me and follow me ! "

" But," says Czartoryski, " she had nothing about her which could inspire or excite devotion, and the foreign accent with which she still spoke Russian was no doubt against her." Unlike Catherine she was always the German, and to the last she had always infuriated Paul by calling him *Paulchen*. Bennigsen, Pahlen, and Elizabeth, whom Alexander reluctantly left behind, in vain did their best to calm her, assuring her that she would very soon be admitted to the death chamber. They urged her in the meantime to follow her son to the Winter Palace. The Emperor, they said, wished to see her at once.

" The Emperor ? What Emperor ? " And she shook Bennigsen by the arm and ordered him to let her pass. " I should like to see you disobey me ! " He resisted, however, and she resumed her course mingling prayers with invectives, now falling on her knees before some official, now falling into the arms of some officer. A grenadier, whose name—Piérekrestof—has been preserved by history, saw that she was on the point of fainting and offered her a glass of water. She pushed him aside. What she wanted was a throne !

It was not until seven in the morning that the dead

man was made presentable and the doors of the room were opened. Marie Féodorovna entered with her children, and abandoned herself to demonstrations of grief which were somewhat theatrical. She then consented to join Alexander at the Winter Palace, and on the way, if we may believe Bennigsen, she kept looking out for some movement in her favour on the part of the troops or of the populace.

VIII

When he reached the Winter Palace Alexander again collapsed. Again he spoke of abandoning the supreme power "to any one who would take it," and then declared that he would only accept it if on conditions and limitations fixed by the authors of the *coup d'état.* On this it is said that two drafts of a constitution were actually produced, and that Alexander was prevented from accepting the scheme by the remonstrances of Novossiltsof according to some, and of Klinger and Talysine according to others. There were other and more pressing concerns which no doubt intervened even more effectually. There were measures of police and military dispositions which required immediate attention, and, first of all, it was necessary to arrange for the ceremonial of the troops swearing allegiance to the new master, which in Russia is the necessary preface to a new order of things. Now at the Michael Palace the Préobrajenski were still expectant, and when Sabloukof, at the barracks of the Horse Guards, announced the death of Paul and the accession of Alexander the men refused to cheer. Leaving the ranks, one of them, Gregory Ivanof, asked the colonel whether he had seen the Emperor dead and had made sure that he had breathed his last. General Tormassof himself, the second in command of the regiment, who was destined to be one of the most valiant fighters in 1812, showed

that he was undecided.   Sabloukof bethought him that
the regiment could not take the oath without its standards,
which, according to the regulations, were deposited at the
Michael Palace.   He sent a few men to fetch them under
the command of a certain Cornet Filatiéf, whom he ordered
to insist on seeing Paul dead or alive.

" When they arrived at the Palace, General Bennigsen,
as commandant of the château, ordered them to fetch the
standards, upon which Filatiéf said that it was absolutely
necessary that the men should first see the Emperor.
On this Bennigsen exclaimed : ' Mais c'est impossible,
il est abîmé, fracassé ! On est actuellement à le peindre
et à l'arranger.' Filatiéf replied that unless the men saw
him dead the regiment would refuse to swear allegiance
to the new Sovereign.   ' Ah, ma foi,' said old Bennigsen,
' s'ils lui sont si attachés, ils n'ont qu'a le voir,' and the
two privates were let in and viewed the mangled corpse."*

When they returned, Sabloukof " first addressed honest
Gregory Ivanof. ' Well, brother (bratiéts), you have seen
the Emperor ; is he really dead ? ' ' He is, your honour,
very dead (kriépko oumier).' ' Will you now swear allegiance to Alexander ? ' ' Yes, I will ; although he shall
be no better, for, after all, whoever is priest is also father
(kto ni pop tot i batka).' "

After this the Préobrajenski also took the oath, and at
the same time orders for the arrest of several persons were
given, but soon remitted.   Generals Malioutine and
Kotloubitski, as well as Obolianinof the Procurator-
General, were set at liberty in the course of a few days.
Koutaïssof had managed somehow to make his escape,
and had taken refuge in the house of Stephen Lanskoï,
a friend of his, who, in later days, became Minister of
the Interior.   He contrived to return the very next
day to his house on the Admiralty Quay without interference.   Mme. Chevalier escaped with a domiciliary

* *Fraser's Magazine*, 1865, p. 318.

visit and the seizure of certain papers. Some days later she applied for a passport, and Alexander gallantly sent to say that " he regretted that the lady's health obliged her to leave Russia, but he hoped she would return soon to be an ornament to the French stage there."

At the Winter Palace the inevitable Trochtchinski drew up another manifesto—a mere paraphrase of the few words addressed by the new Czar to the Siémionovtsy, Catherine's grandson had definitely decided to recommence her reign. He did not long remain faithful to this programme, but without any delay he proceeded to reverse some of his father's last decisions and made certain changes among the high officials, beginning with Obolianinof, who was dismissed. One of his first cares had been to summon the Minister of War whom Paul had just dismissed. When Lieven came Alexander fell on his neck weeping. " My father ! My poor father ! " Then at once he asked : " Where are the Cossacks ? "

He meant Orlof and his comrades, who were on the way to India. A courier was immediately despatched to order them to turn back. This expedition, however, was connected with the hostilities which had been so rashly commenced against England, and Neïson's victorious fleet might any day be expected to appear off the coasts of Russia. Neither Alexander nor his advisers seem to have felt any more anxiety about this than Paul himself. The war was of the dead Czar's making, was it not destined to end with him ? Pahlen contented himself with notifying the new reign to London without a single word which could be taken as an excuse or as a hint at reconciliation. This dignified attitude was completely successful. Pitt had resigned in February, and Addington, who succeeded him, and Hawkesbury, who replaced Grenville, were not men who were likely to be unbending where Pitt had shown so much moderation. They took the first step towards the inevitable agreement by ordering the commanders-in-chief of the British fleets to suspend all hostile operations, and by announcing that they would soon send an Ambassador to St. Petersburg who would do his best to re-establish the old friendly relations between the two Courts. Nelson indeed had got so far that he did not stop till he reached Revel, whence he announced his intention of coming to St. Petersburg " to affirm more clearly," he said, " his peaceful intentions and the cordial sentiments with which he was animated." This demonstration was considered superfluous, and even inopportune, by those to whom it was addressed, but it did no harm.

Lieven was painfully impressed by the self-satisfied gaiety which reigned around the new Sovereign at the Winter Palace. The Grand Duke Constantine alone showed a tear-stained face among these men, who were lost in exultation over their triumph. To Sabloukof he said, a few days later : " My friend . . . after what has happened my brother may reign if he likes, but if the throne ever comes to me I shall certainly refuse it." And this, in fact, he did, as is well known.

He and Marie Féodorovna, however, were the only members of the Imperial Family who showed this spirit. Alexander, of course, looked like a criminal tortured by remorse, but he showed the sincerity of his feeling by choosing the son of the fair Olga Jerebtsof as his envoy to announce his accession to the Court of Berlin, though he could not be unaware of the part his mother had played in the conspiracy. As for Elizabeth, she wrote to her mother three days after the catastrophe that, like all Russia, she breathed again, and that it had been necessary to deliver the country " at any cost " from the tyranny under which it was groaning.

Russia breathed again indeed—at least, what was then meant by Russia. Several witnesses say that in the streets of the capital men wept tears of joy. Passers-by who were unknown to each other embraced and exchanged congratulations on the happy change. On the road to Moscow postmasters sent on for nothing the couriers who carried "the good news." At night, without any orders, the town was illuminated. "The enthusiasm was general and even indecent," says one chronicler. Elizabeth speaks of the "almost insane delight which pervaded all classes, from the nobility down to the lowest of the low." Mme. Vigée-Lebrun says the same. When she came back from Moscow some weeks after the catastrophe, she found St. Petersburg still "delirious with joy. They were singing and dancing and kissing each other in the streets," and the provinces imitated the capital.

If we may believe Mme. Golovine, Marie Féodorovna herself soon shook off her sorrow. When she joined her son at the Winter Palace, and he was about to throw himself into her arms she stopped him with the question : "Sacha, are you to blame for this ? " Alexander protested his innocence, and she embraced him tenderly and placed her youngest children under his care. "You are now their father," she said.

It was not long however before she was leading a gayer life than ever at Gatchina and Pavlovsk. There was a succession of dinner and supper parties, alternating with excursions on horseback, in which she took part. She went on planting and building as in the old days and recalled the misfortune which had fallen upon her only by the portraits of herself in deep mourning, which she distributed to her friends. Paul's widow indeed, with all her affection and her "sensibility," which was after the fashion of the time, was much too fond of life not to be caught up again by the current. The surroundings in which she lived favoured this. Alexander's father was neither regretted nor pitied. No tears were shed at his funeral. What was then called "the public," that is, the Court, the officers, and the Civil Service, genuinely exulted at being relieved of the oppressive regulations and the accumulated restraints of the previous reign. Round hats, high cravats, and cutaway coats reappeared on all sides. Carriages flew over the pavement. Mme. Golovine saw an officer of hussars galloping on the pavement of the Quay, crying : " Now we can do anything we like." This was his idea of liberty !

IX

Alexander soon deceived the high hopes to which his accession gave rise. He did his best in some degree to redress the wrongs of his father's reign. But, in domestic politics he went so far in the other direction that he encouraged a tendency to anarchy which terrified some of his contemporaries. In his foreign policy, on the other hand, though he brought back his relations with his Western neighbours to a more normal footing, he, too, succumbed to the temptation to play the chivalrous part of saviour of Europe to which Paul had sacrificed the vital interests of his country. He scrupulously preserved all the details of his predecessor's military institutions. On the very day after his accession he appeared, at morning parade, still nervous and timid, as if the shade of Paul were still directing the operations, but most careful to preserve the rules in all their strictness. He remained on terms of intimacy with Araktchéief, and accorded neither his friendship nor his confidence to those to whom he owed his crown.

Personally he did not wish, or did not dare, to take any measures against his accomplices in the *coup d'état*. The risk would, in fact, have been great. One of them, Prince Iachvil, went so far as to write him a letter beginning with an energetic justification of the act of violence which had been perpetrated on the person of " an unhappy madman," and ending with a haughty admonition, accompanied by a scarcely veiled threat. " Be an honest man, if you can, on the throne, and do not forget that there is a supreme resource for the despairing ! " . . . On the day of the crime he had accepted Nicolas Zoubof and Ouvarof as his escort to the Winter Palace. The following day at parade he ostentatiously lent on the arm of Prince Plato, which led Mme. de Bonnœil to remark in a letter to Fouché : " The young Emperor walks preceded by the assassins of his grandfather, followed by those of his father, and surrounded by his own ! " Already, however, Prince Plato Zoubof himself had been led to say to Czartoryski, who no doubt repeated it : " The Emperor is discouraging his real friends ! " Already, too, Marie Féodorovna had been pressing for reprisals, not with much intelligence, but with all her habitual violence, and she had to some extent had her way.

When she left the Michael Palace she had not rejected Bennigsen's arm. Afterwards, moved by something more or less true which she had heard, she persecuted Tatarinof —a minor person in the drama—with her hatred. Soon she aimed higher, but always under the influence of some spiteful feeling awakened by chance and served no less fortuitously by the weakness and the duplicity of Alexander. Chance worked for her also in removing several of the principal actors so soon after the catastrophe that they in their turn seemed to be victims to some act of deliberate revenge. Talysine died two months, and Nicolas Zoubof seven months, after Paul. Valerian Zoubof survived him only two years and four months. Several, however, whose guilt was deeper, such as Marine, Ouvarof, Volkonski, and others, remained alive and highly favoured. The widowed Empress at first accepted Pahlen himself and Panine. The former retained all his places; the latter as Vice-Chancellor was recalled to the direction of Foreign Affairs, while Pahlen remained President of the College. Bennigsen's only punishment was a fourth marriage with a young Polish lady who is said to have acquired the charming habit of frequently saying to him, without warning: "My dear, have you heard the news?" "What news?" "The Emperor Paul is dead!"

Pahlen at first thought that he had realised his dream, which was "to govern the Empire and the Emperor." But Panine was not a man to allow himself to be set aside, and the two associates soon found themselves at variance. One of them favoured the *rapprochement* with France, which to some extent was his work, while the other, like the Zoubofs, was a partisan of the English alliance, to which the whole Russian aristocracy was attached. Alexander soon brought them to order. The wily Courlander had calculated that his young master would not be capable of resisting him, and this was so. But the Czar slipped between his fingers and was watching for an opportunity of escaping him altogether. Marie Féodorovna unconsciously, as always, came to her son's help. She had had an icon set up in the chapel of one of the institutions over which she presided which (Mlle. Nélidof says quite by chance) bore an inscription apparently alluding to the event of March 11/23 and the part played by Pahlen. The text was: "Had Zimri peace who slew his master?" (Kings II, ix, 31). This gave rise to talk. Pahlen ordered the icon to be removed and made some offensive observations. Panine and Mlle. Nélidof poured oil upon the flames and the quarrel became serious. Alexander went to Gatchina to arrange the matter, and was told by his mother, after a stormy scene, that she would never set foot in St. Petersburg again so long as Pahlen was there. Alexander temporised; on the following day he worked all morning with his Prime Minister without saying a word about the incident, but immediately afterwards sent for Békléchof, the new Procurator, and ordered him to *advise* Pahlen to set out at once on a tour of inspection in Livonia and Courland.

Pahlen knew what that meant. He set out the same

day, and from Striélna he sent to the Czar a request to be allowed to resign. Until his death in 1826 (he survived Alexander only by a few weeks) he was never to quit his estate in Courland, which he had named *Paulsgnade*. According to Mme. de Lieven he intoxicated himself regularly about ten o'clock at night on every anniversary of March 11/23, and stupified himself with the fumes of wine until the morning of the following day.

Panine had won, but he had only three months in which to enjoy his triumph. After his return to St. Petersburg, Alexander had received him with open arms. " Alas ! " observed the Czar simply, " things did not turn out as we hoped ! " Marie Féodorovna was not at first inclined to join in these demonstrations of affection. She had formerly been very favourably disposed towards the young statesman and had had an almost maternal affection for him. She knew nothing definite about his participation in the conspiracy, but she suspected something. When he came to pay his respects she withdrew her hand which he was about to kiss, and plied him with questions. He replied without apparent embarrassment: "Madam, I was a hundred leagues from St. Petersburg at the time ! " She seemed satisfied, and her letters appeared to show that he had forfeited none of her affection. In June the affair of the icon made their relations even closer, and Pahlen's disgrace seemed to exalt the credit of his rival. But as early as May we find Simon Vorontsof expressing regret that the Vice-Chancellor did not receive all the confidence he deserved, and there were already rumours of the appointment of a Chancellor who would not be Panine. The Emperor and the Vice-Chancellor were at variance on more than one point of home and foreign policy. Panine opposed La Harpe's return to Russia. The Czar disregarded his advice. Their dissensions, however, extended to the subject on which of all others they should have been agreed. On May 28

Panine addressed the following lines to his Sovereign :
" What your Majesty said to me last night on the subject
of the event which placed your Majesty on the throne
has grieved me deeply. If your Majesty regards me as
the cause of an action prejudicial to the glory of your
reign my presence can only be odious, and I am prepared
to relieve you of it. . . . But I shall carry with me to
my grave the profound conviction that I served my
country in being the first who ventured to bring before
your Majesty the terrible danger which threatened the
Empire."

A rupture was inevitable, but it was destined to be
precipitated by a trifling incident. Alexander came to
know of a letter from Panine to Vorontsof in which the
Vice-Chancellor complained of the frivolity of his young
master, who thought more of women than of the State.
The consequence was that Panine was dismissed on
October 3, 1801, and was ordered to travel abroad for
three years. The letter had been sent by courier, and
Panine not unreasonably suspected that his correspondent
had betrayed him. Vorontsof had wished for the end
of Paul's reign, but he doubtless disapproved of the
methods that had been used to hasten it, and in his own
way he avenged his master.

Marie Féodorovna was far from approving of Panine's
disgrace and indignantly protested against it. Alexander
listened in silence, but next day he sent to his mother
with an explanatory note another letter written by the
ex-Vice-Chancellor. This one was addressed to Whitworth and proved his complicity in the plot. Panine
had written too much. The fury of the Empress Dowager
was unchained, never again to be appeased. While she
spared so many others who were guilty, she took care
that he who was still so young should never emerge from
his living tomb. Separated from his family and friends,
he was condemned to vegetate in inactivity, and his

punishment only terminated with his death, which took place in 1837.

" This death had to be," says a French writer, speaking of Paul's end, " but woe to those who were responsible for it ! " *

In these words, perhaps without knowing it, de Maistre pronouced sentence on Alexander I. Amid the many triumphs which followed the trials of the first years of his reign the son of the victim was destined never to find happiness. His conscience, unstable as it was, seems never to have been appeased by the argument " *that it had to be.*" And, indeed, was it really necessary for the son to place his father's life at the mercy of a band of dissolute young men led by two unscrupulous foreigners ? Even if it be granted that Paul's deposition was a measure necessary in the interests of the public safety, it has not been proved that it was necessary to give it the form which it actually took.

It was a consequence of the violently revolutionary character assumed by the changes of reign and of dynasty which for two centuries had taken place in Russia. But twenty-four years later Nicolas was to prove that, given a little firmness, it was possible to break with this tradition. Thus Alexander's weakness once more emphasised the great part which personal and apparently accidental factors play in the development of the laws of history. The temperament of the individual and its influence on our destinies are themselves no doubt merely a resultant of the same forces by which the lives of nations áre governed, but the principle of these combinations almost entirely eludes analysis and has all the appearance of pure chance.

* De Maistre : *Mémoires Politiques,* Paris, 1859.

CONCLUSION

BEFORE Paul succumbed to the blows of his assassins he had already fallen a victim to a combination of circumstances by which his nature and his destiny were alike conditioned. He was a victim in the first place to the crushing task which was laid upon him, or rather which he laid upon himself, and to the vain presumption which led him to suppose that he was capable of bearing such a burden. But this presumption itself, which in him was exaggerated into a maniacal delusion, was a natural product of the extravagance of the position he was called upon to fill and the powers which he was called upon to exercise.

Then, again, he was the victim of his origin, which was more than three-quarters German, of his French education, of the Russian environment of all this, and the inevitable clash of discordant and heterogeneous elements. The romantic and humanitarian ideas of the Latin West were mingled in his mind with Oriental brutalities, the formalism of Prussia with the fantasy of the East: civilisation and barbarism jostled in him. And all this not only entered into the composition of his own personality, but through him penetrated to the people whom he was called to govern.

Finally, he was the victim of morbid tendencies which inevitably resulted from such an abnormal constitution of mind, and were aggravated by the influence which the political and moral exaltation of the age necessarily exercised on so impressionable a temper. When the teaching of the jacobins of the West and the revolutionary tradition of Peter the Great converged in one mind, the end could not fail to be insanity.

Catherine's son has often been compared to the son of Maria Theresa, who also inherited from an omnipotent and glorious mother. He, too, admired Frederick II, and unconsciously imitated the French revolutionaries; he had the same passion for interfering in everything and, like Paul, he finally succumbed to a task which was beyond his strength. Paul's work, however, was much wider in its scope, and its effects were much more lasting. It has, for the most part, survived its author, because in fact it merely exaggerated certain organic traits in the heritage of the last representatives of the House of Rurik and the first Romanofs. Paul's personal eccentricities gave a touch of paradox and caricature to the historic type thus created, and this is still noticeable in certain features of his vast Empire, which is a constitutional and parliamentary country governed by an absolute monarch who professes not to have abandoned any of his prerogatives ! This is one of the most interesting aspects of the reign described in this book. In the history of Modern Russia it is not merely a dramatic episode, it is part of an organic whole and one of its salient points.

The readers of this volume will be in a position to judge of the discrepancy between Paul's effort and his achievement. They are not equally contemptible. Unhappily his nobly-inspired but over-violent and ill-planned reaction against the worst abuses of his age, conspicuous as it was in his lifetime, has proved the least durable of his works. The abuses survived and indeed formed the essential bond of union of the coalition against the reformer. Apart from the calculations of his personal ambition Panine assuredly had in view the safety of the Empire ; but in order to secure it, he had to accept the complicity of such men as Ribas, and more or less directly the co-operation of the " gilded troop " of cynical rakes whom he detested as cordially as did Paul.

The reforms planned by Paul did not all of them die with him. Among his murderers the idlers and the peculators of all ranks were no doubt the first to enjoy the fruits of the victory. But even the triumphant Guard did not succeed in recovering from its earlier downfall and, along with the degrading *caporalisme* which Paul carried to such lengths, there were more praiseworthy borrowings from the tradition of Frederick II which have become a permanent part of the military organisation of the country.

By his dynastic law, promulgated immediately after his accession, Paul hoped to put an end to the periodical crises in the devolution of the supreme power. The maintenance of the autocratic principle made this guarantee a very fragile one in practice, and Paul himself appears to have been on the point of proving how illusory it was. Nevertheless, it has victoriously stood the test of time and has given the political constitution a stability for which credit is due to the reformer of 1801.

Even in the sphere of social and economic interests, maladroit and incoherent as were his interventions, some of the seed which he sowed escaped the ruin of his humanitarian dream, and was destined to bear fruit for his people, who were thereby delivered from one of the bitterest forms of the oppression under which they formerly groaned.

It may be that it was fated that Paul should have lived and reigned as he did in order that there might be created by reaction from the form of government which he inherited, and which he made so intolerable, the movement of emancipation which so soon followed. Alexander was swept away by this movement along with such men as Novossiltsof and Stroganof, and thenceforth the *élite* of his subjects were irrevocably involved in it also. In spite of obstacles, checks, and inevitable reactions this is the path which has since been consistently followed, and if we wish to discover the point of departure it is to the age of Paul I that we must return.

INDEX

Aar, The, crossing by the Allies, 288

Aarau, 288

Abruzzi, revolt, 270

Academies, theological, founded by Paul, 176

Adam, Villiers de l'Isle, 346

Addington, 469

Administrative unification, Paul's policy, 180–181

Admiralty, College of, 107, 162, 182, 206, 207, 412

Airolo, 292

Alembért, d', reply to Catherine, 9–10

Alessandria, 269, 271, 272, 275

Alexander I, education, 19; Catherine's plans for succession, 27–8, 69; military colonies founded by, 34; portrait, 41; and Araktchéief, 56; marriage, 66; and his father, 71, 77, 150, 389, 390, 397, 404–5; consents to scheme for deposition of his father, 72; and Catherine's papers, 78; at release of Kosciusko, 84; orders re-established, 97; and Tourguénief, 98–9; pardons, 115; and Vassiliévitch, 149; trade under, 185; Brünow's summary, 214; eve of Austerlitz, 215; and the Archduke Palatine, 317; and the Indian expedition, 373; letter to La Harpe, 387; accession manifesto, 388; the Secret Committee, 388; the plot, 410, 418, 419, 422, 423, 449, 459; and the exiles, 418; Paul's order for his arrest, 433; complicity proved, 436; the night of 11/23 March, 437, 460, 461; absence from parade, 438, 440; under arrest, 441–3; behaviour on death of Paul, 462–464; retirement to the Winter Palace, 464; arrest of several persons, 468; first measures, 469; Marie Féodorovna and, 471; as Emperor 472–7; dismisses Pahlen, 474–5; and Panine, 475–7

Alexander, Prince, 224

Alexandria, 310

Alexandrina, Grand Duchess, 74, 103, 216–17, 220–1, 253–4, 313–17, 324, 361

Alexis, 155, 181
son of the Reformer, 381

Alquier, d', 367

Amiens, Treaty of, 1802, 241

Amnesty, general, of Nov. 1, 1800, 394, 420, 422

Ancona, 270, 311, 312, 320

Andréievski, 443, 444

Anglo-Austrian League, Paul's position in the, 238–59; end of the Coalition, 291–334; Paul's letter to England and Austria, Oct. 15/26, 307–8

Anglo-Russian commercial treaty of 1797, 215

Anglo-Russian Convention, June 11/22, 1799, 308

Anglo-Russia treaty, Dec. 1798, 200, 249–250–1, 255; Prussia's adherence demanded by Panine in Jan. 1799, 255

Anne, Grand Duchess, 314, 315

Anna, Pavlovna, Grand Duchess, writings quoted, 20

Antoinette, Marie, 35

Antonovitch, Ivan, 8

Antony, Archduke, 314

Appanages, Department of, 163

Apraxine, Stephen, 172

Araktchéief, Paul and, 21, 33, 34, 55–56, 58, 59, 138; Alexander and, 72, 472; and Paul's accession, 78–80, 82; established in the Winter Palace, 88; and the regiment of Ekaterinoslav, 92, 98, 99; banishment, 104, 139, 409; reorganisation of the artillery, 195, 197; recall, 434, 436

Arcola, 212, 219

Argamakof, Peter Vassiliévitch, equerry, 451–2, 454

Arkhangelsk, famine of 1810, 182

Arkharof, General, 80
Nicholas, military governor of St. Petersburg, 110, 112, 128

Army, The, reforms under Paul, 155, 192–3, 392–3; the Guards, 193–5; the artillery under Araktchéief, 195–6; new sets of regulations, 197–8; uniforms, 199–201;

INDEX

military education, 202–3 ; obligation to be present on duty, 203–4 ; Préobrajenski regiment, under Peter the Great, 195–6 ; at the Michael Palace, 450 ; behaviour on death of Paul, 462 ; reception of Alexander, 463–4 ; refusal to take the oath, 467–8 ; Siémionovski regiment, and the plot, 436, 450 ; reception of Alexander, 463–4

Art of Conquest (The), Souvorof, 263

Artois, Comte d', 280, 304

Arzamas, 183

Assebourg, Baron von, 14, 15

Assignats, issue of, condemned by Paul, 187

" Atlas of Navigation," published by Paul, 207

Auffenberg, 300

Augard, Chevalier d', 143

Augsburg, Souvorof's march to, 304–5

Aulic Council of Vienna, Souvorof and the, 263, 264, 274–5, 279, 286, 293

Austerlitz, 215, 427

Austria, and Russian policy, 214–24, 228, 231, 234–6, 257 ; the Malta question, 243, 252 ; action of generals in Turin, 269–70 ; Sardinian policy, 282–3 ; and Pitt's plan, 285 ; Paul's letter of Oct. 15/26, 307–8 ; process of reparation, 324

Autonomy, administrative, Catherine's and Paul's principles, 164–5

Avaray, Comte d', 304

BADEN, Margrave of, Paul and, 282

Bagration, General, 273

Bajénof, Vassili Ivanovitch, 39, 401

Bakounine, 190

Bâle, Treaty of, 213, 218, 245, 257

Ball, Sir Alexander, 241

Bank of Assistance for the Nobility, 146, 168–70 ; 188–9

Bankruptcy, Statute of, 168

Bari, relics at, 112

Bariatinski, 82

Barras, 152, 298, 361, 362

Bavaria, integrity guaranteed by Paul, 243–4, 28 ; annexation to Austria proposed, 314 ; Elector of, *see* Maximilian Joseph

Beaujeu, Maurice, *cited*, 383

Beccaria, 170

Bekhtéief, 9

Bekléchof, Procurator-General, 110, 138 ; compensations for, 162–3 ; message to Pahlen, 474

Belfort, 284, 285

Bellegarde, General, 272, 274
Marquis de, 342

Bellinzona, 293

Benckendorf, 111
Mme. de, 59, 61, 64

Bender, siege of, 57, 416

Bennigsen, the plot, 406, 421–2, 449, 450, 451, 455, 457, 459 ; testimony of, 433 ; Commander of the Michael Palace, 464 ; and Marie Féodorovna, 466, 467, 473–4 ; and the Préobrajenski, 468

Berdskaïa Sloboda, 24

Bergen, Russian defeat at, 309

Berlin, Paul's tour, 34, 44 ; the negotiations at, 225–34, 255–9, 325
Treaty of, 341

Bernardino Pass, 293

Bernhardi, *cited*, 429

Bernstorff, Count, 319, 376

Bernadotte, 222, 267, 276, 298

Beurnonville, General, the negotiations in Berlin, 337, 338, 339, 340, 341, 345–6, 347, 349, 350, 351, 353–4, 357, 365–6

Bezak, 160–1

Bezborodko, Chancellor, 22, 71, 73, 127, 143, 188–9 ; and Catherine's papers, 76, 77–8, 79 ; the new reign, 82 ; titles, 98 ; and Mlle. Nélidof, 143, 144 ; and contraband trade, 183 ; and Paul's foreign policy, 217–19 ; and the proposed Quadruple Alliance, 221 ; the negotiations, 227, 229 ; the draft treaty, 231 ; Whitworth and, 234–5 ; alarm at the Polish agitation, 246 ; and Mlle. Lapoukhine, 250 ; retirement, 255 ; death, 279 ; Alexander and, 388

Bibikof, 26

Bignon, 338

Blome, Baron, 315, 326

Boards of Control, 206

Bobrinski, Alexis, 90–1, 175

Boehme, Jacob, 38

Bohemia, 318

Bolgovski, Nicolas, 458–9

Bonaparte, Napoleon, 45, 72, 389 ; methods, 153 ; Paul and, 179, 214, 325 ; march to Vienna, 212 ; and the partition of Poland, 222, 245 ; victories, 230 ; capture of Malta, 240 ; busts, 269 ; and the Directory, 270 ; Wurmser and, 294 ; seeks *rapprochement* with Russia, 335–47 ; returns Russian prisoners of war, 343–4 ; reception of Sprengtporten, 353, 373–4 ; personal appeal to Paul, 359–60 ; Kalytchof's instructions, 364–5 ; terms to Paul, 366–7 ; march to Milan, 1796, 267–8 ; and Kalytchof, 368–9, 373 ; designs on India, 371 ; Paul's challenge, 374 ; opinion of Paul, 380 ; Austerlitz, 427

INDEX

INDEX

484

INDEX

486

INDEX

487

INDEX

INDEX

INDEX

INDEX

INDEX

INDEX

INDEX

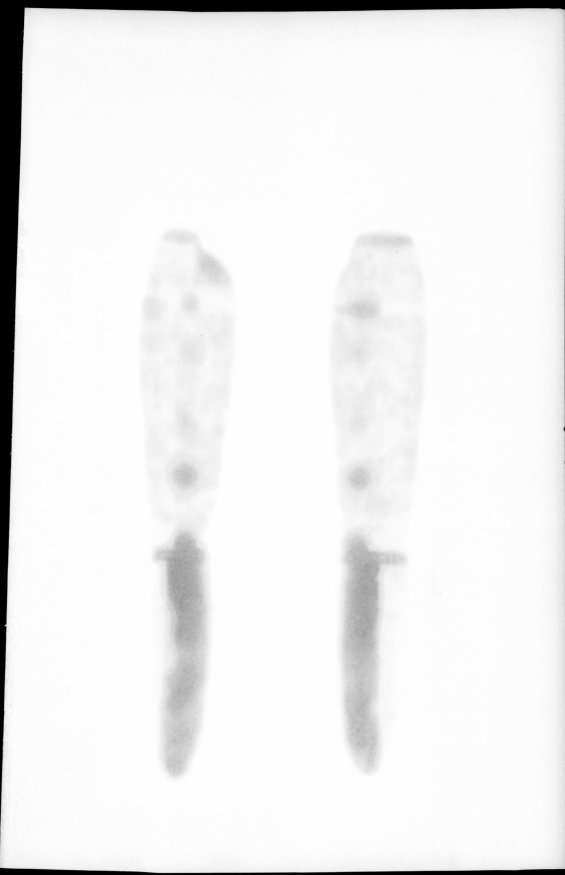

DATE DUE	
JAN 30 2009	

GAYLORD

PRINTED IN U.S.A.